Taken from sketches by Walter Goater, which appeared in *Frank Leslie's Illustrated Newspaper*, 16 April 1881.

THE MEN AND THE MILLS

AND

of the Southern

LAPPER ROOM

THE MEN
THE MILLS

A History
Textile Industry

by

Mildred Gwin Andrews

·MERCER·

ISBN 0-86554-289-9

The paper used in this publication meets
the minimum requirements of American National Standard
for Information Sciences—Permanence of Paper
for Printed Library Materials, ANSI Z39.48-1984.

Library of Congress Cataloging-in-Publication Data
Andrews, Mildred Gwin.
The men and the mills: a history of the southern textile industry.
  Bibliography: p. 313
  Includes index.
  ISBN 0-86554-289-9 (alk. paper)
  1. Cotton textile industry—Southern States—History.
2. Wages—Textile workers—Southern States—History. 3. Business relocation—United States—History. 4. Cost and standard of living—Southern States—History. I. Title.
HD9877.A13A53   1987
388.4'767721'097—dc19   87-29653

CONTENTS

TO
GWIN
AND
BOB

FOREWORD

*As soon as histories are properly told
there is no more need of romances.*
—Walt Whitman,
preface to *Leaves of Grass*

Scholarship without passion seldom produces interesting reading. Dustbins are full of books with backs unbroken. Passion without scholarship is dangerously uneven, inclined to be vaporous and often short on reliable information. A good history consists of passionate scholarship.

Such is the aim of this volume. It is written by one born in the Mississippi Delta. Mildred Andrews spent her life in textiles, holding management positions when women executives were a rarity. She brings an insider's knowledge and technical competence to this book, but she has overcome the handicap of knowing too much and overwhelming the reader. She is, at heart, a storyteller. Anyone raised to the cadence of the Delta knows that it's not things or places or events but people who make a story.

This is a book about people and threads, from the days before Christ to the 1980s. Along with some remarkable achievers, you will meet rogues, pirates, and predators. One man would steal another's invention or his water rights— whatever it took to gain commercial advantage. Mrs. Andrews's account is not a sanitized or sponsored one. Thieves wear white collars too.

The largely nonjudgmental treatment of labor relations leaves one wanting a fuller account of what went on between the textile worker and his mill owner. It is a story that requires judging.

The author has an eye for detail and an ear for anecdote. Her habit over the past fifty years of writing down observations and recording important conversations gave her a headstart in raw material. To that she adds the fruits of her omnivorous reading (see the bibliography) and industrious reporting. An added advantage is her personal acquaintance with the major textilists of the last half century.

Hers is a rendering of one of civilization's most important industries. You learn that manufacturing cloth involved far more than a capitalist, some fiber, and an operative. Whole regions of our country have been influenced by textile development. From the company store to the company church to the company town, textile-related sociology is found between these covers. We talk today of the "progress" in hiring blacks into the mill labor force. Most will be surprised to learn that a Carolina owner tried it soon after the Civil War but had to abandon his idea by 1882.

America long ago was seized by a fever to industrialize. Mass production was the result. With it came immigration, some unions, and the shift from an agrarian economy to one built around the weekly paycheck from the local factory. Our nation was forever changed as a consequence. Mrs. Andrews shows how and tells why.

She gives special attention to how the textile industry behaves under stress— whether it's in reaction to foreign imports, the sudden production demands of a country gone to war, or the migration of spindles from the North to the South.

Withal is a sense of humor. Serious work should never be undertaken by humorless people.

Rolfe Neill
Chairman & Publisher
Charlotte Observer
Charlotte, North Carolina

PREFACE

I was first introduced to the cotton textile industry when I discovered America in Greenwood, Mississippi, and when a trained nurse carefully snuggled me down in a soft, napped cotton "receiving" blanket. All my younger years I heard no conversation but COTTON: the price, up or down; crop failure or bumper harvest; the boll weevil or army worm; labor percentages of the final crop settlement and which planter could or could not pay off crop loans at the banks. When I was about five, after my father had bought one of the first automobiles in the Delta, I remember asking if cotton "had gone up." At our house the conversation was interspersed with music from the Victrola, which was playing Red Seal records of Caruso, Alma Gluck, and other beautiful opera voices that I can recognize today. Until after my debut, I wore fine cotton yarn batiste dresses and petticoats handmade by my mother. Both dress and "petti" were lace trimmed and briarstitched. Even now, to me nothing is more beautiful. As a young child I was interested, as we rode about the plantations, in how cotton grew in the field and was cultivated by field hands and mules. At harvesttime the fluffy staple was pulled by hand from the boll. To see hundreds of acres in full flower bloom in early summer turn into fields of white in the fall was a joy unwarped by economics.

Sometimes I could help pick the cotton, see it loaded on wagons, then on to the gin to start on its way to the mills. It came back, eventually, to the store beautifully finished as cloth, to be handled with love and care and worn with elegance. Nothing made me happier in my teens than to go to Greenwood's historic "Cotton Row" where my lawyer father was a silent partner in a cotton-merchant business. There I learned to "squidge," the first step in classing cotton for sale to mills. I am grateful to those cotton men who had fun teaching a young lady to be a "squidger." No other young lady I know of had such an induction to the trade. When grown, I studied law in my father's office. He was a generous man but a hard taskmaster.

I then married a cotton broker and moved to Gastonia, North Carolina, in 1923 and lived there through 1945. When the Depression hit, it was imperative that I leave the fun of the golf course and get a job. I was employed by the Combed Yarn Spinners (the last job open in the world), thanks to Stuart Cramer, Sr. and Major Cramer, Jr., A. G. Myers, C. A. Cannon, J. A. Groves, Dave Friday, A. C. Lineberger, Sr., R. L. Stowe, Sr. and S. P. Stowe, Sr., and all the members of the board who interviewed me. When hired, I was girl Friday on the magnificent salary of $100 a month. Most of my time during the 5½ days a week was devoted to office and business matters pertaining to reports on manufacturing, finishing and dyeing yarns, and reading the trade publications of the day: *Textile World, Cotton* (now *Textile Industries*), *Daily News Record,* Dave Clark's *Textile Bulletin,* and sometimes Frank Bennett's *American Wool and Cotton Reporter* and the *Wall Street Journal.* To keep my job, because many able men wanted it in those days, I needed to learn more about the machines that made fabrics and yarns so I got a moonlighting job on the 8-to-12 night shift at Loray Mill. The job was under the Vocational Certificate Program, sponsored by North Carolina State College, thanks to dear Dr. Nelson, dean of the Textile College. I worked in the so-called capitalists' office all day, but from suppertime to midnight I was a working "lint-head" in the Loray Mill. Cotton was selling at a nickel a pound, and mill pay was anywhere from 10¢ to 25¢ to 50¢ an hour. Remember, this was in 1930.

The class was wonderful, made up of mill-machine operatives and me, all of us with the same goal: to get ahead. Men were snaggle toothed, tobacco stained, and clothed in greasy overalls. Except perhaps on Saturdays, the men usually couldn't find time for a shave. Women wore their spinner- and weaver-room working clothes; and I, not wanting to look out of place, dressed in my worn riding britches. It didn't take long for class members to make friends and get along, each helping the other to get more from Quigley's "Cotton Mill Mathematics" as well as how to handle a screwdriver or monkey wrench. I learned more about the people who worked in the mills than about manufacturing. The course allowed me an invaluable identification with machines, those who operated them, and the bosses who oversaw the production of the end item. This was probably the most valuable learning period of my life although many more glamorous opportunities existed before and after.

In 1975 it was George McRoberts, with whom I had worked for twenty years on public-relations programs for the American Textile Machinery Association and its exhibitions, who suggested the idea of a bicentennial history of American textiles to be published in *Southern Textile News* (*STN*). I said, "Sure, it would be easy after fifty years in the business." Pat Mullen Smith, who owns the paper, applauded and said, "Great!" Ernie Elkins, the editor upon whose shoulders fell the job of accepting or rejecting the monthly series, was, in the beginning, a bit unsure. He became more enthusiastic as letters from *STN* subscribers and others started arriving on his desk. Many thanks to George, Pat and Ernie, Margie Richardson, and Bill York, who participated in the latter part of the series, which grew by popular demand to forty-one installments. Thanks to those who had an idea that eventually appealed to all phases of the textile industry. One old gentleman wrote, "Thank Gawd you're doing this book. You're the only one old enough to remember what went on, and there's so much to tell." So, I believe I was born to write this narrative.

In compiling this history I have received help from many, many sources. I owe thanks to the following people, both within and without the textile industry, who have been wonderfully generous in supplying photographs, scrapbooks, diaries, family histories, correspondence, vital statistics, company reports, technical information, fabric samples, reminiscences, and, above all, advice:

James Adhead, Jr.
Rita Adrasko
Frank Allshouse
Martha Love Ayres
Edward J. Barnes
Thomas Battle
John G. Beasley
Golvert Bell
Robert Bendheim
Sam Berry
Steven W. Birch
B. H. Bishop
Welsford Bishopric
Margaret Davison Block
Herbert Blueweiss
John H. Bolton
Arthur Borden
Hal E. Brockmann
Morris Bryan
Don A. Bryant
Harry Buzzerd, Jr.
Fuller Callaway
Frank Carter
John A. Carter
Virginia Casey
M. L. Cates, Jr.
Kenneth V. Chace
James L. Chapman, Sr.
Mac Cheatham
William K. Child, Jr.
Laurence A. Christiansen, Jr.
Robert E. Coleman
Donald Comer, Jr.
Edward M. Connell
M. D. C. Crawford
Willhena S. Crutcher
Harry L. Dalton
Robert I. Dalton, Jr.
Mrs. Robert Dalton, Sr.
Sara Davenport

W. H. Davidson
Frederick B. Dent
George Dockray
Ed Duquette
William P. Durst
Robert Edsall
Melvin W. Ellis
James C. Farrow
Maynard Ford
James R. Franklin
Alister Furman
David M. Gessner
Yancey Gilkerson
Lewis M. Goldstein
Ernest Graf
Russell Graham
Diane Greene
Dr. Lawrence Gross
Gordon Hacker
Richard Harris
Charles C. Hertwig
George H. Hightower
H. L. Hodges
Luther Hodges, Sr.
Diane Hoose
James H. Hunter
Tom Ingram
T. J. Jackson
S. Frank Jones
Lillian Katchmer
Alex J. Keller
Eugene Kennedy
John King
Jack Kissiah
Joseph J. Klumpp
Matthew C. Kurtz
Fritz Landau
T. G. Laughman
David Lawrence
W. D. Lawson III

Tom Leavitt
Katherine P. Lee
Frank W. Leitner
Bill Leonard
Samuel Lincoln
J. Harold Lineberger
Walker Lockett
F. Sadler Love
J. Spencer Love
Al H. McCullough
J. Bruce McCullough
Lelah Nell Masters
Paul Mauney
Harold Messmer
Mrs. F. Thomas Miller
Roger Milliken
Walter Montgomery, Sr.
J. D. Moore
James Morrisey
Arthur C. Morrow
Rolfe Neill
Joe Neisler, Jr.
Richard Newell
Haven H. Newton
Boyd Payton
Ted Penn
William J. Pharr
Robert Philip
John W. Powishill
Edward L. Rankin, Jr.
Harry Reimer
Marjorie T. Richardson
Thomas J. Riggs, Jr.
Julian Robertson
William Robertson

William B. Ross
Edward S. Rudnick
William H. Ruffin
George J. Schillinger, Jr.
John G. Schulte
Rose Seisal
J. C. Self
Ray Shockley
W. A. L. Sibley
Ed Silk
Walter Simister
Robert Small
Jack Smith
Melbourne Smith
Michael Smith
Ralph Smith
Morris Speizman
John L. Stickley
Thomas I. Storrs
Bill Sullivan
Harold Swiss
J. Randolph Taylor
R. C. Thatcher, Jr.
Prentice Thomas
Robert L. Thompson, Jr.
Mrs. J. W. Timberlake
R. P. Timmerman
Mae Tucker
Robert M. Vance
Jack C. Werner
Claire B. Whittaker
Dr. Loy Witherspoon
Douglas Woolf
Helena Wright
Joseph Wright II

In addition to these individuals, I would like to thank the many organizations that have been generous with time and information:

Trade Publications
American Cotton Grower
America's Textiles

Trade Associations
Alabama Textile Manufacturers Association
American Textile Machinery Association

Daily News Record
Modern Textiles
Southern Textile News
Textile Industries
Textile World

American Textile Manufacturers Institute
Georgia Textile Manufacturers Association
Master Textile Printers Association
National Association of Hosiery
Manufacturers
North Carolina Textile Manufacturers
Association
Northern Textile Association
South Carolina Textile Manufacturers
Association

<u>Companies</u>
Cannon Mills
Cotton Incorporated
Curtis & Marble Corp.
Davis and Furber Machine Co.
Hunter Machine Company
Lockwood Greene
Ralph E. Loper and Co.
Pendleton Woolen Mills
Riegel Textile Corporation
Speizman Industries, Inc.
Textile Hall Corp.
Whitin Roberts Company

I am especially grateful to the members of our "Book Binders" group, those who actually put the book together: Liz Gwin Kirschten, who typed the original draft some years ago; Arlene Duquette, who typed the rewritten manuscript, working weekdays, weekends, and on call, seeing each chapter as a deadline race; Suydie Upton McLamb and Pat Robbins, who took up the task of retyping the rewrite a number of times; Ann Slesinger, who with her wonderfully trained mind kept the proofreading and research data indexed and in good shape, helped by Joan Rose and D D Littlejohn, Jane McNeary, Ann Woolf, Linda Woolf, Jane Bertolami, and Gwin Dalton, who filled in for typing, research, indexing or any other job when called upon; and Janie White, Loretha Barnes, and Vivian Miller, who fed the crew each day. Many thanks to those faithful members of the Book Binders.

The *Charlotte Observer*, Betsy Brown, and Robert Cannon and Pat Ryckman of the Charlotte Public Library provided their own forms of valuable aid.

When one checks over the list of friends who helped, the narrative is seen not as "Mildred's book," but as one large collection of the firm friendships that we gathered over the years. And best of all, while I was working to be the first lady to reach the level of executive in the textile business, I never met a jealous wife.

And thank you, Rolfe Neill, chairman and publisher of the *Charlotte Observer*, for your clear and splendid foreword.

Mildred Andrews

Edd Rowell, director of Mercer University Press, gave us great encouragement when he said, "This book is all wool and a yard wide." Many thanks to Edd and his fine staff, especially Susan Carini, managing editor, and Margaret Jordan Brown, designer/production manager, for their outstanding contributions. We appreciate the effort they made to keep the flavor and spirit originally intended by the author.

Bob and Gwin Dalton
(the author's family)

Mildred Gwin Andrews

INTRODUCTION

First it was just a rumor in Memphis, Vicksburg, New Orleans, and all through the South that Atlanta was going to stage a world's fair. Atlanta had been destroyed by the Civil War just fifteen years before and had been struggling ever since to rebuild and to go forward. Impossible, folks said, and shook their heads at the thought of such a wild dream. Cotton men who traveled to New England to sell their crops to big cotton mills brought back news that it really was a fact. A big event was being planned by the Northern textile machine builders, and it would be in Atlanta the next year. "That can't be true," said the old-timers. "No Yankee has been in Atlanta since Sherman."

Then the newspapers confirmed the rumor as fact. An International Cotton Exposition would be held in Atlanta, Georgia, from 5 October to 31 December 1881. Every Southerner knew that anything published in the *Atlanta Constitution* had to be true, but even the *Constitution* didn't know some of the facts that led to the big show. Atlanta's population was pushing 40,000 when Edward Atkinson of Boston, a textile executive, banker, and entrepreneur of the first order, came to Atlanta to sell the idea of an enormous cotton exposition that could spell out the future of the cotton industry in the South.

New England mills needed better grades of cotton, Atkinson told a group of Atlanta businessmen. They should attempt to persuade farmers to try improved methods of growing cotton, ginning and baling it for shipment to Northern mills, and thus obtain better prices and raise the economy of the agricultural area. What better way to do this than to show the cotton farmer what his cotton was used for, how it was manufactured into cloth, then cut and sewn into garments on new mill machines up North, he asked.[1]

He said he could not conscientiously recommend investment of capital in Southern cotton mills, but it was still important to have better understanding between the citizens of the two sections of the Union. He believed they should visit each other and became convinced that "in their . . . interdependence is the foundation of their true union."

Atkinson was anxious to heal the economic wounds of the war, and he believed that if the South could redeem itself at all, it would be through a world's

---

[1]Cooper, *History of Fulton County*, 301; *Atlanta Constitution*, 25 August 1880; Garrett, *Atlanta and Its Environs*, 32.

fair in Atlanta. He threw his full persuasive powers and personality into the idea, although he stressed the consensus among Northern businessmen that the South should continue to provide cotton and the North should continue to manufacture it into fabric.[2]

The businessmen of Atlanta enthusiastically went along with Atkinson's plan. The city designated the grounds of Oglethorpe Park, on Marietta Street, bordered by the Western and Atlantic Railway, as the site of the Exposition. The main building was in the shape of a Greek cross with a high vaulted ceiling and a balcony all around for sightseers. The areas between the four sections of the building were landscaped with fountains and plantings. The whole was encircled with a fenced-in roadway, wide enough for carriages and horses. The steam locomotives of the Western and Atlantic Railway pulled their passenger cars up to the Exposition's main entrance and depot where they disgorged excited visitors at periodic intervals.

A large 300-room hotel was built adjacent to the Exposition grounds to house visitors to the big show. The American Hotel, a small three-story hostelry, at the corner of Alabama and Pryor streets, and near the Courthouse and City Hall, was the only hotel to survive Atlanta's destruction in 1864. Smaller buildings for various uses, such as offices, stables for visitors' horses, and machine repair shops were erected on the Exposition grounds in designs that fit the architectural beauty of the whole.[3]

Powerful groups in both North and South supported the plan financially, including textile engineers, cotton machinery builders, Southern bankers and industrialists, and the leading newspapers and journalists of the time. A substantial subscription from the North was made by General William Tecumseh Sherman, who had laid Atlanta low during the Civil War and who now sent penance money toward financing the big event.[4]

The principal Exposition building was designed as a cotton mill of the times. Two Corliss engines were installed, wonders to behold. George Henry Corliss, United States engineer and inventor, had produced this monster of a steam engine that was capable of producing several hundred horsepower. One machine was enough to run an entire mill with its variety of equipment. Exhibits in-

---

[2]Kimball, *International Cotton Exposition*. Description of Exposition from drawings by Horace Bradley, *Harpers Weekly*, 15 October 1881. *Atlanta Constitution*, various issues. The Exposition Cotton Mills Company, *Seventieth Anniversary, 1882-1952*, 1.

[Author's note: Most of the material used, as well as photographs, came from The Exposition Cotton Mills Company, *Seventieth Anniversary, 1882-1952*, which was published by the mill to celebrate the founding of the Exposition Cotton Mill in Atlanta. It includes many details, mostly in the form of clippings from the *Atlanta Constitution*. The mill was bought by J. P. Stevens in the 1940s, then sold and liquidated in the early 1980s.]

[3]The Exposition Cotton Mills Company, *Seventieth Anniversary, 1882-1952*, 10.

[4]Garrett, *Atlanta and Its Environs*, 3:32-33.

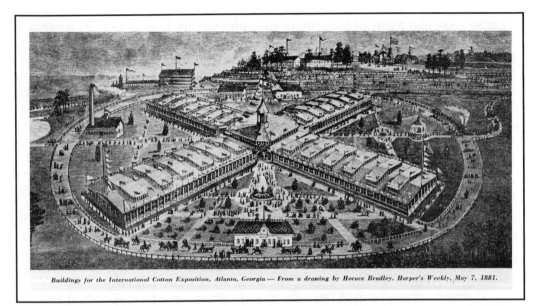

Buildings for the International Cotton Exposition, Atlanta, Georgia — From a drawing by Horace Bradley. Harper's Weekly, May 7, 1881.

A layout of the International Cotton Exposition held in Atlanta, Georgia, in 1881. (From a drawing by Horace Bradley in *Harper's Weekly*, 7 May 1881.)

cluded: an early American patent of the principle of long-draft spinning, which was granted to James Fuller of Norwich, Connecticut; a recently patented "skipping shuttle motion" as well as a patented "new flock-cutter"; a fully automatic circular knitting machine that had been developed by Henry Griswold; a go-through system that had been adapted for lace making; the Ainley-Jacquard loom recently patented; and the IMB wool comber was introduced. Also represented were the George Crompton shedding motion for looms and L. J. Knowles's shedding motion for narrow ware looms; the William Birch machine for smoothing, spreading, and guiding fabrics; the George Draper automatic let-off as well as his ring-spinning frame with the new light-weight spindle; John Whitin's carding engine; the Lowell Machine Shops' speeder frame and other textile manufacturing equipment; William Mason's spinning machines; James Smith and Company's cotton pickers for fluffing and cleaning raw cotton; Philadelphia Textile Machinery Company's pickers; H. W. Butterworth & Sons' machines; Curtis & Marble's finishing machinery for cottons; Lamb's fully automatic flat-bed knitting machine; Birch's new cloth scutching machine; John J. Foss's card-stripping machine. Proctor's new textile dryer was on display and caught the eye of "Buck" Duke who thought it could be adapted for tobacco drying. Also, Proctor and Lindsay exhibited in operation a 36-inch garnett and a 48-inch card, which received much favorable comment from the audience.[5]

[5]Records of the Textile Exhibitors Association and American Cotton Builders Association and Albert Rau's Exhibition Records; Cooper, *History of Fulton County*; Kimball, *International Cotton Exposition*.

These were just a few of the American-built machines on display in Atlanta in 1881; there were many, many more.

The International Cotton Exposition was an enormous success as a business venture and as an inspirational incentive for Southern development. The only recorded criticism was from an old lady, Mrs. Fanny Weaver, of Leflore County, Mississippi, who recalled fifty years later that as a sightseer she loved it, but she contracted typhoid fever at the Exposition, taking the first case of the dread disease back to her hometown of Greenwood, Mississippi.[6]

H. I. Kimball, director-general of the Exposition, reported that 350,000 persons came to Atlanta from all over the Union and from seven foreign countries to see the more than 1,000 exhibits of farming, ginning, and textile machinery. Train fare at Exposition time was only two cents a mile, and many railway systems were back in operation. People who lived nearby or in neighboring counties arrived in spring-wagons drawn by mules or in handsome equipages such as coach and fours or came mounted on their finest horses. Everyone who was "in" or expected or hoped to be "in," or just to make a living out of cotton, made it to Atlanta. Profits of the Exposition were more than $4,000.[7]

The immediate result of the Atlanta Exposition was the disposition and use of the property, and subtly, the public relations and investment gambling that deal engendered. Eleven days after the close of the Exposition, F. P. Rice and H. H. Richards purchased it. The land, formerly Oglethorpe Park, and the entire package of Exposition buildings were purchased from the executive committee of the Exposition. It was proposed by a number of Atlanta business leaders to establish a new mill on the site, utilizing the magnificent building (which had been erected at fifty cents a square foot) and any exhibited machin-

A demonstration of old and new styles of spinning. (From a sketch by Horace Bradley in *Harper's Weekly*, 12 November 1881.)

---

[6]*Reminiscences of Residents of Leflore County.*

[7]King, "International Cotton Exposition," 181-82. At the Atlanta Exposition of 1885, "over $2,000,000 worth of machinery was purchased by the South alone to improve her mills" (*The Progress of Cotton Spinning*, 55).

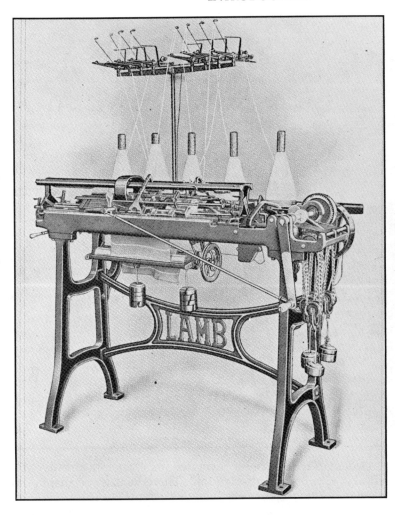

A Lamb fully automatic flat-bed knitting machine. The Lamb Company, founded in 1867, is the oldest knitting-machine company in the United States.

ery that was suitable for textile manufacture. The *Atlanta Constitution* of 11 January 1882 said, "$250,000 was soon raised by 25 men who put up $10,000 each." Actually, 19 men signed the petition of incorporation, but the corporate fund remained at $250,000. Ten thousand spindles and sufficient looms and other equipment were contemplated as minimum equipment for the proposed mill.

On 4 March 1882, a petition was filed with the state of Georgia for incorporation of the "Exposition Cotton Mills." It was signed by H. T. Inman, W. P. Inman, Richard Peters, R. H. Richards, James Swann, T. L. Langston, W. B. Cox, W. W. Austell, W. J. Garrett, J. H. Porter, R. D. Spaulding, J. W. Harie, G. W. Parrott, D. N. Speer, R. M. Clark, L. J. Hill, E. P. Howell, E. C. Peters, and J. D. Turner. Georgia's acceptance of the petition was described by one of the incorporators as "a gigantic move, one that will lift Atlanta from the slough."[8]

---

[8]Quotation by an unidentified reporter from the *Atlanta Constitution,* in an inter-

In 1960 Harold Birch (president, Birch Brothers) celebrated his seventieth birthday at the American Textile Machinery Exhibition-International. There he saw, on display, the original 1878 patent model of his grandfather's scutching machine.

The 300-room hotel built to house visitors to the Exposition was to be converted into a dormitory for mill workers, and buildings other than the actual Exposition building were to be converted into a cotton gin, cotton warehouses, and so forth. One of the investors, interviewed by the *Atlanta Constitution*, said: "We have a considerable little village out there and we shall utilize every bit of it. The Exposition Cotton Mill will prove to be the most important manufacturing enterprise in Atlanta."[9]

The same day in 1881 that the sale of the Cotton Exposition property was announced, it was learned that a new mill was to be started in Mississippi, the

---

view with one of the incorporators, F. P. Rice. From Exposition Cotton Mills Company, *Seventieth Anniversary, 1882-1952*, 7.

[9]Ibid.

Gordon Cotton Mills, located on the Georgia Pacific Railroad near Carrollton, at the foot of the hills and in the delta of the Yazoo River where there were acres and acres of long-staple cotton. At that time Mississippi long-staple cotton was selling at Vicksburg for $1.00 a peck and was being advertised as an "Exposition Cotton Winner."[10] Gordon was investing in the Exposition Mills also.

By 1884 Exposition Mills was listed with capitalization of $350,000, 16,000 spindles, and 480 looms. Sheeting and shirting were the products that were sold through Coffin, Altemus and Company, New York. With the International Cotton Exposition, an economic boom had started for the traditionally agricultural South. The fuse had been lighted for an industrial explosion totally foreign to older generations, totally new and challenging to the younger.

---

[10]Seed cotton was sold by the peck; cotton after ginning was sold by the pound. Seed cotton refers to the cotton seeds reserved after ginning to be planted the following season. In this connection, I should say that it was customary for a planter to allow a tenant farmer to keep the seed from the cotton after ginning to be planted for the next year as his share of the crop. An old tenant farmer met one Memphis train at Greenville, Mississippi, every day and always asked one of the gentlemen getting off the train, "Have you seen my boss, Col. Percy?" Each day he got a negative answer. Finally, in exasperation after several days, he said, "I sho' wish he'd come on home from Memphis and get *his* cotton off *my seed!*"

Reconstruction and Early Entrepreneurs | 1

Historians, all too intent upon political and military phases of events in the South following the Civil War, have labeled the decade after Appomattox the Reconstruction period. These were the years when Federal troops occupied the area, carpetbaggers were in control of state governments, and black labor, by and large, had fled. Most Southerners were compelled to sit quietly and hungrily in looted or half-destroyed homes, or abandoned cabins, slowly recovering from the ravages of the late conflict, taking mental inventory of their meager resources. Many who survived the Civil War and Reconstruction said that the latter was harder to endure than the battlegrounds.

If one acknowledges that the postwar problems of the South were largely economic in nature instead of political, then the period of Reconstruction, in the finer sense of the word, had its beginning in 1880—coincident with the start of the great Cotton Mill Campaign. Men then remembered the road not taken when Southerners listened to Calhoun, the politician, instead of to William Gregg, the builder of industry.

Even before the war, Gregg, of Graniteville, South Carolina, had advocated the building of cotton mills, but the time had not been right. Slavery was still in existence, and the South clung tightly to its agricultural status. By 1880, however, the South had taken stock and realized that its prewar economy had disappeared forever. Editors like Henry Grady of the *Atlanta Constitution* and F. W. Dawson of the *Charleston News and Courier* looked about them and saw deserted fields, charred buildings, and hordes of unemployed. They called for a "New South" based solidly upon busy factories as well as green fields.

The antebellum wealth of the South had been based on the cultivation of cotton, which was shipped to Northern mills for processing. The ambitious entrepreneurs of the postwar South quickly perceived that money could be made by establishing cotton mills closer to the areas where the raw material was being produced. The slogan, "Bring the cotton mills to the fields," animated a whole generation of mill builders and boosters of Southern progress. At its peak, the Cotton Mill Campaign had all the fervor of a religious revival; every city, town, and hamlet wanted a factory and the work, wages, and profits it would bring.

The Raleigh, North Carolina, *News and Observer* editorialized in 1880, "We must make money. It is a power in this practical business age. Teach the boys and girls to work and teach them to be proud of it. Demand all legislative encouragement for manufacturing that may be consistent with free political economy."[1]

Many factors were involved in the South's campaign for cotton mills. Initially, in the minds of some, the demand for profits for the investors was perhaps not as important as the necessity of providing employment. As one observer of the period said, "Community good played a larger part than monetary gain in the founding of a cotton mill."[2]

Teachers, doctors, merchants, judges, preachers, and farmers bought stock in cotton mills, often on the installment plan. Southern mills were conceived and brought into existence by Southerners. The impulse was furnished almost exclusively from within the South, and capital was supplied by the South to the limit of its ability, with some assistance from Northern capital, machinery companies, sales agents, and commission houses.

The Exposition Cotton Mills were not the first postwar mills of the South; a scattered few had been organized throughout the several states. They were small, with limited capital, and the top men had little mill experience. For instance, predating the Atlanta Exposition by only five years was the establishment of the Bibb Manufacturing Company. Hugh Moss Comer, who was in the cotton-factoring business in Savannah, was asked by fellow cotton merchants in Macon, Georgia, to join them in a cotton-mill venture.

Hugh Comer was more than willing since his career, thus far, had been a versatile one. His father died when he was only fifteen and, from that time on, he was the man of the family. Comer took over management of Spring Hill, the family plantation in Alabama where he was born. At eighteen he enlisted in the Confederate army (1861) but was soon discharged due to poor health. After the Civil War, in 1868, he joined his father-in-law in the cotton-factoring business, determined to revive the family's fortune. He developed interests in hotel building, railroad construction, and even cattle raising in Texas. His willingness to join in organizing a cotton mill was a logical step forward to better times.

With a cash outlay of $35,000, three cotton merchants installed 2,500 spindles in an old railroad freight house and started up the Bibb Manufacturing Company. Within two years the company acquired two more stockholders and the Macon Manufacturing Company. A good share of the company's earnings was plowed back into the business each year for expansion and new equipment. The company grew and was prosperous. By 1884 it was listed with capitalization of $115,000, 16,500 spindles, and 140 looms. Its production of shirtings, sheetings, yarns, twine, and rope was sold through James E. Reynolds and Company, New York.

---

[1]Raleigh, North Carolina, *News and Observer*, 1880.

[2]Interview with Donald Comer, Sr., Avondale Mills, describing reasons his father, governor of Alabama, urged building mills in Birmingham.

In Columbus, Georgia, the Columbus Manufacturing Company, Muscogee Manufacturing Company, Steam Cotton Mills, and the Eagle and Phoenix Manufacturing Company had been established before the Civil War and were doing well. After the Exposition other mills were added to the city's roster of textile factories. By 1884 "million-dollar capitalization" was entering the Southern textile economy. The Eagle and Phoenix increased capitalization to $2 million. Its cotton spindleage was doubled to 44,100 and 1,600 looms were producing sheetings, shirtings, osnaburgs, ginghams, cottonades, stripes, checks, and woolens, as well as sewing threads.

In Athens, its three mills were increased to five by 1883 with a total of 30,880 spindles. Other places in Georgia had the same pace of growth. In Augusta, in 1874, there were three small struggling mills with a total of only 5,000 spindles. Two years after the Exposition, they grew to nine mills with 77,312 spindles, including the John P. King Manufacturing Company with capitalization of $1,000,000. Also, there was the Sibley Manufacturing Company with 40,000 spindles and 1,000 looms.

There were numbers of other new mills located in places with unusual names like Maxey's Depot, Parker's Store, Raccoon Mills, Talking Rock, and Too Nigh. The West Point Manufacturing Company, owned by the Laniers, with its original 6,500 spindles and 150 looms was well on the way to becoming one of the greatest mills in the country. In Atlanta itself, two mills, in addition to the Exposition Cotton Mills, were in operation by 1883: the Atlanta Cotton Factory, with 15,000 spindles and 300 looms, and the Fulton Cotton Spinning Company, with 10,000 spindles, established by Elsas, May and Company. Its chief product for many generations to come was bags for sugar, flour, wheat, and other agricultural products. Fulton's bags were popular among the poorer people who used them to make clothing, towels, and dishcloths since they were made from a sturdy, washable fabric.

So, the textile industry of the South grew quickly. Commission merchants and selling agents were playing a big part in the picture of cotton-mill expansion. Most of these companies were headquartered in the North. The textile-trading center known as "Worth Street," New York City, was being established. Also, cotton exchanges were established in New York, New Orleans, and Memphis.

There is no doubt that representation of Southern mills by Northern factors, selling houses, or converters brought in a lot of money for those mills that chose to use trained personnel in selling and financing textile production. Some mills, however, elected to sell their own goods directly to the retailer or consumer, for they were a bit wary of commission houses or converters who sometimes took their commission in mill stock and gained a toehold toward control. The demand for fabric, yarns, and textile products was so great after the Civil War that an astute executive could, and often did, operate his mill and dispose of its products at an equal or higher market price without paying a commission. In the South, a new type of business, cotton manufacturing and direct selling, was making a great impact on its economy.

There are many stories about the brave textile pioneers who ventured into this new, and to them unknown, territory. The story of John Henry Montgomery, a leader in the Build Mills movement, is typical. He was born in 1833 in Spartanburg County, South Carolina. His family, of Scotch-Irish descent, had moved to South Carolina from Pennsylvania, where they had lived since before the Revolution. John Montgomery left his father's small farm and went to work as a store clerk in an establishment near Spartanburg when he was nineteen. His salary was $5 a month and board. Later he went to Columbia, South Carolina, again as a merchant-clerk, all of which provided his training for a partnership with his brother-in-law in general merchandising. That was dissolved and he went into partnership with his father-in-law, David Holcomb. Later he had a financial interest in a small tannery. At the outbreak of the Civil War, he volunteered in the Confederate army and was made commissary of his company with the rank of captain.

Before the war's end, Captain Montgomery was assistant division-commissary. When the fighting was all over and he returned home, his possessions were a small stock of leather left in his little tannery and his burnt-out farm. He tried to eke out a living in those discouraging days, but one day while plowing his field, he stopped in the middle of a row, unhitched the old mule, and went back to the house. "I have too much sense to plow a field," he told his wife. "I'll never waste my time plowing that poor soil again."

The discovery of phosphate rock near Charleston and Anderson (South Carolina) and its use as fertilizer opened new opportunities for him, for no one realized more acutely than he the frustrations of plowing a dead field. In 1874 he became a partner in the firm of Walker, Fleming and Company, dealers in fertilizer. The sale of that product to the farmers of the Spartanburg area became an obsession with Montgomery, and it made him financially successful. In 1881 the firm bought a water-power right on the Pacolet River at Trough Shoals and built a cotton mill there the next year. The new mill, Pacolet Manufacturing Company,[3] had a capital stock of $500,000 and it had 10,000 spindles. In 1887 he doubled its capacity to 20,000 spindles. By prior arrangement, goods were handled by Seth Milliken's selling house in New York.

At Milliken's suggestion, Captain Montgomery had employed the Lockwood Greene Company, very successful Northern-based mill engineers, to help in the planning and building of Pacolet Mills. So, it was only natural that he would get permission to use the services of Stephen Greene from the board of the new mill he planned to organize. In addition to his engineering expertise, Greene had become treasurer and manager of a mill in Newburyport, Massachusetts.

Previously, Seth Milliken, leading commission merchant in New York, and a group of friends had joined together to buy the old Newburyport textile plant, Ocean Mills. They changed the name to Whitefield Mills, did some modernizing, and Greene took over. Soon Greene moved his engineering company and his men to Newburyport where he assumed his new duties with the mill. How-

---

[3]It remained in operation until 1982.

ever, it was an old mill and it soon was evident that the outlook for stockholders was grim. The town itself was found to be unsatisfactory for cotton manufacture.

Then a possible solution to the problem presented itself. When Montgomery called upon Greene to help with the newly organized Spartanburg Manufacturing Company (1888), the name was changed to Spartan Mills by vote of the board. A month after Montgomery and his associates had employed Greene, they received a proposition from him saying that Whitefield Mills was going out of business and the machinery would be sold. He offered all machinery, shafting, and other accoutrements, including brand names, for $200,000. Also, he said, the Whitefield stockholders would take $250,000 stock in the Spartan Mills, provided the capital was $500,000 and all paid in.

Spartan Mills accepted Greene's proposition. As a consequence, it turned out to be the first and perhaps only mill in the South that was in one move transferred lock, stock, and barrel from the North to a new building in the South. It was Plant No. I of Spartan Mills.

The new mill building had a 182-foot-high smokestack that towered over the community and was said to be the tallest structure of its kind in the South in those days. Mrs. Montgomery prepared a lavish dinner for the mill's opening ceremonies to which many notable guests were invited. Some invited guests declined, however, because of their "fear of the dizzying heights of the smokestack."[4]

Five years later, in 1893, Pacolet's capacity was doubled again, bringing its spindleage to 40,000 and its capitalization to *one million dollars*. Then, in 1896, Spartan's No. II Plant, "The New Mill," was opened.

There was a great deal of correspondence between Captain Montgomery and Seth Milliken regarding a plan for a mill to be established in Charleston, South Carolina. The Vestra Mill was built in Charleston in 1892 and operated unsuccessfully for several years due to incompetent labor. Montgomery wrote Milliken that Gainesville, Georgia, was on the main line of the Southern Railroad between Spartanburg and Atlanta, "a fine, high, healthy country similar to Spartanburg, in the Piedmont belt, and inhabited by poor white people of South Carolina caliber. Cotton grown in the area is of the very best grades and staples." He pointed out that there was no other mill of consequence nearby, only two small yarn mills. He enclosed a memo showing where cotton used by Pacolet and Spartan Mills was bought. "Due to competition," he said, "cotton was high in Spartanburg, but in Gainesville, Mississippi and Georgia cotton could be delivered at the mills cheaper than South Carolina cotton," even at $1.25 to $1.50 freight rates. "A 50,000-spindle mill built at Gainesville," he wrote, "would save $30,000 a year on cotton alone."[5] The Charleston plant was aban-

---

[4]In the Walter Montgomery Papers. In the interview with him, he said that the dinner party took place on a large platform inside the smokestack. After the guests were seated, it was hoisted to the top. Knowing this, one can understand why some declined the invitation. *Pioneers of the South* refers to it as the tallest smokestack in the South.

[5]Walter Montgomery Papers.

doned, and the machinery moved to Gainesville, where the Gainesville Mill opened in 1898.

Montgomery's holdings in cotton mills grew steadily as he organized new mills or acquired others. In addition to Pacolet's No. II Plant and the Gainesville (GA) Mill, others were the Whitney (SC) Mills and the Lockhart Mills. In organizing and building these mills, he was assisted and counseled by Stephen Greene and Seth Milliken, both of whom had some stock in the various ventures.

The building of a cotton mill in the South in the three decades from 1870 to 1900 was a far more complicated venture than simply raising capital, ordering machinery, buying cotton, and erecting a mill building. The water-power right had to be obtained, and nearness of a railroad or access to one was an imperative feature. Roads had to be built from railroad to mill and streets laid out for the village. Before the mill could start, a village for the mill workers had to be built and labor recruited. Hardship and difficulties that occurred had to be overcome on the spot. And all of this was in addition to the financing and corporate structure planned in a board room.

Mill houses for the workers were usually one story, although some mills tried the dormitory-type building common in New England. Ellison Adger Smyth, of the Pelzer Mills in Anderson County, South Carolina, tried one-and-a-half-story houses, but found that the workers didn't like an "upstairs," so he went back to what was for many years to come the standard one-story cottage. Wells were dug at intervals along the street, and water for the houses was toted in buckets by hand. There was no village sewerage; instead, "Chic Sales" (one, two, or three holers) were constructed.

Schools had to be built for the children and school teachers employed by the mill. Churches were an important part of the village; a minister was a necessity even if he was a circuit rider. Doctors had to be induced to practice in the village at mill expense. Stores, or commissaries for trade and supplies, were part of the community. Some villages had a company store. Others invited merchants to set up their own business.

Labor agents were employed by the mills to comb the highlands or neighboring states or counties to induce the unemployed or poor nonlanded whites to move to the mill villages where they could enjoy the advantages of village life and a cash payroll. In some cases it was found that the cash was only script issued by the mill, but it was tradeable at local stores and there were plenty of store-bought goods available for trade.

Some fifty years ago, a mill worker who had migrated from the highlands to a village in the Piedmont related this typical story:

> I was just a young-un when the agent came to see us. I didn't know what it was all about, but there wuz a lot of fast words goin' around. Ma, she didn't want to come. Pa, he did. The agent let on that Pa could make fifteen dollars every month workin' in the mill . . . and Pa went to the little chimney-cubby and took out six silver dollars and shook 'em in his hand. I never will forget it. He said he was savin' a dollar every year where he was, but money was mighty hard to 'cumulate. Ma kept sayin' she wouldn't come . . . she'd not work in a cotton mill.

Well, the upshot was that Pa went to work and packed all our clothes and quilts in a big hogshead that had a stick run through the middle of it, stickin' out through each end of the barrel head. We didn't have a wagon, but we didn't have any furniture 'cept wood blocks, neither . . . and this contraption'd roll along. When Ma saw he meant it, she quit her poutin' and we all started walkin', Pa hitched to the barrel with grapevine harness. We walked every step of the way from Yancey, too, Pa pullin' the barrel sometimes and holdin' 'er back another. Didn't mess up a thing, neither, 'cept it wore his silver dollars plum slick![6]

It was not all utopian living that the transplanted Southern workers found in the mill village. There were hardships for those who migrated from worn-out farms and nonproductive mountain sections. It was a psychological hardship to exchange farm or mountain isolation for village living. Moreover, it was hardship to exchange a "do-as-one-pleases" living style for that of the mill bell, which said "come and do it now" and until the bell rings to quit. Then there was the question of people's confinement within the walls of the mill when, before, the great outdoors had been their life. The very worst of all problems was workers' feet. It was painful either to stand barefooted for hours on wooden floors, when people's feet had been accustomed to soft woodsy dirt or the soil of the fields, or encased in shoes that hurt. No matter if the shoes were big enough, barefoot was better.

The Southern nonlanded poor from highland or low-country tenant farms were a sensitive, proud, and stubborn people not found elsewhere. Their change from the old way of life to a textile-mill community was met with a combination of stoicism, courage, and hope; and they did not return to their former farm or mountain homes. They stayed on to work, to become educated. In many cases they became successful and well-to-do, in some cases, rich.

The little town of Greenwood in South Carolina boasted two railroads in 1882: the Greenville & Columbia and the Charleston & Western Carolina. Another was built in 1892, the Georgia, Carolina & Northern. William Lowndes Durst and his brother, John K. Durst, were among an unusual group of industrial leaders of the time who were from the community of Kirksey. Years ago an admirer, with great enthusiasm, described them as "the mill-buildingest boys that ever was."[7] They moved to Greenwood in the 1880s. William Lowndes Durst had enlisted in the Confederate army when only seventeen and fought in the First South Carolina Regiment of Volunteers as part of Lee's Army of Northern Virginia. He was wounded twice. Returning home, he turned to farming and then, with his brother, set up a general mercantile store.

Greenwood had a few stores when they moved there and, of course, the two railroads, but no bank and no industry. J. K. Durst took care of one deficiency by organizing the Bank of Greenwood in 1888; William took care of the

---

[6]Barnwell, *Faces We See*, 13.

[7]Letter from William P. Durst, president of American Loom Company, Inc., Atlanta, and grandson of W. L. Durst.

other by organizing the Greenwood Cotton Mill in 1889.[8] The nearest cotton factory then was at Newberry, where a mill had been established by Colonel R. L. McCaughrin in 1883.

W. L. Durst let his plans "go public" and offered $100 stock certificates in the Greenwood Mill for as little as 50¢ down and 50¢ a week. In this way, 376 shares were represented at the meeting when W. L. Durst was elected president. The capitalization, when the mill was formally chartered, was $100,000, with 1,000 shares, par value $100. The mill building was two stories; the brick was made at the mill site. It had 2,500 spindles, eighty-four looms, seventy-five employees, and fifteen company houses. The mill also had an iron ring built into a side wall for Mr. Durst to hitch his horse. The mill's products of print cloth, sheetings, and twills were largely used for export trade to the Orient.

Another of the mills of the 1890s was the Clinton Mills, organized and built by Mercer Silas Bailey. He, too, was a veteran of the Confederate army. He was born in 1841 and reared on his father's farm. His first job as a young man was as a clerk in a country store, where he received the apparently standard pay of $5 a month. It was considered good pay for the times, but Mercer Bailey quit when the proprietor insisted upon selling whiskey. From there he went to work at the Laurens County Courthouse as a clerk. Here he was paid $10 a month, but even so, he quit—this time to go to school. He joined the James Battalion of the Confederate army at the outbreak of war. After the war he went back to farming, but yearned for a business of his own.

He sold the four bales of cotton that he had raised for 60¢ a pound and, with that money (about $1,200), he went to New York. There he purchased a stock of goods from A. T. Stewart for his South Carolina mercantile establishment. It prospered, so he established a saw mill and grist mill. The South was building and rebuilding as it recovered from the war, so Bailey started a shingle factory to which later was added a sash-door and window-blind factory. When he was only thirty-nine years old, his health broke because of the arduous work and he retired after selling out to his two older sons. After a time he regained his health and again entered business life. This time he was both a cotton merchant and banker. He founded and was first president of the Bank of Clinton. In 1896 he decided Clinton needed a cotton mill and proceeded to organize one.

A site on Sloan's Hill near a spot known as "Lovers' Retreat" was selected for the mill. It was planned to be 80 x 200 feet, to be built of brick (estimates were for one and a quarter-million bricks to be used) with a smokestack 130 feet high. Plans called for 10,000 spindles, but only 5,000 spindles and 140 looms were installed initially. This mill was to have everything modern: engine room, electric lights, and even a telephone. All of Clinton was agog when the wires were installed. A village was built along with a warehouse that held 750 bales of cotton. By 1898 the mill was enlarged to its original concept of 10,000 spindles and additional looms. Its capitalization was raised to $150,000. By 1902 artesian water was available for the village, and a new mill—the Lydia, with

---

[8]Ibid.

5,000 spindles—was built just on the outside of Clinton, on the Seaboard Air-line Railroad. It had a post office and was a flagstop of the railroad. Both were under the management of C. M. Bailey and were able to accept orders for 1,000,000 yards of fine, four-leaf twill, sixty-four square, per year.

Some men from Maine and Massachusetts came down to see these wondrous mills: no indebtedness, a 400-horsepower Corliss compound engine, electric lights, automatic sprinklers, Sturtevant heating and ventilating, thirty acres of land, and a fine mill village with artesian water. They returned home with stock certificates in this venture and wrote to president Bailey that, if he needed cash, they would lend him $5,000 for twelve months, with no interest charge.

In North Carolina, Charlotte was rapidly developing into the textile center of the state.[9] Since the end of the eighteenth century, textile mills had been part of its economy, beginning with Grier's Candlewick Factory on Providence Road, built in the late 1700s. In 1833 David Alexander moved his wool-carding mill to his "lower mill on Mallard Creek" where he carded wool for $6\frac{1}{4}$ cents a pound. In 1839 the Sugar Creek Mill, owned by W. H. Neel, located five miles south-west of Charlotte, was carding wool also. In 1842 Wilson Parks was running a wool-carding machine on McAlpine's Creek eight miles below Charlotte. In neighboring Gaston County, small textile mills were being built, such as the "Pinhook," or Woodlawn, the Lawrence, the Stowe Mills, and Rock Island Woolen Mill on the Catawba.

A public meeting was held in Charlotte in 1870 at which time citizens voted to issue bonds of $200,000 for the Atlanta Railroad and $100,000 to rebuild the railroad to Statesville that was destroyed during the war. That year the Char-lotte Board of Trade also was established with J. Y. Bryce as president.

Efforts were made in 1874 to establish a new cotton mill, but this did not materialize until 1881 when the Charlotte Cotton Mill was built by R. M., J. E., D. W., and J. M. Oates, with capitalization of $131,500. Ten years later looms were added.

The engineer, designer, and actual builder of the Oates brothers' mill, and likewise superintendent of the plant, was a young man of remarkable ability. His name was George A. Gray of Gaston County. At the age of nine years, he was the sole support of his widowed mother and six sisters. An older brother had joined the Confederate army when only sixteen. Before joining the Oates brothers, Gray worked in various capacities in the original Woodlawn, or "Pin-hook," Mill built by the Lineberger brothers.[10] His take-home pay was 13¢ for a "can-see to can't-see workday," six days a week. Eventually he parlayed this salary of 78¢ a week into a large fortune because of his unusual ability, adapt-ability, foresight, and business acumen in organizing textile mills in Gaston County, North Carolina.

---

[9]Tompkins, *History of Mecklenburg County*, 127.

[10]Caleb J. Lineberger and J. Laban Lineberger. Builders included their father, John Lineberger, Jonas Hoffman, Moses H. Rhyne, and John Clemmer. Separk, *Gastonia and Gaston County*, 120.

Circa 1846 the Linebergers and others built the Woodlawn Mill (later known as the "Pin-hook" Mill) along the Catawba River near Mount Holly, North Carolina.

He was a genius with mill machinery, production, and people. In ten years he was running Woodlawn. It was not odd in those days for Civil War children to have a hampered education. Sometimes there were gaps of years between formal schooling periods because schools and colleges were closed, even for several years after the war. George Gray, though, never had a chance at a school. During his days at Pinhook, he broke his arm in an accident. Inadequate treatment for the compound fracture resulted in complications and a long recuperation period. During this period, he gave himself his only "formal education." He committed to memory the entire contents of Noah Webster's *Blueback Elementary Spelling Book* (published 1857) and the famous McGuffey's *First Eclectic Reader* (published 1879).[11]

Gray shortly was called on also by Colonel R. Y. McAden to build a modern textile mill in McAdenville. Gray was then only twenty-one years old, but a veteran in mill operation and in understanding the people of the mills, who were mostly neighbors, all hard up, and all willing to engage in honest and honorable labor. His original contract with McAden contained this clause: "The said George A. Gray is to be the boss of everybody in McAdenville except me." It was signed by McAden in 1882.[12]

---

[11]Young, *Textile Leaders of the South*, 79.

[12]Ibid.

In 1883, only four years after Edison's invention of the incandescent lamp, this new mill boasted a system of electric lights. The 16-candle-power lamps gave off only a dull reddish glow, but the mill, all lighted up, was a marvelous sight in those days. People traveled from miles around to see the McAden Mill at night.[13] Picnickers drove in carriages all the way from Charlotte or Kings Mountain and, after supper on the riverbank, they waited around to "ooh" and "aah" when the mill lights flashed on. As a sightseeing stop in 1883, it rivaled Niagara Falls! This installation was the forerunner of electrification of the industry.

In 1888 George Gray's reputation for mill building, designing, and operation had brought him renown throughout the industry. A group of Gastonians—R. C. G. Love,[14] J. D. Moore, John H. Craig, and others—urged him to build a mill there. There was quite an argument as to where it would be built, on what stream. Gray said to the group, "Why build all these mills on a riverbank? Every time a heavy dew comes along, all the employees have to run to higher ground. Let's build a *steam* plant!"[15] So the Gastonia Cotton Manufacturing Company, miles away from a stream, became one of the first mills successfully operated by steam in the state. George Gray was superintendent and, for the first time, owned stock in a mill he supervised.

George Gray built other mills and operated them. An outstanding one, the largest under one roof in the country, was the Loray Mill, the name a combination of the names John Love and George Gray. He built, in the 1880s and early 1890s, the Trenton Mills, the Arlington, the Avon, the Ozark, the Clara, the Dunn, and the Flint. And he built the Gray Manufacturing Company, which was the parent of the combed-yarn industry of the South, in 1900.

In 1870 James Pleasant Gossett, a ten-year-old orphan, was pretty desperate as he reviewed his situation. The Civil War and five years of Reconstruction had wrecked his family's once-prosperous South Carolina farm. In addition, the almost-simultaneous deaths of his mother and father had left five children to be parceled out and reared by relatives whose fortunes, likewise, had long since gone with the wind.

When a neighboring farmer named Eli Bryant offered him a "contract" to work for "board and keep" until he was twenty-one, Jimmy Gossett signed it. It was not until later that he realized he had sold himself into bondage. The "board" was meager and the "keep" scanty while the hours and labor were unendurably long and hard. There was no further schooling in view. There was no love or friendship at all.

Thus, he ran away and sought help from his father's old friend, C. P. Brown, who was a successful farmer and a merchant. Here with the Browns he found refuge, real sustaining "board" and comfortable "keep," and *pay* of $72.10 a

---

[13]Interview with J. Lander Gray, son of George Gray, 1935. Barnwell, *Faces We See,* 58.

[14]Grandfather of Spencer Love.

[15]Young, *Textile Leaders of the South,* 79.

year, about $1.40 a week. After three years with this good family, he had saved $100 and, with their encouragement, he returned to school.[16]

Jimmy Gossett was splendidly developed physically and had a bright, keen mind. He had become well adjusted to his life of self-reliance and plunged into his studies with zeal. Two great teachers at Wofford College, Professor L. B. Haynes and Dr. John C. Clinkscales, took an interest in young Jimmy as a friend as well as a student. Dr. Clinkscales in later life wrote: "J. P. Gossett, that student who crossed my path and wrote his life so indelibly into my own; in my sixty-two years as teacher, I have touched many young men of different kinds, but no other has driven himself so deeply into my soul as did James P. Gossett."[17]

James P. Gossett. Founder of Gossett Mills of Williamston, South Carolina, and an early president of the American Cotton Manufacturers Association.

---

[16]Ibid., 77.

[17]Ibid.

When Gossett was twenty, Dr. Clinkscales gave him his first real paying job with Rogers and Clinkscales, merchants in Williamston, a small town in Anderson County, South Carolina. He became a successful salesman and remained in that field of activity, always progressing, for fifteen years. He was a "traveling salesman for a number of years and was generally regarded as 'one of the best,' certainly one of the highest paid 'drummers' in the Carolinas."[18] He was making a salary of $10,000 a year, which was extremely high pay in that period of time.

In 1895 he organized and became president of the Williamston Oil and Fertilizer Company. D. A. Tompkins of Charlotte, North Carolina, had inaugurated the cotton-seed oil industry. Cotton-seed meal or cake was found to be excellent fertilizer. He influenced Gossett to invest in this new industry.[19] In 1899 Gossett founded the Bank of Williamston and became its first president.

In 1900 several Williamston citizens attempted to start a cotton mill. The town had the fever, but the venture was doing very poorly, with the building not yet completed and machinery not yet acquired. The distressed stockholders turned to the successful young Gossett. In 1901 he became president and treasurer of the embryonic Williamston Mills at a salary of $100 a month.[20] He went north and raised $200,000 to complete the building and to install 5,000 spindles. The spindleage was soon doubled, and later the mill was enlarged to 32,000 spindles. Williamston Mills was the first unit of what was to become known as the Gossett chain of mills. Afterwards he became president and treasurer of the Brogan Mills at Anderson, followed by the Calhoun Mills at Calhoun Falls, South Carolina.

He had married Sallie Acker Brown, niece of his former benefactors. He had two sons, Benjamin Brown Gossett and Ralph Gossett, and three beautiful daughters.

After college Ralph Gossett established a textile-related business selling mill supplies in Greenville, South Carolina. But it was Ben Gossett who grew up to join his father in textile manufacturing—another notable father-and-son team. Ben had his father's characteristics of self-reliance and adventure; to him, life was one big challenge.

When Benjy Gossett was a little boy, he had to earn his own spending money. During school vacations he went to work as a sweeper at the Pelzer Mills. He swept well, kept the floors clean of lint, and earned promotions. By the time he finished high school, he was head doffer.

Ben had carefully hoarded his earnings and when his fifteenth summer rolled around, he announced he would travel at his own expense. He went to New York to explore the city and its environs. When he had accomplished what

---

[18]Ibid.

[19]Most of this information came from personal interviews with B. B. Gossett in 1940 and from his private papers (in possession of his grandson, Stephen Jones).

[20]Young, *Textile Leaders of the South*, 752.

no other boy in his high-school crowd had done, he wanted his hometown to know that he had been, he had seen, he had explored. When he stepped off the train back at Williamston, he was wearing a huge placard proclaiming, "I have shot the chutes at Coney Island!"

Ben Gossett attended Clemson (South Carolina) College; but the urge to see the world was so strong that he took the Navy route. In 1903 he was at Annapolis in the same class at the Naval Academy as William Frederick Halsey, with whom he formed a lifelong friendship. This was the "Bull" Halsey who gained fame in World War II. Later, Ben Gossett was promoted from midshipman to lieutenant in the Marine Corps.[21]

In 1907 he resigned from military service to return to Anderson County (South Carolina) and to join his father in the textile industry. For the next twenty-four years, until his father's death, the father-son team built the chain that operated twelve mills in three states. Each man was active in public affairs of the industry.

Ben knew textile manufacturing from sweeping to the post of top executive. Like his father, he was a banker, and he had a marvelous personality. At the age of twenty-four, he was assistant treasurer of Williamston Mills, then vice-president of Brogan Mills. He was president and treasurer of Riverside Mills and of Toxaway Mills from 1913 to 1928. The Gossetts then acquired Pendleton Mills.

These mills had a total capitalization of $1.6 million. They had 109,520 spindles and used 23,400 bales of cotton a year. A large work force (1,435) produced goods valued in 1907 at $2.7 million a year. Production consisted of yarns, print cloths, cotton flannels, brogans, and dress goods. By 1910, out of the thirteen mills in Anderson County, the Gossetts had six.

The Gossetts developed the famous LadLassie playcloth made at Brogan Mills. It was a highly successful, popular fabric, the copyrighted name succinctly describing its uses. It was well known in any number of community sewing circles.

Much of the mill building at the turn of the century, and even later, consisted of extension of the plant by means of earnings. Ben Gossett pointed out, in an interview, that there might be a combination of methods. He said, for example, the 5,000-spindle Williamston Mills issued extra stock and raised capitalization to $300,000, increasing spindleage to 15,000; then, afterwards, the plant grew to have 32,000 spindles. "*All,*" he said, "on earnings and credit." In the old days, it took four or five years to pay for a plant if management did not make the mistake of trying to pay normal dividends instead of liquidating the debt.

At any rate, most Southern mills were doing extraordinarily well. General prosperity of the times, newness of equipment, nearness to raw material, cheapness of power and labor costs compared to New England, long hours of operation, and the unexploited home market combined to give substantial

---

[21]Personal interviews with B. B. Gossett.

profits. The mills sprang up, each community endeavoring to have its own textile plant.

"It didn't take too much effort in those days to make the mill profitable," said Ben Gossett. "When a new superintendent took hold at a North Carolina mill, he found half the looms idle, and yet, the plant was making good money."[22] When capable management was added to the manufacturing picture, outstanding results were obtained.

---

[22]Ibid.

Mill Engineers | 2

One of the pioneer cotton manufacturers of the South who had a variety of other business interests, all apparently successful, seemed to his friends and local competitors to be selling his yarn for less than cost—creating, they thought, a buyer's market. They talked it over and decided to have a committee "wait on him" and urge him to uphold the market. On the appointed day, the little group of men went to his office and the spokesman said, "Jim, you're selling your yarn for less than we can make it."

The spinner looked surprised, thought a minute, then pulled out a ledger, opened it up, and replied, "Here's my books. This page shows all I put out and this page shows all I take in. I end up every year with cash in the bank! You can't beat that!"

"No, you can't beat that," they agreed.

Then one spoke up, "Jim, let's see the books. Now, look here," he said, running his finger down a column, "you don't have a thing down for depreciation."

"Nope, I don't count depreciation, just let 'er run."

"And look here, you haven't included taxes. What about taxes, don't you pay taxes?"

"Taxes!" he exploded, "Hell yes, I pay taxes, but I pay them out of my pocket."

The committee was stunned. "Jim," one man said, "you need a mill doctor and, speaking for our group here, we need for you to have a management consultant so you'll stay in line with the rest of us and stop breaking the market by giving away *your* yarn to *our* customers."

Mill "doctors," or mill engineers, were instrumental in the growth of Southern industrialization. Oftentimes they not only consulted on the siting for the mill and oversaw the purchase and installation of the machinery, but also helped line up investors and brokered the financial arrangements.

D. A. Tompkins, one of the earliest to follow this profession in the South, was born on a plantation in Edgefield County, South Carolina, in 1851. He grew up in the heyday of the antebellum cotton economy and he witnessed its collapse and the evils of Reconstruction. He, like William Gregg, was determined to help the South help itself. He studied engineering at Rensselaer Polytechnic Institute and was an apprentice under John Fritz at the Bethlehem Pennsylvania Iron Works. He made connections with some leading United States textile machine builders and went to Germany to introduce American-built machinery to Europe. After a year, he returned to the States and chose Charlotte as his home. In 1882 he hung out his shingle there as "Engineer, Machinist and Contractor."

The financing of new mills was his specialty. He worked out a formula showing that with shares of $100 par value mills could be paid for in full with this method: (1) At the rate of one dollar per week per share, par value would be reached in less than two years. (2) At the rate of fifty cents per week, it would take less than four years to pay for the share. (3) At the rate of twenty-five cents per week, the share of stock would be paid in less than eight years. He stated that all three plans had been tried out and in every case each was successful. The fifty-cents-per-week plan became the most popular.

On the basis of subscriptions of $100,000, the company could start operations in relay with the first subscriptions, receiving about $25,000 the first year. Buildings would be constructed and paid for. In the second year, one-third of the machinery could be purchased and put into operation. In three years, the mill would be in full operation, the balance of the machinery being paid for during the fourth year. Many mills were built on this "patience money" plan.

In ensuing years D. A. Tompkins was the leading spirit and practical visionary who contributed in more ways than anyone else during his time to the growth and development of Charlotte and the textile industry, and the cotton-seed-oil industry of the South.

As sales agent for leading textile machine companies, and with his engineering ability, he designed and equipped textile mills and power plants. One of his greatest fields of activity was building the South's cotton-seed-oil industry. Cotton seed had always been the bane of the planter and ginner. It accumulated at the gin in piles that rotted and stank. If thrown in the rivers, it polluted the waters. Uncracked, it did not decompose sufficiently for fertilizer. It was the South's most objectionable waste product until D. A. Tompkins recognized the potential of crushing cotton seed to produce oil. He built and financed cotton-seed-oil mills and lived to see the Southwide industry be established as one of the more prosperous in the nation. It was backed by capital amounting to hundreds of millions and, in the early 1900s, claimed a comparable annual income. As a food, the oil was clean and palatable. The crushed cotton seed, called motes, was a useful by-product, and the meal derived from the seed was good for a supplement to fodder and as a soil nutrient.

D. A. Tompkins served as a member of the United States Industrial Commission, succeeding Captain Ellison Smyth of South Carolina. He became interested in establishing technical schools for textile study, including the Textile School of Clemson College and the Textile School of North Carolina State College. Mississippi State and Texas Tech established textile schools at his urging. Through the *Charlotte Observer*, which Tompkins owned and which he built into one of the most influential papers in the South, he continually preached the economic gospel of textile industrial expansion in the Southern states.

Stuart Cramer became associated with D. A. Tompkins Co. in 1893. For two years he was engineer and manager of the company. From the time of his first association with Tompkins until 1918, Cramer was engaged in mill architecture and engineering and machinery distribution. He is credited also with having planned or equipped one-third of all the cotton mills in the South. He could furnish management, if needed. It was said that anytime a man could get the money and the site for a cotton mill, Cramer could do the rest. He had the agency for a dozen or more machinery manufacturers, among them Whitin, Kitson and Woonsocket textile machinery, Parsons & Curtis steam turbines, Corliss engines, and Westinghouse.

He was a most active leader in the promotion of the new and growing textile industry. Then, when he took over the Mays Mills, which he built into the splendid Cramerton Mills (later a unit of Burlington Industries), he did something no other engineer had done before. Other mills had housing for employees, but Cramer built the model mill village of the time to surround his own mill, and by doing so, set a new high standard for village housing in the Southern textile industry. He hired a professional landscaper, paved the streets, and built good-looking, English shingle-type houses. He built a community center as well as schools and churches; and as unusual recreation for the mill workers, there was a professionally laid out, nine-hole golf course. It was one of the most progressive steps forward in social planning since the days of William Gregg.

When Cramer died in 1940, he held more than sixty patents on textile inventions. He had coined the term *air-conditioning* and had developed the automatic humidification system, which enabled Southern textile mills to become fine-yarn mills, competitive in quality with those of New Bedford and Fall River, Massachusetts. He wrote comprehensive books on the industry and on cotton manufacture. He had held every conceivable office within the industry, both state and national; and he had served his country, at the invitation of various presidents, by accepting many national committee appointments during military and economic crises.

One of the young men who joined Stuart Cramer's organization in the 1900s was Robert I. Dalton, a graduate of Dalton Academy (founded by his father) and North Carolina State College with a degree in textile engineering. He made many friends among the textile community and was efficient and knowledgeable. One day James William Cannon,[1] a prominent merchant of Concord, called Cramer's office and wanted to talk to "young Dalton."

---

[1]James Cannon was a Mecklenburg boy who, at the age of fourteen, was clerking in a Charlotte store and, at sixteen, went to Concord and got a job as clerk in a general store owned by his older brother David and P. B. Fitzer. He was paid $48 a year and board. When he was twenty, he started a store of his own with his partner, a Mr. Wadsworth. In 1888 he concluded that mercantile trade was too limited for him. He saw farmers selling cotton at around 5 cents a pound and paying 20 cents a yard for

"I'm planning to build a new kind of textile mill and I want you to meet me at Glass," said Cannon.

The answer was, "Yes, Sir!"

A time was set and the meeting duly took place. Glass was a small whistle-stop on the Southern Railway near Concord. Cannon owned the land and outlined his plans for a cotton-towel factory, the first of its kind to be built in the South.[2] Robert Dalton laid out the plans, estimated costs and the machinery needed, as well as seeing to the machinery builders. He sketched the building plans, all of which suited Cannon. Cannon had already raised $75,000 to build the mill and gave Dalton the go-ahead to engineer the company. But Cannon needed more money for this venture, so he went to Boston and sought out a banker there. He wanted to borrow money to buy cotton to run his new towel mill. The banker looked over the statement, looked at this Southern visitor, and said, "Mr. Cannon, you are broke already!"

Cannon, who held the view that a banker should judge a man applying for a loan on his character rather than on his financial standing, took the statement, looked at it again, looked at the banker, and said, "I am broke? Well, I didn't know it!" When he went home that night, he had his cotton money, and the Cannon Manufacturing Co., with 4,000 spindles—the first unit of today's great Cannon Mills—was soon in operation. It was the first mill in the South to produce and sell finished terry cloth towels. It was not long before the Southern's whistle-stop named Glass was changed to the town of Kannapolis.

When Amos Lockwood, founder of a prestigious Northern firm of mill consultants, made Stephen Greene his partner in 1882, the firm of Lockwood, Greene & Co. was born. The textile industry was rapidly expanding by that time in the South through the creation of new companies and in New England by both the establishment of new ones and expansion of existing companies. For the next forty years Lockwood, Greene was the most active organization engaged in textile engineering in New England and in the South. The firm included management, engineering, capital investment, and other activities. Its several divisions carried different corporate names.

By 1910 Lockwood, Greene had designed and built 217 cotton mills. In 1901, at the death of Stephen Greene, his son, Edwin Farnham Greene, inherited the

---

cloth. The margin of profit of the finished goods intrigued him. He decided that he might as well have some of that pie. So he organized the Cannon Manufacturing Co. with capitalization of $75,000, his own savings, and additional money raised in Philadelphia and Boston. The mill had 4,000 spindles.

[2]Cannon had checked the market to find out what fabric was in short supply. It was a very absorbent cloth designed solely for towels. Until then, the aristocracy used linen towels (a flat weave) while the poor used washed-out flour or sugar sacks and the middle-income class used any cloth they might have, embellished perhaps with some embroidery or crochet.

Cannon's decision to make cotton cloth, specifically designed to absorb water, for toweling purposes was one of the greatest comfort decisions in the history of the industry.

Robert I. Dalton, Sr. Designed more than 100 textile plants while employed with Stuart W. Cramer Co. and Whitin Machine Works, where he served as vice-president and Southern agent.

business and became president of the new company incorporated by several of his father's associates. Under his leadership, Lockwood Greene Engineers started purchasing considerable stock in many mills and, under the direction of the new president, a management department was set up to give general supervision to those mills.

Among the more brilliant of the young engineers who joined Lockwood, Greene was J. Norman Pease.[3] He was born 1 November 1885 in Columbus, Georgia, and was educated at Georgia Tech and Washington and Lee. He started his civil engineering career with the railroads. One was the newly organized Southern, for which he was engineer of the Stevenson extensions and the Lookout Mountain Tunnel. Later he joined the Chattanooga and Tennes-

---

[3]Personal interview with J. Norman Pease.

see River Power Co., then the Guild and Co. of Chattanooga. He next became a contractor in Columbus, his hometown, building bridges and a creosote plant, Central of Georgia Railroad underpasses, and bridges at Greenville, South Carolina. He joined Lockwood, Greene in 1915.

His first assignment was as resident engineer for the Hogansville (Georgia) Mills and the La Grange (Georgia) Cotton Mills. Then he proceeded to Burlington, North Carolina, and back to Columbia, South Carolina, where Lockwood, Greene had bid-in at public auction the four plants of the Parker Cotton Mills known as the Hampton Group. These had been purchased for the Pacific Mills and marked that company's first venture in the South, in 1916.

Norman Pease left the company in 1917 to join the war, but he returned to the company in 1919. He was the first manager of the Charlotte office, which he ran successfully from 1920 to 1930, and he became a director of Lockwood Greene Engineers. He resigned from the company in 1932 and within a few years had established his own company in Charlotte—J. N. Pease Associates, Architects and Engineers. At present he is continuing his consulting work though he now is ninety-seven and supposed to be retired. He gives a birthday party every year for himself, and on a daily basis he demonstrates skill in re-

Colonel J. Norman Pease. Founder of J. N. Pease Associates, Architects and Engineers.

partee as he joins the "Bull Pen" for lunch at the City Club. Not long ago he was in an automobile accident that occurred in front of a well-known Charlotte funeral home. Its owner, a friend, rushed out to assist him. He waved him away as he crawled out of the wreckage, "Not yet, boys," he said, "not yet!"

Through the backing and counsel of Lockwood, Greene, plus able local management and as much local capital as could be raised, many fine mills were built. From the early 1880s through 1898, Greene, with this arrangement and additional capital that he obtained from the East (either from the commission houses or the machinery manufacturers), designed, built, and took stock in many large and successful Southern mills.

An early Southern competitor of Lockwood, Greene & Co. was W. B. Smith Whaley of Charleston, South Carolina, a good engineer with progressive ideas who promoted, built, and managed the Richland Cotton Mills, Granby Cotton Mills, and the Olympia Mills organization. He also built family-owned mills and mills that became a part of J. P. Stevens & Co. or a part of United Merchants & Manufacturers. His activities were mostly in South Carolina. He obtained capital from commission houses and from machinery people, and his efforts in those days were regarded as spectacular.

R. E. Barnwell as a young man worked for Whaley and got his first drafting experience with him. After a number of years, he left Whaley to be manager of Lockwood, Greene's new office at Spartanburg, South Carolina, and one of the leading textile engineers of the industry in that day.

From the Southern roster of Lockwood Greene Engineers came J. E. Sirrine, who left that company to establish his own engineering business in 1902. He made great strides, especially in South Carolina. He served as director and counselor for many mills, and aided the growth and development of South Carolina's industry beyond measure. He trained many able men, among them John McPherson, who in 1943 established the McPherson Co., an active engineering firm in that state.

Working with Sirrine's company was a young man named Park Dallis, who in 1908 decided to set up his own business in Atlanta. By tacit consent, Sirrine left the Georgia-Alabama textile engineering to Dallis. By chance, a couple of years later, Lawrence Wood Robert—"Chip" as he became nationally known—started to work for Dallis. The personable young Chip, ranking high in athletics at Georgia Tech, had been engaged by Sam Austin, who during his career was president of many mills in Georgia and Alabama, to join the Whittier Cotton Mill's baseball team and, specifically, to pitch a doubleheader every Saturday. The fabulous pay of $45 a week for his athletic prowess was something Chip could not turn down, so he spent his summer at Sam Austin's mill and pitched baseball on Saturdays.

When the news came to Chip that he could take a postgraduate course at Georgia Tech and play football again that fall, he naturally took textile engineering. After all, he had been around a cotton mill all summer. Then, on the side, he got a job with Dallis's company at $10 a week, a big financial loss from the famous $45, but football and college life compensated. By 1912 he was a partner, the firm being called Dallis & Robert. And when his first real engineering job came along, it was again Sam Austin who employed him. By now, Austin had joined Fuller E. Callaway's organization in La Grange, and he wanted Chip to help build the Unity Spinning Mill.

When World War I broke out, Dallis was convinced that there would be no more textile business; he joined the army and sold out to Chip. For $250, Lawrence Wood Robert bought the firm including the furniture and two office boys, and thus was started the famous Robert & Co., Engineers.[4]

From that time on, Chip Robert was busy selling "the South to the South" and to the North at the same time as he was building industries, especially textile mills for the South. He worked closely with Fuller Callaway, with George Lanier at West Point, Georgia, and with E. T. Comer, brother of Alabama's governor,[5] who was then the head of Bibb Manufacturing Co. He did work for James W. Cannon, helping to build the Cabarrus Cotton Mill in North Carolina for him. He was closely associated with the Hightowers at Thomaston, Georgia, and later with mills in Alabama.

At the close of World War I, Chip watched with tremendous interest the growth of the automobile industry and envisioned the possibilities of the tire-cord business. He coveted that trade for the South, for the yarn (selling then at $2.50 a pound) was being made at only three Northern mills—two in New England, one in New Jersey.

Around 1920, with the South on his mind, Chip disappeared for three months. No one knew where he was, but clearly he was busy with something. When he returned, he had all the answers on tire-cord manufacture. He had worked as a hobo twister-hand and he had gotten himself employed at each of the three mills making tire cord: at Passaic, New Jersey, Pawtucket, Rhode Island, and Easthampton, Massachusetts. He had boarded with the foreign-born mill workers and had drunk beer with them at the corner speakeasy. He had laughed with them, joked with them, and in the process learned from them every secret about successful tire-cord production, from types of cotton to proper drafts and twists.

What he could not learn at one mill, he had learned at another, and he combined his findings to assess the profitability of tire-cord manufacture. He had learned a lot more than that during his hoboing in Northern mills; among other things, he learned the cost of living in the North and how far wages went, or didn't go, and how very cold it got. He was convinced that the South's greatest industrial asset was climate. And on that basis he "sold the South," anticipating the growth of the Sunbelt.

"The South never had cheap labor," he said, "but cheaper living costs on account of better climate." Every time he heard of a new industry that might settle in the South, Robert persuaded the railway officials that he needed a pri-

---

[4]The Robert Co., Atlanta, not to be confused with Pomeranz's The Roberts Co., Sanford, North Carolina, or with the Whitin-Roberts Co. merger. Interviews with Chip Robert.

[5]Braxton Bragg Comer, named for the Confederate general.

vate car to escort the prospects throughout the region. "Why," he said, "we traveled like kings on those private cars the railroads furnished us. There was nothing too good for our prospective neighbors, but those folks we hauled around at the railroads' expense came South to build their new industries, and . . . all on account of climate." It was due largely to efforts of Chip Robert that manufacture of tire cord and fabric was concentrated in Georgia.

Another distinguished textile-engineering firm is that of Ralph E. Loper Co., which has been active in that business since 1914. When Loper graduated from Lehigh University, he worked for several engineering firms and became a specialist in the application of Standard Cost Methods and Cost Reduction Programs for the textile industry. He located in Fall River, Massachusetts, which was then the largest textile manufacturing center in the United States. But with the obvious growth of the Sunbelt, he opened an office and incorporated as a South Carolina business in Greenville. Walter Simister, a registered professional engineer, who had joined him in 1922, became chairman of the company and operated the Greenville office.

Ralph E. Loper Co. pioneered the establishment of Engineered Standard Cost Methods in the textile industry at a time when such methods were generally ignored by mill management. The Loper Standard Cost Systems have as their objective a simple but reasonably accurate relative cost for pricing or merchandising purposes, and for providing a basis for a cost-control system, inventory pricing, and the development of actual costs by periods of time. Loper's Standard Cost System and Reasonable Time Factor System have saved, in sixty-five years of service, millions of dollars for the more than 850 clients they have in the United States and Canada. It is the oldest firm offering continuous consulting and industrial-engineering services to the textile industry.

So, along with actual textile manufacturing, we note a new profession, that of textile engineering. Growing with it, the successful mills have used textile engineers, or "mill doctors," and survived. Textile-research institutes and research departments in textile colleges have been established; in fact, many leading companies today have their own research and development plants, which have made important contributions to the growth and efficiency of Southern textile mills.

Textile Machinery Manufacturing in the 1800s | 3

There are a number of steps necessary before a textile mill is actually a viable, productive unit. First, organizing the mill is largely paperwork plus salesmanship, and it must be coordinated with people's enthusiasm. The movement is started usually by a business leader seeking to improve the community by providing payrolls for the unemployed, or by an entrepreneur who sees a good profit for himself in a venture financed by others. Very rarely does one hear of an individual who is sole founder and owner of a textile mill.

The mill planner lays out necessary organization work for building, equipping, and operating the mill along with estimated costs and then obtains financial resources. Such capitalization is obtained by selling stock in the mill-to-be. Sometimes a few community leaders or well-off businessmen eager for investment put up or pledge cash for shares of stock. At other times, such as in the several decades following the Atlanta Exposition, it took a lot of personal calling on townspeople or farmers or country merchants to raise local stock money in the interests of obtaining a charter of incorporation. Often, in the South, where money was hard to get, Northern textile machine builders installed machinery in exchange for stock in the mill.

Once the mill stock was pledged, a building (usually brick) was erected on a site previously chosen for water power or steam facilities, or in later years available electric power. It could have a smokestack more than 150 feet high, but it was only a stockholders' shell until the textile machinery was actually installed and in operation.

Through the ages, the method of obtaining thread or yarn from raw fiber stock has never changed. It entails drawing out the fibers in parallel fashion, twisting to hold them together, drawing that thread out to a finer thread, and twisting to hold it firm and to strengthen it. That is the principle of the spinning wheel said to have been invented first in India and gradually perfected or refined centuries later. It was the principle of the spinning machine envisioned by Leonardo Da Vinci in the early 1500s.[1] Eventually a machine was

---

[1]Source: L'industria Italiana del Macchinario Tessile.

invented that by water power and a wheel-and-belt system could turn more than one spool of yarn at a time. This was the Englishman Arkwright's spinning system, memorized by his apprentice, Samuel Slater, and duplicated by him in America; he thereby became known as the "Father of the American Textile Industry." Cotton manufacture involves the flow of raw cotton through varying processes until it emerges as finished fabric. Textile manufacturing has a language all its own that is incomprehensible to the layman; but when one observes the machine or the manufacturing process, then the words, coined by the workers through many generations, make sense and combine a bit of folklore with technical progress.

First, cotton fiber that has had its tenacious seed removed at the gin arrives at the mill in a tightly compressed roll weighing approximately 500 lbs. It is taken to the opening room where the bale is stripped of its covering (usually jute bagging) and its metal ties or bands. Then it is laid out on the floor, an intact bale alongside 10 to 100 other similar bales. A portion or layer from each bale is dumped into a machine called the blending feeder where it is thoroughly mixed together or blended, then beat or fluffed up, shedding most of its leaf or gin trash; next it goes to the opening machine where, by centrifugal force and air, it is freed from more leaves or trash that was not removed with the seed at the gin or in the blender.

View of the old Slater Mill in 1840. (Taken from *The Story of Textiles*, courtesy of Walton Advertising and Printing Company.)

From the opening room the cotton goes to the picker where more trash is removed. The fibers are picked fluffier and the first step in paralleling fibers takes place. The cotton emerges from the picker in a flat mass of fiber or bat that is rolled onto a rod the width of the picker machine (approximately 40 inches). The "lap," as it is now called, is transferred to the card machine, which gets its name from olden days when sharp, bent wires were driven through a piece of board or leather with a handle. Two of these, one in each hand, enabled the worker to straighten and parallel the fibers by pulling the mass from one card board to another. The card machine has a larger cylinder covered with card clothing (leather or fabric) from which protrude thousands of fine hooked steel wires. As it revolves rapidly in one direction, overhead is a second cylinder made of narrow, flat pieces the width of the large cylinder, assembled in tandem for flexibility; each piece is covered with steel wires, but its hooks are placed in a direction opposite those of the first cylinder. The entire flat assembly revolves slowly over the large cylinder and in the opposite direction, thus pulling the mass of fibers from the lap, paralleling the single fibers and cleaning them. The product is delivered at the other end of the card as a gossamer web, which merges into a trumpet and is delivered as a single strand of cotton fiber called sliver (accent on *i*), then drawn up and coiled into a can.

This clean, coiled fiber is ready for the next process, which is drawing. Six or more strands or ends of sliver are delivered into a set of drafting rolls and then emerge as one strand or end of drawing sliver. The next process is the roving frame where sliver is drawn into a finer strand and the strand is given its first twist as it is wound onto a bobbin. The twist given to the roving depends upon the length of the fiber; it is used to give the roving strength enough not to break or stretch in the process that follows.

An early example of a Davis and Furber carding machine for wool.

In a mill using combers (machines with very fine teeth that comb out short fibers), the sliver from the card goes to a sliver-lap machine, where some twenty ends of sliver are fed into a set of rollers with a slight draft and emerge as a wide, ribbonlike sheet onto a spool, making a sliver lap. The sliver lap is then carried to the ribbon-lap machine where six or more sliver laps are placed one on top of the other to get a more even distribution of fiber and to obtain the ribbon lap, which then goes to the comber and from there to the drawing frame described above. All mills have cards to make carded yarn. Some mills have the additional process of combing, which produces a higher quality of yarn. Depending on quality desired, ten to fifteen percent of the fiber is combed out by the combing process and the waste known as combing noil is a saleable item for low-grade carded yarns and other uses.

After leaving the roving frame, the bobbin of twisted roving is drawn into a much finer strand, given a harder twist, and put up on a bobbin. This is done on the spinning frame.

To prepare spun yarn for final use, it is wound on a headless spool that, when filled, resembles a round of cheese, and so it is called in the spinning room. The "cheese" contains twice as much yarn as the bobbin. From the automatic spooler, the cheeses (or filled spools) go to the twister. It looks like a spinning machine, but actually it twists two or more ends of yarn into one. Additional processes remain to make yarn ready for weaving and knitting. All yarn is not twisted or plied; some remains as a single yarn. However, in either case it is headed for the loom, or the knitting machine. The yarn may be wound on cones, tubes, and cheeses, or put up in other ways. The mechanical winder lays the yarn on the package in an artistic but regular design, so that when it is unwound in the next process it does not kink or knot up. The many packages—say, 400 to 600 cheeses—are arranged on a warping machine, and the yarn from each is transferred at a high speed to a huge spool called a beam. When the beam is filled, it is taken to the slasher where the yarn is run through a sizing solution (usually starch) and dried and rewound on a loom beam, which may carry 6,000 ends or threads of yarn. The threads must be given the sizing treatment or they would chafe away in the weaving process.

Before the weaving process on the loom, the yarns for the warp (that is, threads that run lengthwise) each must be threaded into the eyes of the dropwires, dents, and then the heddles. This last series of items, each attached to its cross-bar or harness, makes up a reed. The process of attaching the threads is called drawing-in. The harness frame is suspended in the center of the loom. The reed is between the heddles and the point at which the cloth begins. The dropwires are suspended nearest the beam. The warp beam, threaded up to the harness, is placed on the loom so it revolves slowly, unwinding as the warp yarn is criss-crossed by the shuttle carrying the filling yarn or pick between the shed, an area created by the alternate up-and-down motion of each of the harness frames. Thus, the cloth is fabricated by interlacing yarns and wound on a roll as fabric on the far side of the loom. After weaving, the fabric is finished, meaning mercerized, dyed, glazed, or printed.

These are intricate processes that evolved over the years since American textile machine building began. Since the South became industrially oriented, textile machines have been improved, new methods invented, and old ones abandoned as obsolete. New fibers have come into the picture and new approaches have been used to adapt cotton processes to man-made fibers and blends of each.

With the Atlanta Exposition the eyes of the struggling Southern agriculturists were opened to the opportunities of cotton manufacturing with textile machinery. There were machines on display that demonstrated the ingenuity of American blacksmiths and mechanics and inventors of the past four decades. They proved the assertion of Moses Brown, who wrote Alexander Hamilton, then treasurer of the United States, that enough machines could be built and units erected within one year to supply the entire country, making the United States independent of imports.

The ten following early-nineteenth-century prints illustrate the various processes that cotton passed through between bale and finished cloth during the Civil War period. (Courtesy of the Yale University Art Gallery, The Mabel Brady Gervan Collection.)

Willowing

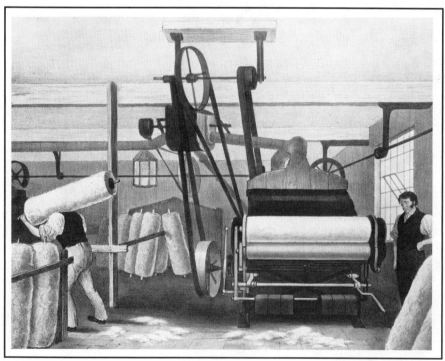

Lap-Frame

Carding

Bobbin & Drawing Frames

Bleaching

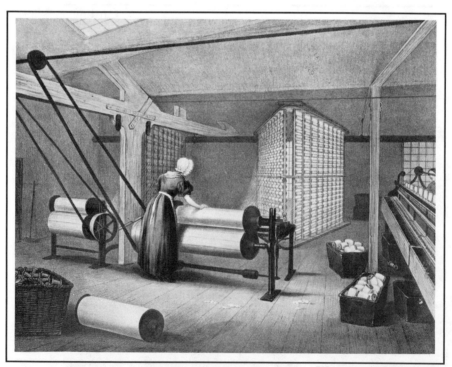

Warping & Winding

Dyeing

Weaving

Printing

From the beginning of the nineteenth century, the textile machinery industry was located in the Northern states. The Boston Manufacturing Co. set a pattern by building a mill with its own machine shop on the first floor. When other mills were being built, the first mill supplied machines for them and thus the Lowell Machine Shop became famous. Paul Whitin first built a textile mill and then a machine shop, and from that point on the tail wagged the dog as Whitin machines became known far and wide. Through the nineteenth century Southern mills bought their machinery in the North, or in some rare cases were able to obtain machinery in England. On the whole, however, Southerners went to the North for their equipment.

Edward Michael Holt of Alamance County, North Carolina, started his first mill in 1837 in partnership with his brother-in-law. He equipped his mill, the first to weave yarn-dyed plaids,[2] with machinery from Goodwin & Clark & Co. of Paterson, New Jersey. In 1845, in order to expand his mill, he went north again and wrote in his diary, "March 26 arrived New York. Went to Paterson. March 27 bought of C. Danforth 528 spindles and preparation and returned to New York in the morning."

A review of some of the great names of earlier times (in addition to exhibitors at the Atlanta International Exposition) starts with the Barr brothers, who built

---

[2]This was the start of the famous Alamance Plaids that later became the product of "Plaid Trust."

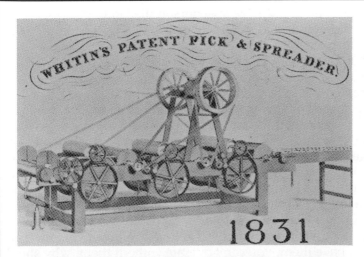

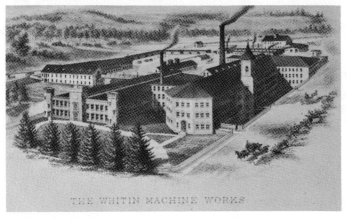

Whitin's first invention (top) and Whitin's first plant layout in 1877 (below).

crude, hand-powered textile machinery for Hugh Orr. In addition to Samuel Slater, there was William Gilmore, whose services Slater rejected, but who built the Gilmore loom to sell for $70.00 compared to the price of $300.00 per loom, or two for $534.69, charged by the Boston Manufacturing Co. at Waltham, Massachusetts. Other machine builders were Dexter Ballou, who made good cards and spinning machines in 1813; John Whitin, who developed and patented his improved cotton picker; Eli Whitney, who invented the cotton gin[3]; and William

---

[3]Whitney's gin model was stolen the night he demonstrated its workability, and he never received a patent or royalty. North Carolina and South Carolina, by legislative action, awarded him several thousand dollars each—his only reward for this great invention. After his model was stolen, every blacksmith learned to copy it and most plantations took advantage of this. It remained for Daniel Pratt, who came south in 1830, to commercialize cotton gins.

Mowry, who in 1816 built the first double speeders in the United States, having stumbled upon England's great textile secret while out walking one night. In fact, he was nearly assassinated for doing so.

There was Jacob Perkins, who was a great mechanic but too busy to take the job of building machines for Francis Cabot Lowell. Paul Moody, who was just as good a mechanic, accepted the job and later invented the warper, improved the double speeder, and patented the filling throstle, among other of his inventions.

Sometimes machines were introduced by happenstance or even necessity. It was in this manner that Paul Moody, a mathematician as well as machine builder, developed the warper. It was imperative that a machine, run by power, be obtained to wind the threads from the bobbin onto the beam of the warper. Lowell, who wanted only the best for his mill, heard that such a machine had been built by a man named Shepherd in Taunton. So Lowell and Moody rode over from the town of Lowell to Taunton to buy the patent or make a trade on the machine. During the dickering, Shepherd refused to lower his price and told Lowell, "You must have them, you can't operate without them, why should I bargain?"

Moody mused aloud, "I was just thinking, I could spin the caps direct upon the bobbins."

Shepherd, seeing his vision of a big sale vanishing, retreated and said, "Well, I will accept your offer."

"It's too late," said Lowell abruptly, terminating the conversation.

En route to Boston, Moody confessed he had no such machine, nor had he ever heard of one. He had only made the remark to assist the trading with Shepherd.

"Well, make one," said Lowell. "You just thought it up." And so Moody did, and the power-driven warper came into the textile machine assembly.

Charles Danforth built the first spinning throstle. Ira Draper made it possible for one weaver to operate two power looms at the same time as a result of his self-acting temple[4]; and he was the first to file for a U.S. patent in 1816. Egbert Egberts along with Timothy and Joshua Bailey pooled their resources and built the first water-powered knitting machines. Andrew Robeson, in 1824, started the first plant for printing calico in Fall River.

Larned Pitcher, a Pawtucket mechanic, with P. Hovey, Asa Arnold, and later (1819) Ira Gray formed a partnership—"Pitcher & Gray"—and built machines on a large scale. Gray invented a dresser and a speeder. Asa Arnold invented a machine for separating wool in the carding process into sliver so that the wool could be spun directly from the cards. In 1823 he took out a patent for a roving machine that increased output of the cotton product at no reduction in the quality of the yarn. An interesting sidelight is that some American machine builders upheld his patent and paid royalties to Arnold, but others did not or would not. Arnold brought infringement suits that resulted in the repeal of the

---

[4]This was the beginning of the Draper family's interest in loom construction, which resulted in the world-famous loom-building company, the Draper Corp.

whole code of patent laws. A new code (1836) was passed by Congress, but Arnold received no redress for the previous infringements.

David Wilkinson, another Rhode Island mechanic and inventor, established the firm of David Wilkinson & Co. in 1817 in partnership with Samuel Greene. He advertised that the company was formed "for the purpose of manufacturing machinery generally: power looms, together with all the apparatus for weaving on the most improved plans; cotton and woolen machinery of all kinds."

In 1864 James Hunter and Son manufactured power-transmission equipment that was sold to nearby mills. They also started building other machines; for instance, a fulling-mill, soaper, and dye kettle were added to the line.

H. B. Briggs, a woolen manufacturer of Clarksburg, Massachusetts, invented a new type of spinning frame. Hunter built it and displayed it in his shop. The *Adams Transcript* described it as a

> valuable invention . . . different from all spinning frames now in use, being a combination of the "Jack" and the old spinning frame. With the same number of spindles, it will do double the quantity of work now accomplished by the "Jack" and will take up only half the space in the mill. Previous machines have been attended with rests and stoppages involving loss of time and production and requiring the labor of able-bodied men to run them, while this machine avoids the rest and secures continuous spinning and can be managed by boys.

The *Transcript* sort of oversold the machine. From its description, it is not hard to understand why "able-bodied men" were reluctant to give their jobs away to boys or to give up their "rests." Northern workers rejected the machine, thus eliminating the high hopes of the inventor and the builder.

When Francis Cabot Lowell returned from England in 1812, bringing with him memorized sketches of the Cartwright-type power looms he had seen, he proceeded to build such machines and put them in operation with great success. Fourteen years earlier, a Frenchman, Jacquard, had made practical the loom appliance (named for him) that did away with the drawboy[5] and automatically produced fancy patterns. There was nothing in between the plain weave of the Lowell- and the Gilmore-type looms and the ponderous Jacquard fancy weaves except a type of limited cam arrangement. There was a great demand for fabric that was a little more dressy than plain, but not as elaborate or as costly as that produced on the Jacquard loom.

In 1837 William Crompton of Taunton, Massachusetts, invented a loom that had the simplicity of the cam operation and approached the versatility of the Jacquard. The patent shows a chain made up of a series of links having high and low rolls arranged to move jacks either into or out of the path of lifter knives.

---

[5]"Drawboy," a small child who, before the advent of the Jacquard loom, sat under the loom and drew the threads down as the weaver called number and color. Jacquard, as a child, had this job and ran away from home to escape it. He vowed to invent a machine that would free children from this hateful and blinding task; the Jacquard loom is the result.

Early etching, by
Harry Morley, of the
first type of Jacquard
loom.

The jacks are attached to warp harness frames that control groups of warp
threads and, in accordance with the arrangement of the rolls, successive movement of the chain determines the pattern. The chain was simple and could be
made long enough to produce a great variety of patterns. This pattern-chain
was a great breakthrough in the art of fancy weaving.

Disappointing news came to William Crompton, however: a financial panic
was then sweeping the United States, and there was no interest on the part of
the textile mills in investing in such a revolutionary machine.

Crompton then went to England, where he received a warm reception and
there he installed his pattern-chain contraption onto a large number of looms
in a British mill. Upon his return in 1839, he found United States mills still un-
interested; not until he wove a fabric for a fancy woolen topcoat did he attain
success. His looms then were installed in the Middlesex Mills at Lawrence,

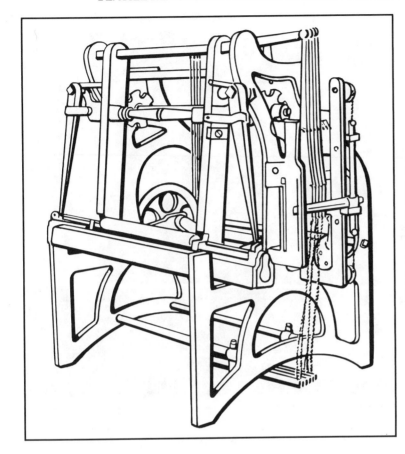

A sketch of William Crompton's U.S. patent 491, which inaugurated the fancy power-loom business in this country. At this time, in 1837, Crompton's establishment was located in Taunton, Massachusetts.

Massachusetts, and a rage for the fancy fabric that was less costly than that of the Jacquard swept the fashion world. Crompton's success and fame were established. Four years later, in poor health, he turned over control of his business to his son, George, who promptly secured an extension of the William Crompton patent, due to expire in 1851.

George Crompton went into business with Merrill E. Furbush, who had machine-shop facilities in Worcester, Massachusetts. The Crompton Loom Co. built a machine to weave a forty-eight-inch-wide fabric at high speed. The shuttle made *forty-five flights a minute*. However, there was one disadvantage to the Crompton box loom. The shifting shuttle boxes were controlled by a chain separate from the harness chain. At times the chains would get out of step with each other and damage the fabric.

In 1856 Lucius J. Knowles patented a device that corrected the defect. The next year George Crompton developed a loom that ran almost twice as fast as his father's loom—a giant step forward in machine productive power. In the meantime, in 1851, William Bickford, expecting William Crompton's patent to expire, had advertised that he was ready to make Crompton looms. George Crompton held later patents so he was able to stop Bickford. But to put an end,

The Crompton loom factory, Worcester, Massachusetts, circa 1865. (Note the shipment of machinery being hauled from the loom works by horse and dray.)

finally, to this type of interference, Crompton bought out Bickford, including patterns and other equipment. This was the first of a continuing pattern of corporate mergers and acquisitions on the part of the company that emerged as Crompton & Knowles.

In 1867 at the Paris Exposition, George Crompton received a medal for the high quality of his box loom, and by 1869 his loom was recognized as "the best worsted loom in the world." One of George Crompton's associates was Horace Wyman, a most ingenious inventor of weaving equipment. Crompton and Wyman developed the Brussels Carpet Loom for a newly established business, the Crompton Carpet Co., a successful venture that became a great industry. Wyman took out a patent on a gingham loom in 1867—a machine considered to be outstanding and one that played a big part in the development of the so-called "Plaid Trust" in Carolina.[6]

A raging controversy and bitter rivalry erupted in 1863 when Lucius J. Knowles took out a patent on a loom that operated the warp harnesses on the

---

[6]See Michael Holt and Alamance.

open-shed principle. Crompton maintained that his closed-shed principle was the only feasible method of box loom weaving. For years Crompton and the Knowles brothers (Lucius and Frank) fought over these conflicting principles. Then, in 1885, the Riverside and Oswego Mills in Providence tested each principle in a trial mill run, made their decision based on quality and productivity, and promptly ordered 200 heavy worsted looms constructed according to the Knowles open-shed principle. It was a momentous decision in which the mill customer was the judge in the controversy. Following this, Knowles's open shed became standard throughout the American textile industry.

Prior to the settlement of this controversy by mill judgment, Knowles had built looms that used certain mechanisms set forth in his 1873 patent. However, George Crompton considered this an infringement on Wyman's gingham loom patent and filed two suits against Knowles. Judge Lowell of the United States Circuit Court (MA) dismissed the suits in 1881, ruling that because of

Lucius and Frank Knowles patented the technique of operating the warp harnesses on the open-shed principle. They are the cofounders of Crompton & Knowles. (Courtesy of Crompton & Knowles Company.)

Knowles's prior patents, he was not guilty of infringement on anything Crompton had invented. Of course, the decision was appealed, but before this appeal could be heard, Crompton died and the appeal was dropped. The company, however, kept on suing Knowles regarding one patent or another, and successively dropped the suits for lack of sufficient grounds.

The Knowles Loom Works, which now had added the word "Patented" to the sign over its door, expanded by buying George W. Stafford's business in Providence in order to secure his dobby for weaving fancy cotton fabrics and his superior Jacquard head.

At long last both companies, exhausted from half a century of feuding and fighting, agreed to call it off and settled their differences by a giant merger that created the company Crompton & Knowles. All resources, patents, patterns, technical know-how, and business contracts were pooled. All personnel were retained. In this way a great team of inventors, Horace Wyman from Crompton and George F. Hutchins from Knowles, was formed. They worked together to build better weaving machines, and together took out famous patents, among them those for the Axminster loom.

One of the earliest companies that built the equipment that helped the textile industries' production power was founded by Winthrop Earle in 1802 to manufacture reeds for looms, spindles and bobbins for spinning frames, and hand cards. From this beginning grew the great Philadelphia company of Proctor & Schwartz. Earle's widow retained her partnership until she married for the second time. Her new husband, Alpheus Smith, took over her partnership and the firm became known as Woodcock and Smith. The name Smith is still carried on some Proctor & Schwartz products such as Smith-Corona typewriters, representing 170 years of succession in the company.[7]

Smith's chief competitors in the 1850s were Davis & Furber, Whitin Machine Works, and C. G. Sargeant & Sons. A daily paper of this period described the Smith Co. as having a completely automated card-clothing operation: "Leather is cut to length and punched, pins cut to length, inserted in the leather and bradded over at high speed. Three men operate 57 punches." This was a very efficient operation at the time. Later Smith took in as partner a young man, Josiah Kendall Proctor, formerly indentured to C. G. Sargeant & Sons. His machinery career was interrupted by service in the Second Massachusetts Heavy Artillery as drummer boy (1862), but after the Civil War was over, he struck out for himself in the business he had learned as an indenturee. He formed the Philadelphia Textile Machinery Co. At this time a machine-shop worker was paid $11.00 a week, a shipment employee $3.00 a week, an office clerk (male) $10.00. The entire payroll, including executives, was paid in gold and silver coins. Minutes of the company's annual meeting in 1885 state the views of the board: "Benefits of a telephone do not justify $100.00 a year. A bicycle rack to hold 50 bicycles should be built at the new plant."

[7]History of Proctor & Schwartz—unpublished manuscript loaned by the company.

C. W. Schwartz was the first college graduate to be employed by the company and to sit on the Board of Directors. Under his direction a new type of cloth-drying (finishing) machine was introduced and converted to drying tobacco at the urging of "Buck" Duke. The company became enormously profitable and so did the cigarette industry.

Around 1831 Albert Curtis was apprenticed to William Hovey at the age of seventeen to build shearing machines. He was a descendant of Ephraim Curtis, the first white settler in the Worcester territory, and had been left fatherless at the age of four. His fellow apprentices were John Simmons and Abel Kimball. The three young men decided to go into business at New Worcester, a nearby village.

By 1831 the company became known as John Simmons & Co. Albert Curtis advertised their products as "Shearing Machines for broad and narrow cloth, carpets, cotton prints, etc., Gigs, Napping and Brushing Machines, Cloth Winders, Shear Grinders, Etc." The variety offered was considerable and each machine was custom built. Curtis was an affable man but a stern taskmaster.

By 1833 he had bought out the other interests and become sole owner. Then Edwin T. Marble joined him as an apprentice in 1845. This young man was said to have such mechanical genius that he could make a "square marble roll." When his apprenticeship ended, Marble sought work elsewhere, but returned to Curtis in 1863 as a partner and general manager. At that time the firm's name was changed to Curtis & Marble.

In 1895, after thirty-two years as a partner, Marble purchased Curtis's entire interest in Curtis & Marble. Associated with him were his four sons, Edwin, William, Charles, and Albert. The five continued to build this business of producing woolen preparatory and finishing machinery for cottons, synthetics, woolens, and worsteds.

In 1816 the first textile patent for an improved fly-shuttle hand loom was granted to Ira Draper, a prosperous farmer of Weston, Massachusetts. It was a superior hand loom, but became obsolete almost immediately with the advent of the power loom. One feature of his loom patent was that it covered his invention of the self-acting rotary loom temple. This device enabled a weaver to tend two looms instead of one, thus doubling his production rate.

The automatic temple was outstanding notably because it became the foundation of the business of Draper Corp., which through five generations of Drapers gave the American textile industry hundreds of machines and devices that have marked the progress of cloth making in this country. The temples were made by the Waltham Co., which energetically pushed their sale. Draper improved the temple and then sold patents and the business to his eldest son, James Draper.

Ebenezer Draper, a younger brother, bought the business in 1837 and moved to Uxbridge, the center of the growing textile industry of the Blackstone Valley. He became greatly interested in the efforts of the Reverend Mr. Adin Ballou, who dreamed of a community where the system of social organization involved common ownership of property. Ebenezer became so enamoured of the plan that he joined Ballou in the founding of Hopedale Community, and there the Draper business established its permanent home. The men would have jobs in the loom works and the women would receive the same rate of pay for their household chores.

Ebenezer made the Draper business one in which everyone enjoyed the profits. When the oldest lady in the village wanted a rocking chair, a community meeting was held and the consensus was that if one person got a rocking chair, everyone would want a rocking chair. As a result, the proposal was voted down.

By 1856 the drain of profits coming out of the business and nothing going back into it produced a hopeless financial condition that would have resulted in bankruptcy but for Ebenezer. Then doing business as E. D. & George Draper, he was forced to take the business back. It was thought that the Drapers had put aside some of the profits for themselves because they were able to pay all bills in the community, pay off investors in the stock of the community, and put the business openly on a successful commercial basis.

History shows that Ballou was a noble, self-sacrificing, Christian man. However, he was working against human nature and the hard fact that the majority of men, once provided with their daily food, clothes for their backs, and a roof over their heads, prefer the rocking chair to a hard day's labor. It is a noted case where an ambitious social experiment failed to compete with the practical economics of the free-enterprise system.

On the last day of 1828, John Thorpe of Rehoboth, Massachusetts, was granted a patent on ring spinning, the method that supplanted mule spinning and is the basic principle of the spinning process in the American textile industry.

In 1853 George Draper moved to Hopedale to join his brother. There he made ring spinning a practical and economical method of producing yarn. George took out his first spindle patent in 1867. With his own inventions and those of his associates, and of men he made his associates by financing their inventions, he produced and developed the Sawyer Spindle and Carroll Double Flange Ring and adjustable holder and later the Rabbeth Spindle. By 1887 he owned the patent rights or controlled the sale of twelve varieties of ring spindles.

The ring spindles in use when he took out his first spindle patent averaged about 3,500 revolutions per minute. On certain yarns they could be run up to 6,000 revolutions, but this was exceptional. The Sawyer spindles averaged 7,800 revolutions, the Rabbeth from 8,500 to 9,200. Both required from one-quarter to three-eighths less power than the old spindles. It has been figured that Draper's ring-spinning improvements saved textile manufacturers of his day millions of dollars. They gave the cotton industry of the United States a tremendous boost on its way to future success and greatness.

Other yarn-preparatory machines received the attention of Draper inventors during this period. Their numerous patented improvements made Draper warpers and spoolers supreme in that day.

James Northrop, who had learned the machinist's trade in England, came to America in 1881. He drifted to Hopedale in search of a job and was hired by the superintendent of the Hopedale Machine Co., one of the subsidiaries of George Draper & Sons. He proved a competent workman and attracted the attention of the Drapers by the invention of a successful thread guide for spoolers. Later he was put to work on a proposed knotter for spoolers. His knotter was not a practical device. So, having become discouraged, he resigned and bought a farm in the neighboring town of Mendon.

In 1886 the three Draper brothers of the third generation decided on a program to research and to develop an automatic loom. Lack of one was a serious handicap to the burgeoning textile industry. When the loom's shuttle emptied of yarn, which was a frequent occurrence, the loom was stopped. The weaver removed the shuttle from the loom, inserted a filled bobbin, threaded the shuttle by sucking the yarn through the shuttle eye with his lips, then restarted the loom—an interruption usually lasting five to ten minutes.

Automatic looms required several years of research and experiment. The first tangible result was the completion in February 1889 of a shuttle-changing loom

Woman operating an early hand knotter. (Courtesy of Crompton & Knowles Company.)

by Alonzo Rhoades of the Draper research staff. This loom was successfully operated at a mill in Fall River.

In the fall of 1888, Northrop had decided that farming was not as profitable as he had expected and had applied for work at his old job in Hopedale. He soon became familiar with Rhoades's work and conceived of an attachment to a common loom that would be much less expensive to build than the Rhoades device and could be sold for less. He had a wooden model of his device in his henhouse in Mendon. On examination, it appeared to have merit, and both the Rhoades and Northrop shuttle-changing looms were completed, patented, and tested in Fall River mills.

While in Fall River supervising trials of the shuttle-changing looms, Northrop thought of changing the bobbin in the shuttle. He returned to Hopedale, explained his idea to the Drapers, and was put to work on the preliminaries that led to the invention of the Northrop loom.

It became evident that a practical automatic loom must have a stop motion. The research on this took longer and cost more than designing the battery. In their search, the Drapers looked at every patent for a warp-stop motion ever granted in this country or overseas and contacted many of the patentees. Several were employed, but neither old patents or the patentees worked out. Finally, a Draper researcher named Charles Roper designed the motion that made the loom successful.

The Drapers named the loom for James Northrop and in August of 1894 the first Northrop looms to be sold to a mill were shipped from Hopedale to Queen City Cotton Mills in Burlington, Vermont. Nevertheless, this shipment did not solve the problem of adoption by the textile industry. The Drapers had to buy mills of their own to prove it could be successfully operated under regular mill conditions.

The ever-expanding Southern textile industry helped too because the new mills needed looms and frequently mill stock was swapped for the new Northrop looms. Eventually this put the Southern mills of the time in the position of being better equipped with modern looms that produced more for less cost than the mills of New England and elsewhere. The Northrop loom was the beginning of a revolution in the art of weaving throughout the world and led to the tremendous expansion of the textile industry in the South. The Northrop loom allowed one weaver to tend sixteen looms instead of two, or four to six.

The South brought cotton mills to the cotton fields, but until the 1960s the textile machinery industry remained a Northern industry that prospered by supplying Southern mills.

Textiles in the New South | 4

There were a number of reasons why the textile industry enjoyed an explosive growth in the South soon after the turn of the twentieth century. They all added up to lower costs per unit of production in comparison with costs of competing mills in New England. The list of these cost items included climate, taxes, land, nearness to cotton fields, cost of building, and other such assets. There was one cost, however, that Northern mills did not have and Southern mills struggled with: the cost of transporting machinery from its Northern source. Machinery moved by ship from a Northern port to a Southern port nearest the mill, by rail to the nearest railroad unloading point, and then by ox cart or wagon and mule team to the mills. This system existed for many years until railroad spurs were built from main lines to the mills and trucking lines developed in the 1930s. Once these costs were taken care of, the Southern mills enjoyed advantages that eventually put them far ahead.

Colonel Elliott White Springs made light of this transportation cost when in 1939, following the death of Charles Schwab, president of Bethlehem Steel Co., Springs bought Schwab's private railroad car, a luxury item if there ever was one. He had it hauled down to his Fort Mill, South Carolina, plant on the Southern Railway, and parked it on the railroad spur that serviced Springs Mills. He promptly adopted the car for his office and formed a pseudorailway line, the "Lancaster and Chester Railway." It was at least twelve miles long and advertised itself as having "all connecting lines," which included every unit of the Southern system. "Lancaster and Chester" had a board of directors comprised of many interesting persons, including Gypsy Rose Lee.

Springs wrote to Miss Lee, a well-known stripteaser, on 15 May 1951.

Agnew Bahnson [of Bahnson Co., Winston-Salem] was here today and said you had ridden on all the interesting railroads of the United States except the Lancaster and Chester, and were anxious to do so on your next trip south. I told him I would be delighted to have you as our guest, and asked him to transmit a formal invitation.

This is to confirm that and to tell you we are building a new terminal station at Lancaster, which will be formally opened on June 2nd. If your trip south can

This rare photograph, taken in 1896, shows a team of two mules and an ox hauling a new Northrop loom to Lockhart Mills, South Carolina, from the nearest railroad. (Courtesy of Northrop Loom Company.)

coincide with this date, I will be glad to have you take part in the ceremony. To make it official, I will appoint you Vice President in Charge of Unveiling.

The railroad-car office was complete with dining room, kitchen, and chef. In it Elliott often entertained his friends and business acquaintances for lunch. He had an interesting menu printed, including such delectable items as: ''Bareback Taxpayer with Drawn Blood, Split Infinitives, Split Dixiecrats with Frozen Assets, Backfire of Misdeal with Sour Alibi, Back Bay Trollops with Harvard Accent, Cannibal Sandwich with Real Collar Buttons, [and] Drawn and Quartered Democrat Roasted in Own Jacket.''[1]

In the post-Civil War days Northern capital certainly helped establish important Southern mills. A promoter of a mill in the South would first get his "home money," but he could depend upon Northern commission houses and machinery builders to contribute forty to fifty percent. In the Southern money market it was said "ponds were dragged and re-dragged." Machinery builders took stock as collateral, and as quickly as possible divested themselves of the stock and did not hold out for dividends. Commission houses demanded and received dividends, and held on to their stock, sometimes getting control of the mill.

For example, in 1876, when Henry P. Hammett organized the Piedmont Manufacturing Co., he contracted with Woodward & Baldwin of Baltimore and New York to be Piedmont's selling agent in return for starting cash: an advance of $5,000 and a $10,000 per annum drawing account. Woodward & Baldwin took a substantial amount of stock also. Out of the entire capitalization, one-third of

---

[1]Source: Elliott White Springs.

the stock was owned in Baltimore and Whitinsville. Whitin Machine Works furnished machines on credit. The product of the mill was for export trade to China, via Woodward & Baldwin.

When the Langley Manufacturing Co. was reorganized in 1870, one-half of the $400,000 capitalization stock was held by the New York commission house, William C. Langley & Co. The balance was held by local Augusta, Georgia, folks, mostly the Sibley family. A ten percent dividend was paid the first year. The Langley commission house was agent, likewise, for Ellison Adger Smyth's Pelzer Manufacturing Co. and had a substantial moneyed interest in the mill.

The Charleston Manufacturing Co., in 1882, was capitalized at $400,000 but $125,000 of that was put up by W. H. Baldwin, of Woodward & Baldwin, and O. H. Sampson, who had a commission house in Boston. Five thousand spindles were bought from Whitin Machine Works, along with 100,000 spindles and 300 looms from Saco-Lowell Shops, all on credit. This mill was built with the intention of using black labor entirely, but the plan did not work.

The panic of 1893 was disastrous to many in the mill business and calamitous to cotton farmers. The unemployment rate soared as a result. In Alabama, in 1895, a move was on foot in Birmingham to build its first mill. The idea originated with the Trainer family, entrepreneurs who operated a spinning mill in Chester, Pennsylvania, and needed additional yarn and fabric. It was promoted heartily by the Birmingham Chamber of Commerce as a way "to give employment to people of the city."

The plan followed the usual formula: the machinery people of the East would take stock for the value of the machinery, while the local people of Alabama would take stock for buildings and equipment. A local man who had $10,000 capital would be elected president. B. B. Comer, president of the City National Bank and the Birmingham Corn and Flour Mills, qualified and was given the office. B. F. Roden, president of the Avondale Land Co., gave the site for the enterprise provided the plant be named "Avondale Mills."

Times were very difficult, and many stock subscribers defaulted. Comer, through his banking connections, was able to borrow enough money from Dumont Clark, a Wall Street banker, to make up for the deficiencies. J. M. Lewis of Talledega took $100,000 in bonds on the property, and some local banks made up the balance needed. The Trainers withdrew from the project before the mill was finished, however, and left Comer holding the bag.

When the first order for goods came through from the designated selling agency, Comer found that the mill's production had been sold for less than 2¢ a yard, and before a yard of cloth had been made! He objected to such a program, which allowed sales agents in the East to sell Avondale cloth without approval or permission of the president of the company, telling the agents he would not honor any sales in the future unless the sales first had his approval. The selling agents then called a meeting of Eastern stockholders to put Mr. Comer out of office, but at the meeting Frederick Jenks, of Fales and Jenks Machinery Co. of Pawtucket, voted with Comer and he remained president and treasurer of Avondale Mills.[2]

His office staff consisted of two men. Comer wrote all the letters in long-hand, bought all his cotton, weighed it, classed it, and sold his own goods. Al-though the experimental type of machinery that had been installed provided continuous trouble and expense, Avondale Mills began operations in 1897 and survived despite all, becoming the nucleus of the present chain. He believed then, as he said later during the depression after World War I, "I'll run this cotton mill as long as I can borrow a dollar!" In that pledge he included his own personal credit and the personal credit of members of his family.

In 1884 Pacolet Manufacturing Co. was organized by Captain John Montgomery of Spartanburg. He went to New York and met with Seth Milliken, president of the big selling house, Deering-Milliken, who put up $10,000 of the $100,000 capitalization "as a starter." This was the beginning of a long and interesting association between the two men, and it was Milliken's first venture in a Southern mill.[3]

Seth Milliken was the son of Dr. Levi Gerrish Milliken, the first physician in New Hampshire to use anesthesia. In Minot, Maine, he had been a miller, schoolteacher, and storekeeper as a young man. In 1861 he took his profits of $8,500 and moved to Portland where he went into the retail business with his brother-in-law, Dan True. In 1865, when Milliken was twenty-nine, he formed a partnership with William Deering to open a general store under the name Deering-Milliken. Additionally, they were sales agents for the Farnsworth Mill of Lisbon Center, Maine.

A terrible fire destroyed the building occupied by Deering-Milliken and all their inventory except potatoes. While a new building was being erected, Seth Milliken took his thousands of pounds of potatoes by ship to Boston. There he found a distressed market and proceeded to New York, where he disposed of his cargo with no trouble. He liked the city and decided to operate from there. Deering-Milliken was established at 79 Leonard Street.

Deering resigned from the company shortly after the move to New York, and headed west, where he formed the Deering Harvesting Machinery Co. The company continued business as a selling house for textiles under the Deering-Milliken banner until 1978 when the name was changed to Milliken & Co.

Every Southern town wanted to build a cotton mill. In 1887, at Fort Mill, South Carolina, a group of citizens—headed by Captain S. E. White,[4] among them Leroy Springs—met, subscribed, and organized the Fort Mill Manufacturing Co. When completed, it had 200 looms. Within a year another mill was organized, and a new addition to the weave mill, a spinning mill, was under

---

[2]Source: Donald Comer, Sr. and Hugh Comer, his brother.

[3]Walter Montgomery, grandson of Captain John Montgomery. Personal correspondence between Montgomery and Milliken.

[4]Elliott White Springs, son of Leroy, was named for him.

construction. By 1892 a third mill was organized, with the list of stock subscribers being practically the same as for the others.

This mill was equipped with secondhand looms (of 1848 vintage) bought from the Graniteville Co. of South Carolina. It had secondhand spinning equipment bought with mortgage money. Its financial statement of 1894 showed capital stock payments of $16,000, debts of $70,000, and quick assets of $1,000. That year David Trainer[5] (the same man who promoted Avondale Mills at Birmingham) placed—on credit, of course—125 secondhand looms in the mill, taking stock for the amount. It was a typical example of Southern industrial ventures of the time.

In 1895 Leroy Springs and his fellow citizens of Lancaster organized the Lancaster Cotton Mills with a capital investment of $150,000. From the beginning, and with Springs as president, it was successful. He organized and subscribed for stock of other plants in addition to loaning money to friends and associates who wanted to subscribe but did not have the cash. By various means he rescued small and almost-defunct mills from financial disaster by re-equipping, revitalizing, and expanding them into the organization now known as the Springs Mills.

When the fever hit La Grange, Georgia, a small mill was built and directorships were auctioned off. Anyone who would put up $5,000 for stock could be a director; and if a widow with a son put up $2,000, the son was given a job in the office. Fuller Earle Callaway, then a merchant of means, warily bought a few shares, then a few more until he had invested $10,000 in the mill's stock. This canny procedure was characteristic of Callaway. Born the son of a Baptist preacher in 1870, he grew up in the Reconstruction-poor era. When not yet twelve years old, he started to supplement the meager income of his family by peddling spools of thread, which he had bought "two for a nickel," for a nickel apiece, thus doubling his money. In a short while he got a job as a porter, sweeping out a local store and delivering goods. He was a born salesman and self-advertiser. By the time he was eighteen, he rented store space, stocked it with household trinkets and sewing notions, and with a sign as big as the entire storefront announced, "Callaway's Famous Mammoth Five and Ten Cents Store." Nothing was priced above a dime, and much to the consternation of other merchants, he undersold them and still made a profit. "A lot of small profits with a fast turnover is better than an occasional big profit and a stagnant inventory," he said. Soon he expanded into the field of dry goods and general merchandise, and had "a little money" to put into the new mill.[6]

The mill was equipped with secondhand machinery shipped down from some New England mills that had bought new replacements. Operations limped along unsuccessfully for a time; however, when Callaway thought he saw his investment drying up, in his customary way he took action. He wrote

---

[5]Elliott White Springs interview.

[6]Interview with Fuller E. Callaway, Jr.; *Who Was Who in America*; Young, *Textile Leaders of the South*.

a letter to every stockholder saying, ''I don't know what I can do to save your money and to save mine but if you will send me your proxy, I will do *something* at the next stockholders meeting.'' When the meeting was held, he had the majority voting power by virtue of his proxies, so he fired the entire mill management and office staff. Then he elected himself president, vice-president and treasurer, and went to work. He bought his own cotton, ran the mill to suit his own tastes, and sold goods through his friends F. Coit Johnson and O. A. Barnard, of J. H. Lane & Co.

At the end of the first year under Callaway's direction, the little mill showed a profit and all the stock was selling at par. He sold his stock for the original sum, $10,000, and got out of the business. He was not long away because his friends, Johnson and Barnard, persuaded him that La Grange really needed another mill—a better one—and that the state, as well as La Grange, needed Fuller E. Callaway's talents to operate it.

That was in 1900, and the result was the organization of the Unity Cotton Mills, with capital of $250,700. Callaway reinvested his $10,000, Lane's company put up $50,000, and local people put up the balance. The city of La Grange gave the land for the mill and the village. Callaway decided to use the same system of personal management and sales in his new mill. Instead of equipping the plant to make standard greige goods, he put in looms to buck and break the Duck Trust. In those days duck was the standard heavy fabric being used for everything from butchers' aprons to horse blankets, and New England mills and selling houses closely controlled the duck market.

Within a year Unity's production had broken duck prices, and the Duck Trust, and showed a 47.68 percent profit on investment. La Grange's other cotton mills were built out of profits, one by one. When Unity Spinning Mill was built, the Unity Cotton Mill put up $1.00 and borrowed the rest at low interest to finance the new plant. When profits paid it out, another plant was built, and so on, until La Grange became one of the most important textile manufacturing centers in the South, and Callaway was one of the most successful mill men.

Callaway was never one to bother with luggage. He'd get on the train headed north with his eye on one thing: business for Callaway Mills. With ''a hail fellow well met'' personality, he soon had sized up every man on the train and, as it passed through textile town after textile town, he carefully watched to see who got on and who got off and where.

At every railroad stop, Callaway checked with the station agent-telegraph operator on the status of the cotton market. So armed, he could talk business easily and accurately as he enjoyed the congeniality and comfort of the dining cars, the smoking parlor, and the lounge of the Southern or the Seaboard. He would meet textile men such as Cassius Bailey of Clinton and Lydia Mills or his brother, William James Bailey, James Gossett of Anderson, John Montgomery of Spartanburg, Leroy Springs of Lancaster, James Chapman of Inman, Stuart Cramer, Sr., Robert Dalton, Sr. of Charlotte, or any number of other men with textile interests. Callaway said, ''If *Cannon* got on, then I'd retire for awhile and refigure my costs.''

Before Callaway reached his New York destination, he had sold in casual conversation with his fellow railway travelers (but with everything so noted in his small black book) enough Callaway Mills products to pay his expenses. This, to him, was a ritual of business: "Don't waste a minute, *sell!*"

He usually timed such trips to fit in with those of dry-goods buyers who intended to replace their stores' stocks or planned a "white sale" to replace local housewives' stocks of sheets and towels. The annual Big White Sale was put on by all retail dry-goods stores. Upon arrival at his hotel in New York, he'd phone John Wanamaker to send over shirts, ties, and underwear, enough for the duration of his stay.

So the railway systems and their excellent accommodations became a marketplace-in-transit because others involved in textile-oriented business also used the cars for pleasure, sales, and profits. Top officers of commission houses were en route to call on customers; textile machinery executives were visiting new and old mills; cotton brokers were lining up the next year's harvest: sales of new crops or disposal of current overstocks.

Given the many facets of industrial growth in the South, there is one example where a man's inventive genius created an industry for his community. That is the story of Roanoke Rapids, North Carolina. When Samuel Finley Patterson was a boy of sixteen or so, he was already 6'3" tall, weighed scarcely 100 pounds, and was thought to have tuberculosis. His grandfather Fries,[7] from near Winston-Salem, North Carolina, sent word for him to come live with him, and he "would cure his T. B." When the boy arrived at his grandfather's, he was put to work in the blacksmith shop at the little cotton mill in which his grandfather was interested.

Two years at the anvil gave the boy great brawn and strength. Hence, by the time he was twenty-one, he weighed 260 pounds and was one of the largest, most powerfully built men in his state.

Two years in the mill community also put him in mind to own and operate mills for himself. He soon had a job as manager of the Roanoke Rapids Mill and the Ilchester Mills in Maryland.

Sam Patterson had a special eccentricity. He hated plain striped bed ticking, then in common use. He conceived of a new way of manufacturing fancy goods to make bed mattresses beautiful, but there was no existing machine for such a purpose. He obtained a secondhand Draper loom and applied to it an old Jacquard head from a Crompton & Knowles loom. In order to make the loom operate properly, he applied to the Draper Corp. for certain changes. The combination was successful, and in November 1900 the newly formed Patterson Textile Co. ordered one new D-Model loom from Draper and a new Jacquard head from Crompton & Knowles Loom Works, with the provision that the two builders should cooperate in providing him a satisfactory loom. Patterson then proceeded to organize a mill with financial assistance from Gustavis Milhisser (a Richmond, Virginia, banker) that would operate solely on

---

[7]His mother was Mary Fries Patterson.

production from his combination-type loom. He assigned his patent to the Rosemary Manufacturing Co.[8] Patterson's idea revolutionized the weaving of Jacquard-type fabrics. As the company profited, it expanded, and over the course of the next twelve years, 264 looms from his specifications were built by Draper and Crompton & Knowles for Rosemary.

It was Patterson who persuaded the Simmons Co. that only a Jacquard fabric was beautiful enough for their new "beautyrest" mattress, and within a few years he had built up a million-dollar annual sales volume in that company alone. The Rosemary continued to expand as other mills were built. Around 1918 W. Lunsford Long and Patterson borrowed $4.5 million and bought all outside interest in the mill. Two years after Patterson's death in 1926, the mills—which then included, in addition to Rosemary, the Roanoke Mills Co.—were sold to Simmons, who then operated them as wholly owned subsidiaries, which was part of their integration plan.[9]

J. B. Duke, whose Southern Power Co. pioneered in furnishing electric power for Southern mills, invested heavily in the newly expanding industrial area, especially in the Carolina Piedmont. Although he did not invest indiscriminately, he was always willing to buy stock in a likely new corporation with a good location and excellent management structure. And he was just as willing to sell out later to the majority stockholder at a figure considered a fair price by the latter.

There was enormous traffic and expense in shipping greige goods north (at one freight rate) to be finished and then back south (at a higher freight rate) or to the west to be sold. This shuffling of millions of yards of cloth and two-way freight costs didn't make sense to Duke. He was actively supporting Southern mill expansion and lending financial assistance. The more mills operating, the more transmission power that could be sold. The less costly the retail market, the more goods that could be sold. He figured that these round-trip freight costs added a big percentage to the final retail price and could be eliminated to a considerable degree.

He enlisted the interest of his brother, B. N. Duke, and Thomas Fortune Ryan of New York, as well as a few Southern textile mill men, and in 1902 they organized the Union Bleaching & Finishing Co. in Greenville. It was built on an uninteresting tract of farmland, but one with a plentiful supply of water available. The building was designed by C. R. Makepeace & Co. of Providence, and was planned to handle ten tons or 100,000 yards of cloth per day in a modern, efficient, and streamlined fashion.

Orders were slow in arriving. The Northern finishing mills were holding onto their customers with grim tenacity and the trade in general was skeptical about the ability of a new Southern plant to do this type of work.[10] Employees

---

[8]Now part of J. P. Stevens & Co.

[9]Interview with W. Lunsford Long, Warrenton NC.

[10]U.S. Finishing Co. was the largest in the United States. It was started under New Jersey laws in 1899 with a capitalization of $3 million.

would report for work at Union Bleaching and find there was none. They'd have to sit out their time on the creek bank until a train brought a cargo of cloth. Then J. W. Arrington took hold. After all, there were eleven up-to-date mills in Greenville and 2,250,000 spindles within a radius of fifty miles. The customers were there if he could capture them. As president, he soon had Union Bleaching on its feet and running at full capacity.

In all the Southern textile areas, none is more interesting in growth and development than the industrial valley of the Chattahoochee, the river that divides East Alabama and Georgia. Immediately after Appomattox, two separate groups of one-time planters and merchants surveyed their ruined plantations and businesses and searched for capital with which to make a new start. This they found by quickly selling cotton, hidden from Yankee invaders, to English buyers in Savannah and Augusta before it could be seized by Reconstruction agents. With this money the two groups decided to build cotton mills along the river. They dug the clay from former grist-mill sites and made brick for the buildings of the textile plants.

The newly elected governor of Alabama and the chief justice of the Alabama Supreme Court went to West Point to preside over the laying of the cornerstone of the Chattahoochee Manufacturing Co. After a noontime barbecue and speeches, and of course a band of sorts, they repeated the cornerstone laying at the Alabama-Georgia Co. a few miles farther down the Chattahoochee at Riverview. The mills equipped with secondhand machinery and inexperienced labor and management struggled, then died in the panic of 1873.

During this depressed era, two young Confederate veterans, Lafayette Lanier and Ward Crocket Lanier, became interested in the old mills. They had long loved the industrial valley since their father, in antebellum days, had operated a successful copper mine in the area. The Lanier brothers had already established a small mercantile business and a bank in West Point.

Lafayette Lanier traded a piece of property for some stock in the closed Chattahoochee mill and set about reorganizing it, determined to re-equip it. He planned to buy new machinery from an English manufacturer who recommended that he employ William Lang, an experienced cotton-mill man from Oldham, England. Lang arrived in West Point, surveyed the mill and ordered the proper new equipment, repairing other machinery at the Lanier Iron Works. He urged his father, Thomas Lang, to join him. The latter became superintendent of the Chattahoochee mill, while his son was superintendent of the Alabama-Georgia mill that the Laniers had acquired. This was about the time of the Atlanta International Cotton Exposition.

The Lanier brothers put both mills on flat duck, a product in great demand. They sold their goods through N. Boynton & Co. of Boston, ship chandlers who had made a great reputation equipping whaling vessels, some requiring 12,000 to 15,000 square yards of duck for one set of sails. With the dwindling of that business, they had turned to meet the demands of the growing Western frontier: tents, covered wagon tops, and housing for workers building the transcontinental railroad lines.

The Laniers organized the West Point Manufacturing Co. with profits from their other two duck mills. There were eight stockholders and a capitalization of $107,000. The company prospered and added new machinery, bought in the East on easy credit terms. They patented the name of the duck product "Magnolia" and found it was the second fabric in the United States to have a patented trade name.[11] In 1886 fire consumed the mill, the Laniers were wiped out, and the sales agent had no supply. After some dickering, a new order was established. The mill would be rebuilt with Boston money. On the new board were two Boston salesmen—Theodore Burnett and William Wellington—who had traveled south for years to buy the Lanier duck. With them came Francis Sears, banker brother of Horace S. Sears.

The business prospered and demand skyrocketed. Lafayette Lanier assumed more and more responsibility for expanding the enterprise in the 1890s. A new mill was built on the Alabama bank of the Chattahoochee. It would diversify production, making sateens, drills, twills, and sheetings. Capital was raised according to the usual Southern pattern: using all the local money to be had, the Lanier money, the Boyton selling-house money, textile machinery on credit from R. P. Snelling, a Massachusetts machine builder. This was Lanett No. I.

In the 1880s the "old mill" at Riverview, which had been limping along, finally was forced to close. Again with assistance of Boston money, it was reorganized as the Galeton Mills, a subsidiary of West Point. It soon became involved in litigation as to ownership. Louis Brandeis, later a Supreme Court justice, argued the case for the Laniers before that court, and the mill obtained its third charter from Alabama, becoming the Riverdale Mills.

As a panic hit the country, with labor plentiful, materials cheap, and other mills closing down, the Laniers expanded and gave employment to those out of work. In the depression of 1890, they organized ownership of the Alabama-Georgia Mill and built Lanett I, Lanett Bleachery and Dye Works, and the Chattahoochee Valley Railway. The latter was really a commuter train, running along the river for $5\frac{1}{2}$ miles to serve the mills and connect the valley towns with the railroad at West Point. It eventually grew to forty-one miles, tying together all the mills along the river and saving the mills excessive freight rates. Previously the mills had depended on barges, which were not satisfactory because of shallow water and shoals.

West Point began its real expansion in the panic of 1893. In 1907, another panic year, West Point began yet another expansion program, another duck mill. This was the Shawmut, adapted to a wide variety of ducks, but later one of the first mills to experiment with the manufacture of man-made fiber.

When the bleachery was built, it was a joint West Point-N. Boynton enterprise. The sales house was, within a few years, reorganized, keeping the name of two of its board members: Wellington and Sears.

---

[11]"Beverly Cotton Mills." Walton, *The Story of Textiles,* 155.

The brothers Moses and Caesar Cone represented the family wholesale grocery company in Baltimore known as H. Cone and Sons. They traveled throughout the South taking orders for wholesale groceries and cigars from the general stores of the small towns. One such country store was the Monroe Racket in Monroe, North Carolina, owned by William Henry Belk. He had started the business after twelve years of apprenticeship under B. D. Heath, with savings of $750 and $500 borrowed from a widow, and a miscellaneous stock purchased on credit from another merchant who was going out of business. Also, Belk could obtain textile goods directly from mills in Mecklenburg and adjoining counties.

He sold easily, and at a profit, the groceries and cigars offered in barter for textiles by the Cone brothers. Belk and the Cones became good friends; he doubtlessly chatted with them as to which new mill would be a good investment and, in turn, Belk won an H. Cone and Sons wall clock given as an award to outstanding cigar customers of the Baltimore wholesaler. Belk persuaded his doctor brother, John, to go in business with him, and the two, using the methods of quick turnover and fast profit, stuck to merchandising, expanding their business as the textile industry grew.[12]

Many of the textile mills had commissaries, or general stores, as a routine setup in the rather isolated villages. Even if the mills were classed as being in a city, roads and transportation were poor, and it was more convenient for mill workers to trade at the mill store, especially if their wages were in script issued by the mill. There was nothing illegal or inhumane about this. There was very little hard money in the South for the everyday worker to spend. This arrangement was the lifeblood of a region still trying to recover from war and Reconstruction.

Like many others, the Cone brothers often bartered their groceries and cigars to general stores and mill stores for textiles: sheetings, drills, plaids, denims, shirtings, yarns, and sewing threads that were disposed of in the national market.

By 1890 the Cone brothers had made many friends among the mill men. They had invested by buying a bit of stock here and there in some mills in North Carolina, and even as far south as Alabama (where they traded with the Tuscaloosa Manufacturing Co.), and in Georgia (where they did business with the Muscogee Manufacturing Co.). It was time, they thought, to devote their entire business to textiles. So, in 1889 or 1890, H. Cone & Sons, wholesale groceries in Baltimore, was liquidated and the funds were invested in a new company called Cone Export and Commission Co. The first headquarters were in New York, but within two years were moved to the small town of Greensboro, North Carolina. The company specialized in ginghams and plaids, and found a good supply from the chain of mills held by the five sons and three sons-in-law of Michael Holt, who built the Alamance Mill in 1837. It was the leading mill of the group.

Alamance had been burned during the war, or shortly thereafter, but was rebuilt by 1871 and was still producing plaids. In the next twenty years the group developed or took many mills in the Alamance area.

---

[12]Lelah Nell Master, director of public relations, Cone Mills, 1978 interview.

The Holt family in North Carolina, including second- and third-generation sons, sons-in-law and nephews, had built upon the original old Alamance Mill and its reputation for managerial integrity and success in the marketplace. The Holts could now boast of an empire of twenty-nine plaid-producing cotton mills in as many years. Their holdings reached from Wilmington on the Atlantic to Asheville in the mountains.

All of these mills were weaving ginghams and plaids on Crompton & Knowles box looms, and all sold through Cone Export and Commission. All were making money. It was a family conglomerate with enormous production of "Alamance" plaids and ginghams, and strong competition among the kins-folk. Each mill owner-relative, in the endeavor to obtain orders for his own mill, completely demoralized the market for plaids.

The Cone brothers persuaded each of these mills to allow the newly founded Cone Export and Commission Co. to sell their output of plaids, guaranteeing five percent commission in exchange for the mills' giving them exclusive sales rights for five years. The Cones straightened out the market through orderly distribution of goods and stabilized prices. Thus was born the "Plaid Trust," so named by Northern politicians in the early 1890s, which under Cone marketing expertise continued to make profit for the mills and to furnish employment to thousands until the Sherman Anti-Trust Law broke up the agreements.

In 1892, W. A. Erwin, brother-in-law of Lawrence Holt, was persuaded by the Duke interests, who were building a mill in Durham, to leave the E. M. Holt Plaid Mills (built in 1884) to manage the new mill. The mill, named for Erwin, was built to make plaids, and Cone Export and Commission was, of course, the selling agent. There was an increasing demand, however, for denims, up until then made only in New England. The Levi Strauss work clothes had become increasingly popular in the mining areas of the West and other Midwest and Eastern industrial centers. So it was that the Cone brothers persuaded Erwin to switch from plaids to denim, while they would continue as selling agents and build a big market in the South, which they did.

For several years the business was profitable and satisfactory to all. Then, for reasons not known, Erwin cancelled his agreement with the Cones. This left Cone Export and Commission Co. with a huge denim market they had built up and no material to supply it.

The answer was to build their own mill. In 1895 H. Cone & Sons pooled the family's personal resources: H. Cone, $70,000; Caesar Cone, $20,000; Moses Cone, $30,000; Dr. Sydney Cone, $10,000, toward a capitalization of $151,000 for a Cone-owned mill. The balance of $21,000 was obtained by sale of bits and pieces of stock held by Cone Export and Commission Co. in various textile mills for which they were selling agents. The Cones' new mill, located in Greensboro, was to run solely on heavy-duty, deep-tone, indigo-dyed blue denim. It was named "Proximity" because it was near the cotton fields and adjacent to the railroad.[13] Additional financing was secured from J. B. Duke. Norman Cocke, of the Duke Power Co., years later said Duke told him:

---

[13]Liquidated 1982.

Caesar Cone came today and said he wanted me to sell out to him. I had only ten shares of the original stock left so I told him I didn't want to sell, but if he wanted me to, I would. I asked Caesar what the stock was worth. Caesar's reply was that it was worth $1,400 a share, but he and his family had talked it over and they thought $1,200 would be a fair price. So Caesar wrote out a check for $12,000 for the ten original shares of Proximity, and I accepted it, and here it is.[14]

The Cones mortgaged Proximity and built White Oak Mill. For twenty years the company did not pay a dividend, but instead plowed all the earnings back into buildings and machinery so that by 1914, the small, 250-loom denim mill had increased to two plants containing 3,500 looms—the largest denim mill in the world. When Moses Cone died in 1908, he had not received one penny in either salary or dividend on his investment in the Proximity Manufacturing Co. The money had stayed in the company building and expansion program. Years later when Herman Cone was raising his sons to lead the Cone group, he had a complete automatic electrified denim loom set up in the recreation room in the basement of his home to teach his sons how to weave denim, fix the loom, and become leaders in the industry.[15]

In Gaston County, North Carolina, when R. L. Stowe and S. P. Stowe, young men of twenty-one and twenty-three years in 1899, decided to leave their family farm to go into the mercantile business, they loaded their belongings onto a farm wagon and drove the two miles from their home to the water stop on the Charlotte and Atlanta Railway known as Garibaldi. The only source of revenue in the surrounding territory was from poor little worn-out red-clay farms, but in Garibaldi there was the monthly payroll of the railroad's section gang, amounting to $115.

After some years of hard work and relative prosperity, the Stowe brothers called a meeting of interested citizens of the neighboring communities with the idea of organizing a cotton mill. They met in the only available place, the waiting room at the depot of the village, which by then had changed its name to Belmont. In the group were R. L. and S. P. Stowe, R. P. Rankin, M. N. Hall, John F. Love, Abel Caleb Lineberger, and G. M. Gullick. First production of yarn was in 1902.

Eventually from small local investors who subscribed stock in amounts ranging from $100 to $5,000, the enormous sum of $100,000 was pledged to build and equip a 5,000-spindle plant that was called the Chronicle Mill, in honor of one of the heroes of the Battle of Kings Mountain who once lived on the mill site.[16]

A national depression, having started in the 1890s, lasted a number of years and affected all businesses, among them the Chronicle Mill. R. L. Stowe ap-

---

[14]Interview with Norman Cocke, Duke Power Co.

[15]Interview with Herman Cone, son of Moses Cone.

[16]Sources: Harold Lineberger (1980) and Messrs. R. L. Stowe, Sr. and S. P. Stowe, Sr. (1940).

The original mill of the Proximity Manufacturing Company.

pealed to his kinsman, D. E. Rhyne,[17] who by then had amassed a small fortune, for financial assistance and counsel. Rhyne thought it over and told them
he would invest in the mill if A. C. Lineberger was put in charge. So, the deal
was made. Lineberger moved his family to Belmont from Tuckaseegee. He was
elected president and helped put the Chronicle on its financial feet.

   In 1905, after earnings warranted it, A. C. Lineberger and R. L. Stowe organized the Imperial Mills. They interested D. E. Rhyne, M. N. Hall, Thomas
W. Springs, J. Q. Hall, J. B. Hall, J. W. Armstrong, Dr. W. W. Davis, and J. A.
Rhyne in the venture, which was capitalized at a quarter-million dollars. All
the machinery was bought from Whitin Machine Works. From then on, Bel-

-----

[17]Although most mills were organized by selling small share holdings to many
stockholders, occasionally before 1910 one might find a closed corporation in small Southern
cotton mills where members of the same family held most of the stock. Sometimes one
found the same man serving as president, vice-president, treasurer, and secretary. Once
a salesman who had taken Daniel E. Rhyne's order for a large block of textile machinery
asked him to have the order confirmed by his directors at the next meeting of the board.
"Young man," answered Mr. Rhyne, "when I walks into this office and takes off my hat,
the Board of Directors has done met."

mont was known as a Whitin town, as new mill after new mill was equipped with Whitin machinery.

Dave Hall, thirty years later in a speech before a large group of textile machinery men, told them he remembered R. L. Stowe coming out to the Hall home to tell of the new mill and to solicit financial interest. Dave said his father bought stock in the mill. Showing the audience a small ragged sheet of paper, he said, "This is it: a ten-share certificate valued at a thousand dollars. It was a hardship for my father to raise the money at the time, but this certificate has helped educate the family, take care of doctor bills, and meet other emergencies. It has grown ragged because of the many trips to the bank as collateral for some urgent family need."[18]

In 1907 A. C. Lineberger, R. L. Stowe, S. P. Stowe, F. P. Hall, W. B. Puett, a brother-in-law of the Stowes, and Thomas W. Springs organized the Majestic Mill, which was capitalized at $400,000 and had 12,768 spindles. The mill used Sea Island cotton or Egyptian long-staple cotton and made fine combed yarns up to 120s on ring spindles. This was a feat that New Englanders had said could not be done in the South. Such fine yarn was used mostly by lace-making mills, both in the United States and in France. A. C. Lineberger was president of this mill, R. L. Stowe was vice-president, and S. P. Stowe was secretary and treasurer.

South Carolina, the last Southern state to be "redeemed" after the Civil War, made a fast recovery. Employees in textile mills increased from 8,071 in 1880 to 30,201 in 1900; the payroll of $1.5 million in 1880 rose to $5 million in 1900. Most of the new mills were equipped with more up-to-date machinery than those in the older textile regions such as New England, and the return on investment in Southern cotton mills in 1900 greatly exceeded that of cotton factories in the North, according to the U.S. Census.

Into this climate of growth came James A. Chapman to organize a cotton mill. Over six feet tall, well proportioned, he was a handsome and engaging man who made plans and carried them out. His ancestral background included many generations of educators, ministers, and patriots. A native of the Spartanburg region, Chapman practiced law in New York City, married Rachel Buchanan McMaster of Winnsboro, South Carolina (1899), and established his law business in Middlesboro, the coal and iron area of Kentucky. But Spartanburg County and the growing textile industry enticed him, so he returned home with his wife, his two young sons, and his daughter.

Apparently he had no difficulty in organizing his mill, the first textile mill of the area to be north of the Southern Railway. About 600 acres of land were purchased from his brother, uncle, and J. R. and B. F. Brown. The latter two took sixty shares of common stock in exchange for their portion of the acreage. The land lay along the right-of-way of the railroad being built from Spartanburg to Asheville, and a nice ploy resulted in a railroad stop for the textile mill being named for railroad tycoon John Inman.

---

[18]Source: Dave Hall.

The financial strategy for the mill followed the traditional Southern textile finance pattern: local investors plus vendors, the latter willing to buy stock in order to have the inside track on the business. The Inman exception to the usual pattern was that no commission house was approached for finance and none was included as stockholder.

Years later, in an interview with Broadus Mitchell, Chapman said that there were instances of bad practices among commission houses, but most had disappeared by then. Whether participation by commission houses in financing cotton mills was damaging or beneficial, it was necessary and the industry owes its establishment as much to them as to any other factor. However, Inman Mills have never sold through a commission house. The machine builders who originally purchased stock were bought out by Chapman as rapidly as possible, in a matter of a few years.

In 1907 the mill's success brought about an expansion of spindles to 19,421, with the looms increasing up to 500. By then the mill had 191 employees, none *under* the age of twelve.

Inman was then consuming 2,732 bales of cotton a year and its annual production was valued at $300,000. Its sheeting was of good quality and was in great demand. To keep up with orders, it was necessary to run longer hours or an additional shift. August Kohn, columnist for the *Charleston News & Courier*, wrote (1907):

> There are very few cotton mills in this state that run at night. . . . As a matter of fact, if the mills wanted to run at night, they could not do so on account of the lack of labor. These few mills that do run at night pay the help from 10 to 20 percent more for night work than day work and, even for this additional inducement, they are unable to get any considerable amount of night help. . . . Within the last few days Inman Cotton Mill has started to run part of its machinery at night. . . . Inman Cotton Mill pays 15 cents per side for its night spinning. . . . A young man or woman can readily run 10 sides. . . . A weaver could operate from 8 to 10 plain looms [nonautomatic].

James Chapman founded his mill, but he also ran it. There is the story of a new hand in the spinning room who asked his foreman, "Who is that great big man in the Panama hat that comes through here so often?" Of course, it was Chapman, the founder and the boss, who was at the same time a reticent person. He had a legal mind of steel and a big heart as soft as putty. The youngster, toddling by his father's side on the daily trips through the mill, was his young son, James, known then to the mill workers as "Little Jim."

During summer vacations from high school, his son worked as a machinery erector. Later, after he had graduated from Wofford College and studied engineering at Cornell, he came back to the mill to work under Gordon Cobb, then superintendent. In 1916 Cobb decided to leave for another job and told Chapman, the president, he wanted to recommend a good man to take his place.

"Who is he?"

"Your son, Jim," was the answer.

"Oh, pshaw," he said. The Inman president whirled his chair around, turning his back on Cobb. He wanted no further discussion.

James Chapman.
Lawyer and founder
of Inman Mills, with
sons Robert (l) and
James (r).

Later, he suggested to young James that he hold things together until he could find a replacement for Cobb. Some months later, on his twenty-fourth birthday, Chapman said to his son, "How does it feel to be superintendent?" He had given him the chance, and Jim had made good.

The executive-superintendent team of Chapman and Chapman brought new success to Inman. In 1920 the mill had 40,000 spindles and 1,000 looms. In 1924 automatic looms replaced nonautomatic, more floor space was added, and the two-shift, around-the-clock operation was started.

Years later, James, then called "Mr. Jim," recalled that it felt fine to be superintendent at twenty-four, in the year 1917. He said, modestly, "Prosperity covered my mistakes and the job was not as burdensome as on today's standards: one-shift operation, producing 39-inch, 72 x 76 4¼-yard goods using one warp and one filling. I took to raising chickens to keep myself occupied." In that, too, he was successful, winning many silver trophies and blue ribbons from various county fairs.

Although most of the commission houses acted in good faith when they took stock in new mills and became their sales agents, some made mistakes that, when uncovered, amounted to chicanery. The Hunter Manufacturing and Commission Co. indulged in a type of finagling that nearly wrecked several of the larger Southern mill organizations and brought disgrace to its own doors. As Donald Comer, Sr. told the story, he said that when Avondale Mills changed its production from print cloth to chambray, around 1907, he changed his selling house and joined Hunter, mainly because of his high regard for the Reeves brothers, who were associated with his company, as well as Mr. Hunter. The Reeves withdrew shortly thereafter and established their own firm, but Avondale Mills, Greenwood Mills, Springs Mills, and others of equal importance remained with Hunter, who specialized in their lines of production.

Southern mills were making profits then of anywhere from 46 to 70%, and commission houses were getting their share of profits and lending money to mills at 6% interest. Also, Hunter paid the mills 6% interest on their money if they left it on deposit with him. It was a good deal for the mills because the bank rate was

James A. Chapman
succeeded his father
as president of Inman
Mills and later
became president of
the American Textile
Manufacturers
Institute. Both of
these posts were also
held by his son Jim.

about 4%, so many of Hunter's suppliers borrowed 4% money and invested in Hunter's depository at 6%. Although Hunter Manufacturing and Commission operated its sales office in New York, most of its preferred stockholders were in the South, largely in the Carolinas.

Donald Comer had a long-distance call from his New York banker saying that it was imperative that he come to New York immediately. Comer explained his daughter was being married in a few days and he couldn't leave home. The reply was, "Forget that and take the next train, this is an emergency."

When he arrived at the bank, representing Avondale Mills and Cowikee, he found James Self of Greenwood Mills, Leroy Springs of Lancaster, Jefferson Evins of Converse and Clifton Mills, and other preferred stockholders. Jim Self had first spotted the trouble during a depressed textile market. Hunter was using the mills' deposit money instead of bank credit to invest in other mills in order to increase his sales volume. Self demanded his money and got out, but by doing so he realized he had made himself a preferred creditor, so he restored some of his money to the company and notified the New York bank. The preferred creditors, a few in number, wanted to get their money but also to have a selling house, so they elected Donald Comer to "take charge of the chaotic situation."

He went to the wedding and then returned to New York with his family to live for three years and have an orderly liquidation of Hunter Co. Hunter resigned; his vice-president and treasurer committed suicide. Under Comer's astute management, creditors were paid in full. The several million shares of common stock Hunter had purchased were a total loss, but of the several million shares of preferred stock, about 30% was saved for the preferred stockholders. The balance of the assets was sold to Jefferson Standard Life Insurance Co. of Greensboro through an arrangement made by Comer with Julian Price, president of the insurance company. Mills that had left money on deposit lost all of it, and everyone had to seek a new sales outlet. Those mills represented by Hunter formed the Southeastern Cotton Corp. and elected Howard Coffin president. Springs established his own selling house and so did Greenwood Mills. Then the Comer interests took over Southeastern Cotton and it was reorganized under the name of Avondale Mills, a selling house to serve not only the Avondale group but other companies selling through Southeastern.

At the time of the Atlanta International Cotton Exposition, young Francis Henry Fries, a graduate of Davidson, had for the past six years operated the F. & H. Fries Woolen Mill, built by his father and his uncle in 1840. It had prospered as one of the first woolen mills in North Carolina. In 1887 he gave up his position in the mill to head up the construction of the Roanoke and Southern Railway between Winston and Roanoke, Virginia, and later, the Winston-Salem Southbound Railroad, a branch that connected Winston with the Atlantic coastline, south and east. About this time, Fries organized the Wachovia Loan and Trust Co. His interest remained in the growth of the Southern textile industry, so as the "build-mill" fever spread, he organized the Mayo Mills and the Avalon Mills at the village of Mayodan, North Carolina, and the Washington Mills of Fries, Virginia. Then he changed the name of the F. & H. Fries Woolen Mills to the Arista Mills. He also organized the Indera Mills and the Oakdale Mills. All six mills were near Salem and Winston.[19]

The urge to build a cotton mill was contagious. The profits from good management were just seen as profits, and to many, made a great and glamorous pie in the sky. There were failures, too, as those with no mill experience ventured their all in a gamble that machinery and buildings would automatically bring success.

Such a venture was that of Warren Coleman, a successful Negro merchant and owner of rentable real estate in Concord. He decided in 1896 that he would

---

[19]Now Winston-Salem.

build a cotton mill to be run solely by Negro operatives and financed by Negro subscriptions to the mill stock. Fifty thousand dollars capitalization was pledged, and the company was organized. It seemed a promising undertaking, and the capitalization was raised to $100,000. This time around, many of his white friends subscribed to encourage him and to reap the future profits. But it took four years to complete the building. Secondhand English machinery was purchased, and much of the Negro-subscribed stock had been forfeited because the poor subscribers could not raise the small capital by "taking in washing" at $1 or $2 a week. Coleman had to assume the forfeited stock. The mill failed due to a depressed yarn market, poor machinery, inexperienced mill hands, insufficient capital, and an untrained administration.

Despite the few failures, however, the textile industry of the South carried the poverty-stricken but willing-to-work South of a hundred years ago into a great new era of progress.

20 October 1905 was a big day for Charlotte, which was becoming the largest textile center in the South. There was a band on every street corner and flags and bunting lined the main streets, where huge crowds had gathered to watch the parade. President "Teddy" Roosevelt was in town to make a speech, and his car (one of the first in the country) led the procession around several blocks, allowing everyone a good look, then moved on to the crowd-packed Vance Park. On the speaker's platform with him and local notables was Mrs. "Stonewall" Jackson, who had met him at the train, along with D. A. Tompkins and S. W. Cramer.

"I rejoice in the symptoms of your abounding prosperity," boomed the president. "I am here in a great center of cotton manufacture. Within a radius of a hundred miles perhaps half of the cotton manufacturing [of the South] is done. I realize to the full, as does every good citizen, that material prosperity, material well being, can never be anything but the foundation of higher citizenship."[20]

Yes, within a hundred-mile radius of Charlotte there were 300 cotton mills, three million spindles, 85,000 looms, with a capitalization of $100 million. This represented one-half the spindles and looms of the South. In Charlotte there were seventeen cotton mills with combined capitalization of $3 million, 3,000 looms, 125,000 spindles, and 6,000 operatives. In Charlotte a weekly textile and ancillary payroll of $30,000 was thought remarkable. There were machinery agents, suppliers and distributors of auxiliary equipment for the textile industry. The average raw cotton trade in Charlotte came to $1.2 million per annum.

The city boasted an iron factory, two hotels, a farm-implement manufactory, three drugstores, a marble works, a bookstore, carriage shops, harness makers, wholesale merchants, a distillery, four liquor dealers, a shoe factory, a tobacco factory, spoke and handle factory, and an ice factory. There was Wadsworth's Livery Stable and a new Opera House that seated 1,000 persons. There was a textile mill at Davidson and others at Pineville, Huntersville, and Cornelius. There were also mills in Gaston County and Lincolnton.

---

[20]*Charlotte Observer*, a special history section, 26 June 1983.

A new road system was under way. Crushed rock roads had been in use, but constant maintenance was costly, so macadam top, considered more efficient, was adopted as the most modern road material. Highways were built to connect all the outlying villages and textile mill communities. But macadam was very hard, it was said, on the feet of horses and mules. So the new roads were built with one-half the width of the road macadam top, the other half-width of clay to accommodate the feet of the animals in the hot summertime.

Charlotte was known as a bustling, prosperous city with an atmosphere of culture. It was a good example of the New South. The manufacture of cotton was the lifeblood of the Piedmont.

Hauling cotton to the mills, Charlotte, North Carolina, 1898. (Courtesy of D. A. Tompkins, *History of Mecklenburg County and the City of Charlotte*.)

Labor | 5

The surge of building new mills throughout the South brought about a labor war because there were not enough workers to go around. Labor agents trekked to neighboring states and to the mountains for labor. Mill men became frantic over the labor shortage and offered competitive wage rates. For example, in Gaston County, North Carolina, fully one-fourth of the working population was on the road moving from one job to another for higher pay. Each mill man was trying to outdo the other in offering inducements to mill workers as he sought to entice his neighbors' help to his own plant. This was a "shootin' offense." Feuds broke out. The labor war culminated in the killing of one mill owner by another with a double-barreled shotgun.

Shocked and sobered by the tragedy, mill owners declared a truce and formed the Gaston County Combed Yarn Spinners Association, agreeing not to steal each other's help, but to work more assiduously on importing labor from Tennessee, Western North Carolina, Virginia, and some from England and Scotland.

Another group, the South Carolina Cotton Manufacturers Association, formed the Committee on Immigration. The association, in cooperation with the state commissioner of labor, E. J. Watson, on two separate occasions introduced foreign labor into South Carolina. The association chartered a ship, the *Wittekind,* and brought from England probably five hundred persons. Skilled textile labor was not recruited as much as industrious, hard-working, and able-bodied people who could be trained to operate mill machinery. Upon arrival, while being questioned by mill men or labor agents, many claimed to be mill hands, although they had never seen a cotton mill. Once at work they seldom stayed long at any one mill, but instead went to Georgia and North Carolina seeking better jobs and pay or just sight-seeing. Some from the *Wittekind* who worked for a time in South Carolina mills wound up on farms in Nebraska. They scattered, but often returned to their original jobs: in Pelzer, Spartanburg, Anderson, Chester, and a few in McAdenville, North Carolina.

Captain John Montgomery of South Carolina wrote Colonel Smyth,[1] who was a member of the United States Industrial Commission, that he would not attend a meeting of the commission because discussion of labor would be the main objective. He wrote that in his new mill (not yet completed), he planned to use Negro help in the mill up to the spinning room, and he was afraid that his plan, if brought up, would start another Civil War. Seth Milliken of New York and New England in turn wrote about labor troubles in Montgomery, saying, "In your section of the country you have better labor than we do."[2]

Some Belgians came to the United States to work in Greenville, South Carolina mills, and one group of twenty or thirty Germans went to Anderson mills. When interviewed by August Kohn of the *Charleston News and Courier*, they said they were getting along fine except for the biscuits. They did not know what they'd do without Mr. Oltman, the German baker who had been in Anderson a number of years and produced bread more to their liking.

While New England's textile industry was struggling to regain its posture after the period 1902-1912, a decade of vicious strikes in the Massachusetts cities of Fall River, New Bedford, Lowell, and Lawrence, the South remained a free land with few and isolated clashes between unions and management.

There had been the strike and lockout of 1886 in Augusta, Georgia, but that only spelled the demise of the Knights of Labor. Then in early 1900, C. P. Davis of High Point, North Carolina, was sent by the International Union of Textile Workers (IUTW) of the American Federation of Labor (AFL) on an "organizing tour." He knew the people of his area, he said, and he knew they were joiners. Many mill workers had no idea what they were joining; it was sort of a club meeting, but Davis was persuasive, to a limited extent.

For example, at Proximity Mills in Greensboro, the new mill built by the Cones, only 150 workers out of 1,000 joined the "union." As soon as the Cones realized what Davis was doing in their community, the mills were closed. Also, the company store, which housed the post office, likewise was closed. This left the mill villagers cut off from the payroll and a place to spend it, and in addition, cut off from daily living supplies or communications. Then, those persons occupying village houses were invited to leave. After a week the mill opened and received employees under the "yellow dog" contract.[3]

---

[1]Ellison Smyth, textile leader, founder of Pelzer Manufacturing Co. I, II, III, IV, and many other South Carolina mills. He was the first man to introduce electric power to textile-mill operation.

[2]Southern labor was native and proud; New England labor at this time was comprised of immigrants from many countries. Doubtlessly they were good, honest people, but confused by language barriers, overcrowded tenements, and other factors.

[3]This type of contract was not solely a textile-mill contract, but was prevalent in all types of construction; it was especially used by the expanding railroad companies of the South. The "yellow dog" contract stipulated that a worker would not join a union or organization in which individual members were governed by the majority on questions of wages and hours. To keep their jobs or to be reinstated or hired elsewhere, the "yellow dog" contract had to be signed by workers.

The Cone strike of 1900 did not work out well for those who participated. The mill lost money too, and no other mill management desired to employ troublemakers. So, the union campaign fizzled out and a lot of unemployed people went back to the mountains because there was no other refuge.

Not long after, the AFL campaigners tried again in Alamance County. But the IUTW organizers didn't know the Holt family. They ran into the solid opposition of nearly twenty family-owned mills, each management group refusing to discuss the matter. This strike had been called because of one worker's alleged violation of plant rules. The operator spit tobacco juice on the floor; this unsanitary habit was against plant rules because it made the floor dangerously slippery for others who might fall into machinery. The rules were posted and he knew of them; he broke them and so was fired. Because one man spit, 4,000 people were out of work, out of housing, and out of town unless they signed the "yellow dog" contract.

The AFL was getting tired of supporting its textile union branch, the IUTW, with its mounting record of strike failures, so a reorganization pattern was set up. All national craft unions except Mule Spinners turned records, funds, everything over to the AFL, and afterwards a new union, the United Textile Workers of America, was formed. The organization embraced the majority of organized textile workers in New England. The IUTW and the AFL abandoned the South as fertile territory after 1902, and their membership in those seventeen states was almost nil.

So it was with appraising eyes that New England companies looked over the area that had better climate, good railroad systems, accessibility to raw materials, and a growing electric-power system. For forty years Southerners, with the help of Northern capital, had founded mills and successfully operated them in many areas to provide work for Southern people. But here was a new slant: Northern capital and Northern management with one central theme: profits for Northern stockholders.

The Massachusetts Cotton Mill in Georgia was a New England company organized in 1894. It was a division of the Massachusetts Cotton Mills in Lowell, which purchased much of the material and provided many services for the Southern mill. Lowell Machine Shops provided equipment. Within five years the Massachusetts Cotton Mills in Georgia had built three mills furnished with old machines from their Lowell plant and some new Lowell opening and spinning machines. Mostly, Draper looms were installed. All of the equipment was designed to produce coarse goods that were unprofitable to manufacture in New England, but were profitable to make in Georgia for foreign export.

This group of mills was located on a sizable tract of land, well over 800 acres, in northwest Georgia, near Rome and the vicinity of Boozville, named for a large landowner. Streets were laid out, and the village was named Lindale by the corporation. Houses and apartments were built for the operatives. The houses resembled those of New England: two-story duplexes with three, four, and five rooms for each family. The entire installation operated according to absentee landlordism, with an "agent" appointed by New England management. It became extremely profitable. Since what was all right for Lindale people was

largely accepted by other mills in the Georgia area as the "standard" procedure, the Lindale Mill kept wages down for decades.

At that time Lindale operatives worked $11\frac{3}{4}$ hours a day, 5 days a week,
and $7\frac{1}{4}$ hours on Saturday. In 1903 a full twenty-five percent of Lindale's working force consisted of children under sixteen. Some children worked as "learn-
ers," but were not on the payroll because they were "helping their parents."
Because children could not reach the machine operations unless they stood on
boxes, the typical paying job for a young child was that of a sweeper, to keep
the floor clear of lint. In 1905 Lindale paid three cents an hour for a sixty-six-
hour week ($1.98); in 1910, five cents an hour ($3.30 a week). A warp spinner,
usually a female, earned $5\frac{1}{4}$ cents an hour, or about $3.50 a week.

An excuse for these low wages was that the cost of living in the South was
much lower than in the North. This fallacy was based on climate, low fuel costs
and, for a long time, on local availability of home-grown food. The fare was
limited, but it was there, and this "lower cost differential" that started at the
turn of the century became a part of the wage picture until recent years. Put
baldly, it was what the mill management could get away with. In the 1930s the
area wage differential became standard through federal legislation.[4]

As to Southern living costs, I quote an 1898 source: "For a large family a
week's supply of food consisting of 100 pounds of flour, a bushel of cornmeal,
10 pounds of meat (salt pork), 10 pounds of lard, 10 pounds of sugar, one dozen
eggs, 4 chickens, 2 pounds of butter cost $4.73, more than the weekly pay of a
'roving hand.' " Also, "Clothing requirements were simple in the South. A man
might wear blue denim overalls and brogans for work and perhaps a clean pair
of overalls on Sunday."[5]

When twenty-nine-year-old Harry Meikleham came to Lindale in 1901 as
the new agent, he had already spent eleven years learning the textile business
in New England. He found plenty to do in Lindale which, in the winter, literally floated in a sea of mud. Families overcrowded the houses and their live-
stock did the same in tiny yards.

It was a rough community, with liquor and shootings prevalent. Captain
Meikleham, a 240-pound former varsity crew member at Columbia University,
moved quickly to clean things up. He arraigned the gunslingers in his office
and told them, "There'll be no more shooting in Lindale. If you want to dispute
that you'll have to whip me; otherwise, I'll whip you. But if you do whip me,
you can shoot the damn things in my office." And that was the end of shooting
in Lindale.

He had the farm animals moved out of the residential section. He brought
pressure on the sloppy householders to clean up or get out. He organized a

---

[4]See Code No. I, in ch. 6, 94–95.

[5]Knowlton, *Pepperell's Progress;* Yorke, *Men and Times of Pepperell; Romance of Pepperell,* 307–19. Interviews with Russell Leonard, president and treasurer of Pepperell
Manufacturing Co.; correspondence and informal autobiography of Jack Smith, retired
superintendent, Lindale.

company of militia to keep the men busy during off-hours, and he organized a burial society to ban the habit of "passing the hat" when a mill worker died. He organized a mill band that became famous throughout the South. Then he started the Boy Scouts and built for their use a clubhouse with a heated swimming pool, basketball court, and other athletic equipment.

G. Howard (Jack) Smith, a one-time agent who in his youth was third baseman on the Lindale baseball team, tells how Captain Meikleham imported "Slick" Moulton, baseball coach of Auburn University, to coach Lindale's team and make it the only "pro" team in the South at the time.

Smith said, "Lindale was losing nearly every game one year, probably because Cap'n was the only honest owner in the league, the only one who stuck to the maximum salary agreement. Well, one day our team was losing badly and the crowd was onto them unmercifully. Cap'n Meikleham refunded all ticket holders their money, paid the visiting team their guarantee, locked the gates, and sat down to view the game alone. He said, 'Our guys are doing the best they can and don't deserve to be booed.' "

Jack Smith recalls other instances of Captain Meikleham's autocratic methods. "He would sometimes blow the mill whistle for his militia company to fall out and go on a long hike. One time he had them swim the Coosa River. And when his company represented Georgia at President Wilson's inauguration, and the militia from another state encroached upon the Georgians' encampment, Cap'n ordered his men to 'fix bayonets and charge.' "

In Meikleham's early days at Lindale he had the streets drained, thus getting rid of the mud. He added to the mill an indigo dye house that was the largest of its kind in the world; also, he added a clothroom building and office building.

During his lifetime he never let an efficiency expert on the premises. He was fair to all employees, but had a rigid code of his own. One time when a case against several young crapshooting black employees was brought before the Floyd County Grand Jury, of which he was foreman, he ruled, "I refuse to indict these boys unless you indict members of my poker-playing club."

Meikleham built Lindale into a "veritable Utopia" for mill workers from all over the South. Five thousand people lived there without a problem. "Lindale was without a slum, without a relief roll, without unemployment, without crime, without poverty, without remediable disease, without illiteracy," said the *Miami Daily News* in 1935.

Captain Meikleham died of a heart attack in New York in July 1937 and was buried at Monticello near the home of his great, great-grandfather, Thomas Jefferson.

The Lindale mills proved extremely profitable. Dividends were paid to stockholders first at the rate of six percent, and later, from December 1906, at the rate of five percent. From 1896, when the mills went into operation, until 1 March 1919, when they were sold to the parent company, Massachusetts Cotton Mills, net earnings—after rent and interest on money borrowed—amounted to almost $4 million. The profitability of the Lindale mills figured greatly in effecting a consolidation with Pepperell Manufacturing Co., which in the meantime (1925) had built its first unit of the Opelika Mills in Alabama, about 100 miles from Atlanta.

To obtain the Opelika Mill, local citizens agreed to convey enough land for the mill and its villages (about 300 acres on the site between the Central of Georgia Railroad and the Western Railroad of Alabama), as well as $62,500 in cash, and promised no taxes for five years and a low assessment thereafter. Pepperell later acquired 400 adjoining acres for expansion of the facilities.

The company spared no expense in the construction of the mill buildings; however, as to machinery, with the exception of four new breaker-pickers, the mill was equipped entirely with old machinery from its plant at Biddeford, Maine, where in turn new machines were installed. Old equipment from Biddeford, Lowell, and Fall River was added to Opelika from time to time. Not until 1934 was new machinery, with its technological improvements, installed.

Opelika paid lower wages than Lindale, the theory being that it cost less to live in Alabama than in Georgia or that lower living standards existed on the west side of the Chattahoochee River. Even so, the workers had a feeling of loyalty to the company and their supervisors, the latter having come from the same areas as the mill hands.

State legislation between 1900 and 1925 overcame some of the wage exploitation, particularly regarding child labor. By 1923 the warp spinner was earning twenty cents an hour, only one cent more than the sweeper who, with the elimination of child labor, was then up to nineteen cents. In those days, each mill set its own wage rates. The lower the better for profit mongers, but each low scale had to be met by other mills in the same line of production. If one mill got by with cutting wages to reduce costs, others had to meet the price to satisfy their customers. Cutting wages was just about the only way a business could lower costs.

These two sets of mills, Lindale and Opelika, produced greater profits for the Pepperell Manufacturing Co. than its better-equipped mills in the North. Both contributed to the flight of the dividend dollar from the South to line the pockets of Northern stockholders.

Another example of Northern-owned mills becoming established in the South is that of Fall River. In that city, between 1907 and 1910, eight new cotton mills were built. *National Geographic* in 1920 described it as America's foremost mill town. "That it can bring coal for power from Pennsylvania and cotton from the South, paying the high freight rates and still compete with the South in the manufacturing of cotton goods is a proof of its energy and efficient organization. . . . Every day the city weaves enough cloth a yard wide to reach from New York to Panama. It produces more goods than any state in the Union except its own (Massachusetts)."

Mill stocks were paying the highest dividends ever. Then in 1923 came the realization that the goose that laid the golden egg had quit producing, or at least the eggs were no longer gold. In one year, 1923-1924, employment fell by 10,000 workers and the total value of Fall River products decreased by $40 million.

At a tax-abatement hearing in 1924 for the Luther Manufacturing Co., an industrial engineer testified that the American Print Works was moving 88,000 spindles from Fall River to the South where everything cost less: construction, taxes, fuel, power, and labor. One important item in the lower cost per unit of Southern production, versus that of New England, was *new* machinery. In 1924 only 21 percent of Fall River's looms were Draper's new modern Northrop automatic looms, whereas in South Carolina, 88.6 percent of the looms were new Northrops, in mills organized and operated by Southerners.

The Bordens, who had figured so prominently in the founding and expansion of Fall River, had virtually left the area. In 1912 M. D. C. Borden and Sons, a very important selling house, was established in New York and successfully operated for many years. In 1924, when Borden announced that its Iron Works cotton mills #6 and #7 would be liquidated and that a new mill would be built in Kingsport, Tennessee, it was the beginning of the end for Fall River's textile domain and definitely established the exodus of the New England cotton textile industry. This single move of two Borden-owned mills displaced 105,000 spindles and 1,850 looms (formerly operated by more than 1,000 employees in Fall River).[6] The machinery was moved to the new Borden mill in Tennessee, thereby opening a new Southern textile area close to an almost untapped labor force. Between 1923 and 1924 total employment in Fall River's textile mills fell by 10,189 workers.

In 1924 there were forty-two labor unions and several newspapers printed in several languages in Fall River. Within the next fifteen years, seventy-three textile mills in Fall River were liquidated.

By the early 1920s Southern troubles were beginning to show also. The days of spectacular expansion and building of Southern cotton mills were over. Ragan Spinning Mills, built in 1922, was the last new combed sales-yarn mill in Gaston County for many years to come. In New England, mill liquidation was under way. Unemployment was already at hand. In the South, there was overexpansion of mill capacity. Inventories had piled up. Therefore, curtailment in operation was necessary. Workers were put on shorter weeks, creating lower payrolls and less inventory. Still, being overinventoried was the governing economic factor.

New machines were developed that allowed one worker to supervise or operate additional machines at no additional pay. Running them required only alertness of mind. The unions called this the stretch-out system.

By 1925 the heyday of textile mill expansion without orderly planning was over. Diversification appeared to some extent in Southern mills with the introduction of knitting, finishing, and increased weaving facilities. But with few exceptions, there was a general decline in profits. The shift of cotton mills to the South was a major development of the decade. About one-third of New England spindles left that area and about half the additional spindles erected in the South were New England transplants.

In 1925 the South had 17,292,000 spindles and for the first time exceeded the North, which was left then with only 15,975,000. Curtailment in the Southern textile industry had started. Weekly earnings of mill operatives were on the decline throughout the area, and some mill villages were allowed to run down. This resulted in some financial support being withdrawn by heavy investors.

---

[6]Ashton, *Of Men and Money.*

For example, one day about this time, J. B. Duke, who financed many cotton mills in the Carolinas' Piedmont area, was driving through a textile section when he found the main road under repair, and the detour took him through a mill village that otherwise he would not have seen. The village was dirty and unkempt, the houses dilapidated and streets almost impassable. Duke said to his traveling companion, "This is a mighty poor village. Anyone who treats his workers like this is bound to treat his business the same way. Let's get back to town in a hurry. I am going to sell my stock in *this mill* before the sun goes down."[7]

Absentee ownership created new problems. The Loray Mill in Gastonia was built originally by George Gray and John F. Love in 1900. The $1 million capitalization was largely local capital, but the cost of the mill and equipment was more than that. George Gray had gone north for some more money, and it was said about $500,000 was subscribed by a Northern woman. Some said it was Mrs. Jay Gould, others Mrs. Jenckes of Providence. By 1907 the capitalization was $1.5 million with 57,000 spindles and 1,660 looms laid out for print-cloth manufacture and export sheetings.

It was never a truly successful venture and underwent a number of reorganizations. Withal Northern capital continued to govern management. In 1919 Loray passed into the hands of the Jenckes Spinning Co. of Rhode Island. It was the first mill in Gaston County to be owned and operated by "outside capital," and somehow, psychologically, it became separated from the town.

Soon after World War I, a local union of United Textile Workers was formed at Loray and about 750 workers walked out, beginning Gastonia's first strike of importance. The workers did not complain about the wage rates or the 55-hour week, but were dissatisfied with the superintendent for not "recognizing" the union. It didn't last long, and in less than three weeks the strikers returned to work, having gained nothing.

Jenckes Spinning Co. immediately started a new community-development project and mill-expansion program. The mill was converted to the manufacture of yarns for tire fabrics, then an upcoming and profitable production located in the South, mostly in Georgia. Loray village was given some 150 new houses, two large dormitories for single workers, a cafeteria, and a laundry. The Community House was enlarged and a playground and nursery were provided. Welfare and community services were inaugurated. A company doctor, a Sick-Benefit Association, a baseball team, a summer camp, and of course, a company store were available to employees.

In 1923 Loray was included in the merger of Jenckes Spinning and the Manville Co., another Rhode Island chain. The new corporation then operated more than 500,000 spindles and close to 10,000 looms. So the future of the Loray Division of Manville-Jenckes was tied in with seven mills in Rhode Island and the relatively small mill at High Shoals, about twenty miles from Gastonia.

---

[7]This mill was absentee-owner operated. Later it was bought by a well-to-do local family. The mill expanded, diversified its products, and the village, still mill-owned, is a showplace of the Southern industrial area.

Capitalization for the new company was $39 million and yet total spindleage remained at the 550,000 level. Stock dividends previously granted by Jenckes Spinning Co. ($300,000 in 1917 and $1.8 million in 1920) had put the stock far out of proportion to productive spindles, imposing on the group of mills a heavy demand for profits in the face of a depressed industry.

In the merger came a number of Northern personnel, including a superintendent, purchasing agent, and others. Workers' wages were about the same as other nearby mills, but although other plants were curtailing, Loray ran two shifts steadily from 1923 to 1928. Employees then totaled 3,500.

There was an element, however, that did not quite fit in with the Southern pattern, and resentment was in the atmosphere. A high chain-link fence was built around the mill, and some said that workers were "locked in" during working hours. Moreover, there was absentee Northern management, and the elaborate community-services program seemed to be an impersonal force for labor discipline rather than a positive force for social activities. None of the compatability existed between worker and "super" that the Southern mill worker had always taken for granted as a matter of pride and principle.

Then the stretch-out system was introduced at Loray. It was one of the first applications of this principle in the Southern textile industry. New equipment was installed to reduce operation costs and to meet new market requirements as "balloon tires" were introduced to the automobile market. Mill workers looked on in absolute horror as old equipment was thrown out the windows and broken up for scrap. No one told them why. To the workers, the machines had been their livelihood. The destruction of their machines, for which they had almost personal affection, hurt them deeply.

Without benefit of time studies, or carefully established job standards, or explanation of any sort to the workers, work loads were drastically increased. Long-time workers, even foremen, were dismissed without cause and replaced by newcomers at lower wages or not replaced as work was redistributed. The superintendent was under orders from Northern owners to cut costs and he did.

Within fifteen months the work force at Loray was reduced from 3,500 to 2,200, while production was kept to its previous level. Two general wage reductions of ten percent each were imposed after the stretch-out began. Twenty-dollar-a-week wages in the card room were down to $13; spinners who earned $18 to $20 a week before the stretch-out were brought down to $10 or $15.

During the new "super's" first three months of management, the mill's total payroll was reduced at a rate that would have saved between half a million and one million dollars a year. Morale in the village dropped to its lowest point. It is said that no one who could get a job elsewhere would work at Loray. Living conditions became miserable.

To show the uptown people what was going on and, in a spirit of bizarre humor, a group of Loray workers staged a parade down Main Street, bearing a coffin in which lay an effigy of the superintendent. Every fifty yards or so, the effigy would sit up and shout, "How many pallbearers are carrying my coffin?" The marchers would shout "Eight!" The effigy then screamed, "Lay off two! Six can do the work!" In describing the situation at Loray, David Clark, publisher, said, "Efficiency has been stretched to the point of being unfair to the employees."

Workers had become increasingly bitter toward the superintendent—to such an extent that he was finally dismissed, but it was too late to mend the situation. Upon word of his dismissal, several truckloads of Loray workers paraded through Gastonia, shouting, laughing, singing, beating tin pans, shooting firecrackers, and otherwise showing their jubilation. On they went until they reached the spacious house of the "super." They turned in his driveway, rode over the lawn and, as one said, "Let him have it." Finally, the police were called to disperse the mob.

A new superintendent from a neighboring state was employed. He was more sympathetic to the human factor. The stretch-out was abolished and management policies were put on a more traditional basis, but it was too late.

The National Textile Workers Union, one of the first national dual unions established by the Communists, had its agent, Fred Beal (early trained in strike technique in Lawrence, Massachusetts), secretly working out of Charlotte. He formed a union at Loray and called for a public meeting on 30 March 1929. At least 1,000 Loray employees attended and most of them joined. Beal and his strike committee were given their vote to proceed and, on 1 April, the entire working force of both shifts walked out of Loray. It was the beginning of a long and bloody business.

Demands made by the strikers were primarily of trade-union character. Yet officials of the Communist party in New York demanded a no-compromise policy and adherence to party lines. George Pershing, representing the Young Communists League, used the Loray walkout as a clarion call to organize 300,000 Southern workers as part of the NTWU.

The strike then became a conflict between Communism and the general community. The AFL and UTW repudiated any connection with the strike. Gastonia folk thought their community and way of life were in danger. The National Guard was called out, but within a couple of weeks was withdrawn. It was replaced by special deputies, many of them veterans of World War I. The *Gastonia Gazette* warned the strikers: "Try to get fresh with an old 1917-18 top sergeant or red-leg who saw service in Belleau Wood or in the Argonne." The paper also urged the expulsion of the Communists from the community.

On 18 April 1929 a band of masked men of about 100 or so destroyed the strikers' headquarters, burning the strikers' stores and all supplies. It was rumored that a couple of leading strikers had been treated to a tar-and-feather bath and taken out of town "on a rail."

The Communists erected a tent colony to house strikers evicted from mill tenements. The Chamber of Commerce and the City Welfare Department launched a campaign for strikers' relief, but not for those who refused to work or who participated in disturbances. Only about $250 was raised.

People were fed up with the whole business: the handbills, the publicity, the noise, everything about the Communist strike. They were furious that Henry Lesesne, a *Charlotte Observer* reporter, had been beaten unconscious by strikers. They were indignant that someone had shot into a van loaded with singing strike sympathizers and killed one of them, a woman from a mill in Bessemer City several miles away.

On 17 June, a carload of officers, supposedly answering a telephone call that there was trouble at the strikers' tent colony, proceeded to investigate. They were ambushed and shooting followed. One striker and four policemen were wounded. One of the wounded was Police Chief Aderholt, who died the next day.

Community feeling ran very high. The night of the Aderholt shooting, about 2,000 citizens gathered at the courthouse and proceeded to get rid of agitators. More than seventy strikers were arrested and taken to the county jail. Fred Beal, six other Communists, and seven other strikers were charged with conspiracy leading to murder. Fred Beal narrowly escaped lynching the next day when news of Aderholt's death was received.

Governor O. Max Gardner sent in 500 National Guard troops to help maintain law and order. The back of the strike was broken, however. The shooting affair and the presence of soldiers scattered the strikers and their sympathizers, who fled in terror. The leaders and the agitators were jailed and Gastonia was willing to allow the final expulsion of the Communist menace by judicial process.

A trial for Beal and fourteen others was scheduled. All the magazines and newspapers, especially the *Nation,* the *New Republic,* and the *Raleigh News and Observer,* were demanding that it be a fair trial. Hence the issue became solely that of murder and the venue was changed to Charlotte.

The city of Gastonia retained Clyde R. Hoey, former congressman and leading attorney who later became governor of North Carolina, and other distinguished lawyers to assist the solicitor in the prosecution. Only one Gaston County lawyer accepted a place on the defense staff; he was associated with Arthur Garfield Hayes, Dr. John R. Neal, and Leon Josephson, recruited by the Civil Liberties Union.

The trial started 26 August amid such demanding newspaper headlines as "Free the Gastonia Defendants" and "Smash Imperialist Capitalism." A campaign had been started by so-called liberals for a million signatures on a petition against conviction, at ten cents per signature. The jury was selected from 408 veniremen. It was composed of seven workers (one textile worker and two others who belonged to trade unions), four tenant farmers, and one grocery clerk.

On 9 September, the solicitor brought into the courtroom a lifesize wax model of Chief Aderholt dressed in the clothes he was wearing when shot, and proceeded to reveal the wounds before Judge Barnhill could order the effigy removed. But the sight of the bloody effigy of the chief so affected one juror that a mistrial was ordered.

New violence erupted in Gastonia since people felt that the mistrial was effectively a victory for the Communists. Several carloads of indignant Gastonia businessmen and Legionnaires caravaned through the county rounding up every strike sympathizer. They destroyed the headquarters and living quarters of the organizers. Three organizers were taken into the country, beaten, and abandoned near railroad tracks so they could get out of the county when the train passed by. Ten days later, another was "ridden out of town" by force.

A special investigation was ordered by Governor Gardner. Five employees of Loray were indicted in the homicide of Ella May Wiggins, but all were acquitted. It was rumored that her irate boyfriend had done her in and thus her death was not connected with the strike at all.

At the second trial, Beal and seven defendants were charged with second-degree murder. By virtue of nolle prosequi, cases against the others were dropped. Beal and his associates were judged guilty and bail of $27,000 was established. They jumped bail, paid by the Civil Liberties Union, and fled to Russia. Years later, Fred Beal returned to the United States to serve his sentence in Caledonia prison. "I'd rather be in jail in the United States than free in Russia," he said.[8]

---

[8]Pope, *Millhands and Preachers*. Interviews with Dameron Williams, Legionnaire.

The Depression | 6

In 1929 the Southern textile industry had hardly regained its composure from the violent strikes in Gastonia and Marion, North Carolina, and Danville, Virginia (the Dan River Mills), and Elizabethton, Tennessee, when the debacle of the stock market occurred on 29 October. The long downward slide of cotton, wool, silk, and rayon began and, of course, affected all mills.

At that time there were 1,281 textile mills in the industry. All were trying to outproduce the others and results were somewhat chaotic from the raw cotton markets to Worth Street, the trading center for cotton goods in New York. Mills slowed operations as orders to ship goods failed to come through, but at the same time, they were accepting orders for "future" delivery. There was no termination date on "future" shipments.

In 1930-1931 the Depression was gaining momentum and, no matter what goods any mill produced, there was almost no market, no matter the type of promotion. Business stagnated. Many mills were idle; most were operating on less than half time. Wages were down to ten to fifteen cents an hour, and hours were very short indeed. Cone Mills in Greensboro, North Carolina, put its employees on a staggered employment basis so that everyone had some work each week even if it was only ten hours. Many mills followed this pattern. Goods were unsold. Raw cotton dropped below a nickel a pound, and yet, at that low price, there was still no market for it. Cloth and yarn inventories on hand at mills prohibited further purchases of cotton for goods that could not be sold. There was just no cash flow. Field workers and tenant farmers, as well as the heavily mortgaged cotton planter, lived on soul food and wild game. One Mississippi Delta lady who lived in a mansion, but in those hard times made good sausage out of wild rabbits said, "If the wolf knocks at my door I'll make sausage out of him."

Profit was a word seldom, if ever, heard between 1930 and 1933. In the first three years, barely 200 mills out of 1,281 reported net income to the United States Treasury Department, and the average annual tax collected by the government from the entire textile industry was reduced to only a scant $1,000,000. The United States Treasury Department figures show that in 1931 the cotton textile industry suffered its greatest net loss—$91,500,000—up to that time.

When textiles hit bottom in 1931-1932, Ben Gossett, then president of Chadwick-Hoskins and the Gossett Mills (a chain of thirteen cotton textile mills), closed his Charlotte, North Carolina, office and went up to New York to concentrate on merchandising technique. He said to his factoring friends, "We have got to move our stocks in order to buy more cotton to run our mills." But how to do it when banks were closing, mills were going bankrupt, credit was all used up? There were few mills in those days with cash resources, and every new day brought more financial casualties.

During this period Ben Gossett went to Washington frequently. He called, in person, on President Hoover. He openly and smoothly lobbied for his industry. "Just move these inventories," he pleaded, "give the stuff away if it can't be sold, and give us cotton to run our mills on. We can't pay our people unless the mills run. The mills can't run without cotton. We're broke and can't buy the cotton," he pleaded, and he and other textile leaders went to Washington to see their senators and representatives.

In April 1932 Gossett was elected president of the American Cotton Manufacturers Association. He threw the weight of the whole association back of his plea. On 2 July 1932, a congressional resolution was passed (as a temporary law) authorizing the Federal Farm Board to turn over to the Red Cross 500,000 bales of cotton that it held, the cotton then being given to the mills in exchange for cotton goods being distributed in the form of cloth or clothing to three million needy families on relief. The bill carried the proviso, however, that no profit could accrue to the mills from the exchange. Profit? No one expected profit in 1932. It was enough to run the mills and to give employment, even part-time employment.

Upon passage of the congressional resolution, George Harris, head of Exposition Cotton Mills, Atlanta, was appointed as the textile expert of the Central Cotton Distribution Office of the American Red Cross to supervise the deal. He, with the cooperation of cotton manufacturing companies and the members of the Textile Merchants Association,[1] soon had the project working, resulting in large orders for mills and garment manufacturers. The legislation of 1932 was supplemented by another and similar resolution in February 1933, which put into distribution, in the same manner, an additional 344,000 bales of cotton and the equivalent in cotton goods and garments.

For some years prior to 1930, the elimination of night work for women and minors had been sought within the industry. In 1928 an effort was made to amend the by-laws of the Cotton-Textile Institute[2] prohibiting its taking part in legislative or political matters in order to enable it to accomplish the reform through legislation. This was defeated, but in 1930, following a conference with

---

[1]The association representing textile merchants, commission houses, and sales agents, located in the Worth Street area of New York.

[2]An association of cotton-textile manufacturers, Northern and Southern, created to coordinate self-imposed rules and regulations directed toward betterment of the industry.

Ben Gossett.
President of
Chadwick Hoskins
and the Gossett Mills,
a chain of thirteen
Carolina mills.
Elected president of
the American Cotton
Manufacturers
Association in 1932.

government officials in Washington, a plan for the institute to propose voluntary action by the mills took definite shape. The first outcome of the conference was the suggestion to the industry by leading mill executives to establish greater uniformity in running time for labor and machinery and to make the night shift shorter than the day shift.

In the fall of 1930 the institute proposed that night employment for women and minors be eliminated. The recommendation was followed by a five-month educational effort concerning the movement by George A. Sloan, then president of the institute, and Walker D. Hines, chairman of the board. In 1930, by personally canvasing the industry mill by mill and group by group, Sloan obtained individual declarations of policy from eighty-three percent of all cotton mills throughout the nation for the discontinuance of night work for women and minors and the voluntary adoption of a fifty-five-hour work week. This action put curtailment on an orderly basis and was subscribed to by all farsighted mill executives. The effective date for this voluntary policy was set for 2 March 1931.

For this achievement, the institute was showered with congratulations by telephone, telegram, and letter. As in all individual efforts, however, the small percentage of noncooperators injured much that progressive leadership had envisaged.

When Franklin D. Roosevelt was elected president in 1932, the second-largest employing industry in the United States was one of the sickest industries in the nation. Even before Roosevelt's inauguration in March 1933, some governmental planning was under way to correct wage and hour conditions in the textile industry and a few other comparably distressed industries. Informal conferences had been held during the fall and winter of 1932-1933 between Roosevelt, General Hugh Johnson, and leaders of industry, among them John Hancock of Lehman Brothers, Alex Sachs, associated with Bernard Baruch, and George A. Sloan, who spoke for the cotton manufacturing industry. Advice from Frances Perkins, industrial commissioner of New York, and from General Johnson had been sought by Roosevelt. Perkins in turn conferred, on several occasions, with some members of the industry as well as labor organizations.

They all knew that some new law, as yet unwritten and as yet unnamed, would be drafted to serve as an emergency measure for all the sick industries soon after the inauguration. Such a law, its effective date only weeks away, created a sudden spurt of activity in the textile market. Orders for yarns and fabrics that had been on the books for years were taken up by the customers as quickly as possible before the legislation-to-come created higher prices. It put the mills back to full operations for a few short weeks. In the meantime, the industry's leaders planned for the orderly handling of business under the expected new act.

Following the appointment of Roosevelt's cabinet, Daniel C. Roper (of the pedigreed cotton-seed family of Hartsville SC), the new secretary of commerce, appointed an Industrial Advisory Board representing all industry and made up of ten members. Walter C. Teagle, of Standard Oil of New Jersey, was chairman; Edward Stettinius was named secretary; and William J. Vereen of Georgia's Moultrie Cotton Mills was appointed to the board from the textile industry. At the same time, Frances Perkins, the newly named secretary of labor, appointed a Labor Advisory Board with Dr. Leo Wolhman as chairman. A Consumers Advisory Committee with Mrs. Charles C. Rumsey as chairman was appointed also. These three boards were set up to approve any codes agreed upon by government and industry under the National Industrial Recovery Act (NIRA).

This act was to become law 17 July 1933 with General Hugh Johnson as its administrator. At President Roosevelt's request, George A. Sloan, chairman of the board and president of the Cotton-Textile Institute, agreed that the cotton-textile industry would submit Code No. I. So, the Cotton Textile Industry Committee was appointed to draft the Code and to guide the industry's policies in cooperation with government planning. All members of the committee patiently negotiated, drafted, and worked out the Code during some of the hottest weeks that Washington's climate could produce, and this was before air-conditioning.

This famous Code No. I served as a model for all the many industrial codes that followed. Under its provisions a minimum of thirteen dollars a week in wages for Northern mill workers, twelve dollars a week for those in the South was set up. Fourteen and thirteen dollars, in the North and South respectively, was the rate for specified finishing operations. Cleaners and outside help were to receive pay at a rate equivalent to seventy-five percent of the thirteen and twelve dollars for machine operators. Apprentices were exempted from the minimum-wage regulations for six weeks. Two shifts of forty hours each on productive machinery were maximum.

Code No. I also set up a Planning and Fair Practice Agency for the cotton-textile industry. The agency was actually a group of subcommittees formed to study various industry problems and to make suggestions and recommendations. Through this planning agency, made up of its own leaders, the textile industry was left relatively free to govern its future.

The cotton textile industry was the guinea pig for the NIRA. At the time of the adoption of Code No. I, the NIRA was so new and events were moving along so rapidly that it was accepted informally. Code No. I, as drafted by the Cotton Textile Industry Committee, was first submitted 15 June 1933, and during the next two weeks hearings were held on it. Some points were bitterly contested by representatives of labor, especially William Green, who wanted a 30-hour week. Following a meeting of the committee on 30 June, the last date on which the Code would be submitted for approval to meet the effective date of July 17, a revised Code was submitted by General Johnson. Johnson's approval and President Roosevelt's executive order making Code No. I effective 17 July were announced in the press on the ninth.

For some strange reason never explained, the Code, *after* being signed by President Roosevelt, contained one or two provisions not previously discussed with the committee. When the terms of that Code appeared in newspapers throughout the country (and other parts of the world), George A. Sloan and Goldthwaite Dorr went at once to the White House and called the president's attention to the discrepancy. Mr. Roosevelt was reminded of earlier conversations in which a partnership relation had been understood, and Sloan pointed out that the Code was doomed to failure unless the newest provisions were removed. The president indicated that he would get in touch with General Johnson immediately to remove the unauthorized provisions. On 15 July 1933 application for final approval of Code No. I was signed by George A. Sloan and submitted to Hugh Johnson.

Daniel Roper's Industrial Advisory Board had left the heat of Washington as had many members of Frances Perkins's Labor Advisory Board. Will Vereen[3] stayed in Washington and had been authorized by Mr. Teagle, chairman of the Industrial Advisory Board, to accept the corrected Code for his committee when it was finally submitted. Vereen, having been told that application for final approval had been filed, found the public stenographer at the Mayflower Hotel gone for the day. In his characteristic desire to get things done, he went down to the hotel office, borrowed a typewriter and, using the hunt-and-peck system, typed out the simple message of acceptance:

---

[3]Interview with Will Vereen, of Georgia, member of the Industrial Advisory Board for the textile industry.

> Having been given authority by our respective Committees, Industrial Advisory Committee and the Labor Advisory Committee, we accept Code No. I.
>
> (Signed) William J. Vereen

He left space for the signatures of the representatives of the Labor Advisory Board and the act's administrator.

He then telephoned Hugh Johnson at his office and told him he had signed acceptance of the Code and wanted to bring it over to him. He then called William Green, head of the American Federation of Labor and a member of the Labor Advisory Board, who said he would meet him at Administrator Johnson's office and accept the Code for his committee. In the meantime, Hugh Johnson called Frances Perkins and asked her if she would approve it. "Approve it?" she said, "Why I have wanted it to go through for weeks. Of course, I approve it." And she added that she had cleared it with Mr. Roper also.

It was late Saturday night when Vereen and Green met at General Johnson's office. Johnson was in a meeting, but came out of it to see William Green add his signature, on behalf of the Labor Advisory Board, below that of William J. Vereen, who had signed for the Industrial Advisory Board. He then added his own signature as administrator of NIRA to the informal document that was to bring about such revolutionary changes in industrial history.

Administrator Johnson left early next morning for a trip down the Potomac with Mr. Roosevelt on the presidential yacht. Johnson took Code No. I with him, hoping to have the president's signature before his return. Most of the members of the committee who had been negotiating all the previous month or so had returned to their homes or offices elsewhere, delegating three or four of their group to stay at the Mayflower Hotel to watch developments.

An executive order, dated 16 July and signed by Franklin D. Roosevelt, made Code No. I effective on 17 July 1933. With the announcement of this executive order, a corrected version of Code No. I, as agreed to by the industry and as worked out in conference with government officials, was given out.

The little group representing the Cotton Textile Industry Committee put in telephone calls to every member of the committee and sent out 1,200 telegrams, one to every mill in the industry, advising them that the Code, agreed upon by the committee and the government, and by the representatives of the Industrial Advisory Board and the Labor Advisory Board, had been signed.

The Cotton-Textile Institute was declared the agency to collect and receive reports called for in the Code. Later, Sloan was appointed by General Johnson as chairman of the Consumers Goods Industries Committee, representing all "light" industries in the United States.

In March 1933 total employment for the industry was 312,000; by November 1934 employment had increased to 416,000. Workers' average hourly earnings increased sixty-nine percent in the first month of the Code, and by the end of 1934, had increased seventy-eight percent over the earnings of March 1933. This acceleration in earnings carried with it increased purchasing power that was instantly employed. So many workers needed so much of the bare necessities such as food, clothing, medicine, and generally small living comforts.

EXECUTIVE ORDER

July   1933

A Code of Fair Competition for the Cotton Textile Industry has been heretofore approved by Order of the President dated July 9, 1933, on certain conditions set forth in such order. The applicants for said Code have now requested the withdrawal of condition 12 of said order providing for the termination of approval at the end of four months unless expressly renewed, have accepted certain other conditions, have proposed amendments to the Code to effectuate the intent of the remaining conditions, and have requested that final approval be given to the Code as so amended and on such conditions.

Pursuant to the authority vested in me by Title I of the National Industrial Recovery Act, approved June 16, 1933, on the report and recommendation of the Administrator and on consideration,

It is ordered that the condition heretofore imposed as to the termination of approval of the Code is now withdrawn and that the Code of Fair Competition for the Cotton Textile Industry is finally approved with the conditions so accepted and with the amendments so proposed, as set forth in Schedule A attached hereto.

Approval Recommended:

Franklin D Roosevelt

Document signed by President Franklin D. Roosevelt pertaining to Code I, 16 July 1933.

There was some cash, too, for cheap luxuries such as cigarettes, Coca Cola, even gasoline for a decrepit car.

The textile machinery industry also benefited from the reforms. When the Wall Street Crash of 1929 occurred, there were 12,067 persons who worked 49.6 hours (without overtime) per week at 41 cents per hour. By 1930 only 9,736 persons were employed by the same forty-four companies. By 1931 only 6,545 persons were employed by the same companies, but a slight upsurge shows up in 1932 when 7,182 were employed. In 1933, first quarter, there were 7,030 on the payroll. The second quarter shows 8,195 employed. With the National Recovery Administration Act (NRA), wages were stabilized at apparently thirty-four cents per hour in New England, twenty-six cents per hour in the South for rough labor. For shop labor, excluding foremen, there was a wage stabilization average of forty-eight cents an hour in New England and fifty-two cents an hour in the small segment of the industry in the South, and a thirty-eight-hour week. Yet there were only 111 employees reported from the South compared to 8,195 from New England.

The cotton-growing industry had been particularly hard hit by the Depression. In 1932 mills' inventories were piling up at their warehouses and raw cotton inventories were piling up or owned by the government through Federal Farm Board dealings. It was then, during President Hoover's administration, that the Domestic Allotment Plan was concocted by W. J. Spillman of the Bureau of Agricultural Economics. By this plan, cotton acreage was to be allotted to farmers according to needs of domestic mills. Cotton from that acreage was to be sold in the United States at a boosted price and cotton for export was to be sold for whatever could be obtained. To finance the subsidy, it was proposed that American mills were to be taxed five cents a pound for cotton purchased by them.

At a special meeting of the American Cotton Manufacturers Association called by its president, Ben Gossett, in Charlotte, North Carolina, Colonel W. D. Anderson, Charles Cannon, and A. Foster McKissick were appointed as a committee to lobby in Washington to defeat this proposal. In order to subsidize the cotton farmer, this proposal would, in effect, place nearly a 100 percent tax on cotton that was selling in the open market for not much more than five cents. The scheme was obviously unworkable and appeared to be grossly unfair to the processors of cotton. The Domestic Allotment Plan of President Hoover's administration finally collapsed.

One of the earliest pieces of legislation proposed as part of President Roosevelt's national recovery plan was the Agricultural Adjustment Act (AAA). It, too, had a subsidy plan for farmers. Its purpose was to raise farm prices to a level that would provide farmers with a purchasing power equal to the purchasing power of agricultural commodities in a base period between August 1908 and July 1914. This was called "parity." To that end, the secretary of agriculture was authorized to provide for benefit payments in connection therewith. To provide revenue to cover expenses incurred in this program, the secretary was also authorized to proclaim a processing tax with respect to particular agricultural commodities.

Many legislative historians felt that the AAA was a revival of the plan concocted by Spillman and his fellow bureaucrats in the Hoover administration. When the AAA and the processing tax were first proposed, Charles Cannon literally stormed Washington in protest. He appeared before the congressional committee on the legislation in bitter anger at this unfair imposition on a seriously sick industry. He started fighting it before industry associations or the industry in general was aware of its portents. And Charles Cannon was a diligent fighter against what he termed "unjust economics dreamed up by a bunch of jackasses."

When Charles Cannon succeeded his father as president of Cannon Mills Company in 1921, he was not yet thirty years old. Many thought he was very young to have such a responsible position, but even then he was already a man of real experience and proven ability in the industry with a decade of hard work and active management behind him. He had struggled during the hard times of the post-World War I depression, mill curtailment of the 1920s, and even a short but bitter strike in 1921—his mill's first, last, and only strike.

He had revolutionized merchandising of household textiles. He had inaugurated, together with national advertising, such things as labeling of goods, high styling and fancy packaging of items that formerly had been simply utilitarian. Until Cannon Mills Company[4] put color and design into towels, the only decor for the stylish bathroom had been the hand-crocheted or tatted borders that more energetic housewives added themselves to the staple items.

Charles had consolidated nine separate corporations into the Cannon Mills Company, and had established such friendly and pleasant relations with the employees that not since that abortive strike in 1921 had there been a hint of misunderstanding. Cannon had been among the first to endorse Code No. I. He worked hard and earnestly to see that fair and equitable wage rates were established for the industry. He urged cooperation between industry and government. However, when the processing tax was levied on cotton mills to provide benefit payments to cotton farmers who had reduced their acreage to raise prices, that was another story!

It also was another story for the mules that plowed and worked the cotton fields. Trained from birth never, never to step on a cotton plant, to plod along in the middle of the rows to prevent injury to the delicate plants, the mules absolutely refused to plow up that third row, which was the way the law decreed that acreage be reduced after it had been planted. Farmers were forced to tie blinders over the mules' eyes in order to force them to plow up the row they could not see.

AAA was enacted 12 May 1933. On 14 July 1933 the secretary of agriculture proclaimed that he had determined benefit payments should be made with respect to cotton and imposed a processing tax on raw cotton beginning 1 August 1933 at the rate of 4.2 cents per pound of lint cotton, net weight. He further

---

[4]Interviews with C. A. Cannon and various Cannon Mills employees.

imposed a floor-stock tax for inventories of cotton goods on hand on 1 August 1933.

The taxes, the AAA decreed, would be passed on to the customer through converters, garment cutters and sewers, wholesale and retail distributors. Since man-made fibers, silk, and wool were exempt, the tax to be passed on was figured on cotton content only. It was a prodigious bookkeeping job at each waystop.

Code No. I was in effect to stabilize wages and hours and to create purchasing power for both mill workers and mill stockholders. However, the processing tax's effect in the cotton goods marketplace was chaotic.

Then in 1934, on the first of September, newspaper headlines announced that all textile workers throughout the United States would go on strike the following Monday. The announcement came from the United Textile Workers of America (UTWA) and had been planned as an organization strike. Also, the movement was combined with that of a group described later by the secretary of labor as "comeouters," those dissatisfied with the UTWA who afterwards formed the core of the Congress of Industrial Organizations (CIO) textile union. The publicized reason for the strike, however, was dissatisfaction with the Code. The strike lasted approximately three weeks. During that time considerable damage was done by the so-called "Flying Squadrons," or mobs of strikers or sympathizers who attempted to terrorize nonstriking workers.[5]

Up and down Highway 29 from Virginia to Georgia, truckloads of demonstrators stopped at each mill located on or near the highway. Upon arriving at a mill, they would storm the place, forcing open doors and running through the mill tearing down the thousands of "ends" and stopping the machinery. Then they loaded into their trucks to speed down the road.

More than one mill man wept in anger and frustration as he saw the damage to his yarn or fabric and saw the dismay on the faces of his loyal workers. An executive of the Southern Combed Yarn Spinners, whose offices were located on the second floor of a Main Street building in Gastonia, had the unpleasant experience every day of seeing a machine gun pointed toward the office from the strikers' headquarters across the street. Others were handed each morning, by a different person, a printed advertisement for a mortician or a cemetery lot.

A climax of the Flying Squadron technique was realized in South Carolina when the Flying Squadron reached the so-called "Upper Plant" of Pelzer Manufacturing Company. (It was called the "Upper Plant" because it was up the river from Plant #1, which was the "Lower Plant.") There they found the loyal workers awaiting them, lined up against the mill and armed with shotguns and .22s. The "Squadron" was armed too and everybody started shooting. No one was killed in the melee, but a salesman, an innocent bystander near the corner drugstore, was injured. South Carolina mill men had begged Governor Olin Johnston to call out troops to prevent disorder and, after this affair, he did.

---

[5]Textile trade papers; *Charlotte Observer; Gastonia Gazette.*

At the start of the strike, Secretary Perkins appointed a panel of three, headed by John Winant, who had just retired as governor of New Hampshire, to negotiate for settlement. It was Winant's first appointment in the Roosevelt administration. Others on the Winant panel were Marion Smith of Georgia and Raymond V. Ingersoll of New York. Since the strike was against Code No. I, the Code Authority met to discuss necessary procedure. During the conference one member of the committee asked, "Has Max Gardner been called in on this?" The result was that Gardner, attorney for the Cotton-Textile Institute, was delegated to represent the industry with the Winant Board.[6]

Many tedious conferences were held by the two groups within the next few days, several in the office of Frances Perkins. An acceptable pattern was worked out, but there was really no "settlement" of the strike. It wore itself out and strikers, most of whom did not belong to any union and who did not know why they had gone on strike, gradually returned to work. The loss in payrolls during that period was a great detriment to the slowly returning prosperity of the nation.

In the meantime litigation as to the constitutionality of the processing tax was begun by the receivers of Hoosac Mills Corporation of Massachusetts. This case resulted in a declaration by the District Court of Massachusetts on 9 October 1934 that the act was constitutional. Appeal was made to the Circuit Court of Appeals for the First Circuit, which on 13 July 1935 declared the act unconstitutional, reversing the District Court. On appeal to the United States Supreme Court, the Circuit Court was affirmed. The Supreme Court finally declared the processing tax unconstitutional in a decision handed down on 6 January 1936.

After the Circuit Court of Appeals decision had been rendered, many mills secured injunctions against collection of the tax, but paid the tax in escrow during the period of the injunction. Since the tax was payable ninety days after the close of the month in which cotton was placed into process, most injunctions were effective to cover the tax imposed on cotton placed into process after the beginning of April 1935. Market conditions became so uncertain during this period that protective clauses of various types came into widespread use in the industry, of which the so-called "Charlotte clause" (so named at a meeting in Charlotte, North Carolina) was typical. The purport of the clause was to require a person who had paid the processing tax to reimburse his customer for the amount of the tax in the goods sold if the tax were ultimately declared unconstitutional.

After the Circuit Court decision but prior to the Supreme Court decision, Congress amended Section 21 (d) of the Agricultural Adjustment Act to pro-

---

[6]O. Max Gardner was a former governor of North Carolina who had established the law firm of Gardner and Morrison in Washington in 1932. He was an attorney for the Cotton-Textile Institute. Later he was assistant treasurer of the United States and then was appointed ambassador to Great Britain. He died of a heart attack before his ship left New York for London.

vide that, in the event of the abolition of the processing tax, only those processors who had borne the burden of the tax should be permitted to receive refunds. In the Revenue Act of 1936, Congress spelled out the procedures for making this showing. The act allowed reimbursement for the amount of the tax to nonprocessors having inventories on hand on 6 January 1936 (the date of the Supreme Court decision) to the extent they could show that the burden of the tax had been passed on to them.

In the same act, Congress included a so-called "unjust enrichment" or "windfall" tax equal to eighty percent of the net income from the sale of articles on which a processing tax had not been paid on the assumption that such net income was due to shifting to others the burden of the processing tax. This provision was designed to cover the taxes paid in escrow during the injunctive period. These refund and windfall-tax provisions resulted in the filing of claims by taxpayers and assessments by the government that were in controversy for a period of many years.

Textile-mill executives were somewhat bewildered by the volume of reports and office checking that became necessary with all this legislative governance of the industry. One mill executive wrote (1935):

> I venture to say that in the last six months we have had to spend between $1,500 and $2,000 for additional auditors' fees in order to have reports made up for Washington. As an example of what we are up against, one day, a short time ago, we had one young man and three young ladies from the Department of Labor in our office checking payrolls, while at the same time we had two hired auditors making up a report for the Federal Trade Commission; and then that same day, along came two men from the Revenue Department to check up on processing taxes, making eight additional people we had to wait on at a time, while our own office force consists of only five clerks.

When the Supreme Court decision invalidated NIRA in 1935, the textile industry tried by general and voluntary effort to uphold the standards and performance of Code No. I. It was a remarkable movement. A year later a survey of the industry indicated that 98.4 percent of the mills continued to conform to previous NIRA standards on wages and hours. Plans were made by the industry's great leaders to "reclaim by persuasion" the few backsliders. During 1936 there was a general wage increase throughout the industry from two percent to five percent, and in less than a year, wages were given a second boost of ten or twenty percent.

Soon after the expiration of NIRA in 1935, the Walsh-Healey Act was passed by Congress as a sort of interim legislation on wages and hours. It provided for compliance with the prevailing wage as determined by the secretary of labor and mandated an eight-hour day and forty-hour week. In addition, it prohibited child labor and prison labor and set up regulations governing sanitary and nonhazardous working conditions. Its provisions applied to all industries on government contracts in excess of $10,000 and it affected, of course, those textile mills that were operating on such government contracts.

Later, in 1938, the Fair Labor Standards Act became effective. In the meantime, during the three years between termination of NIRA and the enactment of the Wage-Hour Act, many inequities existed. Naturally, with strong competition from imported goods as well as domestic goods and with no legal minimum wage in existence except on government contracts, there were occasions of drastic price cutting, which in turn could force a wage adjustment downward at the mill.

It was difficult to resist some of the demands, but the majority of mill men stood firm despite sales pressure from certain sources. A customer telephoned a Southern textile executive long distance, determined to place a large order for 30's[7] single combed yarn at 25 cents a pound. The executive said, "But my price for that yarn is 30 cents." The customer answered, "But the *Daily News Record*[8] quotes 25 cents." The mill executive's patience was exhausted. He snapped, "Then buy it from the *Daily News Record*, my price is still 30 cents."

As the Fair Labor Standards Act came into being, Luther Hodges, then vice-president of Marshall Field and Company and manager of its Manufacturing Division, Eden, North Carolina, reflected the opinion of many farsighted men of the industry when he said:

> Although the maintenance of the wage and hour structure is not the only requirement for profit-making in the textile industry, it is to my mind one of the most important. In the old days, many of the mills which could not compete because they did not have modern machinery or a modern organization did the easiest thing at hand, namely, they reduced wages or increased hours. If it is impossible for such mills to go below minimum standards, it will serve to keep costs more in line and it will help stabilize prices and profits.

With the passage of the Fair Labor Standards Act in 1938, the textile industry was again the first to take the lead in establishing compliance with federal legislation. Elmer F. Andrews, who was then serving as industrial commissioner of New York State, was named administrator of the newly enacted Wage-Hour law.

He made his first appearance before the industry at the annual meeting of the Southern Combed Yarn Spinners Association on 30 September 1938, in Gastonia. He was introduced by O. Max Gardner as "a man from the North who had come down to the South to try to understand the problems of the section, not to tell the South how to handle its own affairs." A tour of the best of nearby cotton mills was arranged for Administrator Andrews before the meeting. He saw at firsthand representative mills of the industry and heard some of the spinners discuss their more pressing problems. His comment, as he walked through mill after mill, was "where are all the workers?" He was seeing the modern machinery and automatic attachments, even those of 1938, that allow one person to operate many spinning frames or looms and other machines in proportion.

---

[7]30's is a medium-weight yarn, with 1's being coarse yarn and 100's being fine yarn.

[8]*Daily News Record*, a Fairchild daily textile trade publication, known among textile mill executives as the "mill man's Bible."

(L to R): Elmer Andrews, Wage and Hour administrator, Fair Labor Standards Act; Claudius Dawson, vice-president of Cramerton Mills; Mildred Barnwell Andrews, executive secretary, Southern Combed Yarn Spinners Association; William Pharr, president of American Yarn Spinners Association and Pharr-Stowe Mills; Cyrus Ching, industrial-relations director, U.S. Rubber Company; Governor Greg Cherry of North Carolina, at an annual meeting of the Southern Combed Yarn Spinners Association.

Dave Hall, Stowe Thread Company, Belmont, North Carolina, and at that time president of the Southern Combed Yarn Spinners Association, presided at their luncheon meeting. He said to Andrews, "We're not really cotton barons. They just call us that. The truth is that we're just ex-school teachers and ex-storekeepers and ex-farmers who thought we could make a living spinning cotton."

O. Max Gardner explained to the group, "You'll find Elmer Andrews not to be a social worker nor a dictator as some have thought, but a business man, a civil engineer, and a man of abundant ability, common sense and methodical determination."[9]

Andrews in turn answered a variety of questions put to him by the textile people. They wanted to know, for instance, what opportunity the new law offered the manufacturers. "More money," was his answer. "As a matter of fact, the Act might well have been called the 'Better Business Act.' It will eliminate many doubtful practices and permit the manufacturers to win profits on merit." They were also interested in whether the wage and hour bases would provide for the physically weak in the industry, those who performed substandard services, and he said "Yes." They asked if different bases would be established for different lines in the industry, and he replied, "That will be worked out." He was asked if a cotton factory truck driver would be rated as a textile worker under the law and again he said, "Yes." They asked about the Negro yard boys, and he said the law would operate without respect to race. He was asked about the indiscriminate complaints made under the old NRA, which were a plague, and he said that the law would be operated impartially, without respect to groups, and that while there would be complaints, he anticipated that that feature would work itself out in time.

On 13 September 1938, Administrator Andrews appointed Industry Committee No. I, with Donald Nelson as chairman, who renamed it the Textile Industry Committee. It recommended a minimum wage schedule that would not be less than twenty-five cents an hour or more than forty cents and that would not curtail employment. There were seven members representing the industry, seven representing the public, and seven representing employees.

The Textile Industry Committee was found to be a hard-working and conscientious group who went about their business in a thorough and studious manner. According to the committee's progress report to the administrator, it received data on wage rates, competitive conditions, costs of living, transportation costs, cost effect, and probable price changes that would follow promulgation of the various minima within the range of the committee's authorization. These data were submitted by the economic section of the Wage and Hour Division and the Bureau of Labor Statistics of the United States Department of Labor. In addition, the committee heard testimony from some sixty witnesses, including representatives of the Cotton-Textile Institute, the American Cotton Manufacturers Association, the National Association of Cotton Manufacturers and other textile-trade associations, the Textile Workers Organizing Committee (of the CIO), the American Federation of Labor, and the New Bedford Textile Council, an independent labor organization.

Public hearings were also held, including one in Atlanta, before the administrator. There, a belligerent witness threatened Andrews, "You adopt these wages, I'll close up my mill, I'll lock up the door and give *you* the key!" The

[9]Southern Combed Yarn Spinners Association Annual Report; *Charlotte Observer; Charlotte News; Daily News Record; Textile World; Cotton* (now *Textile Industries*, a W. R. C. Smith publication).

administrator calmly said to his assistant, "Please step down and get the gentleman's key."

By a vote of thirteen to six, the recommendation of the First Textile Industry Committee was for 32½ cents minimum wage for the textile industry. It was approved by the administrator as a voluntary minimum on the part of the industry. The Fair Labor Standards Act, covering all industries engaged in interstate commerce, became effective on 24 October 1938 with the following provisions:

EFFECTIVE DATE	MINIMUM WAGE	MAXIMUM HOURS
Oct. 24, 1938	$ .25	44 before time & half for overtime
Oct. 24, 1939	$ .30	42 before time & half for overtime
Oct. 24, 1940	—	40 before time & half for overtime
Jun. 03, 1941	$ .37½	40 before time & half for overtime
Apr. 20, 1942	$ .40	
Oct. 24, 1945	$ .40[10]	40 before time & half for overtime
Jan. 15, 1950	$ .70	40 before time & half for overtime

At the time of enactment of the Wage-Hour law, most cotton textile mills were paying more than the act called for and by volunteer action were on the NRA basis of forty hours per shift and a two-shift operation.

The committee's report indicates that the recommendation brought hourly wage increases to only 120,000 of the 365,000 cotton textile workers, as voluntary wage increases had already brought the majority above the recommended minimum.

According to the Fair Labor Standards Act, higher minimum wages automatically became effective again in 1945, but the textile industry did not wait for such mandatory change. The Second Textile Industry Committee, headed by Lessing Rosenwald, was appointed 31 March 1941. This committee recommended a minimum-wage increase to 37½ cents per hour, and this rate became effective 30 June 1941. In less than a year, the Third Textile Industry Committee (Industry Committee No. 39) urged that the minimum be raised to the full extent of the law, so on 20 April 1942 the minimum was set at forty cents per hour.

The Depression had taken its toll on the industry. Many mills closed down or operated under bankruptcy laws, such as the once-great Hoosac Mills. The national textile strike and local union follow-ups took their toll too. The CIO Doffers Union gave the final blow to the Fall River Borden interests. In 1934

---

[10]Acute labor shortage in all fields of industry due to World War II made this figure obsolete. The 1950 provision was set in 1949 and eliminated forever wage differentials in the North and South.

American Print Works[11] was liquidated. Pacific Mills bought its inventory while other interests bought the factory buildings.

Many textile leaders, North and South, had overcome the effects of the Depression, had weathered NRA, and had voluntarily upheld the rules and regulations of Code No. I when such federal laws ran out. They had defeated the processing tax and straightened out the effects of the so-called windfall tax. Now by the late 1930s they were in a reasonably prosperous, stabilized position.

Since retail customers had some money in their pockets to spend on clothing and household goods, a call went out for more fabrics. It was estimated, at the time, that the textile industry had gained sixteen million new consumers of cotton goods, which in channels other than established commercial outlets, took up the slack in an industry with surplus capacity. But a large part of the purchasing power for textiles was within the various government agencies and the military.

The Works Progress Administration (WPA) was buying millions of yards of fabric for its sewing-room activities. In 1936 alone, bids were opened on 150 million yards of forty different types of fabrics for WPA use. All WPA purchases were, like other government purchases, subject to regulations of the Walsh-Healy Act, which stipulated the following: an eight-hour day, forty-hour week, no child labor (under sixteen) or convict labor, no unsanitary or hazardous working conditions, and use of the standard minimum wage when set. During the period 1935-1940, WPA made annual textile purchases of more than $100 million.

With new cash flow from sales in the mid- and late-1930s, mills endeavored to stay modernized. Opelika Cotton Mills in Alabama, for example, installed 7,500 spindles of the newly developed long-draft spinning and Georgia's Bibb Manufacturing Company announced it would spend $1 million for new equipment. Consolidation of the Hart and Fountain Cotton Mills in Tarboro, North Carolina, together with a new annex, made that plant one of the largest print-cloth mills in that section of the state.

The *Atlanta Constitution*, in an editorial of 2 February 1937, said: "The growth of the textile industry in Georgia in recent years has helped maintain a better economic balance in the state between agriculture and industry. The mills have offered a market for surplus farm labor and provide steady work and good wages for thousands of Georgia men and women."

It was pointed out that cotton farmers and mill workers received two-thirds of the cotton-mill dollar. This was generally true throughout the Southern industry. The Cotton Manufacturers Association of Georgia, using its state as an example over a five-year period (1932-1937), said that 1,045,053 bales of cotton were consumed annually by its mills. By conversion into yarn, thread, and fab-

---

[11]Ashton, *Of Men and Money*, 130. American Print Works was chartered by Massachusetts in 1857 with capitalization of $750,000. It became the largest print works in the world and the cornerstone of employment in Fall River. Interview with Arthur Borden.

Aerial view of giant Columbus, Georgia, plant of Bibb Manufacturing Company.

rics, the cotton's value increased to more than $60 million annually, thus making it possible to employ more than 60,000 mill operatives.

Many New England mills had, by this time, gone under. A 40,000-spindle mill in Fall River closed in 1927; a 110,000-spindle mill at New Bedford had closed, and by 1937 it and one other were converted into nightclubs; a 200,000-spindle mill at Lowell was abandoned after a century of operation. In 1936 Amoskeag Manufacturing Company, with 700,000 spindles and 23,000 looms, was ordered liquidated, affecting 77,000 persons in Manchester, New Hampshire. A recent book of interviews of one-time Amoskeag workers by Tamara K. Hareven and Randolph Langenbach[12] consists mostly of rather happy memories. But one man interviewed said being an Amoskeag man was "our life, our mode of living, our ultimate thing." Another said, "When the Amoskeag mills went out the world stopped for everyone."

The South was rising steadily in textile success. It passed New England in spindleage and, in 1930, had nineteen million spindles. Southerners looked with pure horror at any factor that would upset their steady upward growth. Regardless of reasons for the New England plants' downfall—such as labor unrest, general economic conditions, the 1929 Crash, the Depression, competition from the South, or whatever—all mills wanted *no* Japanese competition that could conceivably put them out of business too.

As early as 1933, the specter of cheap imports was haunting the entire textile industry. Prior to the inauguration of NRA and the application of its Code

---

[12]Hareven and Langenbach, *Amoskeag* .

No. I to cotton textiles—which caused a tremendous increase in production costs due to shortened work hours and increased wages—exports of textiles from Japan to the United States had been relatively unimportant in volume and effect upon the American market. But given this new situation, together with a condition of overcapacity and intense competition within the American industry, low tariffs and reciprocal agreements opened the gates of the American consuming markets to other textile-producing countries.

From a gross of less than two million yards in 1933, Japanese exports of textiles to this country jumped to sixteen million yards in 1935 and to approximately seventy-five million yards in 1936. Dependable trade reports toward the end of 1936 made it clear that the amazing rate of increase was continuing and indicated that the first quarter of 1937 would undoubtedly witness a volume exceeding the total of 1936. These startling figures did not include imports of products fabricated from cotton yarns and piece-goods, whose volume would undoubtedly equal that of piece-goods themselves.

The American tariff was inadequate against these inroads of Japanese goods. An attempt at a gentlemen's agreement for limitation, initiated by the United States Department of State and the Japanese government, collapsed because of Japanese misunderstanding and resulted in President Roosevelt's increasing the tariff rates on certain textile commodities from Japan by an average of forty-two percent. At that time, Dr. Claudius Murchison, president of the Cotton-Textile Institute, conceived the plan for direct discussion with Japanese textile manufacturers as a basis for resolution.

The American textile mission to Japan (1937) marked a new era in international trade relations by securing Japanese adoption of a voluntary quota on the number of cotton piece-goods to be exported to the United States during 1937 and 1938. The arrangement, unprecedented in trade history, was effected as a result of a series of conferences held between the American commission and representatives of the Japanese textile industry, in Osaka, Japan, from 15 to 22 January 1937.

Dr. Murchison presented the voluntary quota arrangement, declaring this method to be preferred by "both our government and ourselves (textile industrialists) to any resort either to legislation or to the powers of the United States president." Then it was revealed that orders already in hand for Japanese shipments to the United States in 1937 totalled 155 million square yards, most of which had been booked by Japanese mills prior to 5 December 1936. Many of their big textile tycoons had rushed to sell before the date of the Americans' visit.

With 155 million square yards agreed upon as the 1937 quota, the basic quota for 1938 was set at 100 million square yards. This decision left the Japanese with no further United States export business for that year; so to pacify the smaller Japanese mills, it was agreed to transfer not more than one-quarter the 1938 sales to the 1937 quota, putting 1938 shipments at seventy-five million yards, the same amount as 1936.

The mission was hailed as successful, but textile economists said it paved the way to greater competition from the Japanese in all fields of textile production in future years.

A new agreement was signed by a joint committee of the Cotton-Textile Institute and representatives of Japanese textile interests on 19 December 1938, extending the quota plan for two years beginning 1 January 1939. This agreement limited Japanese exports to America to not more than 200 million square yards for the two years, with basic apportionments of one hundred million square yards a year and the privilege of transferring not more than twenty million square yards from one year to another.

Concurrent with the United States-Japanese "gentlemen's agreement," reciprocal trade agreements had been made by the United States government with Canada, England, and other favored countries in 1936. The agreements were to be effective for three years. Most important were the concessions the United States made to the United Kingdom regarding textile products and manufactures. According to the schedule, reductions in duty were made on forty classifications of cotton manufactures and covering goods that were imported from the United Kingdom in 1937 to a value of $6 million. (The total value of our cotton imports that year was more than $44 million.) Concessions in 1936 covered chiefly yarns of finer counts and cloth in the higher price range. But before the effect of the latter concession was felt by the American industry, World War II had begun and from 1940 to 1947, America was almost the sole supplier of textiles for the world.

Fibers
of the Textile Industry | 7

Fiber is the soul of the textile industry. Search for land in order to cultivate silk for European nobility led to the founding of the Southeastern colonies, but silk did not become a successful crop. Wool was not suited to the Southern climate; rather, cotton was indigenous to the South. Friendly Indians met early explorers with strands and garlands of the spun fiber.

Cotton became the foundation of the Southern economy. It reached fame and brought fortune to the area with Eli Whitney's invention of the cotton gin. Over the many generations to follow, treaties with the Indians were negotiated to obtain more land for more cotton. Mills were built near the cotton fields and ginned bales of the fiber were hawked from wagons in the mill yards. Pedigreed seed, longer staples, more bales to the acre were the trends. At the Atlanta International Cotton Exposition, a big feature was the picking of cotton from a nearby field, ginning it, spinning and weaving the yarn, and finally producing a finished garment.

Cotton has many qualities that make it attractive for yarn and cloth manufacture: staple length, color, trash content, breaking strength, compatibility with dye and finish, silkiness or coarseness and, as E. W. Montgomery used to say, "the convolutions of the coil."[1]

Government standards must be met on each of these qualities; the price per pound at the mill is based on them. In case of a disagreement between buyer and seller, an arbitration board makes a ruling. There are many factors that govern the acceptance of cotton "for the purpose intended." At the mill alone, it must go through several processes to prepare it for the spinning machine.

Man-made fiber has none of these hurdles to cross. It arrives at the mill either in one long monofilament or with staple cut to required length, which means that it is clean and ready for its first machine process. It thus bypasses cleaning processes that are necessary for natural cotton's preparation.

---

[1]E. W. Montgomery, a gifted cotton man, head of his own merchant firm and chief classer and buyer of cotton for Judson Mills, Greenville SC (1920-1930).

Rayon was introduced as a commercial fiber around the turn of the century to compete with cotton and silk or wool. This was the first commercially successful man-made fiber, although it was many years after its discovery that the term *artificial silk* was abandoned and the term *rayon* adopted. A common term today in many languages, *rayon* was coined by Kenneth Lord of the textile merchant house Galey & Lord, who was a member of the committee appointed by the National Retail Dry Goods Association to select a name for the fiber. The name was adopted for worldwide use in 1924.

As to the beginning of rayon, as early as 1664 Robert Hooke, an English naturalist, dreamed of the day when a man-made fiber would be available. Nearly a century later, in 1742, René de Réaumur, a famous French scientist, suggested that artificial silk might be formed from gums and resins drawn into fine threads. But it was still another hundred years before science had the techniques to produce such a fiber.

In 1855 the first patent for making artificial fiber had been granted to Audemars, a Swiss chemist, but his cellulose-nitrate process was not commercially successful. In 1857 Schweitzer had developed the use of copper

Industry officials inspecting the first tire of high-tenacity rayon cord.

ammonium solution for dissolving cellulose; however, this also was not commercially adaptable at the time.

Then another outstanding invention renewed the search for a man-made fiber. When the electric light was invented, a cellulose fiber to be carbonized into filaments was needed. Sir Joseph W. Swan of England, who had the ingenious idea of forcing his solution of cellulose nitrate through tiny holes into a hardening bath, produced in 1880 the first successful man-made fiber. But his interest was only in electric lamps and he did not exploit the textile feature of the new fiber he had produced.

So it is Count Hilaire de Chardonnet, a former student of Pasteur, who is now recognized as being the "father of the rayon industry," for he first produced the new yarn on a commercial scale. He obtained his first patent in 1884, and five years later in Paris he was exhibiting fabric made of chemically produced yarn. By 1891 he had built a plant in Belgium for the regular production of yarn by the cellulose-nitrate process. It was the first "artificial silk" factory. In 1892 Charles F. Cross and E. J. Bevan, of England, discovered the viscose process of making rayon and two years later they secured a patent for making filaments of cellulose acetate. By 1900 a succession of experiments by Weston, L. B. Despaissis, Fremary Urban, and Bronnert had made the cuprammonium process a commercial success.

In America, Dr. Arthur D. Little of Boston had kept abreast of developments in the English experiments and, in partnership with Dr. William H. Walker and Harry S. Mork, was using the new cellulose-acetate compound for electrical insulation. In 1902 these three were granted a patent for spinning rayon textile yarn. It was the first patent on a man-made fiber in the United States and led to the world's first successful manufacture of acetate rayon.

In 1910 Samuel Salvage, a young English yarn merchant who had been in business in the United States, persuaded the English textile firm of Samuel Courtaulds & Company that the time was ripe for full-scale production of rayon in the United States. As a result the American Viscose Company was formed, a tract of land was bought at Marcus Hook, Pennsylvania, and a new plant was built and in production by 1911. That year marks the founding of the American rayon industry with a total production of 362,544 pounds of yarn.

The spectacular rise in consumption of rayon involves Spencer Love and his organization, Burlington Mills. In the four decades 1920-1960, it was the fastest-growing textile company in the United States and is closely identified with and parallels the history of rayon consumption. Although his company is a "first-generation organization," Spencer Love was not the first in his family to be identified with the textile industry; rather, he is part of the third generation of Loves to be active and successful in textile manufacturing. His grandfather, in partnership with George A. Gray, built a mill in Gastonia, North Carolina, in 1887. The Gastonia Manufacturing Company was the eighth mill in a county that for years has boasted more than one hundred. Other mills were built by John Love and George Gray, among them the Loray (1900). This mill broke the fortunes of the two men when the Chinese export business crashed.

J. Spencer Love, founder and chairman of Burlington Industries, was guest speaker at a meeting of the American Textile Machinery Association at the Tatnuck Club (Worcester, Massachusetts) in the 1950s. (L to R): Fred Howe, president of Crompton & Knowles; J. Spencer Love; Frank Lowell, president of Saco Lowell. (Courtesy of the *Worcester Telegraph and Gazette*, Inc.)

Spencer's father, James Lee Love, an educator and philanthropist, after his retirement from the Chair of Mathematics at Harvard University, spent a short time in 1909 in Lincolnton, North Carolina. In association with his brother, Ed Love, he founded the Saxony Spinning Company.

At the close of World War I, Spencer Love, who had served as the youngest major in the United States Army, took his first job with the Gastonia Cotton Manufacturing Company as assistant to the bookkeeper. The family connection with the old mill was the only thing that put him in textile manufacturing instead of some other business, he said. He was simply looking for a job. A year later Spencer Love purchased controlling interest in the little mill that had never made any money except for a short period during World War I. He had obtained $15,000 local capital and had borrowed considerably more from a selling house in New York. His father, who had returned to Boston to live, invested to the extent of one-fifth interest, but took no active part in the business, leaving Spencer as president to run it according to Harvard Business training.

Spencer Love already had ideas about textile diversification that he wanted to put into operation. Other manufacturers in Gaston County had attempted to manufacture rayon fabrics. However, Spencer Love was pretty sure he could make a go of it even with poor equipment, and so it was in the Gastonia Cotton Manufacturing Company that his first experiments were made with rayon weaving.

In 1923 Spencer Love decided to dismantle and sell the dilapidated Gastonia mill and dispose of its holdings. He put the word around that he would organize a new mill in any community that offered good prospects. Gastonia was overloaded with mills and wanted no part of a new venture. But a group of citizens in Burlington, North Carolina, took up his offer and subscribed $250,000. The Gastonia Cotton Manufacturing Company was liquidated and the real estate sold for $265,000, which paid off the mill debts.

Love had $50,000 left over to invest in the new corporation. Also, he swapped the old machinery from the Gastonia plant for stock in the new company. Some new machinery was installed in the Burlington mill, which boasted a new building and a village. Several years later the few remaining acres of the old Gastonia Cotton Manufacturing Company were donated by Love to the city of Gastonia for a park area in memory of Robert Calvin Greer Love and Susan Rhyne Love, Spencer's grandparents.

Thus the Burlington Mills, employing 200, was founded. In 1924, in addition to the cotton it was running, the mill used 106 pounds of rayon. In that year per-capita weight of fibers available for the consumer were: cotton, 22 pounds; wool, 3.5 pounds; silk, .6 pounds; rayon, .4 pounds. Burlington's rayon dress-goods mill was built in 1927, and by 1932 the company had expanded to include 12 mills and to use 10,000 pounds of rayon annually.

Spencer Love began to concentrate on the use of rayon as a spinnable yarn for many purposes. He was aided and abetted by a young fellow from Charlotte named Harry Dalton who had recently joined American Viscose as a salesman. Dalton had plenty of clout. He was in Charlotte looking for a job at one time. As he stood on the street corner talking to one of his friends, a big, black, sleek, chauffeur-driven limousine passed by with a lone passenger smoking a big cigar. "Who is that?" asked Dalton. He was told he was the local tycoon of the textile industry. Dalton made up his mind then and there to go into the textile business.

Harry was born in Winston-Salem in 1895, the youngest of seven children, and is a good example of "how to get rich by really trying." His father was in the furniture business. Since Harry was the youngest child, he had to scrounge a bit to make extra spending money. He was a born salesman and knew the proper pitch on selling the local newspaper, the *Winston-Salem Sentinel*. He hawked his papers by yelling but deliberately garbling his words, "Mrs. 'blub blub blub' says *she* didn't do it!" Passersby would snatch a paper, not wait for change, and hurry home to read the "scandal" that wasn't really there, while Harry hawked papers on the next corner.

When he was in the eighth grade, he moved up to selling subscriptions for the *Sentinel*. He did so well that he won a bicycle for excelling in his sales area and a pony and cart for his citywide selling effort and success. His real salesmanship was evident when he accosted the redoubtable R. J. Reynolds, tobacco king, and persuaded him to buy a subscription although he already had one. Mr. Reynolds probably sold Harry some stock at the same time. Harry says the pony-and-cart deal was great, especially with the young and fairer sex. He described the vehicle as a "horse-drawn rumble seat."

In high school he was a member of the Debating Team and Dramatic Club and helped to bring out the first edition of the school yearbook, "Black and Gold." He had quite a gift for what was then called elocution, and entered a high school contest on public speaking at Guilford College.

About that time William Jennings Bryan was on one of his presidential campaign tours and passed through Winston-Salem. Harry determined to give his speech before this famous man and, through fortuitous circumstances, was able to meet him and recite his memorized speech, "The New South," written by Henry Grady. Bryan pronounced Harry's recitation "the gem of all speeches." In later years when Harry launched into one of his sales talks, he was said to be endowed with the "gift of gab," having been blessed by that silver-tongued orator.

After high school Harry entered Trinity College (now Duke University). While there, he earned part of his expenses at various campus jobs, including delivering students' wrinkled clothes to the cleaners. His little business was designated a "Pressing Club."

After a stint with the *Textile Bulletin*, a post that gave him a broad knowledge of the textile industry and brought him many personal friendships, he joined the Air Service Command in World War I. He was shipped to France. There his sergeant misinterpreted the work of the "Pressing Club" and sent him out as a press reporter to cover G.I. activities at the front.

At war's end he was one of 1,000 Air Corps men to be given the opportunity for further education in Europe. He chose to go to the College of Technology and Owens College, both in Manchester, England, the center of the British textile industry. Both colleges were part of the University of Liverpool.

Back from World War I, Harry got a job with Hunter Manufacturing Company and was sent as a trainee to the Pomona Mill in Greensboro, where he said he "picked up bobbins off the floor." He worked from the opening and picking departments to finishing, learning every step of mill operations. Then in 1921 the Hunter Manufacturing and Commission Company called him to work in their sales office on Worth Street. Pretty soon he was outselling every other company on "twenty-seven-inch-wide cotton plaids" for children's wear. Public demand was so great and it was so easy then to sell that he had spare time to study industrial management at New York University.

But Harry was homesick for the South and so grabbed an opportunity with the Gastonia Cotton Yarn Company, a selling house in Philadelphia representing about twenty-two combed-yarn mills located in that North Carolina city. He opened a sales-yarn office in Chattanooga. He was so good at selling Gaston County combed yarn that he was asked in 1925 to join American Viscose, a relatively new company but already the leading manufacturer of "artificial silk." The company had plans to open an office in Charlotte.

Harry was a salesman of prodigious energy and more than one talent. There were weeks when he spent six nights out of seven in railroad sleeping cars as he called on customers throughout the South persuading them to try rayon: "Try it for knitting sox and ladies' stockings. Try it for weaving. Try it for profits," he would say. Often as not, he concluded a sale en route as he met mill men on the train, showed them samples he "just happened" to have in his pocket, folded neatly like a fancy handkerchief.

Along with a lot of clout, Harry had nerve. One day he arrived at a mill office determined to make a good sale. He found the office filled with other salesmen awaiting their turn to see the boss. He knew he'd never get in before dark. So Harry went out, took off his coat, rolled up his shirt sleeves, stuck a pencil behind his ear and, disguised as a clerk, he walked right into the president's office. The latter, amused by Harry's prank and beguiled by the man's flow of conversation and knowledge, gave him the coveted order for rayon yarn.

Somewhere along the line, Harry acquired the art of mimicry. He could imitate the voice of almost anyone, even the chairman of his company, American Viscose. One day he called his immediate superior and said in Chairman Salvage's voice, "This young fellow, Dalton, he's pretty good. I think we ought to give him a raise." His immediate superior said, "You do? When?" "Well, right now," the pseudochairman's voice answered. Harry got the raise, and later on Samuel Salvage got a hearty laugh out of the story.

In 1936 Harry was called long distance by Chairman Salvage and told he was elected to the Board of Directors of American Viscose. In selecting Harry Dalton as a director of this vast corporation, Salvage was not only rewarding him for outstanding ability, but Viscose was securing the counsel of a man who was one of the most influential salesmen in the textile industry. "This was a great game," Dalton said, "I was on the Board and my immediate boss wasn't."

During the four years of World War II, Harry Dalton was deputy director of the Cotton and Synthetic Textile Division of the War Production Board—working closely with Frank Walton, Spencer Love, and Kenneth Mariner, who were successive directors of the board. He, like many other dollar-a-year men, worked five days each week for the War Production Board in Washington and two days at home at corporation duties. These were the days when Quartermaster Research found that rayon was better than cotton in airplane and automobile tires and that nylon was better than silk for parachutes. These discoveries aided the war effort for the United States and our Allies.

Success didn't change Harry Dalton's down-to-earth personal traits. One time while on the War Production Board, he was asked to visit the spacious Virginia country estate of a member of the Cabinet of the United States. He arrived some hours ahead of his host who, learning that Mr. Dalton was already there, searched the boxwood gardens, the tennis court, and the swimming pool area. He finally found Harry resting on the back porch helping the cook shell peas.

Dalton's clients were industrywide and he helped many to build up their requirements for rayon. His friendship with Huber Hanes dated back to Trinity College days and may have given him favorable audience with the president; at any rate, his first customer was Hanes Hosiery Company. When that company introduced rayon as a hosiery fiber, new hosiery mills mushroomed throughout the South, each one a potential new customer. Dalton persuaded knitters that rayon was good news for hosiery people and persuaded weavers to run rayon on the "upper beam" of the loom and to create such beautiful and fashionable fabrics as woven cotton with satin stripe or plaid overlay—designs that made Hope Skillman famous. Other uses of man-made fiber soon multiplied. Glen Raven Silk Mills was incorporated in 1933 for throwing continuous filament yarn. Their hosiery mill soon followed.

Another large and important customer was Spencer Love. When Burlington Mills was in its earlier stages and needed money to expand its woven-rayon field, Harry Dalton arranged a large loan of several million dollars that in the long run made Burlington the primary user of American Viscose products. When asked, "Why did you make the gamble?" his answer was, "Spencer was a genius, great in mathematical precision of organization and manufacturing, and he was honest. It was no gamble, in that sense of the word. Every cent was repaid."

The successful use of rayon fiber meant adjustments and developments of textile machinery. For example, Draper advertised that its Northrop Loom could be adjusted for rayon weaving and later introduced an all-rayon loom; Saco-Lowell invented a new slasher for rayon use; Crompton & Knowles Corporation introduced its new high-speed, automatic, multicolor loom for cotton and/or rayon fabrics. With machinery adapted for dual use, the rayon market zoomed and fashion adopted the new fabrics.

By 1940 United States rayon production was 482 million pounds. In 1943 Burlington Mills, only eighteen years old but forty-four mills strong, was the largest consumer of rayon: at that time it used ten percent of all rayon yarn manufactured in the United States and was buying heavily into possible nylon-consuming mills. In 1945 production of rayon was 770 million pounds, much of which went to military uses. In 1967 the United States produced more than 4 billion pounds of man-made fiber. Long used in tires for automobiles, trucks, and planes, man-made fiber had entered the carpet field and opened new vistas for producers of such yarns. Nonwoven fabrics had also started to use man-made fibers.

Harry L. Dalton. Vice-chairman of American Viscose Corporation. During World War II he was deputy director of the Cotton and Synthetic Textile Division of the War Production Board.

But there is more to tell about Spencer Love, the man who built the company that in only eighteen years was the foremost producer of goods manufactured from man-made fibers. In the early stages of the South's Reconstruction period and its efforts at textile manufacturing, the name of Love was prominent in North Carolina. It still is. One cannot write the history of textiles without including the background and success of James Spencer Love.

By virtue of native shrewdness and a good educational background, he became one of the business geniuses of this century. He was a gambler, some folks say. If so, he cut his losses when they occurred and went ahead. He had courage when others were discouraged. He had vision when few others could see President Hoover's "prosperity around the corner." He had initiative, was completely a "workaholic." He was a perfectionist and expected everyone associated with him to be likewise. And he was handsome, charming, and somewhat shy in manner. But there was one thing he was not going to do, he said, when he moved to Gastonia in 1919, and that was "spend his life saddled with that old mill just because he was kin to it."

He bought mills that fit into his production pattern. If the mill did not prove profitable, he got rid of it. He believed in rayon and its future, so each mill had to be equipped, or re-equipped, for the lowest per-unit production cost of man-made or other fibers. If that was not possible, then the plant was closed and sold. In the ten years from 1927 to 1937, Burlington Mills set up thirty new rayon-weaving plants. In February 1930 Burlington Mills Corporation was incorporated in Delaware and acquired "all assets, property, goodwill," and so forth of Burlington Mills Company, Incorporated, and its subsidiaries, Rayon Fabrics Corporation and its subsidiaries, and Duchess Fabrics Corporation and its subsidiaries (all now dissolved) in exchange for 350,270.8 shares of common stock in Burlington Mills Corporation.

When Spencer Love was appointed in 1943 as director of the War Production Board's Textiles, Clothing and Leather Division, he found it in a mess and put his extraordinary management ability to work to straighten out the problems by correlating and combining mill production and resources planning, especially regarding rayon tires and the tire program for the military. He solved the many problems stemming from the industry's inability to weave and sew nylon instead of silk for parachutes, and he made the entire procurement program workable. When he returned to his own business life, he inaugurated a program for Burlington to obtain as many mills as possible that were capable of producing woven or knitted nylon items. There was a new fiber that could fill a multitude of needs, he thought.

In 1946 Burlington purchased and established as a new operating division Cramerton Mills in Gaston County, a longtime, outstanding producer of fine-woven combed yarn goods sold through Galey and Lord Company, New York. This acquisition included what was at one time the most famous and beautiful mill village in the United States. But as Love often said, "Textile mills should not be in the real estate business." It was not long before the village houses were put on the block. Many other Burlington purchases, mergers, or acquisitions were consummated in the hectic late-1940s and 1950s. Burlington entered the home-decorating field with the acquisition of National Mallison Fabrics and in this way obtained Jackson Spears, who had worked with the War Production Board. Burlington went into woolens with the purchase of Peerless Woolen Mills for $15 million and 421,900 shares of common stock. Then in May 1953 Burlington acquired stock control of Klopman Mills, Incorporated, producer of greige goods, with plants at Asheboro and Ramseur, North Carolina. With this deal Spencer also brought in Burlington's senior officer for the 1970s, William A. Klopman.

Spencer never stopped. Frank Leslie, a popular member of the merchandising clan in New York said, "We once spent a weekend together with Spencer Love. Now, aside from the hospitality of the house, which is most gracious, charming and considerate, a weekend with Spencer Love is an experience which is about as relaxing as a flag-raising on Iwo Jima." Leslie continued his recollections:

> We watched Spence play tennis which is like having a ringside seat at Pickett's Charge. He plays doubles as though the opposing team were the Gilbert Brothers and the ball was a company that Bob Stevens was trying to buy away from him. It makes you think it's a good thing he has Burlington Industries to rest up on when he's off the court. Also over the same weekend, I discovered why they invented these fountain pens that write under water. That's so he can sign his mail in the shower. Fortunately, they did not have the ballpoints that write through butter at that time or I think he might have written a memo on a piece of toast.
> ....
> Spencer was buying something at the time, I think it was Rhode Island, and when I saw Harry Dalton on the premises, I rather thought that American Viscose might be part of the package. And if you think that is amusing, I would advise you not to laugh. A lot of good men have choked on that laugh.
> ....
> I recall a few years back, when I was still in business for myself, I had to introduce Spencer Love at a textile-industry luncheon. Since he is fairly well known in the industry, and I get to do a lot of introducing, this was the seventh occasion that I had been called on to present him and I was running rather thin on material. So in an attempt to obtain a new angle of introduction, I made up a mild little gag to the effect that he had come down to breakfast on Monday morning to discover that the household had run out of coffee. This was not likely to happen in the Love home again, I said, because on Wednesday, he bought Brazil. Well, two weeks later, there I was in my office, up to my "arse" in coffee beans.

In 1954 Burlington Mills purchased New England's great Pacific Mills.[2] Burlington actually acquired a Massachusetts corporation, but the purchase included mostly Southern properties and a very large net, quick-working capital, excellent management, and a long history of earnings and dividends. The management of Pacific had been active in "moving south" since they first

---

[2]Many thousands of shares of Pacific Mills were owned by Harvard University due to Love's father's tenure there.

bought the old Parker Mills in South Carolina; so what Burlington really purchased in manufacturing properties included large, growing, and successful mills in Southern states, operating with Pacific management and merchandising ability and boasting a high standing in the textile markets.

Burlington next acquired the old, established Goodall-Sanford Mills in Maine, designers and manufacturers of Palm Beach fabrics and Palm Beach clothing and allied lines. Elmer Ward, head of this company, tried hard to keep it going. The original fabric was wonderful for New England summerwear, but Ward could not make it financially.

In 1955 the name Burlington Mills was changed to Burlington Industries, Incorporated. It was more appropriate for wide-range, diversified, decentralized textile operations with more than $500 million annual sales.

Spencer Love always kept his plants modernized if the construction of the buildings allowed it. Thomas West, president of Draper Corporation, greatest loom builders in the world in the 1950s-1960s, said at a dinner where Spencer was being awarded another citation for industrial merit (among dozens he received), "I can testify that he does not believe in obsolescence. In the last ten years, he has spent $25 million with our company alone for looms." That meant buying equipment to make mills work without a stoppage from bottlenecks in opening, carding, and spinning.

Spencer Love had empathy for the causes of the mill operatives. He urged $1.25 as minimum wage when others, including Congress, were discussing 50 cents. He always paid more than the legal wage, considerably more. But his mills could, and did, produce more goods at lower cost per unit and sell them rapidly. There were no inventories, no huge advertising program, just hangtags on garments stating this was a Burlington-quality product.

The early 1960s saw the terrible prison ordeal of Boyd Payton, leader of the Textile Workers Union of America, AFL-CIO, North Carolina Division, due to the Henderson Mills (North Carolina) strike. Much to the surprise of many of his associates, Spencer wrote to Governor Sanford of North Carolina to beg clemency for this man. In a recent interview Boyd Payton said, "Spencer Love was always a fair-minded and strong man." Spencer Love died in 1963. By then he had built Burlington into the largest textile-mill corporation in the world.

Regarding his death, the *Greensboro Daily News* said, in an editorial, "The nation has few men in positions of power—especially in business—who combined the breadth of vision and open-mindedness of Spencer Love. He believed that American Society is open-ended. He had little patience with old prejudices. He was not afraid to espouse unpopular causes. He remained perennially youthful in outlook."

In 1930 a laboratory accident created a new fiber that was destined to have a greater impact on history than any other fiber known. The Du Pont Company has always conducted applied research investigating new products or attempting to improve on old—even when there was no specific commercial end in view. For years, Dr. W. H. Carothers and his staff had busied themselves with this type of work. One day while boiling a mixture for an unnamed purpose, one of the staff dropped and broke a test tube full of hot liquid. Surprisingly,

Tom West. Elected president of Draper Corporation in 1944 and served there until his retirement in 1965. (Photo taken by Fabian Bachrach.)

as the mixture hit the tabletop and the droplets dribbled to the floor, thin strands of a fiber were formed during the fall as the mixture cooled, much like taffy candy as it is being tested by a spoon for pulling consistency. "Look what I've got here," the experimenter cried, "a monofilament of some sort!" The molten polymer could be drawn out into a long fiber even when it was cold.

The chemists soon decided that the discovery might lead to a new textile fiber, but it needed many improvements to make it commercially feasible. After much more work, a particularly interesting fiber was made. The lustrous fiber was strong and pliable. It stood up under heat, dried quickly, resisted attack by mildew, and could be washed and dry-cleaned without harm. In 1938 the fiber was patented by Du Pont, and in the public announcement of the discovery it was named nylon.[3]

So out of a program of pure research came a wholly synthetic organic textile fiber that has opened a new era in textile performance. It is not a single substance, but rather a new and basic class of materials that has many qualities of metals, plastics, and rubber. World War II was about to create many new opportunities for its use.

---

[3]Du Pont de Nemours, *Nylon Textile Fibers in Industry;* interviews with Pierre Du Pont.

The Rise of the Knitwear Industry in the South | 8

A teenage flapper announced to her family one day in the early 1920s that she would no longer wear bobby socks. "I grew up wearing 'Fay'[1] stockings in the wintertime and socks in the summertime, and even cotton stockings with my serge bathing suit. If I am old enough to plan my debut, I'm old enough to wear silk hosiery! McCallum's," she said, reading an ad, " 'You Just Know She Wears Them.' " Her father answered sternly but not unkindly, "Your mother always wears sheer black silk hose because she is a lady. They cost $5.00 a pair. If you wear silk hose, then you must act like a lady, and if I catch you wearing them with a run in your stockings, I'll break your beautiful neck."

And so fashion took over in that booming era, giving great impetus to the fabric-forming industry known as knit goods. It had been slow in developing in the South, although it had gained a stronghold in New England and Pennsylvania. Machine knitting had come a long way since a young former curate at St. John's College in Cambridge, England, had invented a foot-pedaled hosiery frame in 1589 because he couldn't stand the constant clicking of his wife's knitting needles. Two hundred years later a different type of knitting frame was invented by a gentleman farmer named Jedediah Strutt. This machine, superimposed upon the stocking frame, created ribbed hosiery, which was more elastic than plain. The knitting trade became important to England and the machines were prohibited for export. Some were smuggled into the colonies, and all sorts of incentives were offered by the colonials to obtain stocking wear for the growing population.

After 1776, one of the first appropriations made by the Committee of Safety of Maryland was for 300 pounds sterling to Mr. Coxendefer of Frederick County for the purpose of establishing a stocking factory. Pennsylvania had the Dunkers, who brought the art of knitting and their smuggled machines to Germantown from their mother country, and their industry flourished along the

---

[1]Black-ribbed knit long stockings for children, the top front boot extending enough to fasten to buttons on the waistline of the knitted underwear called a "union suit."

William Lee showing his wife the stockings he has just made on his new knitting frame. (Taken from *Hosiery thru the Years*, courtesy of Ira J. Haskell.)

Brandywine; New England had the Leffingwells and their expert machine builders, William Russell and William Cox; Ipswich, Massachusetts, became the home of Benjamin Fewkes and George Warner, who produced the first pair of stockings manufactured by machine in that state.

In 1832 in New York State, Robert Egberts's skill and the Bailey brothers' money started the first water-powered knitting factory and therefore fathered the power-driven knitting industry in the United States. Very fine woolen yarns were used, and the industry sort of migrated toward New Hampshire where the wool was abundant and machines were made by Richard Walker, who obtained a patent on a "rotary-powered stocking loom" in 1832. It was the first practical machine of this type to be patented in this country. Also in New Hampshire were the Aiken brothers, who invented the latch needle, a necessary and delicate component of the knitting machine that required constant replacement.

The invention of the latch needle was the most progressive development in the knitting machine. In fact, its introduction established a new industry: needle-making machines. Such machines, patented and made by Walter Aiken, could turn out thousands of latch needles a day. W. S. Woodward, as a young man, worked for a time for Aiken, then established his own latch-needle firm. In 1862 the advertised price of Aiken's latch needles was $5.00 per thousand.

This gentleman, mindful of his patent rights, made a lot of trouble for anyone who went into the needle business. The result was that Woodward learned he could go up to Canada, where he could buy the British-made needles at a much lower price, and sneak them across the border. The needles were small

The Framework Knitters Company, chartered by Cromwell in 1656, used this insignia. It pictures the inventor, William Lee (l), with an early model of his knitting frame, and a woman spinning yarn by hand.

and several thousand could be brought into the States each trip in a whiskey jug. Woodward would drive his wagon, loaded with hay or some such locally grown commodity, while beside him on the seat were two liquor jugs. One, labeled whiskey, was full of needles and sealed. He would open and offer the hospitality of the other jug to the customs officer. In this way Woodward could buy the English-made, Canadian-imported needles for a very small amount and a swig of whiskey, and then sell them to United States hosiery mills at a comfortable profit.

"Holeproof Hosiery" was one of the first users of Sea Island long, silky, staple cotton in men's hosiery. It made socks with ribbed tops to which leg garters were fastened: "No metal touches the leg." Holeproof was one of the pioneer Western knitwear establishments. Another pioneer was Munsingwear, which made long-legged underwear known as "union suits" and later made T-shirts, undershirts, and so forth. A number of knitwear companies found Midwestern locations excellent for labor supply and market distribution. Southern sales-yarn mills were the largest suppliers to this section of the industry.

Most knit-goods manufacturers had started off selling their products through commission houses in Boston, Philadelphia, Baltimore, and New York. Then from 1880 through World War I, they established selling agencies, by-passing the old commission houses for a neater profit. However, some of the selling agencies invested heavily in knitwear factories or even owned them outright. They would sell their mills' products directly to catalogue houses such as Sears Roebuck, or to a chain store such as Woolworth, Grants, or J. C. Pen-

Model of a
seventeenth-century
stocking frame. From
William Felkin's
*Machine-Wrought
Hosiery and Lace
Manufactures,*
Cambridge, 1867.

ney. A wide variety of sales techniques were used to put hosiery and underwear on every person, young and old, in the United States. Such fine sales-
yarn mills as those in Gaston County flourished because the knit-goods industry was their ever-growing market.

In 1907 circular knit machines were introduced that gave hosiery a neater
fit at the ankle. Further machine developments patented by the Hemphill
Company, Scott & Williams, the Wildman-Jacquard Knitting Company, and
Textile Machine Works allowed fancy pattern knits and introduced embroidered "clocks" or designs up the side of the ankle. As each innovation was introduced, the fashion world became more and more interested in glamorous
legs, even on men. Argyles, English ribs, and cable stitches all added to the
appeal of men's half hose, while women leaned toward sheerness, embroidery, and lace or even sequin inserts.

In 1880 members of the E. W. Holt and the Sellars textile families of Alamance County, North Carolina, decided to build a hosiery mill and utilize the
yarn from their own spinning machines. The product was crude and the mill
short lived, but it was the first establishment in the South in the early post-Civil
War days.

The words "lower Southern costs" brought Northern capital to augment Southern assets and resulted in the most astonishing growth of the knitwear industry in a relatively few years. For example, North Carolina produced 87,875 dozens of cotton hose and half hose in 1890. In 1900 the state produced more than one million dozens; Georgia produced more than one million dozens; South Carolina produced three-quarter million dozens; Tennessee produced more than one-half million dozens; and Virginia was just tooling up with nearly one-quarter million dozens.

At the end of the nineteenth century, two German immigrants, Ferdinand Thun and Henry Janssen, with administrative and technological backgrounds in European-made, full-fashioned hosiery machines, established the Textile Machine Works in Reading, Pennsylvania. By 1900 they introduced a full-fashioned hosiery machine that was quickly accepted by hosiery manufacturers. Thun and Janssen also organized Berkshire Knitting Mills to produce full-fashioned hosiery on their own machines.

By 1929 there were 12,565 full-fashioned hosiery machines in operation in the United States. Full-fashioned hosiery mills had increased in ten years from 92 to 263. Fashion was demanding silk hose, full fashioned, with or without decoration. Consumption of circular knits had decreased by fifty percent while full fashioned, plain, embroidered, or with lace inserts had increased four hundred percent. The fiber favorite, silk, was firmly established as a status and sophistication symbol. No lady would leave home without asking someone who could see the calves of her legs, "Are my seams straight?"

Big names in the Southern textile area became associated with hosiery manufacturing. At High Point, North Carolina, an overall sales agency was organized by J. H. Millis and J. A. Adams, and many of the newly established but small Southern hosiery mills sold through the Adams-Millis Corporation. It became a case of the tail wagging the dog, so the company later went into the manufacturing end of the business. In Burlington the May Hosiery Mills began operations.

Textile-weaving mills added knitting divisions. It was Alonzo Groves, secretary-treasurer of Wiscassett Mills, who persuaded Charlie Cannon to include full-fashioned hosiery as a diversification product of Cannon's wholly owned combed-yarn-spinning subsidiary. The Groves-Cannon connection dates back to the time when Groves was freight agent/station master on the Southern Railway at Concord. At that time, Cannon Mills's payroll was made up every Saturday morning at the Concord bank and delivered to Groves at the railroad station. When the northbound train came through, "Guv'ner"—as he was nicknamed by friends and neighbors—entrusted the padlocked bag to the engineer, who steamed up toward Kannapolis, then only a whistle-stop. Without slowing the train, the engineer tooted the whistle twice as a signal and then threw the payroll bag out the window to the waiting Cannon Mills paymaster.

Later, when Wiscassett was established as a fine-combed yarn mill at Albemarle, Charles Cannon put Groves in charge. When Wiscassett went into hosiery, Groves bought Oakboro, a small mill of about 8,000 spindles that produced 180's fine-combed yarn out of long, silky staple Egyptian cotton for Wiscassett's high-quality lisle hose. During the processing-tax days, Groves reported on the regular government form that Oakboro ran two forty-hour shifts and used one bale of cotton per month, about 500 pounds. That brought a swarm of IRS agents down to Oakboro to catch him cheating on the processing tax. They didn't know that the higher the count yarns, the finer the product, and the slower the consumption of cotton. So they sat with their stop-watches until satisfied that two-shift, full-time production of 180's yarn truly meant only twelve bales a year or 6,000 pounds of cotton, equal to $240 processing tax.

The Valdese Mills and Pilot Mills, founded by the Garous,[2] were flourishing in the Blue Ridge. The Hatch Hosiery Mill, backed by Belmont textile industrialists, was bound for success. Chadbourn Hosiery Mills began operations in Burlington, North Carolina, in rented quarters with a few knitting machines. Its president was Chadbourn Bolles, assistant trust officer in a Charlotte bank. Its greige hose was finished by commercial finishers and sold to chain stores and jobbers under the name "Larkwood." By 1953 Chadbourn had moved its offices to Charlotte and had seven plants in three states.

In 1900 J. W. Hanes of Winston-Salem turned his interest from the lucrative tobacco business to enter hosiery with his Shamrock Mills, making "fancy embroidered and lace, lisle-finished, seamless stockings." Hanes Hosiery Mills was among the first to try rayon. Spencer Love and others followed. Rayon did not have the resiliency of silk, however, and so was used to a large extent only as the boot of silk hose.

Then the Wear Cotton Movement came along with nickel-a-pound cotton. News articles pushed tan, clocked, sheer cotton lisle hose for sportswear and sterile white cotton hose for hospital nurses. The idea didn't really work. A young woman who prided herself on keeping up with fashion trends was wearing cotton lisle when a gentleman friend stopped her on the street and said, "Do you know what happens to ladies who wear cotton stockings?" She looked astonished and said, "What?" In dead seriousness, he answered, "Nothing!" So nothing came of that fashion trend.

In 1939 the industry's total of women's full-fashioned and circular-knit stockings, men's half hose, slacks-socks, children's socks, and anklets was 136,741,480 dozens of pairs for the year and included all fibers: wool, cotton, silk, rayon, and blends. Hosiery production had reached unprecedented numbers. In the past anyone who could buy one new or used knitting machine and had a garage or outhouse to put it in was in business, selling the nameless hosiery through a jobber. This so-called "cottage industry" was banned by the Fair Labor Standards Act.[3]

---

[2]Francis Garou, John F. Garou, and Albert F. Garou—members of an immigrant family who founded Valdese, North Carolina, and the Waldensian, Pilot, and Valdese Mills.

[3]In October 1981 the Reagan administration repealed the ban on manufacture of knitted outerwear in homes. Source, U.S. Department of Labor.

High Point, Asheboro, and Hickory, North Carolina, became hosiery centers. A small fortune was made by the man who invented a machine that printed a brand name on the boot of the stocking, and there were numbers of fancy brand names adopted by jobbers who handled the output of small, so-called "backyard" producers who sold for any price as long as they made a profit to expand.

Then came nylon, the miracle fiber. It was tried out, cautiously, by some hosiery manufacturers. Women were human guinea pigs, wearing them for the mills in order to test longevity, washing, color fastness, comfort, appearance. One woman claimed that a pair of nylons had survived forty-eight days of consecutive wear and forty-eight consecutive washings; but she complained that her legs felt encased in steel. Another woman said that nylons were too harsh unless worn inside out.

So nylons became increasingly sheer and the use of nylon as a hosiery fiber was literally a gold strike for the industry, making silk seem heavy and bulky by comparison. The term *nylons* was synonymous with flattering, sheer hosiery.

World War II cut off the supply of silk and the War Production Board froze all that was available in the States. In addition, it recalled all nylon, regardless of use, from hosiery to toothbrushes. Token amounts only were allocated to hosiery mills to quiet consumer uproar. Nylons instead of diamonds became a girl's best friend. A young woman would sell her virginity for nylons and the black market flourished.

After the war when silk was acknowledged as a thing of the past in knitwear, nylon became plentiful. Manufacturers made hosiery even sheerer. One run and a new pair was bought; the more sheer, the better the chance of a run; and that was the knitters' goal. Then came "panty hose," which brought simplification and freedom of dress. Also, panty hose used more nylon and more often; that is, one run in a leg meant a total loss of the two-legged panty. By 1953 seams were out. Nylon, seamless, preboarded for permanent leg shape, was all sheer beauty. For the elderly or those with varicose veins, sheer "support" hose gave them comfort and some physical security.

There are many types of knitwear other than hosiery. They are popular as well as useful and involve flat-bed machines such as warp knitters, double knits, Leavers, and raschel. "Warp knits" (flat knitted fabric), said Terry Giffen of Courtaulds, "was the most neglected method of fabrication." That statement is no longer true. American Enka, a leading man-made fiber producer from Asheville, North Carolina, sees polyester as an emerging force for the industry, although nylon is still the main component for warp knitters.

Lingerie manufacturers introduced sheer tricot knitting for women's lace-trimmed sleeping and lounging undergarments. The knitting industry expanded its production into outerwear. Double knits were high fashion for men's and women's outerwear until overexpansion and the inflation-depression of the 1970s killed the prosperity of that section of the industry. The knitwear industry survived, however, and is a big part of the Southern textile industry, accounting for almost one-half of its production. It moved south late, but it moved to stay. Knitwear includes cotton and wool, but is predominantly man-made.

　　　Lace is a type of knitting and it—along with netting, the simplest of all laces—is included among knit goods. For many years England had a complete monopoly on machines that made net and laces. The most important machine in this field was invented by John Leavers of England. During the nineteenth century England blocked expansion of offshore net and lace industries by placing export taxes on the machines and removing all export taxes on the manufactured goods, which were dumped on the American market. The United States retaliated by imposing strict and heavy import duties on lace machines and lace.

　　　During the Spanish-American War (1898), many more American soldiers died of malaria and yellow fever than ever died on the battlefront. It was then scientifically proven that the diseases were carried by mosquitoes. A great hue and cry was raised for adequate supplies of mosquito netting for the American people. As a result, the Tariff Act of 1909 stipulated that the forty-five percent import duty on lace machines be entirely lifted for a period of seventeen months. This decree resulted in a rapid expansion of the industry. Machines brought over from England and placed in American mills at that time were in good operating condition in the 1950s. Once the Leavers machines were in place and mosquito netting was in ample supply, netting manufacturers diversified with fancy lace goods.

　　　For years prior to 1940, national efforts at mosquito control and the increasing custom of using wire screen[4] for windows and doors in houses and other buildings displaced the former urgent need for mosquito netting[5] over beds. One of the great achievements of the American textile industry during World War II was in producing this. Many millions of square yards of sand-fly netting, mosquito netting, insect and fly netting, shrimp and fish netting were purchased by the military for use in combat zones and rehabilitation areas. One of the major horrors of the war in tropical areas was the hordes of flies and mosquitoes that attacked the troops. A tremendous effort was put forth to overcome this dangerous nuisance.

　　　One of the strategic war textiles was a very fine, light-weight, mildew-proof, sewable netting of monofilament nylon, made on a Leavers machine for window screening in war-zone tentage, especially in the Pacific theater. This was a top-secret effort and samples were brought down from Wilmington, Delaware, by Pierre Du Pont and one of his research associates to the Office of the Quartermaster General in Washington for approval by General George Doriot's research staff. It was a very tense moment as the "approval" group was told about the screen that could be made at any American netting factory. "Show them the samples," said Mr. Du Pont to his research assistant. There was dead silence. The young developer of the monofilament nylon screen had left the samples on the train! Later, they were retrieved, unharmed, and adopted by

---

[4]Wire screen woven on a loom.

[5]Netting produced on a flatbed knitting machine.

the military for worldwide use. Such knitted screens are now in use in civilian sports and camping areas or wherever tents with windows are desirable.

Lace manufacturers are among the most important consumers of Southern-spun, combed, cotton sales-yarns, or fine-blended yarns, furnishing an outlet for a wide range of counts, from 20/2 to 220/2, from 50/1 to 120/1.[6] Carded yarns are little used for nets or lace except in the lowest counts for heavy laces or fishnets. Combed cotton yarns of best-grade cotton and longest staple are predominantly required. Very fine laces require high-count yarn, mule-spun of Egyptian cotton, which is especially prepared for winding on brass bobbins, a system unique to the industry. Formerly this yarn was imported exclusively from England, but in 1934 Carl Rudisill, a founder of the Carlton Yarn Mills[7] in North Carolina, went to England where in fine yarn mills he studied brass-bobbin yarn preparation. Upon his return, he installed the necessary equipment at his mill in Cherryville, which became the first in the United States to produce brass-bobbin yarn for the lace trade.

A revolutionary introduction to the lace industry was the Raschel lace machine, which produced beautiful narrow lace with selvage interlocking it to the next narrow lace strip in order to make one wide width piece when it came off the machine in the greige. A slitting machine used during finishing cut the selvages and thus produced up to 150 or 200 pieces of narrow lace edging. This was one of the first examples of producing more than one width fabric at the same time on the same machine.

Lace is now made of linen, cotton, silk, wool, or man-made fibers and blends. It is used for lingerie as well as beautiful and feminine blouses and dresses. Brides especially love a lace-trimmed wedding gown with net veiling, particularly if one can be enhanced with a piece of handmade "rosepoint" that has been kept in the family. So we see that lace is not only a modern fashion, made mostly of fine Southern combed yarns, but a collector's item as well. Museums vie for collections of the old patterns, and the new machine-made pieces are copies of them, carrying the same design names.[8]

For a long time there has been a controversy over hosiery, knit apparel, and lace: are they commodities or just fashions? Advertising seems to prove that hosiery is both, especially when Catawba Hosiery Mills "Sells Fashion by the Foot" and pictures a row of fancy half hose. Regarding all fabrics, fashion sways the markets, resulting either in profits and economic expansion, or collapse. Fashion sways with sudden hurricane force concerning knit goods. For example, miniskirts of the late 1960s accelerated production of panty hose. Then the hippie emergence broke the market and jeans were the thing. More than one hundred hosiery mills closed in one year, among them Chadbourn.

---

[6]The higher the count number, the finer the yarn: /2 means two ply; /1 means a single strand.

[7]Now a division of Standard-Coosa-Thatcher, Inc., Chattanooga, Tennessee.

[8]See Leavers Glossary.

R. I. Dalton, Jr., president and general manager of Cocker Machine and Foundry Company, examines lace fabric produced on the company's popular line of Kidde Raschel knitting machines in 1968.

In 1977 more than 20,000 double-knit machines were in operation; the next year there were only 10,000. Springs Mills, of Fort Mill, South Carolina, closed out its knit division in 1978 "to halt a chronic drain on earnings," according to H. W. Close, the Springs Mills board chairman. Some knitting-machinery manufacturers faced bankruptcy because of the disaster of double knits and because newer-model imported machines could operate at two to two-and-a-half times the speed of American-made machines in place in the United States.

Knitwear, however fickle fashion may be, remains a major part of the Southern textile industry. Weave mills have advanced the trend by diversification, or expanding their woven lines to include knit-goods divisions. The National Association of Hosiery Manufacturers moved from New York to establish its headquarters in Charlotte, and its International Hosiery Exposition meets biennially there. The Catawba Valley Hosiery Exposition holds its biennial exposition in Hickory, and the Bobbin Show in Atlanta is one of the greatest expositions of apparel, knit and woven, manufacture.

The varieties of yarns used in knit goods should not be overlooked, especially when the stretchables carry somewhat bizarre trade names such as J. P. Stevens's "Under-Anythings"; Hanes's "Underalls" and "Under-Statement"; Burlington's "Wear-with-Alls" and "Only-Wear"; Kayser-Roth's "Per-Fit." All

Mule Spinning. The illustration is from *Memoir of Samuel Slater* by George S. White (1836). (Courtesy of Slater Mill Historic Site, Pawtucket, Rhode Island.)

the advertisements show glamorous legs and derriers encased in tight-fitting, lustrous knitwear.

On the market today there are countless knit products: velvets, corduroys, dress goods, sportswear, slacks, men's business suits, bathing suits, bikinis, leotards, baby garments, sleepwear, upholstery fabrics (especially automobile), sheets, shoe linings, types of suede cloth for high-fashion ladies' suits and dresses. Knitted man-made fur called "deep pile" is hardly distinguishable from natural mink and is considered high-fashion; it is certainly costly. There is man-made fiber fleece, laminated with knit chamois, to simulate sheepskin for cold-weather wear.

In the medical field there are knitwear bandages, personal hygiene items, and items for surgical uses. Recently the life of a North Carolina governor was saved due to a successful knitted man-made fiber arterial replacement. When NASA was planning its first astronaut program, it was a knitted fabric that served as a protective bio-pack for Sam, the chimpanzee, when he was projected into space. Important life-saving implants such as esophagus and arterial replacements, all made of knitted man-made fibers, have opened up whole new fields.

It would be difficult to face life these days without the contributions of the knit-goods segment of the textile industry. And yet, despite the progress of centuries, on a quiet home evening, one may still hear the click-click-click as someone wields knitting needles, the oldest textile machine in the world.[9]

---

[9]*Textile World; Modern Textiles; Modern Knitting.* Rosatto, *Leavers Lace;* Grass, *History of Hosiery;* Birnbaum, *Legacy in Lace; Antiques Monthly.* Conference with Morris Speizman, Speizman Industries; with Louis Thun, grandson of the founder of Textile Machine Works; with H. W. Close, Springs Mills.

The Textile Industry in Wartime | 9

In May 1940 President Roosevelt appointed the Advisory Commission to the Council of National Defense, which was an emergency committee on defense matters.[1] The commission was comprised of the following members: Industrial Production, William Knudsen; Industrial Materiel, Ed Stettinius; Employment, Sydney Hillman; Transportation, Ralph Budd; Agriculture, Chester Davis; Price Stabilization, Leon Henderson; and Consumer Protection, Harriet Elliot of North Carolina.

Chairman of the Textile Products Division was Robert T. Stevens, of J. P. Stevens & Company, a hard-hitting man whose motto was, "Do It Now." Stevens suggested that each member of his committee make a survey of his section of the industry with regard to productive capacity, machinery in place, raw materiel available. He gave them thirty days. Within a month of his appointment, and with only four days' notice, he called a luncheon meeting for 2 July 1940 at the Mayflower Hotel in Washington of all textile-trade-association executives. He gave an outline of what his committee had assembled and then requested their cooperation in this giant effort to obtain information on the production-performance capabilities of the textile industry and its suppliers of raw materiel.

Attendance was excellent, the enthusiasm great, and Bob Stevens never regretted being personally out of pocket for about twenty-five Mayflower lunches. He recognized that, in this emergency, central leadership should emanate from each group's trade association. So, with the unselfish and farsighted cooperation of individual executives, and properly delegated group leadership, together with the loyal and determined mill workers, the textile industry proved its ability to solve all wartime textile problems in an orderly fashion, although there were unprecedented problems to face and to overcome.

The members of Stevens's committee foresaw several potential problems in war production. First, if the government couldn't get what it needed by ordi-

---

[1]The Act of 1916 established a Council of National Defense, permitting a president of the United States to appoint an emergency committee on defense matters.

Robert T. Stevens, chairman of J. P. Stevens and Company, was named by President Roosevelt to head up the textile products division of the Advisory Commission to the Council of National Defense in May 1940.

nary bidding, it might impose priorities and ultimately take over plants. Second, the government could move to set its own price levels. Third, profits would be merely paper profits because increasing taxes would eat up the excess and, in cases of firms that did not take that contingency into consideration, black ink would turn to red. Finally, every step involved in the national-defense program would inevitably mean a greater concentration of power in federal agencies concerned with prices, wages, hours, and all the other phases that had hitherto been regarded as the prerogatives of individual enterprise.

When the early figures concerning available supply of textile machinery and raw materiel, along with a prediction of future needs, came into the commission's office, the reports called for quick action, especially in grease wool. When decisive action seemed impossible given governmental red tape and reviews, the commission chairman, Bob Stevens, personally underwrote the order for an enormous supply of wool in the grease and the bottoms it was to be shipped in, immediately, from Australia. The wool came into this country just before Pearl Harbor and just before the Australian government placed an embargo on further shipments of wool. The quantity of Australia's fine wool thus obtained was sufficient to serve as the United States' chief backlog source of supply during the war years to follow. But it was a closely guarded secret known only to the Textile Advisory Committee and the quartermaster general.

When war was actually declared, Robert T. Stevens was among the first of Washington businessmen to be called to Fort Sill, Oklahoma, for the military-indoctrination course there, and among the first to resume his former commission of World War I. From then on, Colonel Stevens was in charge of the procurement of textiles, clothing, and general supplies in the Office of the Quartermaster General, Lieutenant General Edmund B. Gregory.

Many top executives from the ranks of industry went to Washington to work for the government, some in uniform, some as civilians. Without their industrial experience, the great production achievement of our textile industry and textile-machinery industry could not have reached the heights they did. It was an honor to be called, and each person accepted the call as such with no expectation of reward except the final victory. The personnel roster of the Textile, Clothing and Leather Bureau of the War Production Board included some of the most distinguished names in the textile industry. Many textile executives gave their full time to the War Production Board. Others acted as special consultants on assignments that lasted from ninety days' service to the duration of the war. Some devoted all the years of the war effort to this patriotic and grueling work, and then remained to "clean up" afterward.

Especially notable were those men who served as directors of the important Bureau of the War Production Board. Frank Walton,[2] who had succeeded W. Ray Bell[3] as director of a similar division in the Office of Price Administration, was the first director of the Textile, Clothing and Leather Bureau of the War Production Board. After he relinquished his post there, he served as consultant to the Office of Price Administration and to the Office of the Quartermaster General. Walton was succeeded by J. Spencer Love in 1943, who put his extraordinary management ability to work at a critical time. He was able to correlate and to combine production and resources planning to speed up the supply for American military and civilian needs as well as those of our Allies. One of his most important emergency accomplishments was the rayon-tire-cord program, which relieved a dangerous bottleneck.

Rayon had never been tried before as a tire cord, but research found it to be more heat resistant and stronger than cotton-cord tires for aviation equipment such as planes that had to land at high speed on flat tops or short runways. Firestone Tire Company, aided by military research programs, introduced rayon as a tire cord, and it saved lives and equipment by its strength and heat resistance during high-pressure landings. Spencer Love was assisted in this program by Harry L. Dalton, head of the Rayon Division of the bureau. Kenneth Mariner succeeded Love and served as director until the end of the war.

Leon Henderson, administrator of the Office of Price Administration, had appointed a Cotton Textile Advisory panel and many subcommittees representing the divisions of the industry. Textile executives and officials who were

---

[2]Frank Walton, director of the Association of Cotton Textile Merchants, 40 Worth Street, New York, and president of Walton Cotton Mills, Georgia.

[3]Ray Bell was president of the Association of Cotton Textile Merchants.

J. M. Cheatham. Many top executives gave up their desk jobs to serve in World War II. Cheatham returned after the war to become president, then chairman, of Dundee Mills. He also served as president of the Georgia Textile Manufacturers Association and the American Textile Manufacturers Institute.

called to serve their country through the War Production Board and the Office of Price Administration committees did so with unstinted effort.

One of the marked trends in the industry during World War II was the development of cloth for the needs of the customer, which at this time was the military. Textile technicians were constantly at work to improve construction of fabric, to make it suitable for the purpose for which it was intended. The climate in which the clothing would be worn had to be specially considered.

Major General George Doriot, a top corporation official, was named head of the Research and Development Division of the Office of the Quartermaster General. He recruited an outstanding group of technicians, scientists, famous explorers, and executives to seek out and to create the very best in every line of materiel. His personality, drive, and imagination kept his textile section in high gear throughout the five years of his service.

Shirley cloth is a famous wartime development made possible by a new application of mathematics to high-sley fabric construction. The principle of manufacture of Shirley cloth was developed by Dr. Fred T. Pierce at the Shirley Institute in England during the bombardment of London and the Battle of Britain (1940). England, however, had not been able to produce it in volume. Supplies of flax or linen for fire hoses were cut off and, to keep down the raging fires of London, a heavy-duty cotton fabric suitable for fire hoses was urgently and desperately needed. No cotton fabric had ever been woven tightly enough to contain such water pressure. Doriot brought Dr. Fred T. Pierce to the Quartermaster Research and Development textile section and things started to move in a hurry.

There were also the wind-resistant, water-repellent, high-sley oxfords developed under the direction of the Research and Development section of the Military Planning Division, Office of the Quartermaster General, and with the cooperation of several outstanding textile firms. The development of this series of fabrics was based on the broad construction principles of the British Shirley fabric, but the American adaptations employed American cottons and yarns of standard numbers that were already in production by mills to make military goods.

Actually, the simple principle of closely woven cotton cloths involves the use of longer-staple cotton, a slightly lower twist in the yarn, and closing of the interstices between threads by using higher sley and picks in balance. When in contact with water, the cotton swells, thus closing the openings. This combination produced fabrics with greater wind resistance and a better affinity for chemical water-repellent treatment than any type of fabric previously known. They are from four to nine times more wind resistant than Byrd cloth (named for Commander Richard Byrd) and, up until the advent of Shirley, the most desirable fabric known for windy, cold, or Arctic-type exposure. High-sley oxfords protect against the wind, but allow body vapors to escape without condensation of moisture within the clothing.

On one of the 600 trial runs to find the exact yarn requirements, the Quartermaster textile-research team thought they had hit the jackpot. So they ordered a combat uniform made up of the new fabric. It was precisely the same in appearance as the G.I. issue; the only difference was its ability to repel water and to resist wind. Word was sent to General Doriot that *finally* success had been attained with this item.

An invitation was issued to him to attend and view the test to be held in the glassed-in "weather room." In this room any weather could be simulated. The audience outside could see the results, but would be protected from the faked elements by heavy thickness of glass. A snow storm, wind storm, hail storm, typhoon—all were possible. The quartermaster general was invited to the unveiling, as were the head of the War Production Board, Pentagon officials, and several congressmen.

But Doriot had plans of his own. He was an impatient man and he wanted no foul-up on this very important project. So he decided to test the uniform himself. There were two identical uniforms, laid out side by side. He thought they were of the same cloth and asked no questions as he quickly changed clothes, donning one of the "demonstrators." He then stepped into the weather room, pushing the button that created a cloudburst and high winds. In about two minutes he jumped out, absolutely sopping wet, wind blown, and cold—and *angry!*

He stalked through the huge main office wing dripping water as he strode to his office and called in the team that had so proudly proved they could produce a proper Shirley cloth. He told them in no uncertain terms what he thought of the cloth. Finally, looking at the distraught, angry, and very wet general, one of the team officers burst into laughter. "General," he said, "you put on the wrong suit, the one we had made up for comparison." Doriot looked at the crowd and then laughed too. "I thought I'd put something over on you all by trying it out myself—I messed it up—so proceed with your original plans to have your unveiling of your improved Shirley cloth."

The result, in less than one year, was the creation of a fabric that revolutionized combat clothing. Twenty-five percent more per loom could be produced of it than other military fabrics using the same yarns. This was the fabric that roofed London and other cities after bombing, and was used for tentage, tarpaulins, pup tents, and uniforms. It was the most versatile fabric produced and was used in every combat theater.[4]

In peace or wartime, as long as history reports, people want cloth. More than a century ago, tribal wars in Africa resulted in prisoners who were sold to slave traders for pieces of red flannel. So it was in the North African campaign of World War II; cloth was even used by United States forces as payroll. Natives building airstrips for the Allied forces insisted that they be paid in yards of cloth. They couldn't spend money, but they could use cloth, big pieces and little pieces. One day the pay-ship arrived and the native workers were in line for their payroll, but some smart bureaucrat had sent, instead of cloth, a shipment of pots, pans, knives, and forks. There was almost a riot when the native workmen heard about it; certainly there was a sitdown! No cloth, no work! A cable, hastily dispatched, brought the cloth in by the next airdrop, so the airfield got finished after all.

The hundreds of experiments run by many other spinning and weaving mills in order to establish construction specifications, and the almost-fabulous quantities of goods that were turned out, combine to make outstanding industrial history. The story of every mill's effort is a saga in itself, and the stories of those "dollar-a-year" businessmen and textile mill workers, who were just as great heroes as those in active service, have been unsung. Without them, the war could not have been won. There was the constant demand for more goods and for acceleration of operations; a terrible shortage of competent workers; production control; difficulties with price control; and the emotional strain of the most dreadful war in all history. And there were always experiments in the quartermaster general's Research and Development Division that, when successful, worked wonders in saving lives.

---

[4]It is still being made. In fact, a member of the team can easily spot Type IV Oxford in rainwear, upholstery fabrics, and sports outdoor equipment.

One scientist-explorer of the Antarctic called in by General Doriot for expertise on fire-protection suits for combat and rescue work was Sir Hubert Wilkins, who had made it to Point Barrow in 1928. When he was a boy in Australia, he was fascinated with sea-turtle eggs he found along the shore in blazing hot weather. He wondered why they did not cook in the sun before being hatched and concluded it was due to the lining of the egg shell. His theory was that fire fighters who died in their asbestos suits were not burned, but had boiled internally, so to speak.

In the quartermaster's Research and Development Division, he concocted a zip-on suit that was fireproof on the outside and boil-proof on the inside. To prove his point, he sat patiently at a large table cutting and sewing by hand the pattern that was to demonstrate his theory. The garment pattern and fabrics used were adapted for all branches of the service and saved countless lives. Wilkins was a hero, as was the volunteer who first wore the suit in practical demonstration.

Another member of the quartermaster's team was the late Paul Siple, the famous first Eagle Scout to reach the Antarctic as a member of Byrd's expedition. He was in the Quartermaster Research Division to teach survival techniques in frozen climates to officers from the field. Among other things, he invented a hand-warmer, small and chemically controlled, that could retain heat for hundreds of hours when worn inside a soldier's glove, thus allowing his fingers to remain facile with a gun.

Conversely, there was Colonel John Dill, who was an expert on man's ability to withstand tropical heat. He had studied the field workers in Mississippi's blazing summer sun and later he traveled to many theaters of war to teach men how to prevent heat exhaustion.

There was a brave, though anonymous, black man located in a mosquito-breeding laboratory in Beltsville, Maryland, who every day kept his big arm—naked, except for one band of cloth—inserted in a cage of voracious mosquitoes while scientists peered through magnifying glasses to see if the mosquitoes could penetrate the fabric and, if so, how far. Smarter mosquitoes bypassed the cloth to attack his flesh. "Naw, it don't hurt," said the man. "At first, it itched a lot, those bites, but it don't bother me now." Textile technicians were developing a mosquito-proof fabric for light-weight jungle uniforms.

Not everyone could serve in the military because it took about nine civilians to provide for one man in uniform. Among the former were those executives who commuted to Washington from the South and from New England to confer with the War Production Board and other agencies. They were veterans of the so-called "Mayflower conferences." They were chairmen of many industry committees, or some labor committees, but in either case were willing, helpful operators behind the scenes—counseling, advising, then going back home to adjust textile production to meet government emergencies.

The Research and Development section in the quartermaster general's office was made up of experts called in to determine new uses for fibers: for instance, recalling all nylon toothbrushes from retail or wholesale shelves so that the bristles could be remelted and the filament recycled for parachutes; or making something useful out of the nylon sweepings on the floor; or ordering duck to be run on sheeting looms; or making tenting out of bedspread yarn numbers; or balancing mill production in one place and unbalancing it in another, but always with the goal to get the goods made and delivered on schedule.

All this was done according to prices set by the Office of Price Administration, and with all government contracts subject to renegotiation. Unfortunately, there were some businessmen who invented excuses to keep part of their production for "their customers." It was they who catered to the black market.

Many leaders, who gave unselfishly of their time and effort, lost their health in good measure as a result. And many, many brave young men—textile workers and their sons—and textile leaders' sons who would have been the executives of tomorrow—lost their lives in the service of their country. Most textile mill workers and most textile management responded as one in the industry's magnificent accomplishment of production without plant expansion, without government subsidy, and with few new replacement machines. Their work stands as one of the greatest industrial feats of all time.

In such a massive effort to satisfy demand and delivery, there were mix-ups. In this war there was the additional problem of clothing the women in the military. The navy was smart and obtained the services of a leading designer of women's wear, so women sailors were turned out smartly. The army had to deal with the imperious Oveta Culp Hobby of Texas, head of the Women's Army Corps (WAC), who had no sense of style and demanded that ladies wear an unbecoming helmet-type hat of her own design. It was uncomfortable and incensed every member of the WAC. The Doriot staff finally got rid of the unsuitable fabric and style of the Hobby uniform, but the hat remained a pain in the neck.

The basic underwear, however, was something even Mrs. Hobby could not alter. Several million ladies' brassieres were ordered in all sizes, but the war went on and none came. There was a great hue and cry from the WACs and from the quartermaster. "Where were the bras?" Apparel manufacturers were accused of nondelivery; warehouses were searched, inventories checked; and finally the bras were located in the mess's chinaware supply department, carefully stored and entered as *Cups, A,B,C,D.*

After Pearl Harbor there was an embargo on silk, but the military still had to have parachutes. Cheney Brothers, silk manufacturers, accomplished a superb achievement by weaving nylon fabrics in a plant that had not previously run the new-filament yarn. Manufacturing the parachutes in a plant that had never fabricated end-items meant tedious experiments in stitching the new fabric, training hundreds of workers unaccustomed to the fiber or the fabric or sewing, and installation of special sewing machines made for this purpose.

The Singer Company sent many of its young executives to help the Cheney operatives, and workers of other companies, with end-items. Two of these trainers were in General Doriot's Research and Development section counting the number of stitches required per inch to get the best and most wear out of any item that had to be sewn. One stitch less per inch of sewing could cost a parachutist his life. One of these Singer men later became a vice-president of the company.

The 100 members of the Southern Combed Yarn Spinners Association enthusiastically pushed war production before Pearl Harbor to meet the new specifications that demanded quality and durability. Ranking high in outstanding work on new synthetics were Duplan Corporation, J. P. Stevens & Co., Hess, Goldsmith & Co., Burlington Mills Corporation, Bates Manufacturing Co., Deering-Milliken & Co., Newmarket Manufacturing Company, Schwartenzenbach, Huber & Co., and many others.

Down in Spartanburg, South Carolina, Walter Montgomery was the first person to put his mill, the Beaumont, completely on war-production fabric. He never made a yard for consumers in that plant until after the war was won. "Number 12.29" and "Number 10" duck were the products. His company won six of the famous Army-Navy "E" Awards for excellent achievements in production.

Spartanburg County mills set an all-time record in 1942 when they produced one billion, ninety-eight million-plus yards for military materiel while consuming 439,085 bales of cotton valued at $38.9 million. In addition, they consumed other supplies valued at more than $12 million. In Spartanburg, 22,564 men and women—all in jobs rated "essential"—worked in forty-one plants with 966,122 spindles.

In May 1943 the town had a big rally called, "Textiles Go to War." There was a parade of soldiers from Camp Croft, a benediction service on the lawn of Converse College, and other ceremonies at the ball park—the only place large enough to seat the crowd. Oveta Culp Hobby, Senator James Byrnes (later justice of the Supreme Court and secretary of state[5]), and Governor Olin Johnston officiated. This was just one example of cooperative enthusiasm by the defense establishment and the textile mill operatives who knew they were contributing directly to the "unconditional surrender" of their country's enemies.

Another example of such cooperation was the Gossett Mills' conversion, in 1942, from manufacturing dress goods to manufacturing 7.9 ounce shelter-tent duck. Although the fabric was extremely difficult to manufacture, the mill became its largest single producer. In 1943 revision in quartermaster requirements terminated all 7.9 ounce orders on hand and, with the mill's consent, this was done without cost to the government. Almost immediately, however, changing requirements of global warfare made it necessary for the quartermaster to ask the mill to resume duck production on a full scale. Without a complaint, Gossett reconverted the looms to the 7.9 ounce fabric, a very costly operation to the mill.

Considering that the United States and England were the only countries supplying the Allies, it was necessary to have some coordination between the producers of the two countries; therefore, the Combined Resources and Production Board was set up. Colonel W. A. Grierson, chairman of Greenhalgh & Shaw in England, was sent over to Washington to represent Britain in allocation of materiel.

---

[5]Supreme Court justice, 1941; director, Economic Stabilization, 1942; director, War Mobilization, 1943-1945; secretary of state, 1945-1947.

Colonel W. A. Grierson, chairman of Greenhalgh and Shaw of England, represented Britain in Washington with regard to the allocation of materiel for the Combined Resources and Production Board in World War II. Shown here is a 1943 meeting with Mildred Gwin Barnwell (later Andrews), who was serving as advisor to the quartermaster general.

Textile executives participated in several overseas fact-finding missions during World War II. One was the Bancroft Mission, so-called because Tom Bancroft, of the War Production Board, was chairman. It included George Lanier, also of the War Production Board, and Walter Montgomery, representing textile mills, as well as Frank Lowell and Hugh Bolton, representing textile-machinery companies. Their mission was to evaluate the potential of the British textile industry in efforts to obtain maximum production for the combined resources program. The Bancroft Mission flew to England on the *China Clipper* and worked with Colonel Grierson, who met them in Manchester. They talked to mill men and with union leaders to urge more production of British-made textiles, more overtime—anything to raise the level of Britain's textile output, or the production per man hour. The mission reported, after returning to Washington, that textile production per worker in England was quite low compared to that of the United States textile worker. In order to find out why, in 1944 the British sent a cotton-textile mission to the United States headed by Sir Frank Platt, cotton controller, Ministry of Supply. He was formerly managing director of the Lancashire Cotton Corporation. This was a top-level group of eight men representing manufacturers and labor groups.

George Lanier was a member of the Bancroft Mission sent to Europe during World War II. He later served as president of Mount Vernon Mills and Turner Halsey Company.

The itinerary of the American tour had been planned in Washington by Colonel Grierson, who was stationed there for the duration. Divided into teams, the group was able to cover the spinning, weaving, and finishing mills of the United States and to study how the American mills were able to surpass British production per man, per hour. Their report concluded that, in spinning, American mills exceeded British mills by eighteen to forty-eight percent; in winding, by eighty to eighty-five percent; in warping, by seventy-nine to eighty-nine percent; and, in weaving, by fifty-six to sixty-seven percent. They found United States mills running a wartime schedule of forty-eight hours per week, three shifts, or 144 hours, compared to Britain's one forty-eight-hour shift.[6] They found the American war-production plan to be continuous production of standard counts of yarn and cloth types, a mass-production system made possible by high-speed, automatic machinery and indefatigable workers. Their report stated also that American management had greater scope than British management in utilization of labor due to the workers' acceptance of scientific methods and the use of a three-shift schedule. There was no evidence of American operatives being overworked in spite of the greater number of machines supervised by them as compared to corresponding British operatives, the so-called Platt Report stated.

The high-speed automatic, American-built textile machinery was the envy of the rest of the world. But new textile machinery was hard to get, indeed impossible without an allocation order by the War Production Board for a specific type of war-emergency fabric. Textile mills and textile-machinery builders are so closely related that achievements of one cannot be explained without comparison with the other. Primarily a peacetime industry, textile-machinery manufacturing firms were uniquely equipped to produce strategic materiel for the military. Their machine tools and patterns, fixtures, jigs, forges, dies, testing equipment and, most of all, 37,000 highly trained metal workers put the industry immediately into successful production of strategic materiel. The contribution of member firms of the American Textile Machinery Association during the war was outstanding. The variety of military items they were scheduled to produce included: 75-mm. pack howitzers, Bendix magnetos, internal grinders, gear shapers, components for jet engines, steam engines for Liberty ships, steam turbines for use in the synthetic-rubber program, and high-octane gasoline refineries. One company delivered 2,500 steam turbines in two years. It may not seem an impressive figure, but each turbine has 1,350 parts, and each part had to be machined and assembled. Then the whole turbine was tested for KW/output, vibration, overload, knock-off, and other performance characteristics. Also, only operating personnel of the ATMA (37,000 persons) made all this variety of precision-tooled materiel. They made the above, plus magnetos for American Bosch, torpedo parts, antisubmarine signaling devices, 50-caliber machine guns, heavy machine tools, and Hanna's "anticipating gyro." So tex-

---

[6]England had junked its redundant spindles during the 1930s to prevent overproduction in a depressed economy, and unions never changed the one-shift rule.

tile mills, screaming for new equipment or more equipment, had to make do with what they had.

As one by one the Allies regained possession of Western European countries, the Technical and Advisory Committee of the War Production Board, assisted by the quartermaster general, sent groups of technicians and scientists into the regained countries as fast as the army would allow. As the Allies moved forward into conquered Germany, in came industrial experts from the United States, under the direction of the War Production Board and the quartermaster general. The purpose of this mission was to find any textile mills that were still in operation and to give each of them 100,000 bales of United States cotton drawn from the government's "loan pool," so the mills could operate and produce cotton textiles for the people of the countries occupied by the recently defeated German troops.

Three textile men—Walter Montgomery, Joe Lanier, and Ames Stevens[7]— were in Rheims when V-E Day was celebrated and, in the midst of that historic city, watched the joyous American/French parade that marked the Allies' victory over Germany. There, too, they received a cable from Senator Jimmy Byrnes, director of War Mobilization and close advisor to President Roosevelt, requesting that they make a survey and evaluation of the damage to Western European textile industries and their possible rehabilitation.

They proceeded to Munich and in this effort, working with Drs. Kellerer and Kohler, distinguished textile scientists, they found in the town of Naila, hidden in a woolen mill, the *Gliederung der Winschaftsgrappe Textilindustrie*. It was the official and complete record of every mill that had been operated under German occupation control. This report covered cotton, wool, worsted, silk, ramie, hemp, flax, and rags as raw material; spinning, weaving, knitting, finishing, and garnetting manufacturing plants. It also detailed the mills' personnel: men, women, children, nationals of conquered countries, and Jews.[8]

Ames Stevens left Montgomery and Lanier in Munich and, in compliance with a government request, continued into Germany to complete the study of the textile industry, or what was left of it there. Their report and substantiating documents, brought back through the ruins of Europe, were invaluable to the War Production Board and other agencies that would assist in the rebuilding of Europe in upcoming years.

---

[7] Walter Montgomery, Spartan Mills, South Carolina; Joe Lanier, Sr., West Point Manufacturing Company (now WestPoint Pepperell), Georgia; Ames Stevens of the Stevens woolen mills complex, New England.

[8] Copy of document loaned for study by Walter Montgomery.

Walter S. Montgomery. Chairman and ceo of Spartan Mills. He has probably served longer in the latter position than any other ceo in the industry. During World War II he was part of the Bancroft Mission and carried out high-level assignments for the War Production Board.

Joseph L. Lanier, Jr. Past chairman and ceo of WestPoint Pepperell. On V-E Day he was in Europe making an evaluation, for the War Production Board, of the damage to Western European textile plants.

Trade Associations and the Trade Press: The Guiding Hands | 10

Since the mid-1800s, there have existed groups of textile manufacturers, or yarn spinners, who attempted to bring cohesive action among their like for the general advancement of the whole. Each association had its own localized axe to grind, or thought it had, and so all united to "lick 'em." Some associations were formed to serve regions, states, or any other purpose of note. Some members laughingly said the groups were largely social clubs, but that is not true.

With the advent of World War I, the textile industry as a whole faced unheard-of problems. For the first time in history, leaders of both Northern and Southern textile interests were brought together to establish a committee for the purpose of industry-government cooperation. This came about through the two big regional trade associations.

Formed in 1854, in Massachusetts, the Hampden County Cotton Manufacturers Association was the earliest of the textile associations. This organization later, through change of name and expanded membership, became the New England Cotton Manufacturers Association and then the National Association of Cotton Manufacturers, later the Northern Textile Manufacturers Association. Although national in name, its membership was from New England and neighboring states. The Northern association confined its effort largely to lobbying for protective tariffs, and in its early days employed Daniel Webster to do the job. Later, Senator Lippitt took up the cudgel in their behalf and his own, since he was a large stockholder in several mills.

In 1897, with the amazing growth of the Southern industry, mill men below the Mason-Dixon line decided they needed an association, too, to fight unfair freight rates and arbitrate cotton problems, so the Southern Cotton Spinners Association was organized. Shortly afterwards, the name was changed to the American Cotton Manufacturers Association, its membership confined to the five Southern textile-producing states. During the early stages of World War I, these two major associations, the American and the National, collaborated and formed the National Council of American Cotton Manufacturers, its sole purpose being to help in the war effort. It was made up of fourteen members, seven from each of the two large associations.

Stuart W. Cramer, of Charlotte, textile engineer and mill owner, was named chairman. Headquarters were established in Washington. This was the first central agency to represent the textile industry in national and international affairs in cooperation with government needs. It performed a great service, notably in regard to protective tariff action, war, and postwar activities. It established a pattern that was followed in greater scale some twenty-odd years later preceding, during, and after World War II.

The council's very active War Service Committee, a group of forty-four leaders of the industry, had Gerrish H. Milliken as its chairman and John E. Rousmaniere as secretary. Both were textile merchants. The War Service Committee gave valuable assistance to both government and industry during the period of materiel procurement and later of textile price control, which became operative about mid-July 1918. It functioned ably and quickly, with its Executive Committee always ready and willing to meet any emergency.

During World War I many other textile executives took active part in the war effort through government positions: Spencer Turner[1] was chief of the Textile Section of the War Industries Board, of which Bernard M. Baruch was chairman; Harry L. Bailey[2] was chief of the Cotton Goods Branch of the Acting Quartermaster General's Department of the Army.

Other future textile leaders were actually on the fighting front. Major Stuart W. Cramer, Jr., West Point graduate and veteran of Mexican border activities (1915), was in France fighting with the Tank Corps along with his classmate, George Patton (who reached his great and lasting fame as a full general in World War II). Major Cramer described his experiences: "Someone had to walk in front of the tank and wave a red flag so the tank navigator could see where to go. I was a Major, so I waved the flag and led the tank! That was what was called modern warfare."

Colonel G. Edward Buxton was leading Sergeant York and learning what marksmanship in the hands of an uneducated Tennessee mountaineer could do to the Kaiser's army. And Colonel Elliott White Springs was spectacularly downing German planes, which earned him distinction as the greatest of aces. Hugh Comer was an officer with the 82nd Division. Herman Cone was an ensign, while Spencer Love, fresh out of Harvard, was the youngest major in the United States Army.

---

[1]J. Spencer Turner, president of J. Spencer Turner Company, member of the board of directors of the Association of Textile Merchants of New York, and later a partner in Turner, Halsey Company. Both companies were textile merchants. Young, *Textile Leaders of the South*, 722.

[2]Harry L. Bailey, president of Wellington, Sears Company, member of the Association of Cotton Textile Merchants of New York. Wellington, Sears is now merged with WestPoint Pepperell. Bailey was a member of the American textile mission to Japan in 1937. As retired chairman of the board of Wellington, Sears, he served on the Supreme Commander Allied Powers (SCAP) Mission to Japan, called for by General Douglas MacArthur, and consisting of five representatives from the United States government and observers from China, India, and the United Kingdom. Ibid.

When the United States entered World War I, Ben Gossett was appointed federal fuel administrator for South Carolina, but a desk job was not Ben's notion of fighting a war. He had attended Annapolis, so he returned to military service—this time, however, in the army, where he held the rank of captain. When Captain Ben Gossett returned to Anderson, South Carolina, at the close of World War I, he was considered a three-time hero, having served in the United States Navy, the Marine Corps, and the United States Army. He was also a local hero as a mill man and was promptly made president of two textile mills. "There was no trouble in those days of getting a person to serve as 'Mr. President.' Textile stockholders just chose a leading citizen or, in my case," he said, "one who had just returned from the wars."

At the close of World War I, to assist the industry in its difficult transition period, the Legislative Cooperative Committee was set up, an outgrowth of the National Council of American Cotton Manufacturers, which was then dissolved. This committee was to guide and to guard national legislation, to promote cooperation between government and industry, and to assist such promotion in any way possible. It proved to be an interim committee serving as a legislative clearinghouse until a new and larger organization was promoted. Indeed, discussions were under way already as to the need for such an industrywide agency and administrator.

One of the broader and lasting results of the wartime National Council was the formation, during Herbert Hoover's secretary of commerce days, of the Textile Education Foundation. There was a fund, in escrow, derived from the sale of impounded German dyestuffs under the war-reparation agreements. No one knew what to do with the money. Hoover had a young colleague named Edward Pickard, whose services on textile matters were so valuable to Hoover that he paid Pickard's salary out of his own pocket. Pickard suggested that the escrow fund be put to use in an educational way for the textile industry. So the Textile Foundation was created and Ed Pickard, appointed by Hoover, became director of the organization. He promptly and successfully put into operation the first planning and promotion of higher economic educational resources for the textile industry, involving such subjects as research on vertical and horizontal mill integration; coordinated research programs by textile schools, including the organization of the Textile School Deans into a functioning association; extension of textile education by establishment of vocational schools; closer affiliation of textile associations via seminars participated in by textile manufacturers and textile-machinery manufacturers. All his efforts were aimed at a better, stronger textile industry through higher education.

"To be a loom-fixer in 1930," said Pickard at one seminar, "one only needs a slide rule and a monkey wrench, but to be a loom-fixer in 1980 a Master's Degree in Textiles, Engineering and Electronics will be the first requisite. A little touch of genius should be helpful."

Between the Armistice of World War I and the mid-1920s, a chaotic duplication of efforts had become obvious when each Southern textile state, as its industry had grown, had set up its own cotton-textile association. The states included Alabama, Georgia, South Carolina, and North Carolina. Each wanted cohesive action within its own group in such matters as state legislation and other state-wide industry problems, but often failed to reach its goal because of competition from another state. The Gaston County Combed Yarn Association, a small group, was set up to eliminate fighting over labor scarcity. The Southern Textile Association was made up mostly of mill superintendents who dealt largely with technical mill problems concerning machines and production.

Each association collected dues, elected officers, and met annually at a convention. By and large, these meetings were mostly annual gatherings with a few speeches and reunions of old friends, and solution of some local problems. However, there was no overall control of general industry problems, even within their restricted areas.

In 1919, a meeting of cotton merchants and textile executives was called in Washington by United States Secretary of the Treasury McAdoo to discuss the nation's postwar economy. President Woodrow Wilson had previously appointed W. E. Beattie of South Carolina and B. B. Comer of Alabama to study cotton prices. Comer (former governor of Alabama and president of the Avondale Mills), who knew the havoc that could be wrought in a cotton panic and remembered that only four years ago cotton had dropped below eight cents a pound, advocated pegging the price of cotton. He championed the farmer and higher cotton prices at the meeting, as a means to stabilize the cotton market and the textile industry.[3]

Such a "ridiculous" proposal as pegging the price of cotton was refused, and the price of the fiber soon was dropping fast. Middling $7/8$ inch average high, on ten spot markets, was 42.26 cents a pound on 17 April 1920, the highest peacetime price ever reached. By 20 June 1921, it had dropped to a low of 9.98 cents per pound. The postwar panic of 1920-1921 was on. Mills that had cotton warehoused at previous highs were receiving cancellations every day on future fabric orders. Mill margins normally fluctuated with the rise and fall of cotton prices, but now the fluctuation was mostly downward. The price of cotton dropped steadily. In the Delta where long-staple cotton, always priced at a premium, had sold for $1.00 a pound the previous year, the price plummeted to 20 cents and the lint remained unpicked in the cotton fields. Cotton field hands wandered about unemployed and many rode the rails headed for Detroit, St. Louis, or Chicago where work perhaps could be found. That was the famous "Buy-a-Bale" year when every little mercantile establishment or business house bought a bale of cotton to help boost the market. One's patriotism was measured by the presence of an actual 500-pound cotton bale at the front of one's store.

The textile market was so badly upset that many who were considered established traders did not sense what was happening. It took a fast thinker to keep up with the vacillations of the market. For example, Charles Cannon (North Carolina), who was in his early twenties and considered "just a mere lad" in the eyes of commission-house elders, was on a sales trip to New York when he received a

---

[3]Comer was ahead of his time. See the Domestic Allotment Plan and the Agricultural Adjustment Act in ch. 6, 98-99.

wire from his father to sell some goods to a man who was considered a "tough customer." Because the market was breaking so rapidly, the price was left to Charles to set because he was there, on the spot.

When Cannon called on the New York commission merchant, he met a barrage of demands barked out in a sharp voice. But Cannon caught on. The "tough customer" was also a confused customer; he really did not know how fast the market was breaking. Cannon quickly quoted a price fifty percent higher than he had intended to quote and, unexpectedly, he closed the trade.

Down in Georgia, from the vantage point of his Moultrie Cotton Mills, William J. Vereen, a young man of great ability and versatility, had more fingers in more pies than the average. For several years he had watched the fluctuating cotton market, watched the accumulation of inventories in mill warehouses, and watched the dumping of goods by selling agents at prices that could only mean a disastrous loss, even bankruptcy, to manufacturers.

"They couldn't do that if we had some proper market statistics," Vereen said when he was elected president of the American Cotton Manufacturers Association. He took the train to New York to consult with the Association of Cotton Textile Merchants. This was a formal group of leading textile-fabric merchants, commission houses, and converters with headquarters at 40 Worth Street. He urged them to collect and compile industrywide statistical information on production, stocks, and unfilled orders. There were some who rejected the service because it meant divulging their "customer secrets" and some who thought the service would be a stabilizing influence in balancing production with shipments. There were many arguments pro and con. The Association of Cotton Textile Merchants employed Ivey Lee, then prominent in public relations work, to analyze and present the problem correctly. But reasonably soon Will Vereen, with the aid of Cason Callaway (of Callaway Mills, La Grange, Georgia), and a great deal of counsel from Harry Reimer (editor of the *Daily News Record*), and the cooperation of Leavelle McCampbell and Arthur Humphrey of the Association of Cotton Textile Merchants, persuaded the merchants' group to inaugurate a statistical service on a sample basis to cover one construction. "I'll never forget it as long as I live," said Will Vereen. "[The sample] was 37 inch 48 square 4 yarn sheeting. We tried to make it simple and took that construction because it was the thickest load on the market." With such a yardstick, statistics on a limited number of griege goods followed. They were compiled by Worth Street and published in the *Daily News Record*, giving the mills a public record of sorts from day to day of the market.

About that time, the North Carolina Cotton Manufacturers Association and the Cotton Manufacturers Association of South Carolina held a joint meeting in Asheville. Vereen called a meeting of the board of the American Cotton Manufacturers Association for the same time and place. There he outlined to the three bodies the principles involved in the statistical service inaugurated by the Association of Cotton Textile Merchants. Eventually he obtained unanimous resolutions endorsing the project. With that backing, the Association of Cotton Textile Merchants proceeded with statistics on a more expansive scale to cover other groups of fabrics.

In 1928 more than 300 types and constructions of goods were included in the statistics. It was a service used by trade and financial groups, published by the *Daily News Record,* and by the *New York Times* in its Business Index, and was weighted along with other statistics of basic industries. It was the first reliable business indicator of the textile industry. The Combed Yarn Spinners, watching the fabric statistics grow, inaugurated their own combed-yarn service. Members reported weekly the poundage, put-up, counts, and finish of yarn on hand. The association office compiled the records and mailed the result each Friday to members who, by Monday's mail, had the statistical picture of the combed sales-yarn industry. Prices, averaged, were indicated.

The work of the National Council on legislative matters along with the response of industry and selling agents and general business to the statistical work of the textile merchants' group proved that cooperation *could* be had and that a central agency might be the answer. Vereen thought if that could be successful, then why not eventual cooperation between cotton growers and mill men? Moreover, why not try cooperation between mill men of the North and South, thus wiping out legendary geographical boundary lines?

Many said it would not work. Antitrust laws and lack of cooperation would interfere. George Harris, of the Exposition Cotton Mills, had established an outstanding record in association success and leadership during his administration with the Georgia group. He believed, with Vereen, that it *would* work. At a meeting of the American Cotton Manufacturers Association held in Atlanta in 1926, Will Vereen devoted his message to the subject of a cotton-manufacturers' institute. He pointed out that uncontrolled production was industrial suicide and let Harris present plans to control mill output within established legal limits.

Harris made his plea for an agency to promote cooperation and unification of ideals. He had prepared charts to illustrate his points and he drew the plan for such an organization on the blackboard. Those present were inspired with its possibilities. A motion was made and seconded from the floor that a committee of three be appointed—including the president, the incoming president, and the vice-president—to handle the matter with expediency. That night, in his hotel room, President Vereen had an informal meeting of what he called his "planning committee" to make further arrangements to promote the plan. The committee was comprised of himself, as president of the American Cotton Manufacturers Association; S. F. Patterson, the incoming president; and James P. Gossett, slated to be vice-president. Floyd Jefferson, Baxter Jackson, and Harry Reimer also were with him. A list of twenty was drawn up that night, all members of the American Cotton Manufacturers Association, to help form the new agency. Patterson, taken ill the next day, died within a fortnight. James P. Gossett succeeded him as president of the American Cotton Manufacturers Association and shouldered the load in getting the new organization under way.

The Committee of Twenty met two weeks later in Greenville, South Carolina, where they had an informal roundtable discussion of the matter. They decided to proceed with the plan for a national institute and invited Northern cotton manufacturers to participate. Two weeks later, they met in Washington.

Herbert Hoover, then secretary of commerce, discussed the project with them at the time and heartily endorsed the general plan.

The National Council was asked to serve as a medium for negotiations. With Stuart W. Cramer as chairman, a meeting was called in Washington of representative textile executives from the North and South. Herbert Hoover addressed the group at a luncheon meeting. At that time Robert Amory, of New England, suggested that a committee of ten be named: five from the North and five from the South, to study the matter and offer a plan.[4]

Through the summer the committee worked, drew up the constitution, held preliminary meetings, and then a temporary organization was set up pending the calling of the first meeting. Will Vereen was named chairman for the Southern membership drive. He dispensed with a formal committee and called in W. M. McLaurine, secretary of the American Cotton Manufacturers Association, then headquartered in Charlotte, North Carolina.

"Come on down to Moultrie," he said, "and get these folks lined up." McLaurine stayed for weeks at Moultrie, Georgia; Will Vereen got on the telephone and took to the road, and together they signed up the South for three years. New England was signed up for the same trial period by Ward Thoron and his committee. The first annual meeting of the Cotton-Textile Institute, Incorporated, was called in New York on 20 October 1926. Even in the name of the organization, Vereen's persuasive planning was evident: "Hyphenate cotton and textile," he promised, "and we'll get cooperation from the growers."

H. R. Fitzgerald, of philosophic mien and scholarly mind, had some years before inaugurated a system of "industrial democracy" at his Riverside and Dan River Cotton Mills (now the Dan River Mills, Inc.).[5] It was an experiment in far-reaching industrial-relations planning. As a teenage boy, "because he wanted to see it grow," he had helped lay the brick at the mill his father was building and of which he was now president. Fitzgerald arose to address the first meeting of the Cotton-Textile Institute. He was extremely deaf and seldom spoke in public, so now all listened attentively as he said, "I feel that we are approaching the most interesting stage that the textile industry has ever experienced in its long and honorable history. Never before has this industry succeeded in creating such unity. It seems to me that we are faced with the opportunity to lift our industry out of the doldrums and carry it forward to the first rank among American industries."

Every effort had been made by the founding group to get Herbert Hoover to serve as president, but he declined for personal reasons. Two years later he was elected president of the United States. He had suggested, however, that

---

[4]James P. Gossett, the new president of the American Cotton Manufacturers Association, appointed the committee: William B. MacColl, president of the National Cotton Manufacturers Association; Andrew G. Pierce, Henry F. Lippitt, Ward Thoron, Edwin Farnum Greene, Robert Amory (all of New England); and Stuart W. Cramer, H. R. Fitzgerald, B. E. Geer, John A. Law, and W. J. Vereen (of the South).

[5]Smith, *Mill on the Dan*, 241-327.

Walker D. Hines, who had served as administrator of railroads during World War I and who was a distinguished lawyer in New York, be approached. On 20 December 1926, Hines was elected president of the Cotton-Textile Institute; George A. Sloan was made secretary.

Ability at self-government and the inauguration of unified action for the best interests of the industry and the nation became definitely established through this first central membership group. It had a succession of able presidents. Sloan, personable and forthright, succeeded Hines and instilled imagination and enthusiasm into the group. He resigned to head up the largest textile mill organization then in existence. Goldthwaite H. Dorr, a member of the Hines law firm and a great statesman and advisor, served as interim president between Sloan's resignation in 1935 and the election of Dr. Claudius T. Murchison of North Carolina in 1936. Paul Halstead was made secretary of the Cotton-Textile Institute when George Sloan became president. He was one of the great statisticians in American industry and a man of great ability in many other respects. His tact and his willingness to take on many hard jobs outside his regular line of duty did much to smooth the way for the industry during the lifetime of the Cotton-Textile Institute.

The Cotton-Textile Institute's role in inaugurating Code No. I has been reviewed already.[6] It was a monumental effort for the benefit of the mill operators and stockholders and the stabilization of the textile sales market. It served, also, as a model for other industries engaged in interstate commerce.

Code No. I was not all the institute accomplished. It assisted other trade associations in obtaining legislative standards on mill production for consumer items. For example, standard-length bed sheets were set by the Government Bureau of Standards at 108" along with specified widths for single, twin, queen, and king-size beds. Up until then, a tired person, looking forward to a comfortable night between his sheets, often found his feet sticking out in the cold or, if the sheets were properly tucked in, he had a cold shoulder. This one action created more employment in the mills, used more cotton, and brought comfort to the sleeping public.

The Cotton-Textile Institute established the annual National Cotton Week, widely publicizing the fine qualities of cotton. It was a successful merchandising stunt. The Cotton-Textile Institute established a fashion division with the famous Catherine Cleveland as director. For the first time, cotton was designed for top fashion by leading couturiers; shows and exhibitions of CTI's "collection" were in great demand throughout the United States and Europe.

A public-relations program was launched to counterbalance the miserable-mill folklore. Labels of content in finished garments and household items were made mandatory to protect the consumer. One young lad wrote his mother from summer camp, "Please send me some name tapes for my clothes. Everyone calls me 'Fruit of the Loom.' "

---

[6]See ch. 6, 94.

Other associations inaugurated additional economy stabilizers. For example, members of the Southern Combed Yarn Spinners Association, by the nature of their manufacturing process, produced a heavy side line of spinnable and reusable waste. The waste dealers bought the various items by bale, sorted and sold them in what was laughingly described as the "junk or ragpickers' " market. But junk it was not. Perhaps one-third of a bale of high-priced cotton, as it traveled through the mill, was lost as waste in process after process. In recycled form, however, it could be sold as useful and profitable products. Mills themselves gained little from this so-called waste, which they treated as such.

One of the best "rags to riches" stories of the early twentieth-century textile mills is based on cotton waste. A most remarkable man emerged from his self-declared "rag-picking business." He was a refugee from the South African Boer War. As Max Goldberg told it, he was one of the Dutch sympathizers captured by the British. He escaped from a prisoner-of-war cattle farm by lashing himself to the belly of one of the animals and so rode to market with the herd, where he quickly got away. He made his way to America and to the South where he heard that opportunities were good. Finally, he migrated to Gaston County, North Carolina, with his two brothers. They made a small beginning in a cotton mill financed by his Southwide waste business, and by group effort they built up a respectable fortune. Max died, and the name Goldberg was dropped for other more "American" names. The three brothers were gentlemen, and the second and third generations of their family were talented and philanthropic by nature.

Another related story is that of Charlie Gray, son of George, the self-educated textile engineer. During the good times of the 1920s, Charlie Gray had one or two of the family-owned mills that made lots of money and were among the mills that integrated into Textiles, Inc. When the latter went into bankruptcy during the Depression, Charlie went into waste dealing. Here he showed his father's business acumen and helped make textile waste a profitable and respectable enterprise.

Stabilization of waste prices was obtained through a "waste column" published weekly in the *Daily News Record* of average sales of each waste item. Thus order was brought to an enterprise that had been more or less a gamble. The column was prepared anonymously by the Combed Yarn Spinners Association, based on figures obtained weekly from mill sales of waste items, which were averaged on Friday and published each Monday. Sales included: comber noils, the shorter fibers combed out of long-staple cotton that are clean, spinnable material; and thread waste, short ends of thread or yarn from bobbins or spindles, now in demand for filters. The international firm of WIX, makers of automobile oil filters, was born when the yarn spinners established the waste market. Other waste, such as floor sweepings, is used for automobile upholstery stuffing or, after sterilization, for mattresses.

When Major Stuart Cramer, a West Point graduate and professional army man, retired from the service and succeeded his father as president and chief operating officer of Cramerton Mills in the early 1930s, he had one obsession. He was determined to have taxpayers' dollars buy quality goods for the military. When he was elected president of the Southern Combed Yarn Spinners Association in the 1930s, he found the opportunity he was seeking. "These old Quartermaster specifications are left over from the Civil War," he said, "or else they were written by a second-hand pants dealer from Philadelphia! I wore shoddy on the Mexican border chasing Pancho, and I wore shoddy in bloody France. If I do nothing else for my country, I'm going to see that the military men get quality goods on their bodies, and that the taxpayers get quality for military dollars."

He had earlier developed the famous Cramerton Army Twill, a specialty of his mill, and a very good combed-cotton uniform fabric that became army standard for hot-weather wear. Bit by bit, with a team of expert yarn men and the backing of the Spinners' association, he had ensured that specifications for military wear were quality cotton yarns, bought at the regular market price. Although not looking ahead to World War II, the Combed Yarn group was already on war production when the time came.

The Combed Yarn group had solved many problems for its members regarding their production-inventory statistics. In fact, it had done so well that the Carded Yarn group organized with headquarters in Charlotte under the direction of Fitzhugh Simmons. He conceived the idea of the Carded Yarn Rules, a manual that set forth contract rules on carded sales-yarn. Later, the Combed Yarn group adopted these rules also, which stabilized production even more for sales-yarn.

It was an outstanding display of self-control by industry to obtain orderly marketing of cotton sales-yarns and to eliminate the chiselers. The Cotton Yarn Rules for buying and selling yarn were adopted by the Southern Combed Yarn Association, the Carded Yarn Association, and the Association of Cotton Yarn Distributors. This was the first successful industrywide form of regulation for those yarns spun for sale in the open market.

The American Textile Manufacturers Institute (ATMI)[7] is now the national trade association for manufacturers of textile-mill products made in the United States. As such, its primary purpose is to provide its members a forum to develop united approaches to industrywide, national issues. ATMI is the outgrowth of a series of mergers beginning in 1949 with the consolidation of the primarily southern American Cotton Manufacturers Association and the Cotton-Textile Institute.

The National Federation of Textiles was merged with ATMI in 1958, bringing in the man-made fibers and silk industries. This was followed by mergers with the Association of Cotton Textile Merchants in New York (the Worth Street group) in 1964, the National Association of Finishers of Textile Fabrics in 1965, and the primarily northern National Association of Wool Manufacturers in 1970. The American Thread Institute retains its identity and independence, but is managed by ATMI. The Northern Textile Association is located in New England and is basically a regional group.

---

[7]American Textile Manufacturers Institute, *1983-1984 Directory*.

Stuart Cramer.
President of
Cramerton Mills and
Southern Combed
Yarn Spinners
Association (circa
1940–1941).

There are other trade associations representing allied industries vital to the coordinated effort of the textile industry, but they operate on their own. For example, there is the National Cotton Council, the result of hard times and surplus cotton troubles in the 1930s. The Agricultural Adjustment Administration, in NRA days, had accumulated in a government "pool" an enormous amount of "loan" cotton that was a constant threat to the cotton market. Actually, catastrophic effects would have resulted had the government dumped it. Most of the cotton was of such low grade that cotton men said it "only had one end," but it was really unspinnable by American standards. However, it was burlap-wrapped, steel-banded, and therefore considered a bale. Oscar Johnston, lawyer, financier, and cotton planter of the Mississippi Delta, was appointed director of finance of the Agricultural Adjustment Administration (AAA) and vice-president of the Commodity Credit Corporation. In those capacities he had disposed of the pool of loan cotton in such an orderly manner that it did not disrupt the cotton market in any way. While in Washington working on this problem, he realized the cotton folk—farmers, ginners, ware-

Robert Jackson.
Served as executive
vice-president of the
American Textile
Manufacturers
Institute in the 1950s
and 1960s.

housemen, and cotton merchants—needed joint representation on a national scale.

Down in the Mississippi Delta, in the Leflore County courthouse, he called upon a group of cotton planters, cotton merchants, bankers, and businessmen to create an organization to look after their interests in Washington. With their enthusiastic support, a meeting followed in Memphis; and there, 21 November 1938, the National Cotton Council (NCC) was born.[8] Oscar Johnston was named president; Rhea Blake, trained by the Delta Council, was named secretary; and Billy Wynn, attorney and planter of Greenville, Mississippi, was treasurer.

The Mississippi legislature voted $9,000 toward its first annual budget, and $40,000 was made up by popular subscription of its prospective membership, composed of cotton planters, ginners, warehousemen, merchants/shippers/ brokers, and cotton mills. Each of these groups paid dues of five cents per bale handled, for a total income to the NCC of twenty-five cents per bale. Many im-

---

[8]Not to be confused with Cotton Inc., of Raleigh NC, which is not a trade association.

F. Sadler Love. Served as secretary-treasurer of the American Textile Manufacturers Institute and succeeded Robert Jackson, upon his retirement, as president.

portant legislative actions affecting worldwide usage and handling of cotton still result from guiding actions of the council.

The council also sponsors the annual Maid of Cotton, a public-relations effort of the first order. A young lady is chosen by a group of judges as ambassadress of the cotton industry based on her IQ and her family's background in cotton. Of course, beauty helps!

Oscar Johnston was a financial genius and a man of wry humor. Some years after founding the National Cotton Council, he suffered an unsuccessful cataract operation. Nevertheless, he carried on, guiding the council from behind black glasses, seldom appearing in public and only then with his dark eye patches. He required a person always at hand to guide him about. Then came his final decision to try a new operation on his blinded eyes. He went to the

W. D. Lawson III. Served as president of the National Cotton Council in 1975–1976. Here he is pictured with a former Maid of Cotton, Gwin Barnwell Dalton.

best eye specialist in New York and learned that the chances were 100 to 10 against him. When the ordeal was over, he could see.

"Hand me the phone," he said, "I want to call my wife."

"Martha," he said as calmly as if he were buying a bale, "I want you to book a front-row table at every night club in New York for tonight. Yes! I mean it, *every one!* I plan to visit each of them, in style, with you. I've seen women by the Braille system so long that I want myself to see what they really look like!"

Through the NCC and cooperating associations, textile manufacturer-farmer relations strengthened, for they were tied in with the orderly program of cotton production and marketing set up by the NCC in cooperation with the U.S. Department of Agriculture.

Another trade association, apart from textile manufacturing yet a vital part of it, is the American Textile Machinery Association. This group, made up of builders of capital equipment (that is, the machines that make the textiles), originated in New England in the mid-1800s. It was really not an organization nor, except on rare occasions, did it emerge to public view. It had no officers and didn't hold any meetings, except once a year some machine builder would suggest that a picnic be held. (Whoever thought that the time was ripe was in charge of the event, which was usually held in the country within a half-day's buggy drive from Boston). The group actually had no name, but was loosely called the "machine builders." Anyone who built a textile machine or one that related to manufacturing textiles was eligible to attend the picnic. There were no association dues and the picnic was dutch treat. If a problem affecting machine builders required financing as its solution, the hat was passed to raise the funds. It was this group that put on the Atlanta International Cotton Exposition in 1881.

During the next fifty years the only recorded activity of the machinery group was an occasional exposition, or legal representation at government hearings on tariffs. With many new machines coming into being, the quiet association dropped its name, American Textile Machine Builders and, in 1913, actually organized into the Textile Exhibitors Association. Stock was issued at $50 a share; one share was allocated to each member company and membership was limited to fifty companies. The Exhibitors Association was put under the management of Chester Campbell, of Fairbanks & Campbell, and his young associate, Albert Rau. The association did nothing of record except exhibitions in Boston in Mechanics Hall and once in New York, where mill customers could see new equipment in operation. Most of the customers were from the fast-growing textile industry of the South.

In 1933, when the National Industrial Recovery Act was in effect, President Franklin Roosevelt declared he would deal with no industry problems except through that industry's trade association. The Exhibitors Association was dissolved, stock cancelled and returned to each subscriber, and a new organization set up: the National Association of Textile Machine Builders. All former members of the old Exhibitors group became members, and any other eligible American capital equipment manufacturer who sought protection or guidance was admitted to membership. David Edwards, president of Saco-Lowell Shops, was elected president, and a constitution and by-laws were adopted.

The machine industry was divided into six groups, each division having its own chairman. A code, based on the textile industry's Code No. I was adopted and, in addition, a Code Authority was set up with W. S. Pepperell as executive director. An office for the association, its first ever, was opened at 38 Chauncy Street, Boston, and William Cliff was appointed secretary of the association. The Code Authority occupied the same premises. About 400 companies making nuts, bolts, screws, bobbins, and such ancillary equipment formed their own association and Code Authority; they too employed Pepperell to handle code matters affecting them.

As soon as the National Recovery Act was ruled illegal, Cliff and Pepperell were dismissed, the Chauncy Street offices were closed, and the American Textile Machinery Association (as it was now called) receded into its former state

First share issued, in 1913, by the Textile Exhibitors' Association, which later became the American Textile Machinery Association.

with an honorary president, drafted from a member firm, and no limitation on time of service. Kent Swift, of Whitin Machine Works, was president from 1935 to 1946.

When a problem came up, it was handled by volunteering members or, on occasion, by an outsider for a fee. For example, during World War II the textile-machine industry, with its forges, furnaces, metal-working equipment, and labor skilled in this field was producing military materiel under government order; only a very small percentage of its total output was for textile mills. Two able executives from this field, W. K. Child and Marshall Newell of Draper Corporation, were drafted for the War Production Board and handled all allocations of production. After World War II, many problems of the industry were handled by member-draftees.

It finally became clear that young executives could not handle their own work and industry problems as well. In 1952 an ATMA office was officially

Kent Swift. Chairman and treasurer of Whitin Machine Works (1936-1947) and an early president of the National Association of Textile Machinery Manufacturers (now ATMA).

opened across the Potomac from Washington with a permanent staff to look after needs of American textile machine builders. In 1950 the American Textile Machinery Exhibition-International had resumed its showings of new equipment every four or five years in Atlantic City, in the only building in the United States that was big enough to hold the heavy equipment. Convention Hall was built by Lockwood Greene, the engineering company that had built so many textile mills and had exerted great influence on the textile industry. In 1959 federal legislation was passed allowing foreign-built equipment to come into the United States, under bond, for exhibit purposes. So the ATMA-owned and -directed Textile Machinery Exhibition became for the first time international, with sixteen countries exhibiting equipment.

In 1969 ATMA decided to relinquish management and ownership of the exhibition and to participate in future machinery shows as cosponsors with Textile Hall (in Greenville, South Carolina) of its world-famous International Exposition. Textile Hall executives served as managers. ATMA since that time has concerned itself only with affairs directly affecting the welfare of its members. Some of those services were seldom publicized, but were vital to the member companies.

In the beginning, ATMA was under the dominance of the "Big Six": Whitin Machine Works, Saco-Lowell Shops, Draper Corporation, Crompton & Knowles Corporation, Davis and Furber, and Leesona. A board of directors included other well-known machinery builders, but on the whole the weight of

William K. Child. Served on the War Production Board in World War II and later became president of Draper Corporation, succeeding Tom West.

opinion of these companies carried the day's discussions and led the way toward solutions of the industry's problems.

There are other trade associations, each serving its own section of the industry, such as the National Association of Hosiery Manufacturers, which sponsors the International Hosiery Exposition in Charlotte, North Carolina, every two years. The National Knitwear and Sportswear Association along with Knitwear Manufacturers Association puts on the Knitting Arts Exhibition, one of the oldest trade shows in the business. Trade associations are the clearinghouse for problems and achievements of each section of the far-flung textile industry, keeping order in the production and consumer worlds.

The guiding hands of trade publications and their editors have been evident for the past century and, as such, tie in with trade associations. The first bona fide textile publication, the *American Wool and Cotton Reporter*, was founded in 1887 in Boston by Franklin Pierce Bennett. David Clark of Lincolnton and Charlotte, North Carolina, began publishing the *Southern Textile Bulletin* in Charlotte in 1911. The two publishers hated each other and fought it out in their weekly journals' editorials. Few Southern mill owners read the Bennett pub-

To gain better understanding and greater recognition, the American Textile Machinery Association inaugurated its Press Tour Workshop in 1953. Leading journalists from trade publications and the daily press were brought by chartered plane to a number of textile-machinery plants for practical demonstrations of research and development in the production of more-efficient machines for all types of textile goods.

lication because Clark accused it of fostering radicalism and unionism. Clark constantly waved the Confederate flag, but managed to give some very good and pithy advice to the rapidly growing Southern industry. To the Southern textile man, what Dave Clark said was gospel.

August Kohn, a textile reporter for the *Charleston News & Courier* at the beginning of the century, was widely read in the South as he wrote of the pitfalls and accomplishments of the developing industry in South Carolina. His column was as informative as a weekly textile paper; however, it limited its subject matter to the industry in South Carolina.

Cotton was founded by W. R. C. Smith Publishing Company in Atlanta in 1898 and was the most widely read trade journal in the South, especially among mill technicians, who followed closely articles on new equipment and how to get the best results from them. Robert Philip, the editor in the 1930s and early 1940s, was so highly regarded by textile leaders that he was asked to go along with them on the first voluntary trade mission to Japan in 1937. In 1947 the magazine's name was changed to *Textile Industries* to include coverage of man-made fibers. Richard

The American Textile Machinery Association Exhibition Committee, 8 July 1954, which included presidents of the "Big Six." (L to R, standing): Kay Schwartz, Hugh Bolton, Robert Leeson, James Hunter, Frank Lowell. (Seated): Roy Ross, Frederick Howe, William K. Child, Mr. Rountsch.

P. Smith, son of the founder, was awarded the Silver Quill[9] at an elaborate affair in Washington in the late 1950s for his leadership in the trade-press world. In recent years George H. Dockray, editor and later publisher of *Textile Industries,* was given international recognition for his outstanding contributions to the textile industry through his leadership and candid advice.

There was Douglas Woolf, editor-in-chief of McGraw-Hill's *Textile World,* who took over from the elderly McGraw and by his friendship with Southern mill men, his respected judgment, and his frequent visits to the mills became one of the most knowledgeable men on mill problems and their economic and personnel solutions. Colonel W. T. Chevalier, publisher of *Business Week,* often reprinted Woolf's editorials on textile problems and their proposed solutions, thereby giving additional status to his advice.

Franklin Pierce Bennett, who founded the *American Wool and Cotton Reporter,* was succeeded in 1920 by his son, Howard Bennett. The policy of the latter was to buy a small bit of stock in every textile mill. One share would entitle him to attend a stockholders' meeting. In this way he gained inside information that many others did not have, and he made the most of it in his cover-page editorials. Sometimes when he could not attend a meeting, he sent as proxy a young man, Randolph Taylor, who started working for him in 1943. It

---

[9]Silver Quill, an annual award by the American Business Press for outstanding achievement in magazine publishing.

Governor Luther H. Hodges of North Carolina cuts the electronic beam that triggered 400 textile machines of all types on display at the American Textile Machinery Exhibition-International. Watching him are (from left) John H. Bolton, Jr., vice-president of Whitin Machine Works and chairman of the ATMA Exhibition Committee; and (from right) William K. Child, president of the ATMA and vice-president of the Draper Corporation.

so happened that Taylor attended a meeting of the Bibb Manufacturing Company in Macon, Georgia. Colonel W. D. Anderson was head of Bibb and he did not believe in giving stockholders a written annual report. He said, "What's the use? It'll cost money and the stockholders can read stock quotations in the paper." Therefore, Colonel Anderson had the annual financial statement read to those at the meeting, and that was all.

Taylor was under instructions to get the statement. Somehow he heard that the local printer ran off the statement, leaving the figures blank; so he got the statement forms, and as it was being read at the meeting, filled in the blanks as best he could. Then, as proxy for a stockholder, he made a motion that in the future annual statements be mailed to stockholders. No one in that audience was going to cross Colonel Anderson's policy, so there was no second and Taylor, branded a Yankee interloper, was in the doghouse in Macon. Still, he had the statement for his boss to publish. Taylor was forgiven later and taken back into "the family."

An American Textile Machinery Exhibition-International in Convention Hall at Atlantic City in the early 1960s.

Frank P. Bennett III succeeded his father, Howard, around 1950 and changed the name of the publication to *America's Textile Reporter*. One of his most poignant editorials was "What Has Happened to the Merrimack Valley," in which he ticked off one by one the great New England mills that had failed, gone out of business, or moved south. It read as if Rip Van Winkle had just awakened to see a vanished, but once great, industry.

In 1968 Randy Taylor, after thirty years with the Bennetts, formed a company, bought and merged *America's Textile Reporter* and Clark's *Southern Textile Bulletin,* changing the name to *America's Textiles,* and moved the outfit to Greenville, South Carolina. It is the official publication of the Textile Quality Control Association, the International Council for Textile Slashing Technology, the International Society of Industrial Fabric Manufacturers, and the American Association for Textile Technology. He also acquired the Bennetts' *The Knitter* and Clark's *Knitting Industry.* He has recently acquired *Modern Textiles* and *Modern Knitting,* founded by Al McCullough, and devoted to man-made fibers. The best thing that Clark did for those affiliated with any phase of the

Douglas Woolf.
Served as editor-in-
chief of *Textile World*
for many years.

textile industry was to publish annually *Clark's Directory of Southern Mills.* Taylor acquired that too and still publishes it annually, keeping the original name.

In the 1930s John M. Mullen was editor and advertising manager of a weekly
textile-news page run by the *Charlotte Observer*. It was timely and very popular.
John realized its growth potential and in 1945 founded the *Southern Textile News*,
a weekly newspaper for the industry. He brought in Charlie Coleman of the
Atlanta Constitution, a brilliant managing editor and ad man, and the paper
flourished. Since Mullen's and Coleman's untimely deaths, Mrs. Mullen (as
president), his daughter, Patricia Mullen Smith (as executive vice-president),
and now his grandson, Mason W. Smith, operate the industry's only weekly
textile publication. They have had a succession of young and brilliant editors
and the inimitable George McRoberts, retired advertising and public-relations
executive, to make it successful.

The *Daily News Record*, a Fairchild publication, had a splendid combination
in editor-in-chief M. D. C. Crawford and textile editor Harry Reimer during the
1920s and 1930s. Both were greatly interested in Southern mill development
and built the paper into what was called the mill man's Bible. No Southern textile executive dared start the day without the *Daily News Record* and his coffee.
There he got the general news and market news in a timely and straightfor-
ward fashion. Crawford authored *The Romance of Cotton* and was seldom seen
outside his office. Harry Reimer was exceptional: genial, knowledgeable, and
infallible in his judgment of what to print and what to hold back. His cooperation with textile leaders made him one of the more respected editors of his time.

The outstanding leaders in the textile-trade press are a very elite group. From
their vantage point, they view world events and textile happenings and fit the
pieces together to see what makes the industry tick, or why the clock is running down. Their guidance has been of inestimable value in peacetime, in wartime, and particularly today when textile mills and textile-machinery builders
face problems undreamed of two decades ago.

George McRoberts of Whitin Machine Works. Worked closely with the author when she directed public-relations for the American Textile Machinery Association. His Christmas poems appeared on the front page of *Southern Textile News* for many years.

War and Postwar Years | 11

At the close of World War II, the textile industry could view with pride its enormous production achievement. It set its own pace when, in one year alone, 1942, an all-time record was reached as more than 12 billion square yards of fabric were produced; twenty-three million active spindles ran full time twenty-four hours a day, seven days a week, to chalk up the unprecedented total of more than 133 billion spindle hours. This was the time schedule throughout the war years, although production never quite reached that peak again.

During the war years, the only time the spindles stopped was when there was a bottleneck in the cardroom. The card machines of that period were able to produce an average of only twenty pounds of sliver per hour, and in many cases they could not keep up with the rest of the mill. These infrequent respites, however, were filled by the spindle hands and repairmen oiling and cleaning and gearing up for the next roll. It was a coordinated effort within the mill for balanced production.

Trade papers had carried notices that the military was issuing bids for items such as these: thirty-nine million square yards of six-ounce uniform twill, forty-six million square yards of 8.2 ounce twill, 6.5 million yards of silesia, one million square yards Byrd-type cloth requiring 80/2 combed yarn for construction of 180 x 100 thread counts per square inch of fabric. The yarn had to be perfect. The fine counts and perfection required had made mill men less than enthusiastic about making either yarn or fabric, but it was done. Five million square yards of 8.2 ounce combed-yarn khaki-uniform twill dyed, finished, mercerized, and ready for cutting into garments were offered at only 63.35 cents per yard.

Major Stuart Cramer, president of Cramerton Mills, said, "We don't want to make war-profits. We want to win the War at the least cost to the United States." This was the general attitude of textile leaders and textile workers.

The general maximum-price regulation issued by the Office of Price Administration affected all sales on deliveries to, or contracts with, the United States War Department on or after 1 July 1942. This regulation kept those who were not so patriotic as Stuart Cramer from profiteering.

One example of purchase by the quartermaster general is Circular #272, which requested bids for 351,300,000 square yards of cotton fabric for uniform twill, overcoat lining-type Oxford, so-called Albert Cloth, canvas padding, shrunk but unbleached drill, sheetings, herringbone twill, overcoat cloth and lining. Orders were scheduled for delivery in intervals of approximately thirty days and maximum completion of the order was 240 days, F.O.B., at point of cloth manufacture to point of designation for item manufactured.

The amount of manufactured items and per-yard quantities needed by the government was appalling but necessary for the long-range goals of all the Allied armies. Large shipments also eased the logistics involved in delivery. Circular #272 is just one sample, quoted to give the reader an idea of what twelve billion square yards meant.

Some of the prices reflect the importance to the tax-paying public of the Office of Price Administration (OPA). Without it, the United States would have gone into a phase of rampant inflation.

The production records established by the industry during the war years served to highlight one of the most remarkable feats in American industrial history: the quick and efficient conversion of mills from war to peacetime uses. Both the war effort and the changeover to peacetime production were done using the industry's own leadership and their expert knowledge of production capabilities and orderly reduction to peacetime needs. There was no government financial aid for the textile industry's reconversion, while "conversion" assistance, totaling more than $16 billion, was rendered to other industries by the federal government.

After the Allied victory, the American textile industry's job of returning to normal was titanic. Reconversion took place in more than one phase. There was the human element as war veterans returned to their mill jobs, glory and all, to take up peacetime life. They were no longer just mill hands. Each returning veteran was something of a hero and entered civilian life on a new psychological scale.

John Quitman Hill, returning to work as a card grinder at Pacific Mills in Lyman, South Carolina, at the same time earned a B.S. degree from nearby Wofford College and went on to a Rhodes scholarship. Rene A. Gagnon, one of the four Marine heroes who raised the Stars and Stripes atop Mount Suribachi at the height of the battle for Iwo Jima in February 1945, returned to his job as doffer at the Chicopee Manufacturing Corporation plant in Manchester, New Hampshire.

Lou Brissie, who grew up in the Riegel Textile Corporation mill village in Ware Shoals, South Carolina, and who was left for dead in the Apennine campaign in Italy, recovered from two shattered legs and multiple wounds to work again at Riegel. He played ball on the mill team, and later became, even with a brace on one leg, one of the great pitchers in professional baseball. Connie Mack said he was "potentially a greater pitcher than Lefty Grove," and the Christian Athlete's Foundation awarded him a scroll as the outstanding major league rookie of 1948.

Inside the mills themselves, poor, beat-up machines that had performed with such gallantry for five years were worn out and tired. They had been severely overtaxed by the demanding schedule that was followed year after year.

The textile-machinery industry, which had been almost entirely devoted to strategic war materiel, had to be reconverted to its original purpose of building textile equipment before it could supply textile mills with anything but spare replacement parts, many of these coming from prewar stock. Rebuilt textile machines were not the new types industry sought, but were better than existing equipment. Textile-machine research had fallen far behind schedule as machinery companies helped the war effort, but some new items were being offered despite government allocations of metal on a priority basis.

Overseas, in Europe and in Japan and other Oriental countries, there was a clamor for American textile equipment and American textiles as well. And the demands of the American public for shirts, sheets, dress goods, and hundreds of other fabrics in short supply created quite a dilemma for the textile industry. Wartime textile and leather allocations were maintained for a time due to the pure necessity of seeing that everyone got as fair a deal as possible in acquiring material for civilian use.

As early as 1940, O. Max Gardner had counseled the textile industry to modernize as far as possible. "Spend all you can get hold of for new machinery," he privately advised his textile friends. In letters he said to them:

> It seems to me that now, in this period, is the time when our cotton spinners should undertake to lay the foundation for a program of modernization. There has been relatively little new machinery acquired in the South and, one of these days, we are going to wake up with the War over and our plants obsolete. It will be in that period when the modern mill will get the business and the old mills will get into the bankruptcy courts. I think of what will happen to American industry that is expanding so rapidly today when a busted world starts on peaceful pursuits.

Prudent and long-range planners had entered orders for new equipment to be delivered "as soon as available," knowing full well it would be years before they received any portion of these orders. Many had their plants surveyed for new equipment for future delivery.

In 1947 it was estimated that total machinery requirements to re-equip America's textile mills amounted to a minimum of $500 million (1947 dollar valuation). Textile-machinery manufacturers figured that a minimum of $50 million worth of new or rebuilt machinery would be installed in the United States each year for a five-year period, and said orders were already on their books. But it would take that long for delivery, with priority being given to existing orders, by earliest dating.[1] Mills were insisting on the latest type of machinery in order to compete with the new equipment being installed in Europe under the Marshall Plan and in Japan under the Supreme Command of Allied Powers (SCAP). Of course, the lower wages in countries long starved for any wages made them competitive in the United States marketplace.

---

[1] Textile machinery manufacturers operated under General Limitation Order L-83 (1942) as amended.

While Japan appeared to have a sufficient supply of cotton goods on hand to eliminate an emergency, Europe apparently did not. Organizations here were formed to send to Europe urgently needed fabric for the millions of displaced persons. The American Cotton Manufacturers Association proposed to its members, representing the majority of the industry, that they contribute, gratis, four million square yards of fabric for European relief. The proposal provided for voluntary contributions by individual mills, on the basis of $1/20$ of one percent of the individual mill's 1946 sales. The cloth was to be handled and distributed by the Friends—the organization designated by former President Herbert Hoover as better equipped than any other for the task.

The first mill promises were magnanimous and included $25,000 worth of cloth from one mill, $39,000 from another, and the promise of 50,000 square yards monthly for six months from a third. Support of the plan was backed by almost the entire industry and the requested four million square yards were easily found. Standard eighty-square print cloth was then priced at approximately 43¢ a square yard.

In 1940 there were 24,940,000 spindles in the United States cotton-textile industry. When new spindles became available in 1946 (see n. 1), new installation, additions, and replacements amounted to 323,056; 1947 brought additional replacements totaling 416,555; 1948, 607,358; and 1949, 858,623 spindles. Really old spindles and looms were junked. When mills could not afford all-new spinning frames, they resorted to "changeovers" or rebuilt equipment. A widespread program of renovation and modernization was inaugurated immediately upon victory and the elimination in 1946 of government controls on machinery delivery. It is estimated that in the five years following the war (1945–1950), the industry spent more than one billion dollars on modernization, renovation, and expansion, with the major portion going toward new buildings and machinery.

In 1945 the once-thriving United States silk industry, including knitters and weavers, faced a real dilemma. During the war, with embargoes on the import of silk and all silk in the United States impounded by the government, the mills had changed over to cotton and man-made fibers, particularly rayon and nylon if they could get them. The United States Post-War Mission to Japan reported that the Japanese silk capacity of 150,845 prewar basins was reduced to 21,800. It was estimated that production of silk would amount to about 180,000 bales, but would increase as cocoon production and reeling capacity increased.

Nylon was released by the government for civilian use in September 1945. By 1947 approximately forty-seven percent of that year's poundage was supplied to the hosiery industry. New nylon-producing plants were under construction. It was estimated that thirty million dozen pairs of hosiery would be made of nylon that year, and this had a terrific impact on the silk industry.

During World War II the United States impounded and acquired all stocks of raw silk in the United States. At the end of the war, the surplus amounted to about 3,300 bales, which were put up for auction. Hosiery manufacturers who had contributed to the stockpile were allocated 1,650 bales (or about 250,000 pairs of hosiery). Sale prices of the stock averaged $11.50 per pound. At the second sale in July 1946, the average price was $9.46 per pound. Compare this with the 1950 price of 30-denier 200 nylon at $2.75 a pound, which allowed the price of one pair of nylon, full-fashioned hose to be $1.25 versus one comparable pair of silk hose at $3.50 to $5.00.

There was another important differential. It took thirteen ounces of silk to make one dozen pairs of full-fashioned hose and only nine ounces of nylon to make the same amount. Silk as hosiery material rapidly disappeared due to economic reasons. Yet it was also the sheer beauty and longevity of nylon that created the fastest changeover in fashion in many, many decades.

Irving Trust Company, New York, formerly the largest finance agency for silk imports, had Dun & Bradstreet make a survey of former silk manufacturers in order to gauge the future of silk in the United States manufacturing picture. Mill after mill was visited, and the consensus was that the American consumer market was used to, and satisfied with, man-made fibers; that it would be very costly to re-equip mills for silk production; and that mill hands refused to go back to operating machines on silk because of stoppages due to fiber breakage and tangling. In the post-World War II era, the manufacture of pure silk-woven fabric or knit goods has become a thing of the past except for a few specialty companies.

Violent price fluctuations of raw silk in the past bankrupted silk mills in an incredibly short time on inventory alone. Conversely, man-made fibers enjoyed a market that was quite stable. For example, from 1945 to 1950, the price of rayon increased only six percent, while raw silk increased by 350 percent. The amount of labor saved in producing man-made fiber was enormous. One plant, during its days of producing only silk, had employed 6,700 persons. When it converted to man-made fibers, keeping the same number of looms, total employment was down to 4,000 despite increased wages. This represented an increased output of yardage at a tremendous reduction in payroll costs, and a lower per-unit cost overall. Labor could handle eight looms on man-made fiber compared to only two on silk. Being paid by the piece, or pick,[2] mill workers liked man-made fiber best.

Price ceilings on textile goods ceased on 10 November 1946; all government controls were lifted by the Civilian Production Administration, which had succeeded OPA (see n. 1).

The all-out effort of the U.S. industry to remove government controls so businesses could get back to reasonable profits and normal relations with their longtime customers resulted in congressional hearings by subcommittees on prices. Charges of big profits in manufacturing were in general refuted by individual illustrations, which caused some investigators to think the cause for

---

[2]A pick is the thread running across the loom from selvage to selvage. An automatic counting machine on the loom totals the number of picks per inch, per minute; this is the speed of production.

high prices might be found on Capitol Hill rather than on Worth Street or Seventh Avenue[3] or in the mills.

Gordon Harrower, treasurer of Wauregan Mills (Connecticut), a company principally making oxford shirting, pointed out to the congressional committee that oxfords remained unchanged from early OPA days when the price was set at 46.23 cents a yard or about $1.16 for the cloth in shirts that retailed from $3.50 to $4.00 each in 1947.

Tracing the rise in the price of raw cotton from 11.06 cents a pound in July 1939 to 38.75 cents in July 1947, he assured the congressmen that cotton of the grade his mill used could be harvested at a maximum cost of 22.75 cents a pound.

"The difference between this harvest figure and mill cost of 1947 cotton," Mr. Harrower asserted, "is represented to a large extent by government parity which takes no cognizance of technological advances in farming (such as automatic picking) between the so-called base period (1909-1914) and the present time, as well as a stimulated shortage through government purchases for export of an already short crop of cotton."

Harrower held that government support of raw-cotton prices, on the basis of parity as computed that year, had been effective in boosting cotton prices to an unreasonable level prior to the 1945-1946 crop. "Since then," he said, "the shortness of the crop itself and the unreasonable demand, including the very large export quotas, has been mainly responsible for the further rise of price levels." Harrower said that wages had increased in his mill from forty-five cents an hour in 1939 to an average wage of $1.05 in 1947, an increase of 133 percent against a cost-of-living increase of 59.4 percent. His own firm, covering the period 1932-1947, had net profits during those years of 2.61 percent and $386,946 in dividends paid, or only $1\frac{1}{8}$ percent of sales.

At the close of the 1940s, many changes were reflected in the overall picture of the textile industry. The United States Bureau of Labor Statistics reported that hourly earnings in textile manufacturing had increased twice as fast as the rise in the cost of living and by fourteen percent more than in the lumber and timber basic-products industry, where the second-largest rate of increase among twenty leading American industries was recorded. According to the bureau's figures, average hourly earnings in the textile-mill-products industry advanced 129 percent from September 1939 to September 1948, while the cost of living rose 62.8 percent within the same period. In Georgia, for example, during that same period, payrolls for the state's textile mills rose 199.7 percent to a new high of $190.9 million. The industry was the state's leading employer, having 108,000 total wage earners out of the state's 480,500.

In 1949 a new minimum wage for all industry was set by the United States Department of Labor, Wage and Hour Division at 70¢ an hour, effective 15 January 1950. Thus, the textile wage differential allowed New England mills over those in the South was wiped out. In January 1950 the Bureau of Labor Statis-

---

[3]Sales areas in New York for textile goods and garments.

tics reported the average hourly pay in the cotton-textile industry to be $1.12, considerably above the new mandatory minimum.

Problems still remained for mill management: the narrow mill margin, the slow profit, obsolete equipment, and the increasingly rapid move to the South. Surrounding Spartanburg, South Carolina, are acres and acres of peach trees. The view of these peach trees in bloom on land rolling toward the mountains is a miracle. In midsummer the peaches are delicious and can be bought at fruit stands along the highway. Thousands of pounds of refrigerated Spartan County peaches are shipped north each day by Southern Railway or truck.

When textile people heard that hundreds of acres of these peach trees belonged to Roger Milliken, now chairman and chief executive officer of Milliken & Co., one exclaimed, "He's planted them to spin peach-fuzz and, with Milliken's research facility, he'll learn how to do it! Then where will we be?"

The Milliken family is not a "new" family in the South; all the ladies in the United Daughters of the Confederacy will agree to that. There was a Milliken in Charleston "long before The War," they say, meaning the Civil War.

In the beginning, Seth Milliken sold for woolen mills in New England, starting with five and finally working up to sixteen. In 1884 Deering-Milliken made

Roger Milliken. Chairman and ceo of Milliken and Company, he has been a longtime leader in the industry and is credited with being the driving force behind the "Crafted with Pride in USA" program.

its first contact with a Southern mill venture when it became the selling agent for Pacolet Manufacturing Company, organized by Captain John Montgomery.

In 1916 Gerrish Milliken, a Yale University graduate, joined the firm. He was a marvelous tennis player. His name is still on the plaque of champions at Jekyll Island off the coast of Georgia. Before World War II, the island was a posh club for millionaires and permitted members to arrive only by yacht, preferably their own.[4] Milliken was also an able businessman and a great success at selling textiles.

Gerrish Milliken was one of the first in the commission-house business to recognize a future for man-made fibers. His first venture in this field was to acquire the huge Judson Mill in Greenville, South Carolina, noted for years as a fine combed-yarn spinning and weaving mill. Every one of thousands of bales of cotton used annually was personally classed by E. W. Montgomery for length, strength, and color of fibers. In his own term, the "convolution of the coil" of the fiber was what counted. On the looms in this mill, the Millikens tested the new man-made fiber, rayon, and decided to try it out on the consumer market.

During World War II textile mills that sold through Deering-Milliken were producing a wide range of textile yarns and fabrics according to government specifications. Certificates of Necessity were issued by the War Production Board in order to obtain goods on the high-priority list for military use. Deering-Milliken was issued such a certificate in 1944 to build a mill to produce tire cord. It was built on the Seneca River across from Clemson College.

It was the first textile plant designed and built to put the newly introduced man-made fibers for tire cord to military use. It was a one-story building arranged to facilitate the flow of raw material through all steps of manufacture and then to the delivery dock for loading and shipment. This was the first textile plant to be built without windows and with complete air-cleaning and cooling systems. It set a pattern that has been copied since then throughout the Southern industry. The mill's design and new, improved equipment added enormously to the cleanliness of the air and prevention of diseases caused by lint-laden air. It is named the DeFore Mill and is the leading producer of tire cord made of man-made fibers.

The company's main line was woolen and worsteds, manufactured chiefly in New England. The demand in the early 1940s was so great that the company decided to strengthen the line of fabrics by buying a few more mills in the South. In the depths of the Depression, Deering-Milliken had acquired a number of plants that it had represented formerly.

Roger Milliken succeeded Gerrish as president of the company upon his father's death in 1947. Two other grandsons of Seth Milliken were given official positions. They were Gerrish Milliken, Jr. and Minot Milliken. It was Roger, though, who took over the job of running the mills, expanding operations and

---

[4]Jekyll Island is now a state park; it was once an antisubmarine base in World War II. Original owners' homes and clubs are still there.

undertaking research that far exceeded anything done before by anyone in the textile industry.

He also undertook building new mills with the most modern machinery and electronic equipment. A well-known textile trade paper stated:

> We printed it a while ago that Deering-Milliken and Company, the great mill owners, operators and merchandisers, have put $50 million of cash into new Southern mills, including cotton and rayon and woolen and worsted mills, within the last two or three years. Fifty million dollars is a lot of money, and, incidentally, when Roger Milliken took that money *right* out of his till without any borrowing or financing, he didn't scrape the bottom of the barrel of his firm; they still have plenty of millions of dollars left.

Roger is a sentimental person, even though he is a tough customer as a businessman. He named a number of mills that were built after he took over in honor of persons who had excelled in the company. When he acquired mills that had well-known names in the industry, he considered that an asset and did not make a change.

His first newly built mill was the Gerrish Milliken Mill, built in Pendleton, South Carolina, and it produced synthetic fiber or fabrics. It was named for his father. It has been expanded several times since first built.

Frank Bennett, then publisher of the *American Wool and Cotton Reporter*, had a lot to say about Roger Milliken, all favorable, but the sentence most remembered is, "Roger is the fair-haired man of the industry today. But watch him, because he is a leader such as we have not known in many a year."

He built the Kingsley Mill in Thomson, Georgia, and named it for the Deering-Milliken executive who had for years handled the unique and exciting Milliken Breakfast Show, an annual fashion show featuring all Milliken fabrics. At Kingsley, specialty fabric is cut and packaged for retail sale to home sewers and others.

In 1958 the big research center at Spartanburg was started. A lovely park is the site for the several buildings of the research center where some of Milliken's fabrics, including rugs, are also on display. In the center there is also a guest house that has sleeping accommodations for twenty-nine persons and a dining hall where 100 may be served. In addition, it has a management-information center. It represents a great advancement in corporate information through a highly synthesized computer setup.

When it was decided to build the Magnolia Finishing Plant, it was designed to be the best and most modern of its kind in that section of the industry. Also, it had to be constructed and in operation in six and a half months. It cost $15 million, but was completed on time. There the age-old art of finishing has now become an exacting science.

In 1965 the company opened offices and mills in Europe for the international trade of France, Belgium, and England. Also that year it built a plant in Laurens, South Carolina, and named it for Dr. Ed Gilliland, head of research at Massachusetts Institute of Technology. That same year the company reorganized into three divisions headed by Ralph Gillespie, Bill Humphrey, and Hal Richey. In this way, better management of direct markets was obtained.

The Milliken & Co. research department developed "durable press" and "soil release." These were developed through the use of electronic irradiation. It was the first time these processes were used in the textile industry and they have added to the usefulness and quality appearance of polyester yarns. Soil is released in the average washing machine, eliminating any dingy appearance of polyester fabrics after relatively short use.

The company went into knit-fabric production and has knitting machines in the Excelsior, Union, Otteray, and Laurens plants in South Carolina and the Golden Valley in North Carolina. Roger wasn't satisfied and wanted to round out his line, so he acquired seven mills known as Callaway, Incorporated. The name of the mills was changed to International Products and Services, Incorporated. In LaGrange is Milliken & Co.'s rug business where, by computer and photograph, patterns are woven into floor covering.

There have been few pitfalls for Milliken & Co. in its steady progress down south. Deering was dropped from the corporate name in 1978. If a mill was acquired that couldn't make a profit, or if it was too old to re-equip to meet modern standards, then it had to go. One example is the Lane Mills at New Orleans. It was old and could not fit into the company's profit pattern, so it was phased out. The other is Darlington (South Carolina) Mills, built in 1883. Deering-Milliken had been its sales agent for many years and finally its chief stockholder. In 1956 the Textile Workers Union tried to organize there, and in September of that year won the vote of workers by a narrow margin. For years the mill had been failing, so when the board of directors met on 12 September, it was decided to liquidate the mill.

In October 1964 the Textile Workers Union sued. For eighteen years the suit was in the courts, but finally the U.S. Supreme Court ruled in favor of the employees, saying that they should be compensated for back pay on a pro-rata basis for all the years since the mill ceased operations. It had long since been dismantled. The case involved millions of dollars and an endless search for employees or their heirs, or next of kin. Many had moved to other employment. Many had died. The ruling of the court was a great blow to private enterprise, which as a result is now unable to exercise judgment on a company's ability to maintain operations profitably.

There is one thing certain about Roger Milliken. If he hears of a new machine, he wants it and is apt to improve upon it for his mill's purpose. He wants the best, the newest, the most productive for the least possible cost per unit of production.

He has made spectacular success and is likable to boot. Southerners are glad he moved down with his family because he has helped to develop the region in a highly industrialized, computerized, humanitarian way.

In 1916 the first real incursion of Northern interests was felt in the South. That year the four defunct mills of the Parker group were sold at auction to Lockwood, Greene and Company for a round sum of $2 million. Everyone wondered who Lockwood, Greene was representing and it was soon learned that the four Hampton Mills at Columbia, South Carolina, would be taken over by Pacific Mills of Lawrence, Massachusetts, as its first Southern venture. A few months later two of the three Parker Mills in outlying districts were sold to Henry Kendall, who already held the Lewis Manufacturing Company, a cotton-batting outfit in Walpole, Massachusetts. One of these new acquisitions was the Wateree Mills; the other was the Addison Mills at Edgefield, South Carolina. These mills fit into Kendall's plans for the Lewis Company to make its own cotton gauze for medical use such as hospital bandages. It was an early example of vertical integration of textile mills.

Henry Kendall was among the first to appreciate the advantages of vertical integration in the textile business. He decided to concentrate on gauze and absorbent cotton sold as hospital supplies. In the next twenty years he had acquired textile properties that consisted of spinning, weaving, and batting companies and were combined into the Kendall Company. He had eight mills in the greige-cloth division; six were in South Carolina operating 283,000 spindles and 6,000 looms. The largest portion of the greige-cloth division was at Pelzer, South Carolina, long owned and operated by Captain Ellison Smyth.

New personal items brought still another vast boom for manufacturers of hospital and medical supplies. The development of Kotex, Tampax, and babies' absorbent diapers in the 1930s and 1940s increased tremendously the demand for hygienic uses of Kendall's products.

In June 1928 the trend of Northern mill interests moving south was an established pattern. In the first six months of that year, fifty new textile companies had crossed the Mason-Dixon Line, and this was regarded as remarkable in view of the generally unfavorable economic state of the industry at the time. In the same period, however, many new companies in smaller towns of the South, financed by Northern capital, were being established. Free mill sites, tax exemptions for a number of years, stock subscriptions by local businessmen, and cheap power rates played a prominent part in influencing companies to move south. Lower costs per unit of production was the name of the game.

The products—silk and rayon, knitted and woven, and specialty goods—made by the new plants of the 1920s added much to the diversity of the Southern textile industry. Especially the Southern silk and man-made fiber industry was beefed up to include full-fashioned hosiery mills and plants that made silk underwear. This incredible expansion was important financially to machinery builders because full-fashioned hosiery machinery was among the more expensive textile equipment.

The South also gained a number of new dyeing, bleaching, and finishing plants, and two rayon yarn-processing plants. One company announced that it would build four plants for producing natural silk yarns for weaving and knitting purposes. Yet there were comparatively few cotton mills built in this period of expansion.

Among the Northern firms that took advantage of Southern opportunities was Frank W. Van Ness and Company, New York, which controlled the Burcot Products Company of New Brunswick, New Jersey. It established a plant for waterproofing and strengthening cotton fabrics for bagging purposes. Floyd

Jefferson and Associates of New York built a new cotton mill in Fitzgerald, Georgia; Kalleman and Mitchell of Paterson, New Jersey, equipped the former Lola Gingham Mills, owned by the Craigs of Stanley, North Carolina, for silk weaving. The Saratoga Victory Mills controlled by American Manufacturing Company of Brooklyn proposed to build two mills of 15,000 spindles and 500 looms in Guntersville and Albertville, Alabama. Hudson Silk Hosiery Company in Charlotte built a full-fashioned unit.

Over the years Northern mills had largely kept old equipment running and old products still standard while Southern mills, being more recently built, had newer and better equipment and were expanding the types of production from plain cottons to other fields.

The final dissolution of the once-powerful New England cotton-textile industry was caused by the high cost of obsolescence. It resulted in a loss of industry, loss of jobs, and loss of tax income to those states that the industry was forced to abandon. Many mills closed because of managers' lack of interest in changing fashion and production through the years.

However, for a long time there had been a steady expansion of one New England company that was owned by the Stevens family. As early as 1918 young Nat Stevens, a born trader, decided to go into textiles. He took the advice of a friend and specialized in red flannels, slowly building a fortune with an underwear item that was necessary for anyone who wanted to keep warm in wintertime. Not until knit goods came into the picture, with a resulting change of style, did the Stevens plants change to other types of woolen goods.

The Stevens Company bought mills at foreclosure sales, repaired them, and continued to make profits. Nat Stevens and his partner, Moses T. Stevens, bought from Edward Hammond, in 1854, the mortgage he held on Ezekial Hale's flannel factory for $16,000. Then they foreclosed and bought the mill itself at auction for $25,000. Hale refused to speak to them for years. Finally he would shake hands, but only with the left, *never* with the right. Stevens renamed the mill the Haverhill Flannel Factory. In the course of time other acquisitions enabled the company to produce fabrics other than woolen and worsteds.

With each modernization effort that Stevens undertook, he tried to do the job cheaply. In 1900, with eleven mills, some of which were forty to sixty years old, a new roof was installed at Stevens Mills. Also added were eleven new 110″ Knowles looms; three spinning frames of 300 spindles each; two sets of cards; new 24″ McCornick wheels; and a 72″ wire napper for flannel and blankets. These were small modernization programs for such a large company.

In 1946 the Stevens Company, led by the broad vision of Robert Stevens, built its first woolen mill in the South, located in Dublin, Georgia. John Baum— a former colonel who had worked with Colonel Robert Stevens in the Office of the Quartermaster General—was put in charge of this new installation, called the Dublin Woolen Mills. It was equipped with the most up-to-date woolen machinery: eight sets of cards, 3,360 woolen spindles, 144 looms, dyeing and finishing. This was Stevens's first incursion in the South. It was only the beginning of expansion in all lines of textile activity and in all areas of the South.

In August 1946 J. P. Stevens effected a consolidation with other old-line and famous Southern mills.

Stevens acquired all textile properties of the Simmons Company in 1956. This company (which made the famous "Beautyrest" mattress) owned, as subsidiaries, Roanoke Mills Company and Rosemary Manufacturing Company in North Carolina; these were merged with J. P. Stevens in 1958. These mills are the group organized a long time ago by Sam Patterson, who thought of the idea of a beautiful mattress covering and made it on a bastard loom created for him by Crompton & Knowles and Draper. He used a Crompton & Knowles Jacquard special head on a wide-sheeting Draper loom. Then he sold the idea to Simmons, who named the mattresses covered with Jacquard patterns "Beautyrest." Today probably no home is without one, and many more people sleep happily on Patterson's idea than on all other types of bedding put together.

In 1960 J. P. Stevens acquired the fixed assets of Exposition Cotton Mills in Atlanta, the place where the Southern industrial revolution was born in 1881 with the great International Textile Exposition. Taking over the birthplace of the post-Civil War Southern industry was sort of like buying the Alamo.

The company operates eighty-three textile-manufacturing plants. Changing from an all-woolen outfit, it now produces fabrics of practically every color, texture, weight, and weave, using a wide range of fibers that includes wool, cotton, polyester, nylon, acrylics, acetate rayon, spandex, and glass. Fifty-two percent of the products are sold to the apparel industry, thirty-one percent to the home-furnishings market, and seventeen percent to the industrial trade.

Thirty-six of the mills are located in South Carolina, twenty-five in North Carolina, nine in Georgia, six in Virginia, and seven in Tennessee, Alabama, and Florida. Only two New England states, Massachusetts and Connecticut, now have Stevens mills. One can indeed say that the company has moved south and wonder why Mississippi was left out of the distribution of mills.

Merger fever began at least fifty years ago, was interrupted by World War II, then restarted, and there seems to be no limit to this financial process.

In the late 1940s the acquisition of sales-yarn and cloth mills in the South by both horizontal and vertical integration stimulated congressional action. Senate Bill 104 (or the Anti-Monopoly Bill) was answered by the Cotton-Textile Institute in a brief filed with the Senate Judiciary Committee strongly opposing the bill and claiming that its enactment would have serious effects upon small-unit industries such as cotton textiles. According to the brief, 164 cotton-textile companies had changed ownership. They were in the business of spinning and weaving or both; they owned 4.5 million spindles and 88,000 looms and represented about twenty percent of the industry.

In 1949 a matching bill, also called the Anti-Monopoly Bill (H.R. 2734), was introduced in the House. It was termed "destructive, impracticable, and unnecessary" in a statement filed with the House Judiciary Committee by Dr. Claudius T. Murchison, president of the Cotton-Textile Institute.

Dr. Murchison's report covered the years of World War II, when everything was under government supervision, and does not include the later years when the textile world was sorely afflicted with merger-acquisitions, conglomerates, and so forth. His table charting the acquisition of sales-yarn and cloth mills for the years 1940-1946 is given below:

	Spindles	Percent Total Spindle Acquisition
New Ownership	1,050,088	23.8
Machinery Dealers for Resale	375,756	8.4
Horizontal-Cotton Mills	775,756	8.4
Vertical-Cotton Mills	311,576	7.03
Vertical Converters	665,616	15.01
Vertical End-Use Other than Clothing	230,588	5.2
Vertical Cutters	277,096	6.25
Vertical Selling Agents	679,577	15.33
Vertical Wholesalers	48,160	1.09
	4,433,545	100.00

These figures were put together before the big liquidation movement of New England plants and before the acquisition or mergers of Southern companies had really started. However, they give a point of comparison for what followed in the 1950s and 1960s.

The bill, according to Dr. Murchison, would prohibit all mergers and freeze small business units or, in other words, remove all incentive for growth and expansion. "The mills would be frozen to their present status, regardless of changes in our economy," he said.

The picture was indeed muddled in the years following World War II. The federal tax structure was forcing family-held and weak mills to be disposed of, and the high cost of production per unit was a major and constant worry to mill and machinery executives as they pondered possible solutions to this problem.

The merging and acquisition fever of Northern mills for those in the South reached a peak in the 1950s. The trade press each day carried headlines about such deals, often quoting millions of dollars involved, Northern jobs lost, and other such details as accompanied a Northern community losing a mill and a Southern community looking forward to a new asset.

With Southern mills changing hands from original owners or builders to Northern interests such as mills, converters, selling houses, and just plain entrepreneurs, one is reminded of the story told forty years before when Fuller Callaway, Sr. was in New York at an important meeting regarding just this problem, which might have created an antimonopoly bill in Congress. He was handed a telegraph in the dining room where he and others were in the midst of a discussion on market analysis. It read, "Hurry home and advise us how to handle this market." It was signed by his son, Cason. He turned the telegram over and wrote on the backside, "Some say it's going down, some say it's going up. For God's sake do something and do it quick." Fuller Callaway tipped the waiting bellhop a nickel and went on with the business at hand.

By 1960 all signs indicated that the mills of New England had seen their best days and the future held little hope. Ten years before, New Bedford and Fall River mill executives met with TWUA-CIO leaders in Boston to discuss a temporary extension of their current contracts beyond the expiration date of 15 March 1957.

"In these eventual negotiations," said Seabury Stanton, industry spokesman,

> both mills and TWUA-CIO must not be misled by present and temporary conditions of peak demand for textiles. If our northern textile mills are to continue to exist after the present situation of peak demand returns to normal, we must depend upon the TWUA-CIO to bring the wages and other working conditions of the southern mills up to standards approaching *our* levels of cost. Otherwise, we will be unable to sell our goods competitively in the New York market and there will be no textile industry in the Fall River-New Bedford area.

It was a hopeless plea from an unrealistic basis. The TWUA-CIO could not stop the trend of lower cost per unit of production in which wages had only a small part.

A long time ago the Merrimack River, in its prime days of industrial use, turned more spindles and earned more textile dividends for its users than any other single river in the world. What happened to the fruitful productive power of the Merrimack Valley? In 1984 one need only look at the long list of one-time famous mills—now defunct or no longer operating in the Merrimack Valley—to see the results of competition from other climes that could, and did, produce lower cost per unit of textile production.

The Merrimack Manufacturing Company, the oldest cotton-textile group (which operated under the oldest charter in the United States), closed in 1958. The Boott Mills were liquidated in 1956. White Brothers, which had 75,000 spindles and 800 looms, is gone. Many others are gone also, some not restricted to the Merrimack Valley: Duchess County (New York) Print Cloth Mill; Crown and Eagle Mills, Uxbridge, Massachusetts; Boston Manufacturing Company in Waltham; the Tremont, Sutton, and Lawrence Mills; the Hamilton Mills at Lowell; the Globe Mills; the Harrissonville Mills, Rhode Island; the Sprague Mill at Cranston; the North Adams Mills; Berman Manufacturing Company, Woonsocket; Greek Revival Mill, Rhode Island; Sister Cotton Company, Eldon Steam Mills; A. and W. Sprague Mills.

The Blackstone Canal opened a new area for industrial development in 1828. By 1844 ninety-four cotton factories lined the banks of the Blackstone River; today, all are gone: the Social Mills, Rhode Island; Clinton Mills, Jackson Company, the Nashua Manufacturing Company, all in Massachusetts; the Indian Head Company in Nashua, York Mills in Saco, Maine; Great Falls and the Dover in New Hampshire; the Amoskeag Mills that once ranked among the greatest; the Dwight, the Cabot, the Perkins, all in Cabotsville, eventually became part of Chicopee, which moved south.

It is a long list and could contain many more closed mills. Many have moved south and are operating there in newer air-conditioned buildings with new equipment. The others are just memories of the past.

The beautiful buildings, each an architectural gem, have been torn down or converted to small shops or filling-station corners. The buildings now are preserved only in photographs.

The mill exodus was well on its way in the 1950s. A meeting of the governors of New England had been held to discuss new methods of saving the industry there. Special reports had been written on methods to save New Bedford and Fall River.

An important one was called the "Blanchard Report," written by Fesseden Blanchard, a prominent textile consultant. The *Springfield* (Massachusetts) *Union,* as a public service, printed it verbatim, omitting only a few statistical tables. Then, the *Union* commented,

> We know, the mill men know, they have experienced it over a long period of years. The professional labor leaders know what's the matter with Massachusetts, they know that they, themselves, are very largely to blame. The State Legislature knows what's the matter with industry. They, themselves, year after year in Legislature assembled are pretty much to blame for it. Too much professional labor domination; too much hampering and degrading legislation; too much expenditure and extravagance creating too many unbearable taxes; and the whole thing adding up to too high unit costs in the industries of Massachusetts and New England.
> ....
> The Blanchard Report is most interesting, not for what it says, but in the fact that the Legislature of Massachusetts appropriated $15,000 to pay for the report and then the Massachusetts executive authority did everything they could to prevent the report being publicized. In fact, one fellow in the State, who one way or another had final hold over the Blanchard Report, nearly went to prison for contempt of the Legislative Committee because he got hold of the original report itself, and kept it hidden for several weeks. The report, amongst other things, *placed* the blame right on the State Legislature for the decadence of industry in the Commonwealth. We're discussing the Blanchard Report at this length because of the fact that the political authorities tried to keep it hidden.

The *Springfield Union* was brave to publish it, but for all practical purposes, the Blanchard Report was at least twenty-five or thirty years too late. There was the Depression, World War II, machine obsolescence, human error, and greed involved—not to mention the constant mergers and acquisitions in the move to the South.

One of the most interesting exchanges of mill ownership, and certainly the most radical, occurred in Georgia and concerned no one except the mills' owner and his employees. From the very beginning of the Callaway Mills, Fuller E. Callaway, Jr., son of the founder of the mill and younger brother of Cason (who made quite a name for himself in the industry), had worked hard and successfully in the Callaway textile business. One by one new mills were organized and old mills were modernized to make them profitable. Finally, in 1932, the Callaway brothers were able to consolidate all their cotton-mill companies into one newly formed corporation—under the name of Callaway Mills Company—through a tax-free reorganization. Each of the old mill's companies received new shares of stock in the new corporation in exchange for their shares in the old.

In 1937 Fuller Callaway, Jr. was made president and selected a treasurer. The entire capital stock of the new company was owned by the Callaway Foundation. The latter, a nonprofit, charitable, educational, and religious organization, was founded and operated primarily to benefit the citizens of La Grange and Troup County, many of whom were Callaway Mills employees.

About this time the Callaway Mills Company Provident Fund was established. Under this plan, twenty percent of all net profits before taxes was paid over to a trustee who held and invested the money entirely for the benefit of Callaway Mills employees. Workers were to receive their pro-rata part of the fund upon retirement. As a sideline, a Fuller E. Callaway Trust was established to support distinguished professorships, the number of which has grown to include chairs in thirty-three colleges and universities in Georgia.[5]

Callaway Mills became a front-runner in the industry in research, design, production, equipment, operations, and sales. Fuller conceived the idea of the Institute of Textile Technology at Charlottesville, Virginia. A plaque on the wall of its administration building testifies to his participation. Also, he worked toward the founding of the Georgia Tech Research Institute.

In 1945 Fuller shocked textile friends and associates with the announcement that he had decided at age forty to take a ten-year leave from the mill. When the ten years were up, he returned to his job as president, which had been filled in the meantime by Arthur Edge. Fuller continued as president until 1965, when he retired.

Around that time Roger Milliken, who had established a textile domain in the South and even moved his residence to South Carolina, needed a mill such as Callaway for his sheet, towel, and rug production. He wanted to buy Callaway Mills.

The deal was finally consummated in April 1968. Only the tangible assets were sold, which did not include the corporation's name, its charter, or accounts receivable. The Callaway Mills Company had leased the mill properties from the Callaway Foundation.

In 1965 Fuller Callaway obtained a charter for a new Georgia pecuniary corporation under the name Callaway, Inc. The entire capital stock of the new corporation was subscribed for and purchased for cash; three-fourths of it came from two other Callaway foundations and the other one-fourth came from the Callaway Mills Company Profit Sharing Trust Fund. Callaway, Inc. then purchased from Callaway Foundations, Inc. the entire stock of Callaway Mills Company.

In 1966 Callaway Foundations, Inc. sold to Callaway Mills Company all physical property that had previously been leased from the foundation at the net current appraised value of the property.

So in March 1968 Callaway Mills Company "spun-off" as a dividend in kind to its parent, Callaway, Inc., all four of its subsidiary corporations. Following the sale to Milliken the corporate name was changed to International Products and Services, Inc., which continued to own and control its remaining subsidiary corporations located in Pennsylvania, Great Britain, Europe, and Haber-

---

[5]Correspondence with Fuller Callaway, Jr.

sham, Georgia. Hence the great Callaway complex was liquidated with honor in 1968. As to the question, What about all the profits the employees were supposed to have in the company's Provident Fund for retirement? the answer is: when the Callaway Mills plants were sold to Milliken, this fund amounted to more than $12 million, which remained in the fund for benefit of eligible employees. Milliken has continued this plan and former Callaway Mills Company employees receive the benefits upon their retirement.

What a way to run a mill, build a textile empire, have fun doing it, and then dispose of it amicably. Moreover, in all those years, neither Fuller Callaway, Jr. nor any member of his family ever drew a penny in salary!

The Textile Mills' Divorce from the Villages | 12

When William Gregg built his Graniteville factory in South Carolina in the 1840s, after he had made a tour of prosperous, well-laid-out cotton mills in the North, he set out to launch a cotton mill that would be an object lesson to the South in terms of its social consciousness and profits. Gregg was an economist who was also determined, from considerations of human rights, to provide employment to poor, landless, white persons only. Gregg stated:

> Shall we pass unnoticed the thousands of poor, ignorant, degraded, white people among us who, in this land of plenty, live in comparative nakedness and starvation? Many a one is reared in *proud* South Carolina, from birth to manhood, who never passed a month in which he has not, some part of the time, been stinted for meat. Many a mother is there who will tell you that her children are but scantily supplied with bread. — These may be startling statements, but they are nevertheless true.
>
> ....
>
> It is only necessary to build a manufacturing village of shanties, in a healthy location in any part of the State [South Carolina] to have crowds of these poor people around you seeking employment at half the compensation given to operatives [of the same machines] at the North. It is indeed painful to be brought in contact with such ignorance and degradation; but, on the other hand, it is pleasant to witness the change which soon takes place in the condition of those who obtain employment.

In 1844 Gregg said, "There are 29,000 white persons in South Carolina above the age of twelve years who can neither read nor write. This compares with about one in five of the white population who are literate."[1]

Gregg built his mill and the surrounding village to house the workers. Other mill founders who built mills had to build houses also, for transportation to and from home and work was a luxury few could afford. Most had given up their

---

[1]Tompkins, *Cotton Mills.*

homes in the far mountain regions and could not return unless such a move would be permanent.

Conditions in the villages varied according to mill management, ownership, and the mill's profit margin. Not until the latter part of the nineteenth century was there much, if any, profit margin for Southern mills. In the post-Reconstruction days, it was a struggle for the mill owners to create employment for the poor, landless whites and at the same time make enough profit to renew their notes at the bank or commission house. The villages of those times reflected that situation. In many cases, the owner, or founder, who had raised money from many sources to build the local mill, plowed profits back into the mill for better machinery or expansion rather than paying big salaries to management or dividends to those who had invested in rebuilding a stricken country. They were striving to keep alive through depressions, trying to keep the mill going on the theory that some employment was better than none.

In the 1920s it became quite a fashion for writers to downgrade the Southern textile industry even though they had never visited the South, or had only hurriedly passed through. There were just enough shameful elements to make it all seem so. There was a village in Gaston County so run down that one passed it with a stench in one's nostrils; yet some of the workers who lived there had emigrated from England on the *Wittekind* and had in their dilapidated houses beautiful antiques, Hepplewhite and Chippendale, that their families had brought with them. There were the stoop-shouldered, undernourished, raggedy-dressed women and smelly, unshaven men—proud but impoverished—who came to a large mill town's Main Street on "Sat'day" while city folks stayed away on the golf course to avoid seeing them. The latter were the "new-rich mill barons."

A new type of social consciousness was developing in the 1930s and a new type of mill grew out of it. Stuart Cramer had built the Mayflower Mills at Cramerton three decades before. Part of the mill holdings included a model mill village, landscaped and beautifully kept. He later added a nine-hole golf course laid out for employees' use only and free to those who wished to enjoy it. Young children of the village, after school or during holidays, "caddied." One beautiful girl grew up to marry, successively, a millionaire, mill owner, and later a member of Congress.

Owners of mills and their villages started installing indoor water and plumbing in each home, replacing the one water spigot per block and the backyard privy. In the mill, bathrooms were installed by locating them in small towers built alongside the mill so there was one to each floor. The water supply was obtained from a tank that was elevated and separate from the fire-protection tank. This sanitation system was not considered adequate, but it was an advance of sorts. Electricity, as it was installed in the mills, was added to village houses to replace the kerosene lamps. Nothing fancy, but a light was placed in every room. One light installed on every front porch burned all night in lieu of street lights.

Typical mill-village houses in the 1920s. They were built in the early part of this century at an average cost of $300 per four rooms.

Houses could be built in the early 1900s at low cost: $350 for a three-room house, $600 for a six-room house.[2] These were rented to the mill worker, before electricity, at an average of twenty-five cents a room a week; that rate was then upped to fifty cents, including electric power. Upkeep of the community—such as garbage collection—and village taxes were the responsibility of the mill. Paved streets and sidewalks (if any), schools, churches, and meeting places were installed or built by the mills whenever the profit margin permitted. Mills that in the early half of the twentieth century had been out in the country were engulfed by expanding towns and cities and soon were taken within their limits, with all the benefits of water and sewage, streets and taxes. Still, many mill villages remain.

The tourist of 1984, traveling interstate highways through the Sunbelt, may be totally unaware that large and flourishing mill communities are nearby. They are seldom seen unless one turns off the interstate onto a smaller, two-lane country road leading to a discount store at the mill. The tourist is probably not fully aware of the benefits that have accompanied the growth of the industry and brought, within the past forty years, an entirely new way of life to the South and to the textile-mill employees and their families. The best outward evidences of this development are the improved mill communities and variety of

[2]Cramer, *Useful Information for Cotton Manufacturers.*

Golf course built for the exclusive use of Cramerton Mills' employees and their guests in the 1930s.

programs and sports sponsored by textile companies for the benefit of the employees and their families.

A few years ago the word *paternalism* was often heard in connection with the early efforts of textile management to offer better living opportunities to the workers. Today the public has begun to realize that *paternalism* is the wrong word. Mills invest money in building better communities. People who live in better communities make better citizens. Better citizens make better business. Plans for better community living are now a vital, integral part of the general economy of the textile industry. Many leading examples of this trend are found in the South. For example, some years ago W. D. Anderson of Bibb Manufacturing Company (Macon GA) in reply to a reporter's query, "What do you make?" answered, "We make, at Bibb, American citizens, and run a cotton mill to do it."

One of the major factors in better citizenship and greater work potential is having a good and pleasant home, in surroundings that please and are suitable to one's economic ability. In the textile industry today, such a home may be found in the mill community or in outlying farm areas populated by mill employees. The mill community, if it borders a town, is a welcome adjunct to the corporate community. Its well-kept streets and homes give an additional appearance of prosperity to a town. If the mill and its village are somewhat isolated, one often finds the community a place of real charm and usually of substantial appearance. Currently the majority of mill communities are governed by the mill operatives who own the houses, pay the taxes, keep up the yards, and plant the gardens. They elect their officials and maintain their police force and firemen.

Mill villages were never planned as sources of revenue to the mills. They were simply an outgrowth of the mill's location, which, in the early days, had to be near water power; therefore, mills were often built in remote places. Transportation was a grave problem, and companies had to house workers or lose them. Nowadays, with excellent roads, wages competitive with other industries, a mandatory shorter work week, wide use and ownership of automobiles, textile mill villages are not the necessary adjunct they once were. At least fifty percent of textile workers live away from the mill town in their own homes or on their farms. Now it is by the workers' choice, not the mills' necessity, that mill communities exist. Before the Wage-Hour law limiting the work day and work week, in addition to establishing overtime pay and a minimum wage, this type of life was unthinkable.

Evidence of a change in the perception of the average mill worker is seen in such things as owning homes, paying taxes, voting and, in general, improving the community. Persons who work for textile mills today are substantial citizens, proud of their work, leading active and responsible lives. In many incorporated textile towns, it is not unusual to find mill workers serving on city councils or working on various community drives. In cities, the same community leadership is shown. This would have been unheard of three, even two, decades ago. In textile-manufacturing towns and cities the distinction finally has disappeared between mill employees and other members of the community. It has been a gradual development, one that is welcomed by all.

Starting in the 1930s, community-recreation projects became joint investments on the part of mill interests and the town. Mill workers and everyone else living in the community share in the benefits and enjoyment of the health and recreation programs, the cultural and intellectual opportunities.

There are several factors that brought about this evolution. These factors include higher pay, more time for recreation, and greater opportunity for broader education. One of the most important factors was the sale of mill villages to employees on a first-choice basis, usually based on occupancy, and then to others if employees did not wish to purchase them.

In 1923, at the beginning of this trend, there was no special long-term plan of action. Spencer Love, who had purchased controlling interest in the antiquated Gastonia Cotton Manufacturing Company, decided to dismantle it and

This half-million dollar YMCA was built by Wiscassett Mills for the citizens of Albemarle, North Carolina, and dedicated to Wiscassett employees.

dispose of its holdings. He said then that the burden of real estate did not fit in with his idea of a well-run manufacturing business. The company was liquidated and the real estate sold for $265,000. He invested the net proceeds in his newly founded Burlington Mills, but again, he found that to get labor he had to provide housing for the workers. He built a new village, although the thought of real estate rankled him for years and he disposed of it as soon as possible.[3]

In 1933, during discussions of Code No. I under NIRA, President Roosevelt suggested that the economic problem of regional wage differentials and the social problem brought about by mill ownership of villages be made the subject of a special study by a committee of the industry. The committee was over-

---

[3]Interviews with Spencer Love.

whelmed by the complexities involved: investment, wages, employee relationships, habits of workers, and the community responsibilities of the mill employer. They despaired of breaking this traditional way of life, so nothing was done about it through legislation.

In 1934, with no fanfare, the Elmore Corporation at Spindale, North Carolina, sold its thirty houses to the mill employees. The next year, Burlington Mills adopted the deliberate policy of getting out of the real estate business. Burlington was expanding rapidly, producing rayon fabrics, hosiery, and other man-made fiber specialties. The better wage scales set up by NIRA, and later by the Fair Labor Standards Act, put more money in the pockets of mill labor. This help, plus easy buying terms set up by the mill or through special agents, made the purchase of a home possible for the first time for many mill workers—homes that had the bonus of being easily accessible to their jobs.

As part of its expansion program in the 1930s, Burlington frequently bought mills that were financially hard pressed because of the Depression. At times, it was able to purchase the mill only. That left the houses of the mill village to be sold by the former mill owner, often through real estate agents or developers. At other times, when housing was included in the purchase agreement, Burlington immediately divested itself of the village.

So Spencer Love, with his genius in finance and manufacturing, established a pattern of separating mill manufacturing from village real estate that eventually was reflected industrywide. By the time World War II began only six years later, twenty-five firms in Virginia, North Carolina, South Carolina, and Georgia had sold some sixty villages, or a total of nearly 7,000 houses.

There was a lull in this practice during World War II because mills feared a possible labor shortage, needed a sure three-shift operation, and new taxes threatened proceeds of the sales. Immediately following the war, however, village sales were resumed throughout the South. In three years, 1945-1948, 5,000 more mill village houses were sold. In 1945-1946, six firms sold sixteen villages. In 1947-1948, seven companies sold thirteen villages.

There was no clause in any of these sales contracts that restricted resale by the mill operatives. Thus they gained not only a house that they could keep up, but also a feeling that is different from any other feeling in the world: "This is my home."

Harriet Herring, in her broad survey[4] entitled *The Passing of the Mill Village*, interviewed many mill owners or managers who had sold villages. She noted in her book that, in the late 1930s, a small percentage of houses bought by mill employees were resold for profit, with the original purchaser investing the profit in a larger house or a small farm. The chance for resales depended upon mill locality and the purchaser's personal circumstances. Given the increase of property values during the last three decades, those who invested in that early "home purchase" movement may, by now, have profited by a remarkable appreciation in their properties.

[4]Herring, *Passing of the Mill Village*, 63-64, 109-10.

After World War II, when the big move from the North to the South began, sales of the villages stepped up. Mergers and acquisitions of Southern mills by Northern interests often hinged on the value of village real estate. One investment company in Greenville, South Carolina—experts in mergers and acquisitions—had to open a "real estate" division to handle both acquisitions of mills and sales of villages.

Alister Furman, head of that firm, recalled that Bob Stevens, of J. P. Stevens, when acquiring a number of mills in the South in the late 1940s and 1950s, said he'd never want to keep a mill unless he could control the village. Furman said, "Bob, the question is not *are* you going to sell?' The question is *when*." The sales of the Stevens villages soon began under Furman's direction.[5] Altogether the Furman Company sold 35,000 to 40,000 mill village houses. What had begun as a trend in the 1930s became accomplished fact by 1960.

Most mills are no longer entangled with real estate. A relatively few mills, however, have held their village areas for the convenience of the workers. The value of the property has been increased by means of planned beautification. But a mill-owned village today is still a rarity.

One mill-owned village that forty years ago was a disgrace is now a shining example of achievement. It has been completely rebuilt by the owner-management and has all-new or rebuilt houses with central heat and modern kitchens and baths. Air conditioning has been installed by the occupants in many of the homes. Paved streets, landscaping, and other improvement plans, such as a lake for recreation, are financed by a foundation set up for this purpose. The long-established mill has itself been rebuilt and equipped with modern machinery, air cleaning and conditioning; and it turns out an outstanding product of man-made fiber yarns. It is a totally integrated, equal-opportunity mill that evaluates workers only according to tested ability.

McAdenville, North Carolina, another mill-owned village, where the first electric lights were installed in a textile mill, is famous for its community spirit, which shows up in spectacular form each Christmas with a fantastic lighting show. The workers decorate and light their own homes, while the mill provides for the communitywide lighting demonstration. This is the twenty-fifth year the Gaston County town of only 1,000 people will glow and twinkle with half a million lights, sponsored by Pharr-Stowe Yarn Mills.

Starting as a small community project, it has grown into a nationally known extravaganza, featured at Christmastime on TV and in newspapers. Thousands of sightseers drive many miles to enjoy the show and admire the people who created it as an expression of pride in their town. Catherine Stowe Pharr and her late husband, William Pharr, planned the village restoration and inspired those who accomplish, in addition to their daily work in the mill, this dazzling annual Christmas production.

Burlington bought, in 1946, the Cramerton mills and village. In the beginning of the century, the property was carefully laid out for beauty as well as

---

[5]Interview with Alister Furman. M. G. Andrews, "Study on Housing Developments in Textile Mill Areas," for Dudley Anderson and Yutzey, New York, 1946.

industry by Stuart Cramer and was considered the model mill village in 1906. All the houses reflected the mansard influence, with shingles predominant in the construction of each. When it bought the mill, Burlington immediately sold the houses according to the usual plan, offering them first to employees of the mill.

In 1975 the Mays plant was closed, leaving the village full of mill workers with no job unless they commuted elsewhere. Three years later the aged mill building was demolished. The tract of land where it stood was graded and seeded, landscaped and converted into a village green; and people who worked in white collar jobs elsewhere bought homes there and became commuters to their work in other nearby areas, including Charlotte.

Those mill operatives who bought homes in the town of Cramerton and who still live there have great pride in their lovely village. Other professional and businessmen bought homes in Cramerton because the one-time mill vice-presidents and other top officials had spacious and beautiful houses. One especially fine place is the Cramer mansion itself on the hilltop, with a view of mountains on the horizon and a large swimming pool that is really the village fire reservoir.

There is a move on foot to have the entire town designated a historic site. C. E. Hovis, an old man of eighty-five, remembers going to the Cramerton railroad station to get telegraphed, inning-by-inning results of the 1916 World Series in which the Boston Red Sox and Brooklyn Dodgers were playing. The Cramerton Historical Society, led by Hovis's son-in-law, Bill Crenshaw, is putting on a drive to have the quaint old railroad depot turned into a historical monument for some village use. The society has 200 members, all of whom joined within a week of its organization. The Cramerton depot was built in 1906 when the Southern Railway made it an official stop. The station was designed with a mansard roof and built in the elaborate style of the times, as adapted to the village architectural plan.

Cannon Mills, founded by James W. Cannon in 1887, naturally had a village around each plant; all mills did at that period of time. He built the towel mill at Glass in 1907 and changed the name to Kannapolis, which is Greek for "city of looms." In his time and during the reign of "Mr. Charlie" Cannon, Kannapolis grew to be the largest unincorporated town in the state.

After Charles Cannon took over from his father in 1921, the one square mile that the mill owned in the heart of Kannapolis was definitely "Mr. Charlie's town." He ran it, and he did a good job. The mill houses were well kept; the streets and sidewalks were in good shape; and the police and fire departments all were efficiently managed. After a trip to Williamsburg, Virginia, with his wife circa 1940, he decided to give the main street and mill office a face-lift. He employed a prominent architectural firm to make the village business area, as far as possible, resemble Williamsburg. When completed, the buildings displayed unusual brickwork based on original Williamsburg English and Flemish bond. It was a source of pride to those who worked in the mill and lived in the village.

Charles A. Cannon. He succeeded his father as president of Cannon Mills Company in 1921 and was a dominant influence in the industry for many years.

The operatives who lived in company houses built in the period 1907-1927 paid a nominal rent of approximately $35 a month for an average-sized house, more for a two-story, four-bedroom house. The utility bill for each house was about $2 a month. They were comfortably situated on lots of one-quarter to one-half acre, on tree-lined streets. Some mill operatives have lived in these houses many years and never considered moving. A number of workers remained after their retirement with an option to buy their homes. By 1983 less than five percent of the mill operatives were living in company houses.

When David Murdock, the self-made, multimillionaire builder and developer from California, acquired Cannon Mills in 1982, the company property in Kannapolis was part of the deal. There was instantly a sense of fear and worry among the villagers as to what Mr. Murdock planned to do. So far, management states that Cannon has 2,600 homes in various locations, of which 1,600 are in Kannapolis. At this time some 640 of the 1,600 will be sold to employees at nominal cost, and directly, not through agents. Others will be reserved to fit in with the plan inaugurated several years ago to nominate the village to the National Register of Historic Places. Kannapolis has been described as one of the most unique and most important historic resources in North Carolina by the state's architectural historian, Peter Kaplan.

Within the short Murdock regime, Cannon Mills has replaced its cancer-screening program by instituting the broadest medical-screening program in its history—perhaps broader than any ever instituted in the textile industry. Cannon Mills has more than doubled the life-insurance benefits for employees, added one more fully paid holiday for all employees, implemented a general wage increase, and inaugurated a dental-care program for each employee. This program alone will cost the company approximately $1.5 million annually. It has also set aside about thirty acres for a community park system and a senior citizens' center has been completed in downtown Kannapolis. The entire downtown is being modernized, but still with a heavy accent on Williamsburg architecture.

So the day of the mill village, in the old sense, has gone with the changing times. Some were good places to live and some were not. Only the better ones have survived as places to live and call home. But the term *mill village* is obsolete. Now the one-time villages are towns. Museums today are busy with projects to erect small replicas of those old-time clusters of houses, bare of ornamentation but complete with privy and company store.

The Textile Machinery Industry: A Changing of the Guard* | 13

J ust one thing, invoked by nature or due to a new invention, can trigger a series of revolutionary developments in manufacturing systems, especially in the textile industry. In the early 1930s the major cotton crop started moving from the fertile, rain-watered Mississippi Delta to equally fertile but irrigated lands in the West. Texas and California became strong competition in the Southern and Eastern mill markets. But in processing the fiber, it was found that Western irrigated cotton did not take the same finishing and dyeing as rain-watered cotton fiber. When the bales were mixed, the fiber looked the same. However, after finishing and dyeing, the result was streaked yarn and cloth—a total loss to the manufacturer.

Textile men demanded one-crop cotton, either Western or Delta. Some people claimed that Western cotton was shipped to Memphis where bale tags were switched to represent the cotton as Delta-grown. Lawsuits were pursued. In the long run, new finishing and dyeing techniques and chemicals developed by textile machinery builders and chemists solved the problem.

When the Cotton Kingdom went down in defeat and field labor had to be compensated in cash or kind, inventors endeavored to find a mechanical means to pick the ripe, fluffy cotton from the boll without damaging the plant or the fiber. Difficulties with finding a suitable mechanical device at times appeared insurmountable. Cotton bolls open at different times; thus fields have to be picked repeatedly. Any machine that injures plants is licked before it starts. Until the Rust brothers' picker appeared, in 1936, no apparatus seriously threatened black field labor, to whom "cotton pickin' time" was the synonym for plenty of money.

Then came two blonde Texas giants who had picked cotton on the 160 acres homesteaded by their father. It was not fun to them; it was drudgery, for they had grown up with it. John went to work in Kansas wheat fields, then later

---

*Author's Note: Data on machinery applies to 1982-1984 equipment. Technological advances are so rapidly introduced that some "modern" machines described in this chapter may be obsolete by now.

For centuries cotton had been harvested with human hands.

worked for a farm-implement company; Mack went to the University of Texas and majored in mechanical engineering. These two young brothers completed their first experimental cotton picker in 1936 and demonstrated its ability at

The Rust Cotton Picker, circa 1940.

Stoneville, Mississippi, before a jury of 200 planters, agricultural experts, and black field workers. The Rust machine showed that it could, under proper conditions, pick a bale (500 pounds) in an hour. The best human hands can do is about 400 pounds in a day.

The Rust brothers had no desire to deprive workers of their jobs. They filed a charter of incorporation for the Rust Foundation in order to aid individuals who might suffer when mechanical picking came into full use in the Sunbelt. However, no deprivation occurred since the Depression had caused a mass exodus of blacks to Northern states. The former glut of field workers was no longer there; 130,000 black workers had left the Southern cotton fields for points north.

"If production costs can be reduced 20 percent," said W. E. Ayres, manager of the Delta Experiment Station at Stoneville, Mississippi, "our markets lost to low-cost producers in other countries can be regained." The early cotton picker was a crude machine compared to today's sophisticated multirow cotton picker with air-conditioned cab that can cleanly pick many, many acres in one shift. This invention started a train of new machine developments.

The person most interested in cotton, besides the farmer who grows it, is the textile executive who manufactures yarn and fabrics from it. The mill man was interested only in how the mechanical cotton picker would affect his business: "What will machine-picked cotton be like? How will it work in my mill? What about leaf trash? Or discoloration? How will its production quality be affected?" He asked, "What will happen at the gin when machine-picked and hand-picked cotton are mixed?"

Dumping the cotton from the Rust Picker to a truck headed for the gin.

Wagons loaded with cotton waiting to be ginned (1930s). With the mechanization of cotton picking came the mechanization of cotton transportation. (Courtesy of Cotton Mills Information Service.)

These questions have been answered, for modern gins are now equipped with dehydrating plants or vertical dryers that remove moisture from seed cotton before it is ginned. It is estimated that cotton which has gone through this drying process at the gin has a considerably increased monetary value because of its resultant smoothness and quality. Pedigreed-cotton-seed breeders realized that years of work lay ahead of them to breed a new type of seed that would produce cotton suitable for mauling by the mechanical picker. Nature would have to meet the challenge of the machine in the field.

The textile machine builders soon became aware of the need for better opening and cleaning systems to handle machine-picked and trashy cotton. The one-process picker[1] introduced in 1928 was one of the most widely heralded developments of textile machine building at the time. It replaced three other machines, but then itself became obsolete with the advent of chute feeding in the 1960s and 1970s.

Around 1938, the time of the introduction and acceptance of mechanized cotton-field harvesting, Eugene Gwaltney joined Saco-Lowell as head of research. His achievements in the improved one-process opening, picking, and spinning operation rescued that company from financial disaster. Gwaltney's

---

[1]Henceforth the term *picker* means a mill process, not field harvesting.

Wagons full of cotton waiting to be ginned, and the baled cotton after ginning (1930s). (Courtesy of Cotton Mills Information Service.)

developments assisted the entire cotton textile industry in adapting to the modernized cultivation and harvesting methods.

Whitin Machine Works had begun work in the 1920s on improved opening and picking equipment for cotton manufacture. An Englishman named Edward Mills joined Whitin for the sole purpose of developing a new opener-picker. He remained in Whitinsville about ten years and initiated the company's important role of building opening and picking and other preparatory equipment for cotton manufacture. Then came Dr. Zoltan S. Szaloki, who developed the centrifugal opening/cleaning system in the early 1950s. His system was the best and cleanest yet introduced.

By 1939 only twenty-two percent of the nation's cotton manufacturing machinery—measured at that time by "spindles in place"—was left in New England. Two-thirds of the machinery was in North Carolina, South Carolina, Georgia, and Alabama. The close geographical association of the majority of spindles to cotton fields, and mechanical harvesting, brought about formation of an aggressive group known as the Spinner-Breeder Conference.

Representatives of the cotton planters, seed breeders, and cotton spinners met to discuss their mutual problems and work toward solutions. Mills ran special spinning tests. W. H. Garrard, general manager of the Staple Cotton

Cooperative Association[2] in Greenwood, Mississippi—the largest cotton sales agency in the South—wrote the Southern Yarn Spinners: "We are sending ten samples of cotton harvested by the Rust picker. I think the Experiment Station at Stoneville would be willing to sell ten bales at any reasonable price the mill would pay in order to have spinning tests made." Actually, one mill volunteered to run the tests for free, and the Delta Experiment Station donated the cotton. Machinery builders strove to develop more efficient opening-pickers, cards, and cleaning apparatus.

One can look back a couple of decades and see how a strictly New England industry, textile machine building, gradually became Southernized. It was a long, tedious, and expensive trip for Southern mill men to travel north to choose machinery they needed. Out of their dilemma, around 1900-1910, a type of informal cooperative marketing system for textile machinery began operating. For example, the first was the Charlotte Machine Company, a small repair shop, but primarily a textile machinery manufacturers' agent. It served Pettee Machine Works, which made cards and drawing frames; Providence Machine Company, which made roving equipment; Fales and Jenks, which made spinning frames; Cohoes Iron Foundry and Machine Company, builders of slashers; Easton and Burham Machine Company, which made winders and spoolers; Knowles Loom Works, which made looms; and Curtis & Marble Machine Company,[3] which made finishing equipment. So the company had a complete line for any mill customer. It was a lucrative business.

D. A. Tompkins—engineer, textile mill president, and publisher of the *Charlotte Observer*—decided he would like a piece of that pie and became the Southern agent for Whitin Machine Works. That was great for him, but not great enough. He wanted to "round out his line" so he could offer a mill any kind of machinery needed, from opening to spinning, through weaving and finishing. He made such arrangements, and took in S. W. Cramer as a salesman. When Cramer succeeded Tompkins, he too endeavored to enlarge his field of supply in order to have a "complete line." However, he insisted upon salary and expenses rather than commission. The Charlotte Machine Company faded out of the picture when Tompkins and Cramer entered the business.

Lowell Machine Shops refused to go into any such arrangement. The same was true of Howard and Bullough-American. Each made such a complete range of products that each preferred to deal directly with mills.

As a temporary expedient, the group marketing was highly successful. It was not a stable arrangement for machine builders, but it made the Southern agents, Tompkins and Cramer, who were hard salesmen, very rich.

Whitin Machine Works perfected the Nasmith Comber by simplifying the design of the machine and introduced its first high-speed comber[4] in 1905. In

---

[2]Now known as Staplcotton.

[3]None in business in 1984 under original name.

[4]Combs out shorter fibers and parallels longer fibers into a flat ribbon.

1910 Marston Whitin stated that four-fifths of all combers being sold in the United States were made by his family's company.

One of the most important new developments in the industry during the 1930s was long-draft spinning. It was originally developed by Fernando Casablancas, a cotton-mill superintendent in a mill near Barcelona, Spain. His discovery meant that a good deal of the drafting[5] work done formerly on roving frames could instead be performed on the spinning frame itself, eliminating one of the three roving operations. This opened the way to substantial savings in labor and machine costs.

In the meantime Saco-Lowell Shops (formerly Lowell Machine Shops) had concluded that the French LeBlan-Roth system was better and negotiated a licensing agreement with the French company and adapted that system on Saco-Lowell spinning frames. Not wanting to let Saco-Lowell get ahead of it, Whitin concluded an arrangement with American-Casablancas that gave Whitin sole right to manufacture Casablancas's attachments in the United States. Thus Whitin obtained exclusive American manufacturing and sales rights to the finest drafting system then known, and incidentally added fuel to the competitive feud between the two companies.

The textile mills were still battling effects of the Depression and would not acknowledge the merits of the new system by installing it until after 1933 when money flowed more freely. Then there was a deluge of orders for the attachment to be installed on existing equipment although mills preferred new spinning frames with the long-draft built in.

It was not long before spinning-machinery builders realized that the long-draft system could be applied to the roving complex as well as to spinning. There was violent rivalry between Whitin and Saco-Lowell during the decade following the introduction of the long-draft systems. Suits and countersuits on patent infringements and "breach of faith" were filed by both companies and the original developers of the long-draft roving systems. For example, for twenty years the case of *Whitin* vs. *Reynolds and Terrell Machine Company* (a Charlotte company, incorporated in 1917), involving the quarter turntable on the roving system, was open. It went through court after court up to the Supreme Court, which finally in 1948 refused to review it. It had been a bitter fight between a Southern company and a Northern company, but the South won the case.

Saco-Lowell introduced the one-process picker to the market in 1928. It was an immediate success, with mills clamoring for it. Textile engineers and inventors from the Shirley Institute in England traveled to Gastonia, North Carolina, to see its installation in the A. M. Smyre Manufacturing Company. The one-process picker eliminated two other processes and reduced production costs accordingly. Many improvements during the next two decades met the difficult challenge offered by the modern, highly compressed bales of cotton and the problems of mechanically harvested cotton.

---

[5]Extending and paralleling the fibers.

Whitin Machine Works had stolen a march on its rival, Saco-Lowell, when it introduced the Nasmith Comber, named for its developer. Twenty-eight years later (1933), Saco-Lowell added combers to its production line. It bought certain assets of a wholly owned subsidiary of Atkinson, Haserick & Company, the Alsatian Machine Works. The latter was the American division of the British firm of Dobson & Barlow, which built combers. Fortunately for Saco-Lowell, the machine's chief designer, Joseph Fosch, and his staff went with the deal. This acquisition, transferred to Saco-Lowell's plant at Biddeford, Maine, became the nucleus of its comber department. The transaction was completed without the expenditure of any cash. David Edwards, president of Saco-Lowell, paid a percentage of the difference between cost and sales price on all combers built by the firm until the specified purchase price of the Alsatian assets was reached.

Up until World War II, most of the textile machine builders were centered in New England, but there were a few very good machine builders in the South. They were alert to the introduction of man-made fibers in the 1920s-1930s, which opened a whole new field of developments in machinery. There were machines suitable for man-made fiber alone and those that could spin and weave both natural and man-made fiber. Man-made fibers, being very clean, could bypass the opening-picking and start with a system of blending fibers that is almost the universal textile manufacturing process as we know it today.

Among the Southern machine builders were Cocker Machine & Foundry Company in Gaston County (North Carolina), founded in 1913 by George Cocker, a machinist who had moved south to start a business. A young and talented Gaston County man, Dave Friday, became associated with Cocker. His inventive genius and business vision made the company outstanding and Dave became executive vice-president. In 1934 Cocker built a spindle-driven warper, the first warper designed expressly for man-made fibers. Within the next three decades, Cocker Machine, under Dave Friday's astute management, became the leading builder of high-speed warping and slashing equipment and added a line of knitting machines. Upon Friday's retirement, John Cocker, son of the founder, took over. The company was bought by Walter Kidde & Company around 1965, and in 1967 Robert Dalton, Jr. was named president.

One of the most distinguished, longtime native Southern textile machine builders is the West Point (Georgia) Foundry and Machine Company, manufacturers of warping and slashing equipment for weave-process preparation, and bleaching and dyeing machines.

Gaston County Dyeing Machine Company is another native Southern engineering and textile machine company that in recent years has become internationally known under the presidency of Max Craig, with Gordon Hacker as executive vice-president. This company was the first to apply control automation to its textile machines and first to develop the jet-type fabric-dyeing machine. Its machines produce quality goods in a cost- and time-effective manner.

Southern mill men were well aware of the unsightliness of cotton waste on the floor and of the necessity for lint-free machines in order to maintain the quality of the product. To anyone who has seen the methods of cleaning the floors by sweeping and hand cleaning lint from a machine that has been stopped, it seems miraculous that the modern traveling overhead vacuum cleaners, blowers, and filters keep the air, ceiling, walls, machinery, and floor as clean as a well-kept home. This was happening in the better mills long before the regulations of the Occupational Safety and Health Administration.

The trend for clean mills and clean air had its beginning back in 1907 when the G. M. Parks Company of Fitchburg, Massachusetts, acquired rights to an industrial humidifier and began pioneering in this direction. In Charlotte, Stuart Cramer, Sr. was doing research on textile-mill humidification and air cleaning. He is credited with originating the term *air-conditioning*, which now includes a cooling system. His research led to new devices and methods related to humidification, air-conditioning, and psychometric control.

Ultimately, a conflict about patent rights arose between Parks and Cramer. In 1918 G. M. Parks bought the S. W. Cramer air-conditioning business and, since Cramer was well known in the South, also acquired the use of his name. Thus Parks-Cramer Company was formed and incorporated with manufacturing facilities in both Charlotte, North Carolina, and Fitchburg, Massachusetts.

In 1920 the company built a new factory in Charlotte to meet the increasing demand for humidifying and air-cleaning equipment. The demand came especially from Gaston County where the mills had installed combers and were attempting to compete with the high quality of New England fine-cotton yarns. For a century a strong belief prevailed in the trade that high-grade cotton yarn could be produced only in New England cities such as Fall River and New Bedford that were blessed with humid sea air. Until the automatic humidifier was developed, Southern mill workers in the spinning and weaving rooms threw buckets of water on the floor at regular intervals to create humid air.

A self-propelled traveling cleaner was first conceived at Roxboro (North Carolina) Cotton Mills in 1925 by its superintendent, William B. Walker. He built a track system over a winder, from which he suspended a traveling, self-propelled, down-blowing fan. Walker worked with W. J. Smith of the Firth-Smith Company of Boston. Together they designed the ceiling-suspended, automatic cleaner for spinning, twisting, winding, spooling, and high-speed warping. Thus they pioneered a new textile process to deal with the lint generated by yarn- and fabric-making machines.

Meanwhile, Cullen L. Lytton of Flint Manufacturing Company, Gastonia, North Carolina, had been working on a similar idea; he mounted the track on the spinning frame. Parks-Cramer's research and development department worked with Lytton. In 1932 the company acquired his patent rights, and in 1934 took over the business of Firth-Smith. Today Parks-Cramer is considered a longtime Southern establishment with a plant in the North. Installations per year of Parks-Cramer traveling cleaner units throughout the textile industry grew steadily from six units in 1931 to 514 units in 1937, then to 600 units in 1946. Meanwhile the Bahnson Company, Winston-Salem, had introduced its own machine- and air-cleaning system and became a vigorous competitor of Parks-Cramer.

World War II and its restrictions on textile production virtually halted research on textile machines that made civilian goods. Postwar problems and continued government restrictions slowed machine builders' research and factories' conversions from materiel output. The Marshall Plan in Europe and the Supreme Command of Allied Powers in the Pacific placed heavy demands on textile-machine production. Each plan entailed rehabilitation of the conquered countries, and so demanded a large share of American-built equipment.

American machine builders were working against terrific odds to produce new equipment for American mills while war-torn countries under rehabilitation plans were moving forward, rebuilding plants containing the newest foundry and metal-working equipment. Within a decade three countries would pose stiff competition for American machine builders. Their munitions plants were converted to peacetime production, usually the development of textile machinery. Such a company was Krupp in Germany.

Although the big Northern-textile machinery companies had had Southern offices and Southern agents for some time, not until the 1950s did they realistically face the fact that the goose now laid its golden eggs in the Sunbelt.

Saco-Lowell, the original Lowell Machine Shops and one of the largest preparatory and spinning machine builders, started its move south in the late 1950s by buying a company in Sanford, North Carolina. Then in the 1960s it built a complete, modern, and spacious one-story plant and foundry at Easley, South Carolina, not far from Greenville. It closed its large New England operation with the exception of the Biddeford, Maine, plant. In the meantime, it had been acquired as a division of Maremont Corporation, machine tool builders.

Whitin Machine Works (founded in the early 1800s and established at Whitinsville, Massachusetts), the other New England preparatory and spinning manufacturer, was merged in 1965 with White Consolidated of Ohio. Shortly thereafter it closed out its vast Whitinsville establishment—which included luxurious executive homes, a full-fledged town, foundry, and plant—and moved its operations south. Its sales office was located in Charlotte, North Carolina. White Consolidated then acquired the recently bankrupted Roberts Company of Sanford, North Carolina, builders of competitive spinning equipment. Whitin Machine Works, founded by Paul Whitin nearly 150 years before, had only one Whitin kinsman in the organization when it changed hands. He remained at home in Massachusetts.

In 1960 someone asked W. K. Child, vice-president of Draper Corporation, located at Hopedale, Massachusetts, if the company was planning to move south. "Move South? We're moving every day!" was the answer. Child was referring to Draper's closing its Pawtucket, Rhode Island, plant and its acquisition of a modern subsidiary, Marion (North Carolina) Industries, along with Burns Tool Company of Louisville, Georgia, and their sales and parts facility in Spartanburg.

Draper was one of the six greatest United States machine companies, known for its early development of ring spinning, its Northrop and automatic high-speed looms for cotton and man-made fibers. In 1952 Bracket Parsons, president of Pepperell Company, said of Draper:

Following the sale of Whitin Machine Works to White Consolidated Industries (a nontextile company), most senior management departed. R. I. Dalton, Jr., the vice-president (r), left to become president of Cocker Machine and Foundry Company. At left is Maynard Ford, president of Parks Cramer Company and a senior member of the board of the American Textile Machinery Association.

The weaving operation in a textile mill is one of its greatest costs. We are fortunate in having Draper help us out. Draper has to compete with 150 other types of machinery for the textile mills' dollars. In running those looms on a single shift basis [8 hours and/or overtime], it is amazing that the total annual cost of repairs runs probably about 3% of its purchase value. When you consider an average loom making 300,000 interlacings of threads per minute and having that loom run with a mechanical failure averaging only *once* in 72 million interlacings or a loom stopping for any reason, such as a broken thread, once every 27 million interlacings of thread, it is certainly a wonderful machine.

At that time Draper was building its newest model loom, X-3, at the rate of one every nine minutes and also producing its quota of machine tools for the Defense Department. It had at least a two-year backlog of orders on the X-3s. Draper operated on a mass-production schedule that was an indigenous part of the American industrial pattern and the envy of the world.

The noise and clatter of 200 or more looms of any model in a weave room was deafening, actually shocking, to an outsider entering a weave area for the first time. Draper was already researching a shuttleless loom that to a great extent would eliminate the racket caused by shuttles moving back and forth across the loom's warp to make the interlacings. Its research department was successfully operating an automatic doffing machine for spinning frames and tests were being run in Southern mills.

To the shock of the industry, Draper was acquired by North American Rockwell in 1967 and its headquarters established in Spartanburg. It became the Draper Division of Rockwell, a company noted for research and development in the aerospace program. There was no longer a research program for Draper, or its affiliate companies, Textile Machine Works and Wildman Jacquard, which became the Knitting Division of Rockwell.

Gone with the change of ownership were the marvelous and huge foundry and machine shops, the beautiful and historic village of Hopedale, whose model homes had won four medals at World Expositions. Gone from Draper were the 150,000 acres of forest lands in four Northern states that furnished wood for loom parts, and the dozens of saw mills in the South that cut dogwood for shuttle making at Hopedale. It seemed that, almost overnight, Draper had become only a division of an international company not interested in textile machinery building.

Crompton & Knowles was another of the outstanding leaders in machine building. This company made looms too, but not in competition with Draper's. Crompton & Knowles made looms for fancy cloth, or special-purpose fabrics ranging from narrow looms that produced ribbons, tapes, and elastics to immense long looms that made rugs and broadloom carpets, and looms that produced the multicolored, yarn-dyed fabrics, ginghams and plaids. With the Jacquard head superimposed on the Crompton & Knowles loom, rich brocades were produced: multicolored or color-on-color damasks.

The company started with a patent by William Crompton in 1837. A mechanism in his machine frequently got out of order, much to the consternation of the weaver. Twenty years later this fault was corrected by Lucius Knowles, who took out a patent on his correction of the defect. Years of litigation by Crompton over patent rights on the Knowles device and others finally ended when Crompton and Knowles agreed to stop feuding and become one company. Many improvements were made in the fancy, multipurpose loom, and general acquisitions of other patents or companies put Crompton & Knowles in the forefront of loom building.

During the Eisenhower depression of the mid-1950s, textile mills were facing obsolescence. Textile-machinery people were pointing out, in 1953, that a mill still in operation with obsolete equipment needed seventy employees per eight-hour shift to produce the same amount and quality of combed "four-yard broadcloth"[6] that forty-three employees could produce with new equipment. This also meant savings in the payroll and other operating costs. In addition, yarn would go through only thirteen processes on new equipment compared to eighteen on obsolete machinery, an elimination of capital investment on five preparatory and spinning machines. They would need only 417 X-3 Draper looms compared to 500 obsolete Model Es, a saving in the investment of eighty-three looms, floor space for more productive equipment, fuel, energy, and other operating costs.

American textile-machine builders were at that time spending more on research and development in ratio to value of sales than the national average of

---

[6]"Four-yard broadcloth" indicates four yards per pound.

other industries. They pointed out in briefs filed with the United States Treasury Department that as soon as any machine was successfully introduced to lower the per-unit cost of production, the other machine, regardless of physical age, had outlived its profit life. Obsolescence is a terrible creeping disease that no industry can survive for long. Textile mills (and the Treasury Department) joined in the plea of the textile-machinery people to the United States government to adjust depreciation rates that had been in the IRS code since 1937 concerning textile machinery. Machines available in 1957 were not even in existence in 1937.

President Kennedy announced on 11 October 1961 that tax officials had been ordered to speed up depreciation rates on textile machinery from twenty-five years to fifteen years, and for some types of equipment to twelve years. On a case-by-case basis, it could be lowered even more. This legislation was incorporated as a permanent part of the United States tax laws. It was widely hailed as a stimulus to textile business and the textile-machinery business as well. At the time of the president's announcement, only twenty percent of the industry's spindleage had been in place less than twenty years; 37.46 percent had been installed at least forty years before, around 1920, at the peak of new mill building in the South.

In the four years after the effective date of the investment-credit clause, passed as a permanent part of the tax structure, textile mills doubled expenditures for modernization on a long-range program basis. Even so, fifty percent of the industry's capital equipment was more than five years old and the mills had a long way to go to modernize completely. Then abruptly, under President Johnson, the investment-credit clause was cancelled.

Looking at the narrowing mill margins, executives sought other means to produce goods at lower cost. About this time the American textile industry was introduced to a supposedly new type of spinning frame, built in Japan, that could spin yarn directly from sliver, eliminating one process. There was quite a ruckus about this at the time. The American machine builders pointed out that there was nothing new about the machine; U.S. patents had been issued on the same spinning principle in 1885. A new mill had been built in Fitchburg, Massachusetts, equipped with Saco-Lowell's sliver spinning, but it was not prosperous and closed due to economic factors.

Charles Cannon wrote a blistering letter to George Dowdy, then manager of Belk's department store in Charlotte and a member of a panel appointed by the National Retail Merchant's Association. He had been invited to Washington to work on problems of general agreement regarding tariffs and trade (GATT). Cannon wrote:

> The Japanese equipment had been on display in the United States for more than a year. It does not equal the improved spinning frames made by American companies, many of which we are using. The truth of the matter is that the textile industry has so little money that they do not have sufficient capital to invest in what the American machinery builders have been able to produce. The attraction to foreign equipment is the cheaper price.

At that time the members of the American Textile Machinery Association represented ninety-five percent of the gross expenditures for capital equipment by the textile industry. Easy travel to overseas points, international textile-machinery exhibitions, subsidized research and development programs in foreign countries, and lower prices made European- and Japanese-built equipment not just enticing but a must if the textile industry wished to survive. More and more new developments from overseas were replacing obsolete equipment in American mills. Teams of research engineers and purchase executives from American mills were not an unusual sight in foreign textile-machinery markets.

The picture was indeed muddled in the 1960s and 1970s. The federal tax structure was forcing family-held and weak companies to be disposed of, and the cost of production per unit was a major and constant worry to mill and machinery executives as they pondered possible solutions to these problems. Northern textile machinery companies continued to move south in an effort to cut their costs, to be close to their customers, and to stem the tide of foreign-built equipment. One by one, foreign machine companies formed American divisions and established Southern offices, chiefly in Charlotte, Spartanburg, and Greenville. Highway I-85 between Charlotte and Greenville was called Machinery Mall as new overseas offices and assembly plants sprang up. And, besides this situation, new government regulations on the health and safety of workers were issued to the mills.

In 1973 Crompton & Knowles moved the headquarters of its Textile Machinery Group to Charlotte, North Carolina, but retained its manufacturing facility in Worcester, Massachusetts. It had expanded within the textile-machinery industry by acquiring James H. Hunter & Co. of North Adams, Massachusetts. It also built a new plant at Mauldin, South Carolina. It had, around 1950, entered the dye-stuffs and fiberglass fields. But within a decade of its move south, James Hunter Machine Co. was bought back by the Hunters. The fiberglass involvement had long since gone by the boards; its Worcester facility was closed in 1980; and in 1981 Crompton & Knowles sold its Loom Division to Leesona Corporation, located in Warwick, Rhode Island. Another giant company had bitten the dust.

All but a few of the 475 former employees were relocated in jobs with other textile or machinery firms. David Schrom, head of the Textile Machinery Division of Crompton & Knowles, said the closeout was due to imports of weaving machinery from Japan, Switzerland, West Germany, France, and Italy. His statement was backed up by Dame Hamby, dean of the School of Textiles, North Carolina State University, who said, "Nearly every new loom bought today is made abroad."

Leesona, the only one of the so-called Big Six of the textile-machine builders to elect to remain in New England, had made its southern move ten miles or so south of Providence to Cranston, Rhode Island, in the 1950s. It bought what was left of Crompton & Knowles, but Leesona was already in trouble and had been acquired by John Brown & Co. of London in 1980. Despite changing fortunes, the company's earlier contributions to the textile industry are too important to overlook.

Dame Hamby. Dean of the Textile School at North Carolina State University until his retirement in 1987.

Joseph Leeson, an ambitious immigrant from England, founded the company in 1893 to develop and market his invention—the first winding machine that could produce a self-contained, completely wound package of thread or yarn, supported on an inexpensive, flangeless container. It became so popular in textile mills because of its advantages and adaptability in winding commercially used yarn that he patented the device under the name "Universal Winding."

Robert Leeson, grandson of the founder, was made president of the company after his return from service in World War II, and soon changed the name of the company to Leesona. By means of his vitality and vision, Leesona Corporation broadened its output and introduced some machines that revolutionized the industry in terms of saving floor space and manpower. One of these is the Unifil Loom Winder. This remarkable device, fully automatic, and attached to an existing loom, eliminated seven steps in the preparation of filling yarns. The Unifil Loom Winder displaced two machines formerly required to do the work: a manually operated filling-winder or an automatic filling-winder, and an automatic bobbin-stripper. Also, it replaced the rotary-loom battery and accessories.

Reduction in payroll costs due to installation of the Unifil Loom Winder on each loom is about forty-five percent. By 1980 the Unifil Loom Winder had been

Joseph R. Leeson.
Founder of Universal
Winding Company,
which later changed
its name to Leesona.

installed on practically every one-color loom in the United States and had been improved to handle more than one color, and with speeds of more than 12,000 rpm. With the advent of shuttleless looms, however, the market played out.

Robert Lesson resigned as president of the company in 1969, and then resigned as chairman of the board due to ill health, from which he did not recover. At the time Brown acquired the company, no Leeson was affiliated with it.

In 1972 Platt International introduced its open-end spinning to the United States, a much more advanced development than an earlier Japanese model. This machine had the ability to spin both short- and long-staple fibers, and each unit had its own trash-removal system. This special device gets rid of the "pepper trash" such as fine dirt that remains in the cotton immediately prior to spinning. The trash-removal device enables mill management to take advantage of the use of lower grades of cotton and, consequently, gives the mill a wider margin of profit.

A year later Stone Platt Industries of England acquired the Saco-Lowell Division of Maremont. In 1977 the newly formed company, Platt-Saco-Lowell Corporation—then the largest textile-machinery company in the world—added 47,000 square feet of space to the Frank Lowell plant. But within three years, the British-owned Saco-Lowell Division of Platt was bought by a native Southern company, Hollingsworth-on-Wheels.

The first model winder developed by the Universal Winding Company.

John D. Hollingsworth started out in the textile field as a card grinder (one who sharpens metal wires on card clothing) and card-clothing supplier to textile mills. His office and equipment were in a van mounted on truck wheels. The name of his company was, appropriately, Hollingsworth-on-Wheels. He drove from mill to mill and rendered excellent service. Indeed, as one mill executive said, "He had the best wire in the business, and he was at your mill as soon as Wheels could make an answer to a phone call." Hollingsworth did not believe in patents. He said that where there is a patent, someone will copy it; then one must go through litigation and lose a lot of time and maybe the case. So he kept on improving machines, repairing them, and purchasing textile-machinery stocks anywhere he found a good bargain. He is now a tycoon of the machinery industry.

Barber-Colman, a Rockford, Illinois, machine company, moved its textile-machinery division to the South when it bought Cocker Machine Company from

Robert Leeson, in 1960, examining his grandfather's invention, which in 1891 revolutionized yarn packaging, a vital operation in textile manufacture. At the time Mr. Leeson represented the third generation to head the Leesona Corporation (formerly Universal Winding Company).

Kidde. Howard Colman, inventor, with his benefactor, Barber, founded the company in 1919 and acquired the American Warp Drawing Machine Company to satisfy patent difficulties arising from Colman's experiments with warp drawing. This is the process of drawing the ends of threads of the warp through the eyes of the heddle that is a part of the loom harness.

Heddle eyes used to be made of cotton cord and, before that, of silk. In 1945 Barber-Colman shipped the first all-steel heddle warp-drawing machine for operation in an Alabama mill. To replace a tedious hand job with automation was a great achievement in this field. Since Cocker introduced the first warper for man-made fibers, the merging of the two companies made sense. Barber-Colman transferred its textile-machine marketing division to Cocker's location in Gastonia. It has, since that merger, acquired the textile-machine division of Warner

Robert Leeson. Grandson of the founder, he broadened the company's output and introduced the Unifil Loom Winder.

& Swasey Company of Cleveland, Ohio, and that company's pindrafter and long-staple drafting machines (used for yarn preparation of long-staple fibers). Barber-Colman's triaxial weaving machine forms fabric through interlocking three equally spaced ends of yarn at 60° angles. The fabric produced has uniform strength in all directions, high tear resistance, and no bias weakness.

To the trade, Barber-Colman means warping systems. Its new models meet any yarn-preparation demands, with a production speed of 1500 yards per minute. The machines also are enclosed and carry safety guards for operators.

One by one, machine builders moved south. Birch Brothers, one of the oldest, went to Waxhaw, North Carolina; Fletcher Industries went from Philadelphia to Southern Pines, North Carolina; Marshall & Williams went to Greenville, South Carolina; and Whitinsville Spinning Ring Co. went to Gastonia, North Carolina, to join those companies that were already there, either natively or due to relocation.

Entrepreneurs arranging leveraged buyouts entered the picture in the early 1980s. One example is that of Derrick A. K. Smith, a Scotsman who came to the United States via Canada and is a former president of Centennial Industries. He first bought Abbott Machinery Company in New Hampshire, then moved

Howard D. Colman as a young inventor working on the first warp-drawing machine.

south in 1983 to buy out White Consolidated's Whitin-Roberts Division. He promptly reduced three plants in Sanford to two, sold off surplus equipment, reduced inventories, and sold surplus real estate to pay off mortgages. Now Whitin-Roberts is renewing its efforts in research. The company recently introduced a new wrap spinning machine especially suited for coarse count yarns that make items such as carpet and upholstery. It is said production speeds may be increased sixfold. The wrap process can eliminate the twisting that produces two-ply yarn.

The methods of textile spinning have grown from ring spinning, developed first by Thorpe in 1818, to rotor spinning or open-end spinning, to air-jet spinning and friction spinning. In the traditional ring spinning, a spinner has problems "piecing up" (or attaching two ends of yarn to one another) at speeds of more than 200 rpm of the front roll, which is about 16.1 meters per minute. Platt-

Saco-Lowell's "PSL" frame with 144 positions may spin 100% cotton-weaving yarn, size 34s, at 210 meters per minute. Air-jet spinning will replace older ring spinning and open-end spinning as rapidly as the mills can afford to invest in the equipment. Already a number of mills have so invested, but with the exception of this one American machine builder, the equipment must be bought today from one of several foreign builders who produce such sophisticated spinning machines.

Increased automation, quality control, and greater production ability are the technological goals of every new type of machine. Every department of every mill must be equipped with technological advancements to meet rigid controls set forth by the United States Occupational Safety and Health Administration (OSHA) in 1970 and upheld by the Supreme Court in 1981.

Two of these regulations have brought financial hardship on Southern textile mills. One regulation involves controlling cotton dust in the mill because of a disease known as byssinosis. The other regulation involves the control of noise, and is especially applicable to the weave areas. The standard set by OSHA in 1978 on dust control is a maximum of 200 micrograms of respirable dust per cubic meter of air, eight-hour time-weighted average, in yarn and preparatory manufacture areas and 750 micrograms of respirable dust per cubic meter of air, eight-hour time-weighted average, in slashing and weaving departments of a mill.

The compliance date was 27 March 1984. However, on 24 February 1984 OSHA announced a six-month extension for areas of ring spinning, through winding, twisting, spooling, beaming, and warping if the yarns being run are fifty to one hundred percent cotton and if the yarn count by weight is 18/14 or coarser. The original regulation date applied to all other departments.

Byssinosis is a lung disease long associated with asbestos fibers, but not until OSHA's regulations were issued did the disease become connected with cotton-textile mills. There is varied opinion as to where the cotton dust comes from or whether it causes the disease, which is curable only in the first stages. Mill men say the dust comes to the mill in the bale as a result of modern machine cultivation and harvesting procedures and use of pesticides and chemicals that permeate the cotton before it reaches the mill. Others claim that smoking is as great a contributor to byssinosis as cotton dust. OSHA claims the dust is the result of manufacturing processes. The controversy raged for fourteen years before that 1984 deadline, but in the meantime the textile industry had spent $1.2 to $1.5 billion on new plants and equipment to eliminate dust and to reduce noise.

Mill spending for capital equipment to ensure employee safety has reached phenomenal proportions in a relatively short time. For example, one company alone spent $50 million in 1983 for new capital equipment and modernization and will continue to spend from $15 to $25 million in the next five years. At the same time, it has disposed of seven obsolete mills that were part of its chain. This is a typical pattern.

It is estimated that to meet final compliance with OSHA will cost $1.1 billion in manufacturing equipment alone. Some older mills are just so out of date, they actually cannot be modernized to meet requirements and consequently are being torn down or put to uses other than textile manufacturing.

One South Carolinian refused to try to meet OSHA's regulations, saying he resented government interference with private enterprise. "If you give in to socialistic laws that are eroding your freedom, you're a damn fool," he said. So he sold his ninety-two-year-old mill full of mechanical corpses, and the new owner says he is spending the millions it will take to comply with the standards.

Automatic bale openers—entire systems of opening, blending, and carding—have been developed to reduce operational costs and improve dust and noise control. All the machines in the new systems are enclosed units or have operator-safety designs. Sales of this type of equipment have been enormous within the past five years, as mills faced the stark situation of "eliminate dust or go out of business." One native Southern machine company sold 360 chute-feed units in one order, while one overseas company installed 1,400 of its opening-carding systems and related equipment in fifty-one Southern textile mills within six months and continues to fill orders booked far ahead.

New and more sophisticated air-cleaning and machine-cleaning systems became increasingly important throughout manufacturing areas of the mills. These systems also must adhere to noise regulations of ninety decibels per installation area. Parks-Cramer's high-velocity cleaning system is one that conforms to OSHA's regulations. In the spinning room the Endsdownlocator system is incorporated into the unit and enables the traveling unit to patrol and observe each spindle as it cleans. The Parks-Cramer EDRS system patrols, detects broken ends of yarn, interrupts roving feed, and then reports to the operator by flags, lights, panel board, and computer printout, indicating which spindles have been stopped by a broken thread or whatever. Air-cleaning systems were in use long before the regulations pertaining to cotton dust were issued, but they are mandatory now because of the presence of OSHA.

In North Carolina, through the first quarter of 1983, 2,417 textile workers had filed brown-lung claims and employers had paid $16 million in damages in 1,174 settled cases. Mills also paid huge litigation costs in each of these cases. In April 1983 a North Carolina Supreme Court ruling made it easier for workers to file compensation claims for byssinosis when it held that this lung disease, caused even partially by on-the-job exposure to cotton dust,[7] could qualify the victims for total compensation even if other factors—such as habitual smoking—were involved.

Actually, today's mills are very clean establishments. A group of visitors to the South in late 1983 was taken on a tour of a large textile plant. Upon reaching home in New England, one described with delight her interesting trip through

---

[7]On 18 April 1984 the North Carolina Court of Appeals ruled for the first time that exposure to synthetic fibers can aggravate lung disease in textile workers and entitle them to worker's compensation benefits. The court's recognition that synthetic fibers can contribute to chronic obstructive lung disease reverses a 1982 Court of Appeals decision.

the towel mill. "What about all that dust? Weren't you afraid of byssinosis?" asked her amazed listener. "If the air in my house, with all our pet dogs and cat and visiting smokers, was as clean and breathable as that cool, air-conditioned factory, I'd be one happy woman!" was the answer. Certainly most Southern textile mills have such broad medical surveillance programs that employees should not become disabled with byssinosis.

New shuttleless looms—of the advanced rapier, air-jet, and water-jet types—are being installed throughout Southern mills to replace shuttle looms as rapidly as cash flow can be had. What is important, these new looms meet OSHA's requirements about noise level. At the 1983 International Textile Machinery Exhibition in Milan, a visitor reported that for some time before the show opened, it looked like a battleground for new weaving technology. One European manufacturer of looms booked orders for 1,000 weaving machines the first day. This company produces a terry-cloth weaving machine that carries, at the same time, three different widths of toweling on one beam, 3,300mm wide, therefore tripling production by weaving three towels at the same time and greatly increasing the production rate per minute.

Another weaving-machine company, best known for the rapier-type shuttleless loom, offers to convert its earlier shuttle model to newer rapier weaving. Another company builds water-jet looms for man-made fibers only that produce at the rate of 600 to 700 picks per minute, and air jets for cotton and man-made blends that produce at a rate of 600 picks per minute. The jet (water or air) propels the filling yarn across the loom to lay the thread between the warp yarns, and in this way replaces the shuttle and is said to reduce the loom noise level in the weave shed to less than the OSHA-required ninety decibels.[8]

A foreign loom builder says one textile mill has assigned 120 water-jet looms on filament yarns to one operator, one fixer, and necessary auxiliary hands. The jet loom takes up less floor space, uses less energy, has easier machine adjustment and a simpler mechanism, thereby making the work less arduous for its operator. One operator is assigned to thirty-five air-jet looms on spun yarn, but a fixer can take care of 100 looms.

For a Southern textile mill to obtain any one of these new weaving machines, it must place its order with a foreign company, although that company may have an American division, with offices and assembly plants. American loom builders have not given up, however. In 1982 the managers of the Draper Loom Division of Rockwell got together and bought back the division at an approximate price of $30 million. They established offices in Greensboro, North Carolina, but kept the foundry in Spartanburg, South Carolina. They reinstated Draper's research program and entered into a licensing agreement with a West German firm to obtain its air-jet technology. In late 1983 the revived Draper Corporation sold twenty of its new sixty-four-inch-wide, air-jet X-3000 weaving machines to Kendall Co. for use in its Pelzer, South Carolina, plant.

---

[8]The Hearing Conservation amendment to the OSHA regulation on noise sets the level at eighty-six decibels in some cases.

Management is concentrating on converting the old Draper shuttle looms still in place to the new rapier- or air-jet method that will operate at close to 500 picks per minute. In sheeting widths, the Draper jet loom will cost less than $20,000, which is at least $5,000 less than air jets from overseas.

They've come a long way since Ira Draper's first patent (in 1816), the automatic loom temple, that allowed one weaver to tend two looms. In 1894 the Northrup automatic loom allowed one weaver to tend sixteen looms whereas in 1961, the best Draper allowed one weaver to tend 100 looms. With the new X-3000, a weaver can handle up to 400 looms. Leesona, in 1981, introduced its own method of converting Draper shuttle looms on print cloth to an air-jet operation. However, the new Draper setup is to be multijeted (versus Leesona's single jet) and will cost about $8,000 per loom for conversion.

Media and government attacks on textile mills' safety and health programs and the costly struggle on the part of mills to meet or beat OSHA's regulations resulted in disastrous repercussions for American textile-machinery builders. The industry was losing due to the technical achievements of foreign companies.

Then came the unexpected attack from lawyers who discovered the lucrative loophole in the Workmen's Compensation Law that allowed a person injured on the job to sue the manufacturer of the machine involved in the accident, regardless of the age of the machine or the number of times it had been rebuilt or sold. In 1970 there were no product-liability suits against textile-machine builders. In 1980 seventy percent of the machine builders were mired in such suits, amounting to millions of dollars. One suit was based on the injury of a person working on a machine built in 1903 that had been rebuilt and resold many times. It was pure junk, but was still operating, with the only original portion being the section that carried the builder's name.

Such suits have become so widespread and so vicious that at least five large American machinery companies have been forced out of business. The idea that a textile mill's owner or the corporation using the machine could be bypassed and the suit filed against the family of the original builders was both astonishing and debilitating.

The Hunter Machine Company for six generations has been a family-owned corporation. The company filed for reorganization under U.S. bankruptcy laws (Chapter 11) in 1983, citing as its reason thirty-one product-liability suits against it. Product-liability insurance rates have increased dramatically during the past decade, for some industries by as much as 7000%. The costs of these premiums are expected to continue to rise, especially for capital-goods manufacturers. Hunter and many other companies had dropped this type of insurance. However, Hunter had been operating on a self-insured basis with a reserve of up to $500,000 to meet product-liability contingencies.

In 1982, at the Chapter 11 hearing, Hunter said that the company had to pay $175,000 to settle its share of a single suit that involved two other codefendants. In addition, the company's share of the legal fees was $125,000. It faced twenty additional product-liability suits at the time of the hearing. The company made machines for the manufacture of home-decorative textiles, automobile parts, paper felt, and nonwoven fiber fabric used in road building.

Another example of the product-liability debacle is the liquidation of Davis & Furber Co., one of the Big Six of American textile-machine builders. It was the largest builder of machinery for manufacturing of wool and woolen goods in the world. It was founded in 1835; but in 1981, faced with vanishing customers and product-liability suits, it closed its doors.

In 1984 five capital-goods industry associations, concerned about increasing competition from foreign firms and product-liability suits, were awarded a federal government grant to conduct a comparative study of U.S., European, and Japanese product-liability systems and costs and their effect on competition in international markets. The American Textile Machinery Association (ATMA) is one of the five groups awarded funds for the study by the U.S. Department of Commerce.

The only way to analyze the market standing in textile machinery is to evaluate the membership list of the ATMA, the voice of the industry. This association until recent years had a strict regulation that confined its membership to American-owned companies that built complete machines for the manufacture of fibers into finished fabric. A small group of makers of ancillary or auxiliary equipment were associate members without a vote. The membership list today is like a patchwork quilt.

Textile machine building in this decade is a new industry. Also new is the layout of the textile mills themselves. Automation is part of the makeup of every machine. Modernization includes computerized manufacturing, automated systems, mechanization, computer controls, and even robotics. New finishes give the consumer perma-press, nonflammable, and soil-resistant fabrics; computer-formulated color batches in dyeing match shades precisely. Patterns of color and design are photographed on rugs and also transferred to fabrics. A mill no longer buys machines, but rather "systems." A spinning machine is no longer described by the number of spindles per side but by rotors or positions.

In earlier days a machine "simple enough for a child to operate" was considered a capital asset, and consequently many young people grew up working in a mill to the detriment of their education. In the 1920s, although mill villages boasted schools, rarely did a mill worker have an education beyond the eighth grade. Many had not even reached that level of schooling; some middle-age workers were illiterate.

During the Depression, the WPA conducted free education classes for all who would attend. Some mill hands enrolled. One was asked how he was getting along in school. "Just fine," he said, "on the road signs I can read 'how far,' but I can't tell 'where to' yet." In the 1980s a high school diploma is a requisite. Now even the job titles are different. No longer are there "mill hands" or "mill workers" or "lint heads"; they are called machine operators. A loom fixer is now a "weaving machine technician." A background in textile engineering has become more and more important, if not absolutely necessary, to make good. A textile mill job now ranges in pay from $5 to $6 per hour, nearly *twice* the legal minimum-wage rates paid by many other jobs.

Out of ATMA's 1960s membership of 118 capital-equipment companies, largely located in New England, in 1984 there were only fifty. Of these, thirteen New England companies have moved south; seventeen New England companies have been liquidated; fifteen have been bought by other companies and moved south; and five are native Southern capital-equipment builders. Some of the original members have been swallowed by others. One small-time repair business of the 1960s now owns eight large capital-equipment companies and chunks of stock in others. The designation of Charlotte's Douglas Airport and Greenville-Spartanburg Airport as international has been a marked assist in importing foreign equipment, for entire machines can be loaded in cargo planes, flown in ready for erection in a mill. One cargo line has routine daily landings in the Carolinas, bringing a complete machine and parts from Europe on each trip.

Present ATMA members include nine German-owned capital-machinery companies with Carolina-based assembly plants, and three Swiss and two English companies. The balance of the members includes those manufacturing ancillary and auxiliary equipment such as computer and control systems, mostly located in the South. Japanese manufacturers of capital goods for textile mills have not yet become members of ATMA, although they are prominent in the Southern textile picture. Due to many factors beyond the control of the old, established machine builders, the picture for native American manufacturers looks bleak.

In order to compete in the world market, the textile mill of today must be modernized in every department in order to obtain greatest production at the lowest possible cost per unit and at the same time meet all government requirements in safety, health, wages, and hours. The mill owner, or chief executive officer, really has no choice; for some items in some departments, he must buy foreign equipment.[9]

---

[9]ATMA records; *Textile Industries, Textile Reporter;* American Textile Manufacturers Institute; personal interviews.

The Southern Textile Industry—1984 | 14

On 1 February 1979 the Crescent Limited, the last privately operated, overnight luxury passenger train in the United States, made its final run from Washington to New Orleans.

It was a historic event because it was the end of the great train era. The Crescent was a symbol of the new industrial South, which could not have come about without the famous Southern Railway system and connecting lines. For years and years it was the lifeblood of the textile mills. The Southern abandoned its luxury passenger train because it was losing passengers and money ($6 million in 1978). A different era of planes, automobiles, buses, and trucks, as well as four- to six-lane interstate highways, had made passenger train travel practically obsolete.

Amtrak, the federally subsidized national railroad, agreed to take over the Crescent, but it speedily announced that it may have to be scratched in an economy move. The train's transfer leaves the Southern Railway without regular passenger service for the first time in its eighty-five-year history. On that fateful last run, Clifton Mattox was the engineer. With his hand on the throttle, he took the Crescent through the New South that the Southern had helped to build, a South of phenomenal industrial growth, particularly in textile manufacture and allied industries. The South's history and growth are spelled out by the textile facilities strung along the steel rails of the Southern that, for such a long time, have swung in a shining arc from Washington, through eight Southeastern states, to glamorous and bustling New Orleans.

More than fifty years ago, the textile mills' big move from North to South was just beginning through mergers and acquisitions. The trend was accelerated by the 8,000 miles of the Southern's system that covered the area south of the Potomac and east of the Mississippi like a net. By one connecting line or another, it got into every Southeastern state except West Virginia, and served every major city below the Mason-Dixon line except Montgomery, Alabama, and Nashville, Tennessee.

The "Queen and Crescent" route ran from Cincinnati through Chattanooga to New Orleans. Other arms stretched westward to St. Louis and Memphis, and eastward to most major ports on the Southern Atlantic coast and the Gulf of Mexico. It is estimated that, one hundred years after the great Atlanta International Cotton Exposition, ninety percent of the textile industry lies within that network, with mills' privately owned spur lines leading from their sites to the nearest conjunction stop.[1]

The Crescent, though, ran on the Southern's main line. In earlier days, it was on the Crescent that passengers met and bought and sold textiles and machinery. You'd be surprised how much business could be conducted between Greensboro and Charlotte, for example, or Spartanburg and Atlanta, and so on.

About two hundred railroad buffs rode the Crescent on its final run, and when they were not reminiscing, they had a good long look at the New South. Those who ride Amtrak over the same route today may learn how New England and New York textile interests had invaded the area little by little, until they owned or controlled most of the textile mills they were passing; and the same is true, of course, of other industries.

After crossing the Potomac River into Virginia, leaving Washington for the old Crescent run, if it were not for the skyscrapers, offices, and condominiums built in the last decade, one could see the beautiful meadows and rolling hills that mark the beginning of the Piedmont. There, around the turn of the century, lived the famous horses that financed the operations of a large textile mill. The absentee owner was Harry Smith, obsessed with steeplechasing and internationally known for his sportsmanship. Smith had been carefully educated for a textile career and, although he had at least forty patents on loom mechanisms and his mill was the only American one to produce polished cotton fabric for sleeve linings, he stayed ensconced in the Piedmont hunt country. Smith devoted his time to arranging international steeplechases for rich and sporting people who flocked to watch him win them. All his winnings bought new machines for his mill, met the payrolls, and paid for the cotton.

A great feud began when as Master of the Hounds of the Loudon (Virginia) Hunt, he discovered that E. H. Harriman, railroad tycoon and founder of the Orange County Hunt, had leased all of the Piedmont farms for hunting solely for his hunt. This action was against all traditions of the sport, and Smith protested violently. When his letters to Harriman went unanswered, he was enraged and sent copies to every member of the Orange Hunt, to every Master of Hounds in the country, and to leading sports journals.

Despite enormous winnings from his pursuits with horses, his mill stockholders complained about his continued absence from his desk. Smith answered that his horses kept the mill; the mill did not support the horses.

The Avtex Fibers Co. is in nearby Front Royal. The company manufactures man-made fibers, including rayon staple, industrial yarns, and polypropylene fiber. The name of this company came about when John Gregg acquired the fiber division of Food Machinery Corp. (FMC) in 1976 and named the company

---

[1]*The Southern Serves and Sells the South;* Andrews, *Southern Railway System.*

Avtex, a derivative of the name American Viscose, which was acquired by FMC in 1963.

In Charlottesville is the Institute of Textile Technology, founded by Fuller Callaway, Jr., and carried on by other textile leaders, particularly Roger Milliken. It is a cooperative research center and the only graduate school in textile research. Also in Charlottesville is the recently built filament-woven goods mill of Frank Ix and Sons. They are longtime Northern manufacturers of silk who now run a man-made fiber plant that has more than a thousand looms.[2]

Further south, at Buena Vista, is the Vulcan Division of Reeves Bros. This mill makes coated fabrics for industrial uses. Bernson Mills, a relative newcomer, manufactures novelty goods from man-made fibers and cotton. Georgia Bonded Fibers, a producer of nonwovens, makes products developed as disposable items since World War II. And at Alta Vista are two plants of Burlington Industries, one making glass fabrics for high-temperature insulation, the other making man-made and blended woven and knit fabrics.

The Crescent's next stop is Danville. "It was not '38' but 'Ole 97' " that wrecked near here, an accident that has been immortalized in song. "It's a mighty rough road from Lynchburg to Danville / a line on a three mile grade / It was on this hill that he lost his airbrakes / you ought've seen the jumps that he made!" It was Steve Brodie whose hand was on the throttle that day. Tragically, he was scalded to death by the steam.

"Dan River Fabrics" is what the sign says as the train passes the mill, but it doesn't have space to announce that the river is named for Daniel Boone, or that the mill was built there for the water power, or that millions of yards of fabrics are turned out each month at this mill. Dan River Mills maintains two textile schools, each operating a fully equipped, miniature mill with a staff of specialist instructors. Years ago a full four-year high school course was made available to mill workers and was popular. Fourteen hundred employees successfully completed such courses. Those "students" fortunate enough to be selected for the research division had the great experience of working under Russell Newton, who for many years headed that division.

The Riverside Cotton Mills, built in 1882, and Dan River Power and Manufacturing Co., built in 1895, became incorporated in 1909 by merger and consolidation as Riverside and Dan River Cotton Mills. In 1946 the name was changed to Dan River Mills.

The mill on the river Dan was organized in 1882 when Thomas Burton Fitzgerald (a Civil War veteran, contractor, and brickmaker), Dr. H. W. Cole (a physician, coroner, and drugstore proprietor), Benjamin F. Jefferson (a Confederate veteran, coal, wood, and lumber dealer), and the three Schoolfield brothers met at the home of J. E. Schoolfield. They authorized R. W. Peatross, attorney and counselor, to draw up a contract binding them to form a joint stock company to manufacture cotton and woolen fabrics, rope, and other items. The initial capital was $75,000, of which Fitzgerald owned the largest single inter-

---

[2]M. G. Andrews, a study of the silk industry for the Irving Trust Co.

est, $21,000. He was elected president and was engaged to build the mill at cost plus ten percent, but received no salary as president.

The Riverside Cotton Mills, with 2,240 spindles and 100 looms, began to produce yarn and cloth in April 1883. In less than three years, the mill had reached its capacity of 260 looms and 6,000 spindles and employed 200 operatives. They made sheeting, shirtings, drills, warps, and twine.

In 1890 Riverside was merged with Danville's other mill, the Morotock, which became Riverside Number 4. By 1900 there were 67,000 spindles and 2,772 looms; 192 of the latter were classified as "broad looms." The firm had built a dye house also. Most important, it had built a town and the mill was its heartbeat. It was said that every person in town had at least one share of stock in the mill, so everyone was a part of it.

Fitzgerald died in February 1931 and was succeeded by Robert Rout West, a farsighted man who believed in modernization. He started investing huge sums in new machinery of the time and was dismissed for doing so because the expenditure cut dividends for stockholders. During his tenure, the American Federation of Labor and the United Textile Workers Union chose Dan River to launch a Southern organization drive. The strike was a failure; the mill reopened in a few months.

The next years were turbulent, for the company had several presidents in relatively quick succession. George Harris was named president, but when the textile bubble burst after the peak period following World War II, Harris was stricken with a heart attack. Russell Newton, a textile engineer who had straightened out manufacturing problems and inaugurated research programs under Harris's presidency, was elected to succeed him. Wrinkle-Shed cotton fabrics were the result of Newton's work. He insisted on modernization of equipment, even obtaining a long-term loan of $9 million for the purpose. He brought in a well-known "head hunter" firm to evaluate the company, and the result was an unbelievably rapid change of personnel.

One man lost his job due to an outside activity. The *Saturday Evening Post* carried a lead story (24 November 1951) about a mobster gang in New York City that built a secret hootch factory on an isolated farm in New Jersey, supposedly financed by "Legs" Diamond. The mob, according to the story, had a "fixer" who arranged things with an agreeable farmer who was not averse to having a profitable still on his place. The farmer was very careful of his own position, however, and went to the Alcohol Tax Unit of the IRS to get its blessing in writing so he would be "clean." The gang hired a general handyman to assist in building and operating the still. It just happened that he was an agent of the Alcohol Tax Unit who blew the whole scheme.

When Dan River's administrative officer at its New York sales office picked up the most recent *Saturday Evening Post*, he was thunderstruck to see a featured picture of his personnel executive identified as the "Mob's Fixer." The personnel executive caught the next elevator down and *out* of Dan River's office.

In the midst of the Korean War, when the industry was working under Federal Wage and Hour regulations, Emil Rieve, president of the Textile Workers Union, attempted to organize the South, beginning with Dan River. After months of negotiations and picketing, Cy Ching, director of the Federal Mediation and Conciliation Service, settled the attempt by telegraphing the mill management and union that "industrial peace to the fullest extent possible is essential to our national safety and welfare." The strikes threatened elsewhere were called off by the union two days later.

Suddenly Russell Newton was asked by the mill board to resign. He did and quickly was asked to join Milliken's Research Center. Harris had recovered from his heart attack and had joined Burlington. In 1953 William J. Erwin was appointed president, and during his time Dan River's huge expansion and profitable period were under way. Among the mergers and acquisitions was Woodside Mills of South Carolina. It was said that Dan River acquired Woodside to get Robert S. Small. It was not long before greater expansion took place along with corporate realignment.

In the midst of this, Small was trying to comply with government civil rights regulations in order to make Dan River an equal-opportunity company. Supposedly Department of Labor and civil rights officials told him to step it up. He passed the word along. A few days later, his personnel and industrial relations director came to him and said, "Mr. Small, we have a horse applying for a job."

William Erwin. Served as president of Dan River Mills in the 1950s and 1960s, until his retirement.

Robert Small.
President of
Woodside Mills when
it was acquired by
Dan River Mills. He
subsequently became
president of Dan
River Mills and also
served as president of
the American Textile
Manufacturers
Institute.

"Then *hire* him," said Small. "But, Bob" was the answer, "this is the first time a *whole* horse has applied for a job!"[3]

When the Crescent passed Dan River Mills on its final trip, the mill had 409,136 spindles, 6,506 looms, and was one unit of a far-flung, four-state textile complex formed within the past twenty-five years.

The office of Dan River's chairman, Small, was for a time in Greenville while the chief research center was in Danville. Since Small's retirement, the corporate management has returned to Danville. The move has been financially successful by reducing overhead, eliminating duplication, and making the entire operation more responsive to production needs and to employees. Dan River has its sales office in New York. The company divested itself from Iselin-Jefferson Financial Company, which it sold to Iselin-Jefferson Factors, a subsidiary of Manufacturers Hanover Trust Company. Thus we see an original Southern company that expanded by acquiring additional plants in other Southern states.

---

[3]Cross, *Dan River Runs Deep*, 134.

Bob Small served as president of the American Textile Manufacturers Institute and his prime worry was what the import situation would do to the American industry.

Dan River celebrated its 100th anniversary in 1982, claiming to be the sole survivor of industrial firms founded in 1882 that had achieved 100 years of continuous independent operation. It is also one of the *Fortune* 500. At least two attempts to take over the firm have failed. This is the story of an attempted leveraged buyout by a Northerner.

Dan River had, at its 100th birthday celebration, 5.8 million shares of stock outstanding. Shortly after, 29% was held by Carl Icahn, a forty-six-year-old New York investor or, as some said, "boardroom battler," who coveted the balance or at least a majority of the stock.[4] Dan River's board of directors did not take kindly to Icahn's advances. He had already run Dan River's common stock prices up from $16.50 a share to $18 and was planning to offer more.

Dan River's board fought back hard and fast and filed suit against Icahn's tactics. It voted, also, to establish a new series of cumulative, votable preferred stock, and issued 1.7 million such shares to a stock-bonus plan for employees. The stock was to be held for five years in a trust fund controlled by Dan River

An aerial view of the greige manufacturing and finishing plants in Dan River's Schoolfield Division, located in Danville, Virginia.

---

[4]*Dan River* vs. *Icahn*, a suit filed in U.S. District Court in Danville, Virginia, 6 October 1982.

An aerial view of Dan River's Riverside Division, located in Danville, Virginia. When combined with the Schoolfield Division, these plants form the largest single-unit textile operation in the world.

management with the requirement that any merger proposals would have to be approved by holders of two-thirds of the new shares. As a practical matter, any merger could be blocked by Dan River management. The new stock issue of 1.7 million shares represented 22% of Dan River's outstanding securities. A federal judge ruled that Dan River could continue to buy its own stock, for which $15 million had been allocated by the board.

Icahn filed countersuit, then made a new offer to pay $55.8 million for 3.1 million shares of common stock, which would give him sixty-nine percent of all shares. His plan didn't work.

Dan River's suit accused Icahn of a "pattern of racketeering" in his bid for Dan River stock acquired with "proceeds derived through prior acts of extortion, mail fraud and securities fraud, violating rules of the Federal Securities & Exchange." Of course, Icahn denied the charges. It was a bitter battle. Dan River's third-quarter earnings during this late-1982 fight dropped, but David Johnston, Jr., chairman, predicted a rise because of a seven-day-a-week operating schedule at its new $25 million denim plant, twenty miles west of Greenville.

In the meantime, the company sold 475,000 shares of its common stock to a British concern that was called "an ally" for $8.7 million. After a five-month battle, Dan River and Icahn reached a truce: Dan River would remain an independent concern, but would pay Icahn $9 million to buy back his shares in the company.

In April 1983 Dan River converted from public ownership to employee ownership. Its Employee Stock Ownership plan (ESOP) has worked out very well, says Dan River president Lester Hudson. To make the employee stock plan work, employees had to forgo pension rights; however, employees now own seventy-one percent of the stock, and managers and Dan River's investment banker, Kelso Investment Association, own the remainder. It is predicted that within eight or ten years, an employee retiring under ESOP will have three to four times greater benefits than under the old plan.

Already Dan River has paid off $55 million of its $148.9 million debt, putting the company ahead of schedule. It exceeded its 1983 projected profits and had sales close to $600 million. "This is due largely to the increased interest in company productivity inspired by employees who now have a clearer stake in the company's finances," says Hudson.

When Dan River became employee-owned, it had twenty-six plants in the South, twelve in the Carolinas. A year later Dan River announced the sale of its Woodside Division to Alchem Capital of Greenville. The Woodside Division included plants in South Carolina. Alchem is a Southern company, part of a Greenville-based diversified holding company.[5] The purchaser said all employees in both manufacturing and administration would be transferred to the new company, which would continue as a supplier of greige goods to apparel and industrial trades.

About thirty miles west of Danville, the formerly sleepy town of Martinsville, Virginia, has grown to have six textile companies of considerable size: the huge plant of E. I. Du Pont de Nemours and Co., where nylon yarns are made; a fleece fabric plant; three well-known companies making knitted athletic wear; a twisted heat-set plant that produces multicolored yarn for carpet and upholstery. Also located there is the Sale Knitting plant of Tultex Corp., which boasts an apparel group at Roanoke, a yarn group at Gastonia, a group of mills making athletic-wear textiles, an international group, and an associate group, Dominion Surplus—all selling through Tultex Factors of New York. In its annual report of December 1983, Tultex reported earnings of $14.6 million on sales of $288 million.

From Eden, North Carolina, where Fieldcrest Mills is headquartered and some other plants (including Spray Cotton Mills, privately owned and operated by Welsford Bishopric) are located, one has to drive to Danville to catch the Southern. Fieldcrest Mills, making high-style sheets, towels, bedspreads, and Karastan rugs was, until 1947, called the manufacturing division of Marshall Field and Co., Chicago. Luther Hodges went to work sweeping floors before and after school hours in this mill when he was nine years old. He saved every dime and, after graduating from the local high school, he went to the

---

[5]Alchem Capital is controlled by R.S.I. Corp. of Greenville, South Carolina, a diversified holding company.

University of North Carolina at Chapel Hill where he continued to work and to save.

One who knew him in those days said, "Luther would work at any job to pay his way through the university, cut grass, wait on tables, sweep dormitories, then go back to work in the mill during the holidays and vacations." He became the head man, but would never accept the title of president. He was manager, chief executive officer, and head of sales. He raised the company's style and quality standards and profits, and changed its ponderous name to Fieldcrest. To those who worked in the mills, he was affectionately called "Mr. Hodge."

After forty-five years in the mill, he retired to enter public service. First, after World War II, he went overseas to facilitate the Marshall Plan, then to serve North Carolina as lieutenant governor, then governor for seven years. Later he served his country as President Kennedy's secretary of commerce, and remained there for a time with Lyndon Johnson. He was a great help to the depression-ridden industry of the 1950s and 1960s. He returned to North Carolina to take on the presidency of the Research Triangle, which he had established while governor. He was paid $1 a year, but insisted that he be paid in "quarterly" installments.

In 1953 Fieldcrest Mills was incorporated. It was sold by Marshall Field and now is controlled by D. B. Dumaine and F. C. Dumaine of the old-time New England Amoskeag Co., which owns 40.8 percent of the stock according to Dun and Bradstreet. This, then, is how the once-great Amoskeag Mill moved south. Fieldcrest has eighteen mills in North Carolina, two in Georgia, three in Alabama, one in Virginia, and the Delaware Wool Scouring Co. Fieldcrest remains a leader in its field of production.

The Crescent's first stop in North Carolina is Greensboro. It is the home of Cone Mills Corp., founded in 1895 by Moses and Caesar Cone, and one of the largest weavers of denim and corduroy in the world. The Cones' first mill, the Proximity, was spun off in 1978. Long gone were the cotton fields that inspired the name. The seventy-five-year-old plant had become too obsolete for installation of the modern mill equipment necessary to meet health regulations set by OSHA.

Cone Mills is considered a company of progressive ideas and plans. In 1981 it announced that Luz International, a Los Angeles outfit, would build one of America's largest industrial solar systems to furnish energy for its Cliffside plant in Rutherford County, North Carolina. The collector system was described as covering an area equal to eight football fields with moving, curved mirrors that track the sun, then focus the sun's rays onto pipes carrying a liquid that converts the heat into steam for use by the mill. North Carolina Governor James Hunt said it would be the third-largest solar-energy system of its kind in the world. As big as it was, it could only supply a third of the heat required to manufacture and dye Cone's output of denim. The project's estimated cost at the time was between $2 million and $3 million, but was expected to be a cost-saving investment for the company.

Secretary of Commerce Luther H. Hodges congratulates Mildred Andrews, executive secretary of the American Textile Machinery Association. She had been selected to serve on the Commerce Department's Trade and Industrial Equipment Mission to The Netherlands (April 1963).

Over the years Cone's denim and Levi Strauss work clothes have become synonymous. In the 1960s-1970s, ragged, bleached-out, woven denim blue jeans became hippie high fashion, and the market widened accordingly. Then in 1980 a slow reversal set in as cheaper imported denims encroached upon the market. At the same time, exports of Cone denims dropped from thirty-three percent of the company's sales to eight percent. Stock prices declined much lower than their book value.

When Caesar Cone, son of one of the founders, was approached by a broker who offered him $50 a share for his holdings, it was tempting to consider such a large profit. Caesar had retired from his mill position as president at the age of sixty-five; he was, in 1983, seventy-two years old, and his only connection with the mill was as a member of the board based on his inherited stock of some 600,000 shares. So he sold his Cone stock for $30 million. Unwittingly, he

Greensboro plants of Cone Mills Corporation in foreground, with the city in background.

handed Western Pacific Industries of New York the lever by which it expected to buy out Cone Mills.

A mighty battle ensued. Dewey Trogdon, the second man outside the Cone family to be president of the company, immediately set in motion a ways-and-means plan to block Western Pacific's takeover. He filed a federal court lawsuit to block further purchases by the stalking company. James Martin, chairman of Ti-Caro of Gastonia, said, "I don't know how he's going to do it, but no one's going to run over Dewey Trogdon." Trogdon was elected president of the North Carolina Textile Manufacturers Association in November 1983, but was too busy saving Cone Mills to go to the annual convention, and so had to accept this signal honor by telephone.

By that time Chairman Trogdon had obtained the backing of ten banks, with Morgan Guaranty Trust Co. named as agent for the group, to finance a loan enabling the mill management and employees to buy out Cone Mills. Then Herman Cone, Jr., who had been inactive in mill affairs for years but remained

Caesar Cone.
President of Cone
Mills until his
retirement in 1976.

a member of the board, resigned his position. He sold his inherited stock, but
not to Western Pacific. Other third-generation members of the family followed
suit. Before the close of 1983, management was able to obtain all outstanding
shares of the company at $70 a share; and in this way Cone Mills changed from
a public company to a privately owned company.

In view of Jeannette Cone Kimmell's active interest in the company's welfare, the new board of directors elected her, the granddaughter of a founder,
as a member although she now owns no stock.

Cone Mills Corp. reported sales of $687.8 million in 1983, a 13.1 percent in-
crease over 1982. Earnings before taxes and unusual expenses were $28.6 mil-
lion, a 39.5 percent increase over 1982. But it had cost Cone $37.2 million in
contributions to the Employee Stock Ownership Plan, $9.5 million in expenses
connected with its reorganization, and $4.3 million related to closing the old
Hillsboro plant and disposing of Union Bleachery in South Carolina—all of
which totaled an $8.8 million loss for this unusual administrative fiscal year.
"Despite those figures, it was an improved operating year," said Trogdon.

In 1983 the company spent $50 million in modernization programming,
which the chairman says will continue on a long-range basis. New fashions in

Dewey Trogdon. Chairman of Cone Mills. He was successful in blocking a takeover attempt by Western Pacific to acquire Cone when he obtained financing to enable management and employees to buy out Cone Mills.

denims have increased consumer demands; sportswear and home furnishings are "up"; and, all in all, Dewey Trogdon and W. O. Leonard (vice-president) believe that the new Cone Mills Corp. is headed for better days than in many years.

Ironically, Levi Strauss & Co., which helped build Cone, closed its Greensboro plant in mid-1984, just as Cone was beginning a new life. The San Francisco-based company blamed imports for higher-than-normal inventories, resulting in decreased earnings, layoffs, and its final closeout.[6]

---

[6]In March 1984 Blue Bell, apparel manufacturers of Greensboro, paid $144.1 million to Lee and Sid Bass of Fort Worth, Texas, to avert a potential takeover battle. The Bass brothers had accumulated three million shares at an average $33 a share, giving them a 23.3 percent stake in the company. Blue Bell bought back the stock for $48 a share, giving the Bass brothers a $45 million profit. "It's a bitter pill," said Edward Bauman, president and chief executive officer of the nation's second-largest apparel maker. This type of operation is called "greenmail" and is sort of a first cousin to blackmail. A bill is pending in Congress to prohibit such tactics (1984).

Greensboro is the base of Texfi Industries, manufacturers of apparel fabrics. After the worst year in its business since the Depression, it rebounded in 1983, and Joseph Hamilton, then president, had a very upbeat attitude about Texfi and its future despite the threat of imports.

In Greensboro is the corporate home office of the giant Burlington Industries, the largest publicly owned textile concern in the nation, founded in the nearby town of Burlington by the late Spencer Love. It is said that during the days of Burlington's mass acquisition plans, Spencer Love could go through a mill and in thirty minutes decide whether or not he would buy it. That probably is true, but he had, as well, a crew of excellent engineers, cost analysts, and market analysts under the direction of Robert L. Huffines, president and head of Burlington's marketing. His crew had for weeks or months studied every possible angle of successful production and profitable marketing for that specific mill before Spencer walked in for the final decision. Joseph Wright II was vice-president and assistant to Bob Huffines at that time. His grandfather, at the turn of the century, had founded the largest textile finishing company in the world. In 1983 Burlington continued its record of profits with a sixty-eight percent increase on a four percent increase in sales.

In the same county is High Point, an internationally known furniture and hosiery center, but only a flag stop for the Crescent. The city's twenty-six textile mills turn out many types of goods, mainly hosiery for men, women, and children. Much furniture shown in its annual "Mart" requires upholstery fabrics, most of which are produced in the Carolinas. Chief among the hosiery manufacturers is Adams-Millis Corp.,[7] with nine manufacturing facilities in five North Carolina locations. It recently announced an agreement-in-principle to acquire Silver Knit Industries and its Drexel Knitting Mills Division and Hayward-Marun at a purchase price of $25.4 million. Silver Knit's earnings after taxes for 1982 were about one-fifth the acquisition price.

Just north of High Point, and on a connecting railroad, is Winston-Salem, home of the Hanes Corporation,[8] founded three generations ago by the Hanes family, who were textile leaders in every sense of the word. Feature stories a few years back described its modern equipment as "ten million needles, each making hundreds of stitches a minute. In 8 hours, one machine could knit enough fabric to stretch to England and back." Such machines are considered obsolete now since newer equipment allows even greater production. The only member of the Hanes family now in an executive position with companies founded by this distinguished family is Philip R. Hanes, Jr., vice-chairman of the board of Hanes Dye and Finishing Co.

---

[7]In mid-1982 Adams-Millis obtained a court order restraining Robert Pace Scholfield, Jr., retired businessman and investor, from buying additional shares of Adams-Millis stock. Already owning $300,000 worth of stock, he planned to purchase 125,000 additional shares, all on borrowed money (approximately $1 million).

[8]Hanes Corporation, consisting of Hanes Hosiery Mills and Hanes Knitting Company, is now a wholly owned subsidiary of Sara Lee Corp. of Chicago.

South of High Point, the train whizzes by the Lexington Division of Park-dale Mills (head office in Gastonia). This mill marks the eastward line of the fine combed sales-yarn industry. Under management of its president, Duke Kimbrell, it has become the largest single unit in the country manufacturing 100 percent combed cotton yarn as well as a 50-50 blend of polyester and cotton combed yarn. Highly modernized, it averages more than 400,000 pounds of combed sales-yarn each week, chiefly for knit goods. Frank Ix and Sons have a plant here too, weaving all types of synthetic filament yarn fabrics. Dacotah Cotton Mills, family-owned for many years, is also located in Lexington, making industrial fabrics.

Sandwiched in between Lexington and the town of Salisbury is Spencer. Anyone familiar with railroad lore knows the town of Spencer. A line from the ballad of "Ole 97" says, "You must put 'er in Spencer on time." During the heyday of railroading, it was the home of the throbbing Southern Railway shops where more than 2,500 men and machines kept steam engines rolling throughout the first two-thirds of the twentieth century. It was named for Samuel Spencer, the Georgia-born railroading genius. He and fellow Georgian John In-

Duke Kimbrell. President of Parkdale Mills, a director of Inman Mills, and former president of the American Yarn Spinners Association.

man, president of the Richmond Terminal Co., rescued the deteriorating Richmond and Danville Railroad and other small, dead-broke railway lines by building them into the Southern Railway system for the financier J. P. Morgan.

Diesel locomotives made the Spencer shops obsolete, but not the name. A new $48 million switching system about ten miles north of Salisbury is now a Historic Trust monument, and there is a museum dedicated at the Spencer Yards in memory of the Southern's greatest hero and railroad network.

Fred W. Morrison was born in Spencer and naturally railroad minded, but his chief business affiliation was with the textile industry. He and his law partner, former North Carolina governor O. Max Gardner, left the state for Washington to form a prosperous law practice about 1932. Among other noted clients they represented was the Cotton-Textile Institute during its founding and halcyon days. Morrison, a gentle, quiet man who prefers to stay in the background, has done much for the industry, for North Carolina and, not incidentally, the University of North Carolina.

Textile mills comprise the major industry of Salisbury, which also profits from granite quarries and iron deposits in the vicinity. The combed-yarn spinning sector of the textile industry continues here with the Rowan Cotton Mills, one of the Gaston County Lineberger group and its neighboring combed-yarn China Grove Cotton Mills. A Cannon sheeting plant is within whistling distance. Salisbury also has one of the finest finishing plants in the South—North Carolina Finishing Company, owned by Fieldcrest.

A little further south, the Southern passes through the small town of Landis where Linn-Corriher Mills has been for many years the town's only mill employer. In days gone by, if one went to Landis to call on old Mr. Corriher, he would quite likely be dressed in overalls, a shirt with no collar but a gold collar button, and wearing a greenish-black aged derby hat. He might be up on the mill's water tank with hammer in hand. "Go on in the office," he'd call down, "I'm just fixin' a leak up here." After a time he'd come down, push his derby back on his head, lean back in his swivel chair, and ask most courteously, "What can I do for you?" He became very wealthy and left the Landis holdings to younger family members, who sold the five plants to Dominion Textile, a Canadian corporation. On the old Crescent's last run, Fred Corriher, a grandson—young, rich, and retired—boarded at Salisbury. He was a nostalgic passenger, helping the club-car attendant, J. McMichael, collect money for drinks and serve fellow passengers.

Kannapolis was not even a flag stop according to the Crescent's schedule, but it always stopped there during Charlie Cannon's days. In the days of heavy railroad travel before the Depression, and when Highway 29 was called the Main Street of the South, a huge, electrically lighted sign was erected on the outskirts of Kannapolis. It could be seen from the train and the highway and proclaimed to all that Cannon Mills Co. made towels and sheets and was the "World's Largest Manufacturer of Towels." In the daytime one could not fail to see it; at night it was lighted by 1,800 incandescent bulbs. During World War II it was blacked out. After the war the sign was changed to read "Leading Manufacturer" in lieu of "Largest," and it was modernized to neon. When

Charles Cannon died in 1971, exactly fifty years since he had taken over the mill after his father's death, the sign was darkened and has been ever since. The Crescent then discontinued its stops to Kannapolis. It was the end of an era.

Three Cannon presidents and eleven years later, in 1982, things started to change. A man named David Murdock came out of the West and found large chunks of Cannon stock for sale. In the past decade Cannon products had slowly become established in the consumer eye as bargain-basement-type goods. Other names in household items had a greater reputation in styling and quality. The mill-owned part of Kannapolis wasn't looking well kept and the interior of the plants looked a little seedy. The company had spent $20.5 million for new equipment in the years 1980-1981, chiefly to meet standards set by OSHA. It sounds like a lot of money, but in these days when one machine may cost $1 million or more, and the company has nineteen manufacturing plants, one wonders how far that modernization went.

In January 1982 the dickering between David Murdock and Cannon's board started when he offered $40 per share for Cannon stock. A few days later, through his Pacific Holding Company, he upped his bid to $44 for each of the 6.8 million shares already offered him and set his limit at $413 million for all of the 9.38 million shares. That included shares in the four trusts and a foundation set up by Charles Cannon. For a number of years, no member of the Cannon family had been active in the mill. Charles's eldest son had been killed in World War II, and his other son had been fired but still remained a member of the board. William Cannon sold out for $4 million, the trustees followed suit, and Cannon Mills became a wholly owned private company before the month was out.

Speculation ran high among industrialists, bankers, mill workers, and indeed the whole textile industry as to what the self-made millionaire from California planned to do with this ninety-five-year-old company that had been the bedrock of Western Carolina for so long.

In the olden days of the wild, wild West, Murdock might have been a two-gun, shoot-from-the-hip guy. Maybe he is in his heart, but his story of personal achievement, astute planning and management belies that. He is a man of many interests and humanitarian instincts. Within a short span of months, people realized that they had nothing to fear. He was not going to gut Cannon; instead, he was "going to put it into the twenty-first century."

David Murdock was born in Kansas City, Missouri, and spent most of his youth on a farm. He attended public schools, but after a year of high school, he dropped out to go to work. He joined the U.S. Army Air Corps right after Pearl Harbor and was a gunnery instructor until World War II ended. A year later he founded the David H. Murdock Development Co., got backing from a bank, and plunged into real estate development and building.

As he built, he acquired companies that made products needed for building. In addition to being sole proprietor of David H. Murdock Development Co. and a privately owned corporation, the Pacific Holding Corp., he is a large investor in a number of publicly held corporations such as Occidental Petroleum. It was as an investor in the future that he bought Cannon Mills. One of the best things about this purchase is that he brought his young associate and attorney, Harold Maximillian Messmer, Jr., with him and made him president of Cannon. Max Messmer's enthusiasm about rebuilding Cannon is equal to that of David Murdock. Together they have already started the ball rolling to upgrade Cannon's twenty plants and thirteen communities scattered through three Southern states.[9]

In 1983-1984 they spent $100 million on new equipment, including twenty-four Murata jet looms, sixty open-end Schlafhorst spinning frames, and the only Reggiani silk-screen printing machine in the United States. The machine costs well over $1 million and is designed electronically so that one technician and three helpers can operate it and print designs on 576 dozen towels per eight-hour shift. It runs three shifts a day, five days a week, but may step up to seven days.

Max Messmer, who was born in Mississippi, grew up and went to college in Louisiana, and earned his law degree in New York. The company is contracting its modernization-expenditures program of $210 million over a five-year period to two years and will settle down to spending a steady $28 million annually. Quality improvement of goods includes 100 percent cotton content, long-staple Pima cotton, and a 50/50 cotton polyester developed by Celanese. The company's ads are proclaiming to the top consumer clientele who read the slick magazines that the most renowned persons are bathing, sleeping, or cooking with Cannon. Its customer line now includes all high-quality household domestics such as closely woven, deeper-pile terry cloth items, 250-square-count percale sheeting, and novelty kitchen decor. These goods are being designed by ten of the most outstanding stylists in the business, including French, Japanese, and American fashion names.

David Murdock, upon his first visit to his new domain, immediately spotted the lack of accommodations for visiting salespersons and buyers. As a builder, he soon had a luxurious and spacious lodge ready for them. It is a twelve-bedroom guest house done with great taste and architectural beauty. The stairway itself is a noteworthy gem of design and craftsmanship; but the greatest gems of the establishment are the talented Guy Ferreri, former assistant manager of the Charlotte Country Club, and his wife, who serve as manager and chef respectively. Lodges for visiting notables are not unusual assets for big Southern mills because most of them are located in the country or small towns. For example, Fieldcrest's lodge was renowned in the trade. Now, with superhighways and their elaborate motel systems, lodges are considered unnecessary.

Murdock and Messmer agree, however, that the Cannon lodge is the greatest selling tool that a major manufacturer and marketer of household textiles

---

[9]See Kannapolis story, ch. 12. Personal interviews with Harold Maximillian Messmer, Jr., president, and Ed Rankin, vice-president of public relations, Cannon Mills.

can possess. Here the customers not only see the goods, they live with them. Murdock predicts that Cannon sales will reach $1 billion, at least, in 1984; thus the company will join the Big Four in that figure: Burlington Industries, J. P. Stevens & Co., WestPoint Pepperell, and Milliken & Co.

To be a successful builder and developer, a person must have vision. David Murdock has that and push: when he wants things done, he wants them done *now*. At first his mill colleagues found his pace frenetic. They no longer do; they have stepped up their own. "How does all of this improvement get done so quickly?" a junior officer was asked. "Well, a couple of decisions are made and then it happens" was the answer. Murdock is used to bossing, and in a loud voice, but he is also capable of relaxed talk. In a casual, get-acquainted conversation with one of the company's security guards, the latter told Murdock that he had worked at the mill for years, having stopped school at the eighth grade to work there. "Well," said Murdock, "I had to stop school at the ninth grade and I've worked hard but now I am a millionaire and paid $413 million for these mills." "Yes, sir, Mr. Murdock, but if you'd gone through the tenth grade, you might not have wanted to do that!"

The half-century-old Cannon sign was torn down in January 1984. It was a safety hazard due to neglect and old age. It was symbolic of bygone times.

The Crescent doesn't stop at Concord, halfway between Kannapolis and Charlotte, but passes some of the oldest mills in North Carolina. One of these is the ancient Randolph Mill, built in 1836 and long abandoned as a manufacturing unit. It is on the National Register of Historic Places and is now part of an $8 million plan to turn it into 166 high-priced condominiums, surrounded by boutiques and professional offices. Its location, twelve acres in the heart of town, makes it an ideal site for the development. The old mill was part of the Odell chain, family-owned mills of prominence for more than 100 years.

A few miles northwest of Charlotte on a Southern connecting line is Mooresville. Here history was made in 1961 when Templon Spinning Mills and Chemspun Yarns launched an expansion program including a new unit to complement production of the other two plants. "It is the plan of the company to hire black workers solely for this new manufacturing unit," said Rufus Dalton, president and chief executive officer of the two mills at the time. "We plan to use an all-black work force with the exception of foreman and plant superintendent. I have great confidence in the ability of black employees to handle the work," he said. Most of the jobs were operating high-tech production equipment and involved considerable training. (Three months is the customary "learner" period.) Only high school graduates were considered for employment. All applications went through the North Carolina Employment Securities Commission. This agency made available a representative one day a week, in the Mooresville courtroom, to process applications.

This was the first Southern, white-owned mill since 1865 to employ voluntarily an all-black operating force and meet all industry standards of work and pay. It was the first mill unit of the textile industry to train blacks to operate modern machines. Later on Rufus Dalton expressed great satisfaction in both the work performed and the attitude of the black force. By 1980 all businesses were operating under Title 7 of the Equal Employment Opportunity Act, passed 2 July 1965.

The only Southern passenger train stops at Charlotte, the nerve center for the most highly industrialized area of the state. The city was once a large textile mill community; now it's a textile-influenced community. The old cotton mills disappeared during the merger and acquisition period that began in the 1940s; abandonment and fires have taken their toll of the old buildings. Chadwick-Hoskins, for example, part of the Gossett mill chain, was sold to Textron of Rhode Island in 1946 along with the twelve other Gossett mills in South Carolina and Virginia.

Ben Gossett, son of the founder, said at that time that he had to sell. "Under the United States tax laws of today, if I should die suddenly, my family would be wiped out. There's no other way, and Textron has offered a good deal." But Ben, who loved the mills and the people who worked there, did not know of Royal Little's proclivity to gut out the industries he purchased. This was Textron's first try in the South. The Gossett name disappeared and the company was named Textron-Southern. It existed long enough to be liquidated at a huge profit to Little.

Around 1880 W. E. Holt, fifth son of E. M. Holt of Alamance, founded the Highland Park Mills in Charlotte with associates J. S. Spencer and C. W. Johnston. From this single mill, a chain of seventeen plants grew under the name of Johnston Mills, a landmark industry for Charlotte. The Johnston Mills Co., once powerful, was merged in 1976 with the Washington Group in Winston-Salem. After considerable litigation between the Washington Group and the Securities and Exchange Commission, the Group's textile mills were sold in 1983 to Bassett-Walker of Martinsville, Virginia.

Many new types of textile companies have sprung up in Charlotte, manufacturing hosiery and knit goods, carpet backing, narrow fabrics and laminates, man-made-fiber textile yarns, nonwovens and batting, spun woolen yarns, and multicolored printed towels (such as Floyd Hansen's Hydro-Prints). One such company, PolyGrinders Corp., a diversified producer of polyethylene compounds for coating textiles, has a 100,000-square-foot facility in the city's Arrowood industrial complex.

Charlotte is the home office of Celanese Corp., a company only sixty years old that was started by Camille and Henri Dreyfus, Swiss brothers who developed acetate yarns.[10] The Celriver plant of Celanese Fibers at Rock Hill, South Carolina, is only about twenty miles away from Charlotte. When the wind blows from the southwest, however, Celriver smells a lot closer.

Textile-machinery builders who are old-time natives of Charlotte include: Parks-Cramer, Terrell Machine Works, and Speizman Industries; the latter makes knit-goods machines and dyeing equipment. Speizman's newest-model knitting machine, the Carolina Amy for production of athletic socks, is respon-

---

[10]On 15 May 1984 Celanese Corp. renamed its Celanese Fibers Operations' Research Park in honor of its founder, Camille Dreyfus. *Charlotte Observer*, 15 May 1984, 14A.

sible for the company's sales increase in 1984, says Morris Speizman, president and founder of the company.

Twelve foreign-owned branches or subsidiaries of textile-machine companies have come to Charlotte, the main shipping point for textile and machinery companies to nearby areas and adjoining states. In January 1984 the North Carolina Ports Authority established Charlotte as the state's first inland port. Ports officials say some shippers can save as much as half their transportation costs to and from the port at Wilmington by using Charlotte's Intermedial Terminal, located on a twenty-three-acre site on the edge of town. Textile machinery and parts, finished and partly finished textile goods and wearing apparel pour into this regional distribution center each week from European and other foreign countries.

E. K. Fretwell, chancellor of the University of North Carolina at Charlotte, wears a railroad engineer's hat all the time, especially when playing golf. "There's nothing like it to keep the sun out of your eyes," he said. A longtime member of the National Railway Historical Society, he has a chronic case of railroad fever. "When I was working at night and I heard that whistle blow at 12:27 A.M., I knew that was the Crescent leaving Charlotte. I'm going to miss it. The idea of the midnight passenger train is part of the folklore of America which is going to be lost."

Charlotte is the terminal for branches of the Southern Railway system that serve the major Southeastern Atlantic ports. One route passes near Lancaster, South Carolina, home of Springs Industries, which was founded in 1887 at Fort Mill by Samuel Elliott White, Colonel Leroy Springs, and fourteen other original shareholders.

Springs Industries was made famous by Leroy's son, Elliott White Springs, a brave and colorful character. An ace in World War I Air Services, he chose, after the war, to amuse himself by such stunts as flying under the Catawba River bridge as well as writing novels and naughty ads about Springmaid cottons. The latter put his inherited mills, wavering on the brink of failure when he took over, in the black. He was an astute businessman who always maintained a humorous side. His Springmaid ads were the best of the time and provide good reading today. In addition, he was a great humanitarian. He believed in the better things of life for family and friends, especially his mill workers.

In his later years Elliott built his second fantastic office at Fort Mill.[11] The exterior of the building is of two successively overhanging floors; the exterior walls, instead of supporting the roof, are suspended from it. All the furniture in the building was made from old mill equipment, an early example of the modern art of today. The executive desks were supported by simulated cotton bales. Chair legs were revolving top-clearers. The wastebasket was an old humidifier; lamps were made of winder cones; and lampshades were made of doffer boxes. The sofa was made of a Draper O-model loom and weighed 1,800 pounds. The hat-rack lamp was part of a crankshaft, boat wheel, and roving

---

[11]See ch. 4, 57–58 for a description of Elliott Springs's first office.

Colonel Elliott White Springs, president of Springs Mills, flies his plane under the Catawba River Bridge.

can. But the real eye-catcher was Elliott's own office where, by some elevator-type contraption, part of the desk sank into the floor. The space became the directors' room with the directors' table rising from below to formal desk level.

Elliott was an unforgettable character and businessman. At his death he was succeeded by H. W. Close, a brilliant executive as well as his son-in-law. He carried on the Springs Mills in an interesting and successful way, modernizing existing plants and building many new ones.

Bill Close was a humanitarian who spent a great deal of his time in efforts to improve the quality of life for Springs workers and their neighbors as well. Foundations and trusts were set up to make all this possible. They include recreation facilities in the mill towns and an unusually fine South Carolina beach resort; health-care facilities; higher-education visual and performing arts opportunities with foundation grants.

During the 75th anniversary luncheon of Inman Mills in South Carolina, Bill Close was paged for an urgent telephone call. The many guests at this important industry affair looked at one another wondering what calamity could have befallen his family. Then a smiling Bill Close returned to the dining room and proceeded to the head table and the microphone. "I think my friends deserve an explanation," he said. "The message informed me that I have a new grandchild. [There was applause.] My daughter, Crandall Bowles, presented me with this sweet package, but Crandall is always in a hurry to get things done; she

Zany outfits were a trademark of Elliott Springs. This photo was taken in front of his home in Fort Mill, South Carolina, and was used for one of his famous ads.

couldn't wait to get to the hospital in Charlotte. She had the baby on the median of Providence Road! She and the baby are doing fine.''

Bill Close died in 1983; Springs is now headed by a professional management team, led by Walter Elisha. Close's daughter, Crandall, took over the nontextile operations as chairwoman of the board and president of the Springs Company and its affiliates, which include insurance agencies; a realty company, property and development companies; three foundations; a newspaper publishing company; and the Lancaster and Chester Railway Company. Through the latter, Elliott Springs's railway-car office was donated to the North Carolina Transportation History Museum, where it is a showpiece among other railroad relics at the Spencer Yards.

Crandall Bowles, great-great-granddaughter of the founder of Springs Mills, is a rare species: an efficient and attractive manager of family assets who is a young and charming Southern belle too.

Gaston County has the largest concentration of combed sales-yarn mills of any area in the country. As the Crescent, on its final trip, left Mecklenburg County and, crossing the Catawba River, entered Gaston, quite a change was

As a gag, Elliott Springs posed as a mill hand in one of his plants, tending this Saco-Lowell picker (c. 1930s).

obvious in McAdenville, Belmont, and adjacent towns. A fresher look, signaling better maintenance than in previous years, is now apparent.

A sleek new edifice near the Catawba bridge at McAdenville belongs to Pharr Yarn Mills. This is an international business owned by the family of the late W. J. Pharr and his wife, Catherine Stowe.[12] Belmont has been solidly held by Stowes and Linebergers since their original mills were built at the railroad watering stop of Garibaldi. Some swapping has occurred in the last few years as the third generations of the two families move over to make way for the fourth. In 1972

---

[12]W. J. Pharr died 2 May 1981 at age eighty-three; he was president of the Southern Combed Yarn Spinners Association, 1944–1945. See ch. 12, 200. On 10 June 1984 Mrs. William James Pharr gave a carillon to the First Presbyterian Church, Belmont, North Carolina, in memory of her husband and dedicated it to the people of the surrounding community.

H. W. (Bill) Close, popular son-in-law of Colonel Elliott Springs. Elected president of Springs Mills following the death of Colonel Springs in 1959. He later served as president of the American Textile Manufacturers Institute.

Climax Spinning Co. (est. 1915), Majestic Manufacturing Co. (1907), Stowe Thread Co. (1928)—all operating 52,000 spindles—and the Belmont Knitting Co. and Belmont Mills, Inc. merged and changed the name of the group to Belmont Heritage Corp. It is one corporation, but the original mill names are on the letterheads. Bill Pharr, a son-in-law of Robert L. Stowe, Sr., in 1959 purchased full control of Imperial Yarn Mills. In 1973 he acquired Sterling Spinning Co. and Crescent Spinning. These three, plus Stowe Mills and Pharr Yarns, are operated by the W. J. Pharr family.

At the turn of the century, A. C. Lineberger, R. L. and S. P. Stowe had joined the Chronicle Mill and its 10,368 spindles in an executive capacity. By 1920 they had organized eleven additional mills, all in combed sales-yarns and with a total of 174,804 spindles. It was the beginning of a textile dynasty. More mills were to follow.

In 1924, when other combed-yarn mills were curtailing, the Lineberger-Stowe mills were expanding. In that year, in order to bypass the converter (a middleman who converts natural yarn to dyed yarn), Belmont Processing Co. was organized to mercerize, dye, and bleach two-ply yarns from several spin-

Crandall Bowles. Great-great-granddaughter of Elliott Springs, she is the chairwoman of the board and president of the Springs Company, which is the nontextile sector of Springs.

ning mills supplying the capital. After a few years of operation, they realized they were competing with their best customer, Aberfoyle Manufacturing Co. So a deal was made to lease Belmont Processing to Aberfoyle on a yarn-purchase plan; and after fifteen or twenty years, Belmont was sold to Aberfoyle, a major mercerizing company.

Then, to diversify a bit more, the Stowe Thread Co. was formed by R. L. Stowe, who was elected president, and S. P. Stowe, who was made vice-president. R. Dave Hall was assistant secretary and treasurer.

By extending these holdings to include Rowan and China Grove, the total of combed-yarn spindles inaugurated by A. C. Lineberger reached 296,452 as of 1979.[13]

There were community activities too. The Belmont Converting Co. was organized by A. C. Lineberger, R. L. Stowe, S. P. Stowe, and associates to provide an ample supply of clean water for the community. This was an early

[13]See ch. 4, 69-71.

The late William J. Pharr, president of Pharr Yarn Mills, was an early manufacturer of long-staple yarns using the shortcut "American System" (as opposed to the French and Bradford Systems).

instance of mills' efforts to improve the environment. The facility is still operated by their heirs.

Sensing the rise of knit goods in the consumer market, Knit Products Co. was built in 1929 by A. C. Lineberger, his son, Henry A. Lineberger, A. F. Dichtenmueller, and S. H. McDonald. They issued $108,000 common and $22,900 preferred shares of stock. The mill had twenty full-fashioned knitting machines for ladies' hosiery, a style greatly in fashion. Later Hatch Hosiery and Knit Products were merged. A. C. Lineberger was president and Henry A. Lineberger was secretary-treasurer.

The Art Cloth Mills, set up to use the new man-made fibers, was started in Lowell, North Carolina, by R. L. Stowe, E. T. Switzer, A. C. Lineberger, and J. B. Reeves, with capitalization of $200,000. This was in rayon's early days, actually before Judson Mills had gone in for rayon weaving in a rather big way. Charles Geer, nephew of Judson's executive officer, B. E. Geer, came from Laurel, Mississippi, to take over management of the mill. He could not make a go of it, however, and it was sold to Beaunit.[14]

---

[14]Beaunit closed its last textile plant, a rayon-filament facility in Elizabethton, Tennessee, in 1978. Others in North Carolina closed after losing money for seven out

S. P. Stowe, Jr.
President of Belmont
Heritage
Corporation.

In 1927 the Geers and A. C. Lineberger, Jr. organized a new mill for a new process of dyeing: Thies Dyeing and Processing Co. in Belmont, with Charles Geer and A. C. Lineberger, Jr. in charge of operations. This was the first time in the South that the Thies method of dyeing packaged yarn was tried. A. C. Lineberger, Jr. assumed management when Geer resigned as manager, and the company was reorganized as Piedmont Processing Co. Spindles were added and, after several years of successful operation, it was merged with Textiles-

of nine previous years: Hamilton, Clinton (purchaser, WestPoint Pepperell), Rockingham (purchaser, Avondale Mills), Statesville (purchaser, an investment group headed by Richard Altman), Lowell (purchaser, Guilford Mills), and Fountain Inn in South Carolina. Beaunit had employed 3,000 persons in the mills and about 200 in its research center in Raleigh, North Carolina. The Elizabethton plant was the last rayon-filament mill in the United States and was sold to a group of stockholders who planned to operate it as North American Rayon Corp.

Inc. (now Ti-Caro). A. C. Lineberger III is assistant vice-president of Ti-Caro, Piedmont Processing Division.

But that was not all. In 1931, the beginning of the Great Depression, South Fork Manufacturing Co. (originally known as Belmont Fabric Co.) was organized by A. C. Lineberger, Henry A. Rhyne of Mount Holly, and D. E. Rhyne of Lincolnton. The mill was to weave spinnable waste from other Belmont mills, an arrangement comparable to "using all the pig except the squeal" except in this case, the squeal was the spinnable waste. Spinnable waste from combed-yarn mills is mostly comber noils and card strips. Since these items were bringing a low price in the waste market in those days and goods woven in this mill were of salable quality, there was opportunity for considerable profit.

The mill had 200 looms and was capitalized at $1 million. Under Henry Rhyne's management, however, it did not prosper. Rhyne was allowed to resign, the looms were taken out and 6,120 spindles and complementary combers installed, just five years after its opening. D. P. Stowe succeeded Henry Rhyne.

A. C. Lineberger had four sons, all of whom succeeded in the textile industry: A. C. Lineberger, Jr., Henry A. Lineberger, J. Harold Lineberger, and Joseph W. Lineberger. A. C., Jr. and Henry died in their middle years. In 1984 Harold, the patriarch of the family, is president and treasurer of Acme Spinning Co.; treasurer of Linford Mills; and president of Belmont Throwing Co., Perfection Spinning Co., South Fork Manufacturing Co., and Rowan Cotton Mills. His only surviving brother, Joe, is president of Linford Mills and Outlook Manufacturing Co., a hosiery mill making ladies' high-style seamless hosiery. He is vice-president of other mills.

Walter S. Lineberger, son of Henry A., is treasurer of Outlook Manufacturing Co. and president of Knit Products Corp., both of which make ladies' seamless hosiery. Clayton Lineberger, younger brother of Walter, is secretary and treasurer of Belmont Throwing Co. Thus, within the Lineberger-Stowe mills group, we have four generations who have followed their fathers' footsteps in founding companies while continuing to manage and modernize the original mills. They have made these mills rank among the greatest producers of combed sales-yarn. Among all the textile-mill groups of 1984, this is one of the few that, from its founding 138 years ago, remains in the hands of the same families.

As David Hall said to a government official some fifty years ago, "We in Belmont are not 'mill barons,' we are hard-working ex-farmers, trying to make a living, and to give a good living to those who work with us." Just ask Raymond Helms, eighty-two years old, who has spent sixty-nine years working in one of the Belmont mills and does not plan to quit. His sharp blue eyes smile kindly through his silver-rimmed glasses; his crisp white hair is neatly combed.

> I came to Belmont from Charlotte when I was thirteen. I was making fifty cents a day in Charlotte and heard Mr. R. L. Stowe was paying $4.50 a week. I figured that was a good raise. I never have left the Chronicle. . . . They didn't ask me to retire when I was 65 so I go in every day and oil the combers. The work is easier now, everything's automatic. I've outlasted two generations of Stowes and

J. Harold Lineberger. President and treasurer of Acme Spinning Company and other Lineberger-affiliated textile companies.

I'm working on the third, Robert Lee Stowe, III. I don't know how long *he's* going to work, but I'm not aiming to quit.

Harold Lineberger and members of his family have long been heavy donors to the North Carolina Textile Education Foundation. Also, a recent editorial in the *Charlotte Observer* noted the generosity of the Lineberger family in giving two million dollars to the University of North Carolina Endowment Fund. One-half the income from the Lineberger gift is to go to professorships in cancer research, one-fourth to strengthen teaching of the humanities, and one-fourth to improving library services. The cancer-research gift enlarges a program begun in 1975 through a family foundation: the Lineberger Cancer Research Fund. This gift to the University of North Carolina establishes benefits that will last for many generations.

The Southern's engineer blew a long wail as the train neared Gastonia, and the engine groaned and sighed as it stopped. It always does, as if remembering how this flag stop was established. Back when railroads were just being laid, the Southern planned to go through Dallas, then the county seat, just five or six miles north. The citizens of Dallas, however, did not wish to be disturbed

Robert L. Stowe III. Chairman of R. L. Stowe Mills, Inc. In the 1986–1987 period, his company acquired the South Fork and Eagle Mills and in 1988 will complete a new, automated spinning plant in Belmont, North Carolina.

by the noise of the train and the nighttime whistle-blowing, so they protested. The Southern, to accommodate them, moved the planned railroad stop to the then unheard-of Gastonia, leaving Dallas to its quietude while Gastonia became the combed-yarn center of the world.

In Gastonia, by 1920, family dynasty mills were clearly formed. There was the Gray-Separk chain. These several mills were owned and operated by children of George Gray, the self-educated textile mill builder, and Joseph Separk, a professor who married George Gray's daughter. There was the Armstrong group of fifteen mills, founded by C. C. Armstrong, one-time clock peddler and three-time sheriff of Gaston County; and the Rankin group, formed by Grady and his brothers. There were also mills founded by the Loves, Rhynes, Ragans, Groves, Dixons, Smyres, Robinsons, and Myers.

During World War I the need for combed sales-yarn increased. In some cases, Gaston County combed yarn was sold before the cotton to be used was planted or the mill was yet in operation. Earnings, actual or estimated, generated new mills. Indeed, in some cases a group would organize one mill in the morning, another in the afternoon, or at least in the same week. By 1920 Gaston County had 103 combed-cotton sales-yarn mills. Huge fortunes had been made and extravagantly spent. Separk made regular trips north to consult Evangeline Adams, the famous seeress, as to his future business moves.

By the end of the decade, New England mills in the fine-yarn business were beginning to fear that their industrial back was broken. With the Crash of 1929 and the beginning of the Depression, the Gastonia bubble burst. However, Gastonia produced one of the largest horizontal mergers of all time in the midst of the Depression. In 1931 the best-known Gastonia combed-yarn mills owned by the Grays, Separk, and the Armstrongs decided to merge into one unit and pool their troubles and assets in order to work out something for the future. Three mills of the Armstrong group withdrew and were sold to the Goldberg brothers, but managed by Clyde Armstrong.

The Rankin group and A. G. Myers and Associates decided to join the merger, and there was great talk of success for the twenty-one plants involved. Each of the top executives of the groups was given a title and a high position. These mills were only the beginning of Textiles, Inc., as it was called. Each mill was on combed yarn. Eventually, Textiles, Inc., with a total of 303,000 ring spindles, represented about twenty-two percent of the total combed-cotton sales-yarn in the South.

Albert G. Myers, who owned the least stock of anyone in the several groups, was a prominent banker who emerged as president after the consolidation was complete. He employed J. C. Roberts of Ernst and Ernst as comptroller. It was soon evident to these two financial minds that the mills' economic position was not only deplorable, but beyond repair, and the group filed for bankruptcy under Chapter XI. Myers was named receiver and Roberts remained as comptroller. Many former executives resigned; their textile fortunes spanned only two other generations.

During the receivership, Textiles, Inc. stock sold for five cents. For $1 one could buy a certificate of twenty shares. The company came out of receivership in 1941 and has prospered ever since. The officers of Textiles, Inc. formed a wholly owned subsidiary, Threads, Inc. Textiles, Inc. acquired Rex Mills, a division of Aberfoyle, in 1963; then in 1968 it acquired Caro-Knit, a knit-fabrics company of Jefferson, South Carolina, followed by the 1972 acquisition of Clyde Fabrics, a producer of fabrics for gloves that is located in Newton, North Carolina. Later in the same year it acquired Piedmont Processing Company of Belmont, North Carolina, a producer of dyed yarns.

In 1978 the name Textiles, Inc. was changed to Ti-Caro because its line of production, which once was only combed sales-yarn, had now expanded into other fields and other regions (South Carolina, Tennessee, and Puerto Rico) and had become a vertically integrated corporation. From 1976 to 1982, Ti-Caro was listed by Ralph E. Loper Co., consulting engineers, as the most profitable of the nineteen largest publicly held textile manufacturing companies in the United States, and fourteenth in size.

It was no surprise to knowledgeable persons in the textile industry when, in early 1984, Ti-Caro's executives announced a proposal for private investors to buy out the company's 8.2 million shares of common stock at $23 a share and

Albert G. Myers. The first president of Textiles, Inc., which subsequently became Ti-Caro.

its 78,000 shares of preferred stock at $25. There were some unhappy stock-holders who filed suit, but in the end (4 May 1984), Ti-Caro announced it had been acquired by a group composed of the current management team, Lazard Freres & Co., and the Equitable Life Assurance Society of the United States.

Under the agreement, holders of common stock would receive $23.12 in cash per share. Preferred stock was priced at $25.28 per share. It also announced a court-approved settlement of the stockholder class action in opposition to the deal. James Fry (who as a young man worked for the American Textile Man-ufacturers Institute in Washington, then as executive vice-president of the American Yarn Spinners Association, then as a vice-president of Ti-Caro) was named president of the company after the $190 million management-led buy-out. Other members of the management group are Albert G. Myers III and thirty-nine additional group, division, and corporate officers. Myers repre-sents the third generation in this conglomerate.[15]

---

[15]Since 1953 the Albert G. Myers Foundation has awarded 184 college scholarships to deserving children of the company's employees.

Parkdale Mills, founded in 1916 by J. Lee Robinson and J. H. Separk, operated with success until the Textiles, Inc. merger. There was quite a squabble then among the stockholders as to whether Parkdale should participate. After Lee Robinson's suicide, the Robinson family finally secured control of Parkdale, refused the merger plan, and turned its management over to Fred L. Smyre, Sr., brother-in-law of Mr. Robinson, who continued its record of success.

Its current president is Duke Kimbrell. Duke, in his fifties now, began his career as an errand boy at Parkdale when he was fourteen. He is a 1949 graduate of North Carolina State University, with a degree in textile engineering. A fast-rising executive, he is a past president of the American Yarn Spinners Association, a director of Inman Mills (South Carolina), and a director of the American Textile Manufacturers Institute.

In recent years Parkdale Mills bought Erlanger Mills of Lexington, North Carolina, Amazon Cotton Mills of Thomasville, and Mauney Mills of Kings Mountain. All were made divisions of Parkdale. Today Parkdale Mills is a privately held company owned by the family of W. Duke Kimbrell, president and chief executive officer, and by George F. Henry, each representing fifty percent ownership of the firm. D. R. LaFar and Associates formed a successful conglomerate of financially troubled out-county yarn mills with headquarters in Gastonia, LaFar's hometown.

A few big outsiders have come to this region with success. Decades ago Firestone bought the Loray, which was bankrupted by Manville-Jenks Co. Among others who tried to buy Gastonia mills were Royal Little of Providence, which in 1927 bought the Carolina Dyeing and Winding Co. By 1957, though, it was out of business. U.S. Rubber Co. established a textile division with two successful mills, but they have now been liquidated.

Other changes in the county's combed-yarn industry, at one time controlled by a small group of mill barons, include the sale of Ragan Spinning Co. (est. 1922), which was sold to J. P. Stevens. Carlton Mills (est. 1922) acquired Cartex, in Salisbury, in 1931. It then had 67,699 spindles. In 1975 it was sold to Standard-Coosa-Thatcher Co. of Chattanooga. Peerless Manufacturing Co. (est. 1906) was Gaston County's smallest cotton mill with only 2,048 spindles. It was sold circa 1982 to Tultex of Martinsville. The Arrow Mills, Gray Mills, Melville Mills, and the Gurney group of spinning mills, once good companies, are closed. However, one novel mill is Rauch Industries, makers of Christmas tree ornaments, bright rayon-filament yarns wound on styrofoam balls. It is a 14.5 million-dollar business; Christmas takes place at Rauch fifty-two weeks every year.

There is another group of importance in Gaston County that should not be overlooked. In 1874 the Mount Holly Mills were built by A. F. Rhyne and D. E. Rhyne. Later the name was changed to Alsace Mills. In 1892 C. E. Hutchison built the Nums Mill; in 1916, the Adrian Mill; and, in 1918, founded the American Processing Co. It was chartered by Hutchison, I. (Ike) C. Lowe, and C. I. Burkholder. Two years later its name was changed to American Yarn and Processing Co. and included Hutchison's other two mills. It was the first warp-processing plant built in North Carolina and was primarily for the mercerizing and finishing of yarns from its own and other mills. It had a capacity in 1936 of mercerizing 200,000 to 250,000 pounds of yarn weekly, considered then an enormous production.

In 1952 American Yarn and Processing of Mount Holly and Efird Manufacturing Co. of Albemarle merged to become the American & Efird Mills. A thirteen-million-dollar corporation operating 144,000 spindles, it is one of the largest producers of combed, carded, and mercerized sales-yarns in the United States. A. K. Winget was named president of Efird Mills in Albemarle, North Carolina. He had been cotton buyer for the Armstrong group in Gastonia for years before it was sold to Gurney/Girard (Goldberg).

Winget was a man of great integrity and strong aversions. In his early business career, around 1910 or so, he clerked for Gastonia's Belk store. For the rest of his life he greatly disliked a prominent Gastonia socialite. One day he confessed why. "She always messed up the ribbon box, and I'd spend hours sorting out the colors," he said. When he joined the Armstrong mills as cotton buyer, he proved to have unusual talent for classing cotton, and the Armstrong group was buying enormous quantities of Delta long staple. A young cotton broker who represented Delta and Memphis cotton firms forgot to invite Winget to his wedding. From that day on, he never sold another bale to an Armstrong mill.

Winget resigned from the membership of the Southern Combed Yarn Association because he had a special distaste for green peas, which were standard fare at the association's luncheon meetings. He rejoined upon the promise that never again would he be offered green peas. He was an outstanding mill executive and became internationally known when serving on the Cotton Arbitration Board of the American Textile Manufacturers Institute.

Active in the formation of the American Yarn and Efird merger was Rush Dickson, prominent in the investment field and a large stockholder in the merged company. After his company, Ruddick Corp., acquired American & Efird, the Efird mill was sold to Union Underwear Co. Alan Dickson, Rush's son, is now chairman of the board of American-Efird . The company purchased Groves Thread Co., a family-owned mill established in 1916.

Speeding south, one can see historic Kings Mountain from the windows of the Crescent. A good-sized textile company there, the Neisler Mills, owed its beginnings to the Southern's luxury dining cars. It happened this way. In 1894, Charles E. Neisler, Sr. became superintendent of Andrew Mauney's Mauney Mills, but in 1910 he left to build the Pauline, his first mill. Shortly thereafter, he and Mr. Mauney went to Kings Mountain to call on a man named Jenkins who operated a whiskey business near the Revolutionary War battlefield. They told Jenkins they had secured a fine lifetime contract from the Southern Railway to provide tablecloths and napkins for its luxurious dining cars. Neisler intended to build a cotton weaving mill with Crompton & Knowles Jacquard looms, use the cotton yarn from Mauney's mill, and make the finest cotton damask for napery. All he needed was a loan of $10,000.

Old Mrs. Jenkins was listening to the talk and watching her "old man" shakin his head in a negative fashion. She "wanted in" on the deal. She hauled a crockery jug—not as big as a churn, but on that order—from the kitchen,

Rush Dickson. Chairman of the board of American-Efird Mills and Ruddick Corporation until his death.

and it was full of coins. She stood by the table and counted out $10,000 in gold to invest in the new mill. This was coin minted by the Swiss family Bechtler[16] from gold mined in Carolina before the California gold rush and hoarded by her family for many, many years. So Neisler built the Pauline Mill, installed 400 Crompton & Knowles Jacquard looms, and supplied the Southern Railway with napery until Amtrak switched to paper napkins. During World War II, under government contract, Neisler mills supplied the Navy with table linens and developed military fabrics of strategic use.

From that beginning, Mr. Neisler and his five sons built the Margrace and the Patricia, and acquired the Belmont, the Mayo, and the Palmetto in Pageland,

---

[16]Swiss miners who were licensed by the U.S. government in 1834 to assay gold and mint coins of locally mined gold. The Bechtler Mint was the only significant private assay and gold-minting operation in America until the 1848 California gold rush. It produced the first gold dollar in America, a currency not issued by the U.S. Mint until seventeen years after the Bechtler dollar was struck. The Bechtlers returned to Switzerland very rich and invested their gold in money-making ventures and art. Today Andreas Bechtler has returned to North Carolina to head some family-owned textile-electronic-equipment companies located in Charlotte.

Alan Dickson.
Current chairman of
the board of
American-Efird Mills
and president of
Ruddick Corporation.

South Carolina. They also had a mill at Ellenboro, North Carolina. These mills specialized in upholstery, drapery, and bedspread fabrics. Of course, they started using man-made fibers for the latter, although they stuck to fine-combed cotton for table napery.

The Neislers sold their seven textile plants in 1955 to Ernest and George Horvath, who had previously acquired textile holdings in New England. The Horvaths became heavily involved financially with the Teamsters Union, borrowing at least $4 million from them. The Teamsters spun off or sold the mills without regret for displaced workers. The Neisler family is now no longer connected with the mills, but a granddaughter cherishes one of the Southern's damask napkins.

The Crescent feels at home as it pulls into South Carolina. It is in the land of its forefathers. The first locomotive built in America for actual service on a railroad was The Best Friend. In 1830 Nicolas Darrell became the first locomotive engineer on the first commercial railroad, the South Carolina Canal and Railroad Co. Later a notice in the *Charleston Mercury* (7 December 1830) stated, "The locomotive will start from the Lines at one and half past three this afternoon with cotton and cars for passengers." The railroad eventually extended 106 miles from Charleston to Hamburg (a village across the river from the cotton mills of Augusta and close to William Gregg's mills at Graniteville, South Carolina). The railroad later was extended to points west and was known as the Louisville, Cincinnati & Charleston Railroad Co.

After the railroad's destruction during the Civil War, its owners attempted to rebuild and extend the line west, north, and south as the South Carolina and Georgia Railroad. The venture encountered great financial difficulties and was acquired by the Southern Railway Co. around 1890 but remained a separate corporation. In 1902, along with several other lines, it was consolidated to form the Southern Railway-Carolina Division and leased to the Southern for 999 years.

Passing Rock Hill, one sees the first mill of M. Lowenstein & Sons, a New York selling house that came to the Sunbelt. Ninety years ago, Morris Lowenstein and his brother, Abram, founded a small textile-marketing business in New York. Their merchandise consisted mainly of fabrics. Morris's young son, Leon, started to work for the firm when just a lad, and by the time he was eighteen, the business had grown to the point where their initial headquarters was too small. They moved to larger quarters, which they shortly outgrew, so they rented the empty store next door. Leon's father handed him a sledge hammer and told him to get busy and knock out the walls between the two buildings so they really could enjoy the expansion. The company of M. Lowenstein & Sons was incorporated in 1918. Sixty-five years later it had twenty-five divisions as well as a number of affiliates and joint ventures.

In the early days of the company, the Lowensteins found there was money to be made as a jobber buying firsts and seconds, fabrics with slight flaws that could not be delivered to regular garment cutters. However, these fabrics could fill a demand from household users or even large-order cutting houses, since they could easily use cutting patterns that evaded the defect. The Lowenstein philosophy was, "Where there is cotton cloth, there is a market."

Leon became a full partner after he had turned twenty-one and finished two years at the City College of New York. He worked hard and saved every penny for the company. Once, arriving in a large city on a sales trip, he checked into a fine hotel, rather pleased to be able to afford it. At the end of the day, he had received not a single order. Finally, his last customer offered $6^3/_4$ cents per yard for a fabric that should sell at 7 cents. Leon took the order, then promptly checked into a cheaper room to save the $1/_4$ cent he had lost on the deal. The company passed the million-dollar mark in 1909, and in 1918 was incorporated with a net worth of $2.7 million.

In the meantime, Leon had joined the Army and went to officers' training camp. World War I ended too soon for him to face combat in his family's native land. "It was just as well," he said, "our family of emigrants had found fortune and friends in the United States, and it was their adopted country."

It was about this time that Leon decided the only sure road to success for his jobbing company was by means of vertical integration. He wanted to build a bleachery, dyeing, and finishing plant in the South. He persuaded Archie

Joslin, lawyer by training and textile finisher by avocation, then working at the Imperial Printing and Finishing Co. in Providence, to join his company.

They chose Rock Hill, where there was electric power, water, efficient labor, and the Southern Railway. They erected a plant that would employ 500 people and could be expanded to 800 employees. Rock Hill Printing and Finishing Co. is now known throughout the industry as one of the largest plants in that line of business, with more than two million square feet, printing machines and screen printers, and all auxiliary equipment.

Lowenstein's next step into the Sunbelt textile field was in January 1946 when he bought the greige-goods mill at Huntsville, Alabama, that was owned by the Merrimack Manufacturing Co. of Massachusetts. This was during the restricted years of World War II when government priorities limited shipments for consumer use. In June 1946, just six months later, he acquired control of the Entwistle Manufacturing Co. in Fayetteville, North Carolina. He changed the name of the mill from Entwistle to Aleo Mills. Four of Lowenstein's merchandising subsidiaries—Classic Mills, Plisse Corp. of America, Lenworth Corp., and Wearever Fabrics Corp.—were merged with Aleo and operated as a division of Lowenstein.

In 1947 Lowenstein acquired Hamrick Mills and Limestone Mills along the railroad in Gaffney. These became known as Limestone Manufacturing Co. and Summit Manufacturing Co. In 1952 Lowenstein sold its subsidiary, Kerchiefs, which was soon liquidated. It was the last of the quality handkerchief producers in the United States. Kleenex put them out of business. None may be found today on the retail market, except for imported items.

Lowenstein's Southern mills make fabrics and household goods using the name of once-great New England companies. In 1954 Wamsutta, that famous and wonderful New Bedford fine combed-yarn fabric mill, was sold to Lowenstein. The mill was liquidated except for the prestigious name; its machinery was shipped south. Wamsutta products are now made by Lowenstein at Wamsutta I and II mills in Anderson, South Carolina. Both new plants have a total of half a million spindles and nearly 1,000 looms.

During 1955 Lowenstein purchased the great Pacific Mills. Four of these mills were from the Parker Group located in Columbia. They also operate a finishing plant at Lyman and a large research and development organization there and at Anderson. Lowenstein also owns the Orr-Lyons Mills at Anderson. All of these concerns are on important connecting lines of the Southern.

In 1960 Lowenstein built its first fiberglass factory at Anderson in cooperation with R. F. Clark and J. P. Schwebel. It is equipped with new machinery engineered specifically for fiberglass weaving and shipping.

Fiberglass fabrics are utilized in reinforced plastics, aircraft electrical insulation, filtration of dust and aluminum, and a great many other uses that require insulation from heat, cold, or fire. Research has not been left out of the

Lowenstein plan of vertical integration. Lowenstein has an additional plant in Alabama and one in Georgia.

It is a New York company that moved into the South by acquisition or new mills. Its sales office, however, is in New York. That's where the buyer goes and the money flows, where style and fashions may change overnight because, by and large, they are made on Seventh Avenue. M. Lowenstein & Sons Co. is a firm that tried the vertical game and made it a successful venture, modernizing equipment and increasing sales as it went.

The Southern whizzes by Gaffney, a mill town populated with branches of companies such as Milliken, Montgomery, Lowenstein, and the surviving mill of the Hamrick family. These mills make print cloths and sheetings. Soon the Southern is in Spartanburg, headquarters of two great companies, Milliken & Co. and the Montgomery family's Spartan Mill chain. The former has twenty-seven plants in North Carolina, South Carolina, and Georgia in its Menswear and Fine Goods Division; seventeen in the three states in its Fashion Fabrics Division; twelve in the three states in its Industrial Division; and six in its Home Furnishings Division, located in La Grange, Georgia.

Milliken & Co. is the largest solely family-owned company in the textile world. All of this has come about since Roger Milliken, described by Frank Bennett of *America's Textile Reporter* as the "fair-haired boy of the textile industry," moved south in the 1940s. He has firmly established this three-state dynasty through astuteness and constant modernization. The Milliken Research Center in Spartanburg is the finest facility of its kind anywhere and has developed outstanding new methods in textiles, most of which are being used by Milliken & Co.[17]

Spartanburg is also the home of Walter Montgomery, Sr. and his family-owned and operated mills. For many years they were associated with Seth Milliken of the well-known New York textile-selling house. The story of the Montgomerys, pioneers in the first "build mills" movement, has already been reviewed (see chapters 4, 5, and 11). In 1983 Walter Montgomery, Sr., patriarch of the Montgomery clan, was named Textile Man of the Year.

Just northwest of Spartanburg is the Chapman family-owned Inman Mill, built in 1901, along the right-of-way of the railroad connecting Spartanburg and Asheville. It was the first mill to be built north of the Southern, and was named for John Inman, who was president of the Tennessee Coal, Iron and Railway Co. He was called by some the "Southern Carpetbagger of Wall Street." He built the connecting line from Spartanburg to Asheville, conveniently including a stop at Inman. This line was later part of the Southern Railway network.[18]

James Chapman, son of the founder, never used the term "Jr." He died in 1964 and was succeeded by his son, James III, who was known as James, Jr. This splendid man, who had all the qualities of his father and grandfather, made an outstanding success of the family mills, Inman and Riverdale. James Chapman, Jr. was dedicated to making the industry a better place for people to work

---

[17]See ch. 11, 183-84.

[18]See ch. 4, 71.

and a better place for business to work successfully. Once when questioned as to reasons for Burlington's closing the great F. W. Poe Co., a Greenville-based company, Jim said: "Burlington is a huge company. It had modernized the plant, but Burlington tends to close a mill when a family would not."

Jim didn't spend his time in the office and boardroom. As one friend said of him, "It was a pleasure to walk through the mill with him. Occasionally he would stop to take off a 'roll lap' or piece-up an end, but he always had a smile for everyone who walked by." He served as president of the South Carolina Textile Manufacturers Association and was nearing the close of his term as president of the American Textile Manufacturers Institute when he died in 1983 of cancer at the age of sixty-two. Under his presidency, ATMI inaugurated an industrywide program to label all textile-industry products, household goods, industrial goods, and wearing apparel with the emblem "Crafted with Pride in USA." This was a campaign to fight increasing textile imports at the grass roots, the consumer level; and under the strong leadership of Jim Martin—chairman and ceo of Ti-Caro, who moved up to the presidency of ATMI following Jim Chapman's death—the program gained widespread support throughout the country.

James A. Chapman, Jr. was serving as president of Inman Mills and of the American Textile Machinery Institute at the time of his death in 1983. His brother Marshall succeeded him as president.

Jim Martin, chairman
and ceo of Ti-Caro,
Inc.

Greenville is one of the most important textile sites where the Crescent stops. Not many years ago, passenger trains on the Southern were so timed that an executive could board the train in the morning in Charlotte, have a comfortable air-conditioned ride to Greenville, conduct business over lunch at the Poinsett, and take the late-afternoon train back to Charlotte. The passenger trains also had day coaches for the less-affluent.

That was in the days when railroad depots had "White" and "Colored" waiting rooms. One top textile person returning to Charlotte on a hot summer day found the "White" waiting room crowded, stuffy, and full of noisy and screaming children. After a long day's conference, he needed peace and quiet. The "Colored" waiting room was empty and the ceiling fan inviting, so he settled in comfortably to read the paper before the train arrived. Soon a uniformed railroad official came in and said, "I fear you have made a mistake. This room is for Colored." "I'm comfortable," said the executive, "I prefer to stay where it's cool and quiet." "You may, but at your own risk," said the official. "To hell with it," sighed the executive, and resumed his reading. Today most passenger depots all along the line have been abandoned or moved out of the city to the freight yards, where a ticket counter in a bare room and a parking lot replace the old-time accommodations.

Greenville is the headquarters of J. P. Stevens, the second-largest publicly held company in the industry, ranking next to Burlington.[19] For two decades the industry had watched Stevens, with seventy-five plants throughout the South, struggle with unionism. It started when Stevens bought Roanoke Rapids' seven plants, including a subsidiary apparel company. The conflict became a hot subject for the media, especially when some churchmen, the governor of Maine, a hostile Massachusetts legislature, the Los Angeles city council, the mayor of Atlanta, and the governor of New York went on record urging their respective constituents to boycott Stevens products. A mile-long human billboard in New York protested against Stevens. Pro-Stevens parades were held in mill towns by SPFF, Stevens People and Friends for Freedom.

The feeling was high and bitter on both sides. Suits and countersuits were filed, and a small victory for the Amalgamated Clothing and Textile Workers Union (ACTWU) was obtained after seventeen years, with the signing of a contract with Stevens covering only ten plants, seven in North Carolina. The boycott campaign had cost the union $5 million a year. Stevens reported a net loss in 1980 of $36.6 million; but despite the boycott effort, sales were $1.457 billion for the first three-quarters of the year, up some $45 million. The boycott was a failure because consumers like Stevens's products and admired the company's resolve.

In 1980 Whitney Stevens, great-great-grandson of Nat Stevens, the founder, became the company's president and chief executive officer. In 1983 Stevens and the ACTWU and the National Labor Relations Board negotiated a comprehensive agreement to resolve all remaining labor charges and related court cases. This finally concluded the long, drawn-out, and bitter battle between the union and Stevens, the company that had been labor's primary organizing target in the textile industry.

Early in 1983 it appeared that Gulf and Western might attempt a leveraged buyout with its 3.97 million shares, or twenty-two percent, of Stevens's outstanding eighteen million shares. Quick action on the part of Stevens regained the shares of $96.7 million in what was described as the sixth-largest New York Stock Exchange transaction in its 114-year history. In May 1984 J. P. Stevens purchased 914,000 shares of its stock from an unidentified seller in a move to forestall another buyout plan. So-called "insiders" owned only one percent of Stevens stock; its pension plan owned another six percent.

Another company that has brought textile renown to Greenville is Riegel Textile Corp. A manufacturer of upholstery and apparel fabrics, athletic wear and disposable diapers, Riegel has kept up modernization at a rate of about $20 million a year, and according to its chairman, Robert Coleman, Riegel remains committed to modernization. In May 1984 Riegel announced it had approved in principle a $140 million buyout at $35 a share by management and Wesray Corp., a New Jersey-based investment group headed by former U.S. Treasury

---

[19]See ch. 8, 132; ch. 9, 143; ch. 11, 186-87.

Whitney Stevens. Great-great-grandson of the founder of J. P. Stevens, he serves as chairman and ceo of the company.

Secretary William Simon. A month later Riegel announced that the deal was off and offered no explanation.

United Merchants & Manufacturers maintains divisional headquarters in Greenville, and a number of other companies have offices there with mills in nearby towns. Reeves Bros. has fifteen mills along the Southern's route from Buena Vista, Virginia, to Eastman, Georgia. Just south of Greenville is the small town of Easley, but it is big in mills. There are five mills of the McKissick family—leading industrialists since Captain Ellison Smyth, the great-grandfather, established the domain that passed to his daughter's children. Also at Easley is one of the Mayfair Mills, whose president and treasurer is Frederick Dent, a former U.S. secretary of commerce.

And so the Crescent whistles on its way to Georgia, stopping at Gainesville, home of the Chicopee Mills, makers of surgical gauze and industrial synthetic woven fabrics. This is another Northern company that moved south.

Atlanta is the hub of the South. According to today's airlines, to get anywhere, one goes to Atlanta first. It was the same way during the prosperous heyday of passenger trains, especially when traveling salesmen were drumming up trade.

Robert Coleman. President of Riegel Textile Corporation and former president of the American Textile Manufacturers Institute.

A connecting railroad line takes one to Macon and its big mills; another takes one to Columbus and south to West Point where the far-flung WestPoint Pepperell empire is headquartered. Its thirty-eight plants extend up and down the valley of the Chattahoochee, the river dividing Alabama and Georgia.[20]

Columbus is the home of Swift Textiles, which began life in 1882 as Excelsior Mills and recently celebrated its 100th anniversary under the name Swift.

The Crescent continues from Atlanta to Birmingham, home of the Avondale Mills and the Comers who live mostly in Sylacauga,[21] and arrives finally at New Orleans. Atlanta was the starting place for the postbellum industrialization of the South, and it's the stopping place for this narrative. We get off here.

Many good mills and interesting stories could not be included because of space limitations. There are many case histories indicating a continuity of Southern development and the determination of the people who worked to make it possible with their frailties, foibles, and genius.

---

[20]See ch. 4, 65-66.

[21]See ch. 4, 59-60, 73-75.

Ellison McKissick, Jr. Chairman and ceo of Alice Manufacturing Company. He served as president of the American Textile Manufacturers Institute during 1985-1986 and received the Man-of-the-Year award at the annual meeting of the textile section of the New York Board of Trade in November 1987.

History moves fast when one is living it. Now 103 years have passed since Atlanta's International Cotton Exposition kicked off the "build mills" drive. This century has seen the explosive growth of Southern textile mills. There has been financial struggle and success, reorganization, changes in raw materials and finished goods, depression and recovery, war and peace—and each has had its impact on the textile industry. The mills have brought about social changes, community development, better communications and industrial relations, and challenges from competitors (once Northern, now overseas). But all these developments have combined to create a more vibrant Sunbelt.

Passenger days may be over for the railroads, but as long as there are textile mills strung along the rails, the railroads will survive hauling freight. With continuing demand by the mills for new models of advanced machinery and a growing market for fibers of all types, there should be sufficient business to keep the railroad and trucking lines busy and healthy for many years.

An editor of the *Charlotte Observer* wrote in 1984, "Capitalists Have Returned to the Mills." He's wrong. They were always there and still are. Opportunity, from the beginning, is there for any mill worker, floor sweeper, or electronic engineer to climb to the top and make a fortune. In his heart, everyone plans to be a capitalist. Southern textile mills will continue to show the way. The climate is very good.

EPILOGUE

"He that wishes to be counted among the benefactors of posterity must add, by his own toil, to the acquisition of his ancestors."[1]

Recently Mercer University Press invited me to update this book, which was completed by the author just prior to her death in October 1984. The publisher's perception that so much has happened since that time, involving technological advancements and corporate reshuffling, warrants that an epilogue be written updating the book.

Since the author's primary asset was her personal experience in working closely with many of the men who shaped the industry in her lifetime, my only purpose is to inform the reader of the important developments that have occurred between October 1984 and the end of 1987. As one whose profession was rooted primarily in textile-machinery marketing over a period of twenty-five years but whose course was reset in the field of mergers and acquisitions during the past sixteen years, I hope that Mrs. Andrews would have approved the decision to have me add this epilogue.

The invitation to write this piece arrived at an appropriate time because the author would have been traveling—as I just did—to the International Textile Machinery Exposition. She not only attended but directed many of the machinery exhibitions in the past. As executive director of the American Textile Machinery Association, she had managed exhibitions on behalf of the American firms at Atlantic City, New Jersey; Greenville, South Carolina; Milan, Italy; Hannover, Germany; and Basel, Switzerland. In the introductory chapter of her book, she sets the scene at the first International Cotton Exposition in Atlanta, Georgia; hence it would seem a fitting finale to describe the most acclaimed and far-reaching textile-machinery exposition ever staged: the International Textile Machinery Exhibition at Paris, France, in October 1987.

After commenting on the technical advances exhibited in Paris and their potential impact on the future of the American textile industry, I would then like to note some of the many mergers and buyouts that have continued to reshape the industry since the author passed away. Finally, I will list the names

---

[1]George S. White, *Memoir of Slater and History of Manufactures* (1836) 71.

of those friends of Mrs. Andrews who were mentioned in the book as being active at the time of her death but have since died also, turning over the reins of their companies to others.

THE INTERNATIONAL TEXTILE MACHINERY EXHIBITION

Among the bustling crowds that jammed the 1,300,000 square feet of floor space at ITME 1987, it was said—and often repeated—that the Paris exhibition was to a textile executive like a giant toy store to a child. Whether a visitor came to the show to view a specific machine or process such as weaving or dyeing, most agreed that the long and expensive trip to Paris was more than rewarding. Indeed, those to whom I spoke came away with a feeling of excitement and wonder.

Due to the enormity of the show and the countless numbers of machines on exhibit, it was virtually impossible to visit every exhibitor's booth and judge where the longest technological leaps had been made. Still, teams of reporters from the various textile publications and staff members of the large textile schools poured through the halls, lifting machine covers where possible, recording published data, and interviewing exhibitors. Thanks to their thorough work, the month of November saw a flood of articles by the trade press and the establishment of seminars by textile schools aimed at highlighting various processes and providing an overview of the show.

Realizing that I might have missed some important development, I signed up to attend the seminar sponsored by the School of Textiles at North Carolina State University. It consisted of two fast-moving days kicked off by Dean Robert Barnhardt and followed up by four members of his faculty who must have stayed at the show from the opening to the final bell ten days later, judging by the immense amount of data they brought home with them.

This epilogue cannot attempt to document all the many technological advances shown in Paris. Rather, at some future date, someone will probably write a lengthy book covering the show and its impact on the American textile industry. It is proper, however, to make a few general observations on what has happened technologically since Mrs. Andrews completed her book and on how these developments might affect the face of the textile industry in future years.

As Dean Barnhardt correctly pointed out in his opening remarks at the Raleigh seminar, "The textile industry is in the midst of a technological revolution. Concepts that were radical departures a few years ago such as in-process machinery linkage, artificial intelligence, and on-line quality and process control are in fact a reality." At the author's death, these things were in prototype stages only, but today they appear ready for the market. New terms relating to job responsibilities and manufacturing processes are slipping into popular usage: terms like robotic vision, computer-integrated manufacturing (CIM), computer-aided design (CAD), and bidirectional communication. To an old-timer who is accustomed to talking in terms of hanks, doffs, and ends down, these new terms are mind boggling to me!

The new developments will no doubt have significant implications for the U.S. textile industry. Mill owners will need to staff their plants with people having new and different skills. For example, in past years the industrial engineer assigned to the mill's payroll usually kept himself busy determining pay rates for a given job, working out process specification, and determining manufacturing components of production costs. Today, with much fewer operators in the plant, there is little need for rate determination. Process-performance data are now available on-line, and with modern computer softwear, cost data can be displayed instantaneously.

Already now, a number of the more modern, fiercely competitive American mills have installed computer-controlled equipment and are bar-coding their products to maintain more efficient levels of inventory. Process-linked machinery—which, for example, links the spinning process to the winding process—is on order and will be operational in the U.S. by 1988. When I began work in the industry in 1945, there were eleven processes between the bale and finished yarn. The more modern mills had narrowed the number of these processes to just four by 1986; and ITME 1987 flashed signs that there is hope for narrowing this number to one or two before ITME 1991, scheduled for Hannover, Germany.

While excitement was in the air for most of those who attended the exhibition, I felt a certain sadness as I remembered earlier years when large American companies dominated the exhibitions. When these shows—which occur every four years—were started in 1951 at Lille, France, in an exposition hall containing 115,000 square feet of floor space, the exhibitors were primarily American, British, and Swiss—with American technology standing at the forefront.

At the Paris show, 85 percent of the floor space was occupied by the Europeans—mostly German exhibitors who were barely in evidence at the 1951 show. On the other hand, the large American machinery companies such as Whitin, Draper, Crompton Knowles, Barber Colman, Leesona, and others were missing either because they have been acquired or redirected into other product lines. Saco Lowell, a dominant American player in earlier years, was at the Paris show by virtue of the fact that it was acquired by John D. Hollingsworth, Inc. of Greenville, South Carolina.

At the time Mildred Andrews was running the American sector of the exhibitions in the 1960s, she was associated with an industry in its prime. In 1960 U.S. textile-machinery makers supplied ninety-three percent of the domestic market. In 1987, for the first time, imports captured more than fifty percent of the U.S. textile-machinery market. When the final tally is in for 1987, it is expected that U.S. textile companies will have spent a record $2 billion outfitting their plants.

To many industry observers, it is a moot question whether the majority of the remaining American textile-machinery firms can survive foreign competition in the future. Dame Hamby, who retired in 1987 as dean of the North Carolina State School of Textiles, was quoted in the 7 December 1987 issue of the *Charlotte Observer* as saying: "I'm not sure we'll ever get back on top in all areas. To do so would require a leapfrog in technology. I don't think we'll be able to do it." The same article reports that "virtually no state-of-the-art weaving and spinning machines are made in the United States anymore. Few of the major

U.S. machinery manufacturers are left. Employment has steadily declined from 32,700 workers in 1972 to around 15,500 today."

But all is not doom and gloom according to Harry Buzzerd, Jr., executive vice-president of the American Textile Machinery Association in Washington, D.C. He disagrees with the current pessimistic forecasts and rightly points out that several American companies—such as John D. Hollingsworth and Gaston County Dyeing Machine Company—are offering state-of-the-art machines with large backlogs of orders in their particular fields. Part of his enthusiasm and optimism stems from the fact that this summer the members of his association launched "Campaign Springback," which is designed to help the industry recover lost ground. At about the same time, he received news that the federal government had approved a $195,000 grant for further research. Then, too, he holds out hope that a textile-machinery modernization bill recently introduced in Congress will pass, generating $10 million annually from tariffs levied on foreign-machinery imports. Whether all these aggressive steps can rebuild the textile-machinery industry to a competitive level remains to be seen.

RESHAPING THE TEXTILE INDUSTRY
THROUGH MERGERS AND ACQUISITIONS

Chapter 11 speaks of the "merger fever" that spread throughout the textile industry over a fifty-year period beginning in the mid-1930s and was interrupted only by World War II. But Mrs. Andrews would have been shocked, I believe, had she lived long enough to witness some of the huge mergers and acquisitions that have taken place since her death. Giant corporations like Burlington, Cannon, Collins & Aikman, Avondale, and others have either merged or have been bought out by other companies or management groups. At the same time, smaller but well-known lesser companies—who were considered modern with strong balance sheets—have been gobbled up by determined pursuers who must have been driven in part by the same conviction that drove Samuel Slater more than 200 years earlier. Entrepreneurial acquirers like Duke Kimbrell of Parkdale, Stephen Felker of Avondale, R. B. Pamplin of Riegel, Joseph Ely II of Fieldcrest Cannon, Dewey Trogdon of Cone, Joe Lanier, Jr. of WestPoint Pepperell, Erwin Maddrey of Delta Woodside, and Dan Frierson of Dixie could be those, among others, who have through their own toil added to the acquisition of their ancestors.

Such men have changed the makeup and profile of the industry. Whereas Burlington, Milliken, and J. P. Stevens were major companies in the industry for many years, only Milliken today has the dominant image that was enjoyed by all three during a forty-year period. Being a private company, Milliken publishes no information about its sales, earnings, or net worth. Yet it is obvious to all industry watchers that the company remains strong and profitable. How else could it continue to spend millions each year to update its well-maintained plants with the latest technology while generously supporting community projects in the area where its plants are located?

As for Burlington and Stevens, they present case histories that would seem ideal material for business-school studies. Both companies were highly successful and aggressive acquirers of other mills following the end of World War II, but in 1985 the management of J. P. Stevens & Co. made a decision that appeared diametrically opposed to the management philosophy of Burlington. It decided to spin off divisions that it felt were too marginal for its own purposes but might be able to prosper in a more entrepreneurial environment. Therefore, it sold its finished fabrics and Stevcoknit divisions to Alchem Corp. (now Delta Woodside Industries) and spun off its narrow fabrics and woolen and worsted divisions to management groups, thereby sharply streamlining the company.

At the same time Burlington pursued acquisitions, paying $115.9 million for C. H. Masland & Sons (a carpet manufacturer), a price of 2.9 times the book value and 16.89 times earnings. W. T. Grimm and Company, one of the oldest firms specializing in mergers and acquisitions, reported in its 1986 edition of *Mergerstat and Review* that the Masland price of 16.89 times earnings compared with an average multiple of 14.4 times earnings paid by other textile acquirers. In more stark contrast, an investor group led by George A. Swift acquired Columbus Mills, another large carpet manufacturer, at a price of 12.8 times earnings and a premium over book value of only 1.4.[2] At the same time Burlington was unsuccessful in finding buyers for its weaving operations at Post, Texas, and Asheville, North Carolina.

Using part of the cash generated by the sale of its various divisions, Stevens acquired the sheeting and bath-products division of Burlington which, when added to its own lines, made Stevens a major competitor in the domestics field. That transaction, completed in February 1986, poured $110 million into the coffers of Burlington and no doubt eased its capability to pay a premium for C. H. Masland & Sons. Hindsight reveals, however, that it might have been better to reserve the money in preparation for what many view as the bitterest and costliest war ever to be fought over the control of a textile company.

When the top officials of the American textile industry gathered on 8 April 1987 at the Fairmont Hotel in New Orleans for the annual meeting of the American Textile Manufacturers Institute, the usual conviviality was evident. Members checked their invitation lists to the various parties staged each year by the big suppliers of money, fiber, and technology; there was no hint that one of the registered guests, Tom Bell (chairman and ceo of Dominion Textiles), was about to stage a takeover attempt of the largest textile company in the United States: Burlington Industries. Burlington's previous chairman, William Klopman, and current chairman, Frank Greenberg, as well as Don Hughes, executive vice-president and chief financial officer, were all registered for the meeting, indicating they had no forewarning of what was about to happen.

On the very day that guests were checking in the hotel, an obscure published report appeared in the financial press stating that a group headed by Dominion Textiles and New York financier Asher B. Edelman had acquired 4.9 percent of Burlington's stock and was considering a possible takeover.[3] The next

---

[2]*Mergerstat and Review* (Chicago: W. T. Grimm & Co., 1986) 139.

[3]*Daily News Record*, 12 September 1987, 12.

day none of the Burlington officials was to be found anywhere, and the rumor that Dominion and Edelman were making a bid for Burlington spread like wildfire. It was not until 24 April that the general public received confirmation of what was happening.

On that date the Edelman-Dominion partnership, called Samjens Partners, filed with the SEC disclosing that they had accumulated 7.6 percent of Burlington's stock and were going to seek control. Press reports said Samjens also sent a letter to Burlington suggesting a friendly transaction at $60 per share. (Stock had been selling at $48 per share.) But it soon became obvious that Burlington's directors were not going to play ball with Samjens. On 29 April Burlington officials issued a press release saying they would study the Samjens proposal and consider other alternatives.

A series of lawsuits ensued. Samjens went to court to knock out Burlington's poison pill and in another suit claimed misleading disclosures had been made. Burlington filed suit in North Carolina charging a former Burlington official had provided inside information to the buyout group. U.S. Senator Terry Sanford and North Carolina Governor James Martin sprang into action on the side of Burlington, pushing for laws to protect North Carolina corporations against hostile takeovers.

On 6 May Samjens pushed its offer to $67 per share, but Burlington's directors rejected the offer and decided to make a partial tender offer for its own stock at $80 per share. However, they later withdrew the offer in favor of an offer that emerged from Morgan Stanley for all stock at $76. Samjens inched its bid to $77, and this move was followed by more lawsuits. Federal courts in Richmond and New York blocked Samjens from proceeding with its $77 per share bid, so Morgan Stanley's final bid of $78 stood up. Along the way Samjens had accumulated 3,408,813 Burlington shares at an average price reported to be $51 per share, providing a gross profit of $88,629,138, to be divided by Dominion Textiles and investor Asher Edelman.

Burlington Industries, the "victor," now was in the hands of an investor group led by Morgan Stanley, which paid $2.129 billion in cash to the selling shareholders. The price represented 190 percent of book value and a price-to-earnings ratio of 37.5 to 1. The now-private company found its debt quadrupled and subsequently announced that it needed to generate $900 million from asset sales in order to meet principal and interest payments due within the next two years. At the same time Burlington announced the elimination of 900 jobs, mostly white-collar workers and middle management.

In early October Burlington announced that it was seeking a buyer for its $300 million industrial-textile business and in late November it announced that it was seeking a buyer for its international plants. As of this writing, no buyers have stepped forward to acquire these divisions although Burlington did sell, to Dominion Textiles, the crown jewel of its denim plants located at Erwin, North Carolina. The sale of the Erwin plant was completed on 27 November at a price of $205 million in cash.

Thus we see today a vastly different Burlington, whose management will be highly challenged to structure the company so that it can meet its debt requirements. The recent market crash on 19 October 1987 will make Burlington's task extremely difficult because the value of the various divisions it wants to sell will probably be lower than expected. Capital-spending plans will no doubt have to be delayed or canceled. And in a capital-intensive industry hungry for higher speeds and more innovations each year, the future of Burlington will remain in question for some time.

Considerable space has been given to the Burlington transaction because it has been, without question, the most dramatic and largest buyout ever to occur in the textile industry. Nonetheless, other important acquisitions or divestitures have occurred that have helped reshape the industry since 1984.

Springs Industries, Inc. When Walter Y. Elisha left his post as vice-chairman of Jewel Companies in 1980 and joined Springs as president and chief operating officer (becoming ceo in 1981), many industry people felt that a big acquisition was imminent. Although a series of smaller acquisitions occurred in the years 1981-1984, it was Springs's acquisition of M. Lowenstein Corporation that projected the company into the arena of large acquisitions. Lowenstein—a large public company with sales in excess of $600 million annually—was producing many of the same product lines as Springs. It is thought, however, that what attracted Springs's attention was Lowenstein's highly profitable fiberglass operations. Springs announced on 11 October 1985 that it had offered $63 per share to acquire all the stock of M. Lowenstein Corporation in a transaction amounting to $286.2 million. The sale was concluded the following month.

Parkdale Mills. Forbes was impressed enough with the acquisition skills of Duke Kimbrell, president of Parkdale Mills, to run a feature story on him in its issue of 2 November 1987. During 1986 Parkdale acquired *Perfection Spinning Company, Linford Mills, Rowan Cotton Mills,* and *Acme Spinning Company.* These acquisitions increased Parkdale's production to 3.5 million pounds weekly and sales to more than $300 million annually, making it the largest yarn spinner in the U.S.

Fieldcrest Cannon, Inc. As noted by Mrs. Andrews, David Murdock, through his Pacific Holding Company, acquired *Cannon Mills* for $413 million in 1982. On 5 December 1985 Cannon sold its principal businesses (sheetings, towels, and rugs), as well as the world-renowned Cannon name, to Fieldcrest Mills of Eden, North Carolina, for a price of $250 million. The transaction closed on 31 January 1986.[4] Max Messmer, mentioned as the one who helped David Murdock engineer the Cannon acquisition and later became Cannon's president, soon moved out of the industry. He became president and ceo of Robert Half International of San Francisco. Doug Kingsmore, who succeeded Messmer as president of Cannon, left Cannon following its sale to Fieldcrest and accepted the job of president and chief operating officer of Graniteville Company.

To prove there was still plenty of financial muscle available after the Cannon acquisition, Fieldcrest moved aggressively to acquire *Bigelow-Sanford, Inc.,*

---

[4]David Murdock, through his Pacific Holding Company, retained Beacon Manufacturing Company and Wiscassett Mills Company.

a large manufacturer of commercial and residential carpeting, closing the sale on 22 December 1986.

Walton-Monroe Mills. While the fight over control of Burlington Industries will likely dominate the merger scene in the textile industry for many years, the sale of Avondale Mills to much-smaller Walton-Monroe Mills and its associates was equally dramatic. To most industry people, it seemed that the solidly entrenched Avondale Mills would be around as long as there was a Comer to run the company. However, when Donald Comer III, president and ceo, turned in his resignation on 31 December 1981 and the company looked to the outside for a new man to fill the vacancy, there was a feeling that Avondale would soon be ''in play'' as an acquisition target. But Avondale's board didn't seriously consider the flirtations of several would-be acquirers until its new president, Doug Kingsmore, left Avondale to accept a contract from David Murdock to serve as president of Cannon Mills. In late 1985, after the company experienced its first substantial annual loss (which exceeded $14 million pretax), the Avondale board was willing to talk.

On 6 February 1986 Avondale entered into an agreement to be acquired by Walton-Monroe Mills for $23.41 per share. Subsequently Dominion Textile, Canada's largest textile producer, made an unsolicited tender offer to acquire Avondale for $24 per share. Avondale's directors chose not to respond to Dominion's offer in order to see what other offers would surface and to honor its agreement to pursue a negotiated transaction with Walton-Monroe. Following the Dominion tender offer, the Avondale board received an offer of $26 per share, or $104 million, from Spectrum Dyed Yarns, a Kings Mountain, North Carolina, textile concern. On 27 March 1986 Walton-Monroe Mills purchased on the open market, in a private transaction, fifty-one percent of Avondale Mills at a price of $28.20 per share and entered into an agreement with the Avondale board to purchase the balance of the company in a cash merger at the same price. Other buyers withdrew, and the transaction was consummated on 2 July 1986, with Walton-Monroe having paid $113 million for the equity of Avondale plus $52 million of assumed debt and transaction cost for a total purchase price of $165 million.

To many, the acquisition of a large, publicly owned company like Avondale by a small, privately owned mill like Walton-Monroe was almost unbelievable. It was not so to me since I had had previous experience negotiating with Walton-Monroe's young president, Stephen Felker, when he acquired Dacotah Cotton Mills, a family-owned mill at Lexington, North Carolina. It was plain to all who participated in the transaction that the keen mind and gentlemanly ways displayed by that thirty-three-year-old executive would take him to much higher plateaus in future years.

WestPoint Pepperell, Inc. Perhaps the most interesting restructuring of a textile company in the past three years is that of WestPoint Pepperell, which in November 1985 reached agreement to acquire Cluett Peabody and Co.—a large, publicly owned apparel company—for a price of $375 million in cash and stock. An investment group from the West Coast headed by Paul A. Bilzerian accumulated 187,500 shares of Cluett Peabody stock, representing 2.25 percent of the outstanding shares, and announced in the fall of 1985 that it intended to seek control of Cluett Peabody. The intentions of the Bilzerian group were of little or no interest to Cluett's directors, and its chairman, Henry H. Henley, Jr., went searching for a "white knight." He found one in Joe Lanier, Jr., chairman and ceo of WestPoint, whose family had founded WestPoint generations ago and guided it to the strong and dominant position it holds in the industry today. Lanier and Henley, along with their respective boards, reached agreement on 4 November 1985, and the transaction was completed on 15 January 1986. At the time of closing, it was reported that WestPoint Pepperell's annual sales volume was $1.3 billion while Cluett Peabody's amounted to $949 million, thus boosting the total sales volume of WestPoint Pepperell to more than $2 billion. The Bilzerian group sold its 187,500 shares to WestPoint Pepperell for $7.5 million.

In the spring of 1986 Joe Lanier took a look at his moderate-sized denim operation at Lindale, Georgia (sales $60 million). He decided that in order to be truly successful in denims it needed to be very large like Burlington, Cone, or Dominion. Otherwise, it should get out of the business. Lanier chose the latter and sold the Lindale operations to Greenwood Mills, which had previously acquired the relatively small denim division of Dan River Mills.

In the fall of 1987 WestPoint Pepperell sold its carpet division to Shaw Industries for $381.5 million. The sales of the denim and carpet divisions were both at a profit and have allowed WestPoint Pepperell to reduce debt while positioning itself for what some believe may be a major acquisition in 1988.

Dixie Yarns, Inc. Another acquisition of major significance was that of Ti-Caro, a major producer of yarns and threads, by Dixie Yarns. In early 1984 a private-investor group led by Lazard Freres and members of Ti-Caro's senior management acquired the company in a highly leveraged buyout. The new owners felt it was to their advantage to sell while the market was strong. Ti-Caro was sold to Dixie Yarns of Chattanooga, Tennessee, in a transaction involving the issuance of three million shares of Dixie's stock (valued at $21 a share) and the assumption of $350 million in debt, which Dixie refinanced. To industry watchers, this transaction was a good one for the sellers, the buyers, and the lenders. It also permitted Dixie to get out of the commodity-yarn business and to concentrate instead on the thread and carpet-yarn markets believed to be more profitable.

Mount Vernon Mills. R. B. Pamplin had acquired Mount Vernon Mills in May 1982, and in October 1985 Mount Vernon Mills acquired Riegel Textile Corporation for a price of $90 million. Mrs. Andrews wrote: "In May 1984 Riegel announced it had approved in principle a $140 million buyout at $35 a share by management and Wesray Corporation." Subsequently, when Riegel's earnings dropped sharply, the deal was called off. Riegel then resorted to closing and selling off unprofitable operations, and on 7 November 1984, the *Daily News Record* reported the stock had dropped to $25\frac{1}{8}$ after the company showed a loss from continuing operations of $11.5 million for the year. Mount Vernon's timing could not have been better. It acquired a slimmed-down Riegel at a price that was $50 million less than the price Wesray had offered in 1984.

Delta Woodside Industries, Inc. Following Delta Woodside's acquisition of the unfinished woven-fabrics division of Dan River (Woodside Mills), it moved to acquire the knit-fabrics division of Cannon Mills at Maiden, North Carolina, in September 1985. On 15 July 1986 E. Erwin Maddrey, president and ceo, announced that Alchem Capital Corporation (later Delta Woodside) had completed the acquisition of the Delta Finishing and the Stevecoknit Fabrics Division of J. P. Stevens. Erwin Maddrey had resigned as president of Riegel in 1983 and on 1 January 1984 announced the formation of Alchem together with Buck Mickel of RSI and Bettis C. Rainsford of Edgefield, South Carolina. In less than four years, they had put together a company employing 6,700 employees in twenty-three plants. For the year ending June 1987, Delta Woodside reported sales of $418 million and earnings of $1.31 per share. It was a truly remarkable achievement considering that the company was started in early 1984, when many mills were running part time and imports seemed out of control.

American Thread Company. One of the real bargains that came out of the frenzied merger and acquisition activities of 1986 was American Thread's decision to acquire Standard-Coosa-Thatcher (SCT) Co. of Chattanooga, Tennessee. SCT was a major producer of threads and yarns and had gone from a public company to a private company in 1982. When the rumor got out that American Thread was negotiating to acquire SCT, another major thread producer tried to set up negotiations with SCT, but to little avail. The owners of SCT saw an opportunity to make a deal that they felt they could not make with anyone else. An inside source told me that American Thread paid $53 million to SCT and then turned around and sold off all the production plants, except the Rossville Dye Plant, to the sellers for $18 million. This would indicate that American Thread paid $35 million to obtain the excellent name of SCT, the Rossville plant, and the customer list, with an agreement by the sellers not to compete any longer in the thread business. In the end the sellers of SCT acquired production facilities located at Jefferson and Washington, Georgia; Piedmont, Alabama; Chattanooga, Tennessee; and Salisbury, North Carolina. The transaction was completed in December 1986, and the timing of the repurchasers could not have been better because 1987 probably proved to be the best year in the history of the yarn-spinning industry. It was considered a "bargain purchase" on the part of the sellers, who bought back most of the physical assets at a price far less than replacement cost.

Texfi Industries, Inc. In recent years many people in the industry have regarded Texfi as a real loser after seeing its sales fall from a high of $250 million during the years of the double-knit explosion to just a little more than $85 million in 1986. But under a new management team headed by Terrell Sovey, chairman and ceo, Texfi arranged some imaginative financing and acquired Marion Fabrics, a weaver of blended apparel fabrics, and Highland Cotton Mills, a well-known spinner of combed cotton and synthetic yarns. Both transactions were closed in October 1986 and added $60 million of profitable sales annually to Texfi. A few months later it acquired the Elastex Division of Stedman Corporation, all of which helped boost Texfi's sales to $162.8 million for the year ending 30 October 1987—an increase of 91.5 percent while profits jumped from $142,000 to $9,037,000.

Collins & Aikman Corp. When Burlington agreed on 22 May 1986 to pay a price of 2.9 times book value to acquire C. H. Masland and Sons, a Collins & Aikman insider was heard to say: "At that kind of price, I believe Don McCullough [chairman and ceo] would be interested in selling C & A." Don McCullough did even better for his shareholders, however. Six months later, on 10 November 1986, he and his board agreed to accept an offer from Wickes Companies to sell Collins & Aikman for a price of $1.1554 billion, representing a price to book value of 3.14, the highest premium paid for any of the major textile companies in my memory. The transaction was wrapped up on 10 December 1986.

My remarks have concentrated only on transactions involving the spinning and weaving segments of the industry. To write about mergers and acquisitions involving cut-and-sew companies like VF Corporation's acquisition of Blue Bell, Inc. or the acquisition of the large cotton-ginning operations of Anderson-Clayton Co. by the Julien Company would probably go beyond the scope of this book.

Suffice it to say that the robust level of mergers, acquisitions, and corporate spin-offs will continue into the future although premiums paid by buyers will certainly moderate. The "meltdown" of the stock market this year caused potential buyers to assume a more cautious approach to acquisitions, but the easy availability of financing will continue to fuel merger and acquisition activity into 1988 and beyond.

Several men of importance to the industry who in 1984 were reported as alive and active have since passed away. After checking with various trade publications and friends in the industry, I am—with feelings of respect—listing the following names of men who helped shape the industry and are no longer with us:

• *Morris M. Bryan.* President of Jefferson Mills and past president of the American Textile Manufacturers Institute and the Georgia Textile Association.

• *J. M. (Mac) Cheatham.* Chairman of the board of Dundee Mills and past president of the American Textile Manufacturers Institute, the Georgia Textile Association, and the director of the Bibb Company.

• *Donald Comer, Jr.* Chairman of the board of Avondale Mills and a past president of the American Cotton Manufacturers Institute and the International Textile Manufacturers Association.

• *Caesar Cone.* Chairman of the board of Cone Mills Corporation.

• *J. Harold Lineberger.* Chairman of the board of Acme Spinning Co. and Linford Mills and president of Perfection Spinning Co., South Fork Manufacturing Co., Rowan Cotton Mills Co., and Belmont Throwing Corp. Mr. Lineberger was also a founder and president of the Combed Yarn Spinners Association.

• *Col. J. Norman Pease.* Chairman of the board and founder of J. N. Pease Associates, mill engineers and architects, designers of many textile plants. He lived to the amazing age of 101.

• *Morris Speizman.* Chairman of the board and founder of Speizman Industries, a company specializing in designing, building, and marketing a wide range of knitting machines, primarily for the hosiery trade.

R. I. Dalton, Jr.
President, Tech-Tex, Inc.
December 1987

GLOSSARY

For the convenience of the reader, I am providing a glossary of terms included in this book. There are several good textile dictionaries that cover textile terms in detail. They are: *Callaway Textile Dictionary*, *The Modern Textile Dictionary*, and *Fairchild's Dictionary of Textiles*.

A

Acetate Rayon Process: Fiber, yarn, or material made by the acetate process and differing from other rayons in that it is not a regenerated cellulose, but an ester of cellulose, namely, cellulose-acetate. It has different physical and chemical properties from other rayons, especially in its reaction with dyes. It is not affected by most dyes, so a whole new set of dyes had to be developed for it. The principal development work was done by two brothers, Camille and Henri Dreyfuss of Basel, Switzerland.

American-Egyptian: Crosses of American-Upland and Egyptian cotton. Also known as Pima and SXP.

American-Upland: Domestically grown cotton other than Sea Island and American-Egyptian.

Asbestos: A general term embracing a variety of fibrous minerals that are silicates of magnesium and calcium and usually mixed with iron and aluminum. The most common minerals include the fibrous varieties of serpentine and hornblende. Most commercial asbestos is mined in Canada and is a variety of serpentine known as chrysotile. Italy produces a variety of hornblende known as amphibole. Asbestos is valuable chiefly for its resistance to heat and flame. The best fibers are several inches long, rather curly, white, and lustrous.

B

Bale: A standard package of raw cotton wrapped in cotton or jute baggings and bound with narrow steel bands. A square bale averages 500 pounds in weight, a round bale, 250 pounds.

Basis Buyer: Purchaser of raw cotton who buys strictly on prevailing basis figures (for certain staple and grade), which are added to futures market price.

Basket Weaves: Weaves made by extending the plain weave both in width and length. Characterized by various-sized squares and rectangles of warp and filling floats. Cloths made with these weaves tend to be loose in texture. Also known as matt and hopsack weaves. (See Weave.)

Battery: A device on a loom that holds the supply of full bobbins.

Beam: The Gudgeon beam, or large metallic roll 40″ to 60″ in length on which warp yarn is wound preparatory to weaving, fits at the back of the loom. The length of the beam governs the width of the cloth.

Beef Tubing & Stockinette: A knitted fabric used for meat packing.

Bleaching: A chemical process of "finishing fabric" that turns yarn or fabric from its natural color to white.

Bobbin: A highly polished wooden spool on which roving or yarn is wound at its respective productive frames.

Box Cotton: That equal to government standards or the government box, against which raw cotton is compared for grade and color.

Bread and Butter Cotton: Medium grades and staples easily sold.

Breaking Strength: The number of pounds of pressure that may be applied to a length of yarn before it breaks.

Broadcloth: 1. A closely woven (see Weave) fabric made with plain weave and having a very fine rib fillingwise. The best qualities are achieved with combed ply yarns in warp and filling. Cheaper qualities use combed cotton single yarn in the filling, or in warp and filling, and some even use carded yarns. 144 threads x 76 threads per square inch is a standard construction for broadcloth, and for a 37″ width cloth the yards per pound run from 4.00 to 4.75. Also made in colored stripes, end-and-end effects, novelty yarns, dobby loom, and Jacquard loom woven effects. Usually mercerized, sanforized, and given a soft, silky finish. Widely used for shirts, dresses, pajamas, and other wash goods. In England a similar fabric is known as shirting poplin. 2. A similar fabric is made of man-made fiber in dress and shirting weights. Also called Fuji. 3. A high-grade, lustrous woolen cloth made of fine merino yarns using the 2/1 twill weave. It is heavily milled and given a dress-face finish with the nap lying in one direction. It is a dense, smooth-faced fabric, usually dyed black, having a velvety feel and silky gloss. When well made it is one of the best of all woolen fabrics.

Brown Lung: See Lint.

Buggy Whips: Cotton difficult to sell.

Bumblebee Cotton: Shortest staples.

Burlap: A coarse, heavy, plain-woven jute fabric made of coarse singles yarn. Largely used in the natural state as a wrapping or bagging material. Cotton bales ginned in the U.S.A. are usually wrapped in burlap.

Buzz-Fuzz: Very short staple cotton.

C

Calendering: A process that smooths and irons fabric by passing it between several sets of hot rollers.

Canvas (Duck): A term applied to a wide range of medium- and heavyweight fabrics, commonly made of cotton, including the heaviest and strongest of all single-woven fabrics. There are three main types: number duck, "army" duck, and flat duck.

Canvas Cloth: A plain-woven woolen dress fabric of an open character made with ply yarns—usually 3-ply—in warp and filling.

Card: Machine for carding cotton that parallels fibers by passing raw cotton between large rollers covered with card clothing.

Card Clothing: A triple thickness of cotton, wool, and cotton fabrics from which protrude many thousands of steel points per square foot. This covers the flats and cylinders at the carding machine.

Carding: Pulling cotton fibers between myriad steel points as a means of cleaning them, paralleling the fibers, and preparing them for further manufacture.

Card Strips: A salable waste item; the waste lint from the carding machine.

Carded Yarns: Yarns in which the manufacturing processes did not include the combing process.

Casein Fiber: A synthetic protein fiber made from casein that has been culled from skim milk. It is cut to staple lengths and has properties somewhat the same as wool.

Chalks: Quotations chalked up on a futures market board in cotton exchanges.

Chambray: A popular cotton fabric made with the plain weave and using colored warp and white filling yarns. Fairly coarse carded yarns are used and the picks (threads) per inch run about 2/3 of the yarn ends per inch. The warp is usually blue and the cloth is a standard material for work shirts. Lighter-weight fabrics made from finer-count carded yarns are made plain as well as with stripes, checks, and dobby (woven) designs on a chambray background. These are known as fancy chambrays and are used a great deal for women's and children's clothes.

Cheese: A package of yarn shaped much like a round, flat cheese.

Cheesecloth: A loosely woven, lightweight, open-construction cotton fabric made from carded print cloth yarns and using the plain weave. The cloth is thin and flimsy and the threads tend to slip badly if subjected to any strain. The name is derived from its original use, which was to wrap pressed cheese. Now widely used for bandages and surgical gauze. Also called gauze, scrim, tobacco cloth.

Cheviot: 1. A breed of sheep native to Great Britain and raised in the Cheviot Hills of Scotland and England from time immemorial. Very prolific and noted for their ability to withstand a rigorous climate. Useful for crossbreeding. The fleece weighs six to eight pounds per yard and the shrinkage is around thirty-five percent. 2. A term generally applied to woolen suiting fabrics having a rough, shaggy face. Originally made from wool of the Cheviot type, but crossbred wools are now used and the cheaper qualities implement reused wool, cotton, and man-made fibers. Various twill weaves are used and the cloth is well fulled and raised to give the characteristic rough surface of wool.

City Crop: Loose, or waste, raw cotton from floor of the cotton-classing room.

Classer: A person who classifies raw cotton as to staple length, quality, and grade.

Cloth Broker: A proprietorship, partnership, or corporation that arranges sales between textile buyers and sellers on individual transactions for a brokerage fee, usually one half of one percent.

Collateral Cotton: Cotton bought at a cheap price to keep an average in a mill's bank account.

Combed Yarns: Yarns whose manufacture includes the combing process.

Comber: Machine that combs cotton fibers, removing short fibers and paralleling the longer fibers that remain.

Comber Noil: The short waste fiber that emerges from cotton in the combing process; a salable waste item.

Commission Buyer: One who buys cotton or fabric with the intention to resell it on commission.

Cone: A conical-shaped package on which yarn is wound.

Corduroy: A stout, durable fabric, generally cotton, of man-made fiber having pronounced cords running warpways the length of the fabric. The cords are made of cut pile and are termed wales. They are separated from one another by narrow cut lines known as welts. The wales per inch may vary from one to twenty-two. The material is woven with two systems of filling, ground and pile, and has a high number of picks (threads) per inch. In the finishing of corduroys, the pile picks are cut to form the tufted cords. A very satisfactory fabric for outdoor wear of all kinds, sportswear, slacks, children's clothing, and in the fine-wale type as a dress fabric. From the French, *Corde du Roi,* or king's cord, since only royalty could then afford to buy it.

Cottonade: A twilled cotton fabric made in colors and patterns similar to worsted suitings. Dark background colors are usually used with lighter colors for the stripes. It is a stout, serviceable fabric, often napped on the back. Used for trousering and cheap suiting.

Coutils: A cotton fabric made with a 2/1 herringbone twill. They are strong and firmly woven, somewhat like jeans, but of a higher count and heavier weight. Made from medium-count yarns, carded or combed. Usually piece dyed and used for corsets, brassieres, and so forth. The name comes from the French word for drill.

Covert: 1. A closely woven, stout cotton cloth made with a 2/1 twill and having a characteristic mottled or flecked appearance. Singles carded yarns are used. The warp is of mock twist yarn, usually a dark color and white, and the filling yarn is generally the same color as the dark warp. Commonly used for work clothing of all kinds. 2. A lighter weight, cheaper cloth similar to that above, but made with the plain weave. 3. A closely woven mixed-effect woolen fabric. Usually made from two-ply warp, one end dark and one end light. Filling may be the same or a singles yarn. The weave is a warp-face satin of the buckskin type and gives a fine upright twill line. Usually made in shades of tan or brown and very popular for top coats and men's suiting. Also made of rayon staple and blends.

Creel: Arrangement of full bobbins on higher level of a machine, the creel being the source of yarn supply or roving for a machine.

Cuprammonium Rayon: Rayon made by the cuprammonium process in which the filaments are composed of a regenerated cellulose that has been coagulated or solidified from a solution of cellulose in ammoniacal copper oxide, or ammonium hydroxide with copper salts. This process is used in manufacturing Bemberg rayon.

D

Damask: A firm, lustrous fabric with more or less elaborate Jacquard designs woven into cloth. Commonly made with warp and filling-face satin weaves, one for the figure and the other for the ground. Somewhat similar to brocade, but flatter and reversible. Made of linen, cotton, rayon, silk, man-made fiber, or various combinations. May be all white, piece dyed, or warp and filling in different colors. Used for napkins, tablecloths, draperies, upholstery, and so forth. See Double Damask; Single Damask.

Deeps: D. & P. L. cotton, a type originated by Delta and Pine Land Company that has become widely popular among growers of cotton and yarn spinners.

Delivery Rollers: Between these rollers the machines' product is delivered to a bin.

Denim: A stout, serviceable, twilled cotton or man-made fabric made from coarse singles yarns. The usual weave is the 3-harness warp-face twill (2/1), although the 4-harness (3/1) is used for the heavier weights. The standard denim is made with indigo blue-dyed warp yarn and gray filling yarn. Denim is the most important fabric of the work-clothing group and is extensively used for overalls, coats, caps, and so forth.

Dobby: The mechanism on a loom that controls the harness frames and thereby the patterns of the weave.

Doff: To remove.

Doffer: One who removes filled packages such as bobbins from spinning machines. These are replaced with empties that are to be filled. Automatic machine doffers are now being installed in the machine themselves.

Doffer Wagon: Small wagon that a human doffer pushes to hold the filled packages being removed; or which travels with automatic doffer to receive filled yarn bobbins.

Dogs: A very low grade of raw cotton.

Double Damask: Table damask woven of comparatively fine yarns and using 8-harness satin weaves.

Doubling: Running more than one strand of yarn, sliver, or roving through a machine to get one strand delivered.

Draft: The relative amount by which a strand is drawn out in length and reduced in weight per yard as it passes through a machine.

Drawing: A process to straighten and parallel cotton fibers.

Drawing Frames: Machine on which drawing is done.

Drills: Stout, medium- to heavyweight twilled cotton cloth made from coarse carded yarns. The weave is the 2/1 left-hand twill, but similar cloths made with a 3/1 twill are often called drill. Also made in herringbone patterns. Ex. 30″ wide fabric, 72 x 60 threads per square inch = 2.50 yards per lb.

Drop Wires: The ends of warp yarns are threaded through drop wires on a loom; if an end breaks, the wire drops and the loom stops automatically.

Duck: See Canvas.

Duvetyn: A twilled fabric characterized by a very soft, velvety nap usually produced by emery rolls. Originally a soft down woolen fabric, but now also made of rayon, silk, cotton, or various combinations.

E

Egyptian Cotton: That grown in the Nile Valley in Egypt. Long and silky fiber used in very fine goods.

Enameling Duck: A term often applied to flat duck, especially the double-filling type, because it is used extensively for coating purposes: e.g., oilcloth, imitation leather, and so forth.

End: A strand of roving or yarn.

F

Fabric: A woven, knitted, or laminated (bonded) piece of cloth.

Fair Labor Standards Act: Federal legislation providing standard hours and wages for employees.

Farmers' Hedge: Long on both spot cotton and futures.

Feed Roll or Rollers: Rollers that carry the textile material forward and feed the machine.

Fell of Cloth: Edge of woven cloth near the reeds in the loom.

Fiber: A single hair of mature cotton or man-made fiber, its length being from 1,000 to 3,000 times its diameter.

Filling: Yarn or threads that run crosswise a piece of cloth from selvage to selvage; the woof of the fabric.

Filter Fabrics: There are more than 100 types of cloth known by this name. They range from fine filter fabric made of silk to very coarse cotton or man-made filter cloth. Plain, leno, or twill weave may be used to make the cloth, which varies greatly in yarn count, texture, and weight. Used for filtering purposes in the candy, chemical, food, paint, petroleum, and similar trades.

Flannel: 1. A widely used term in the woolen industry applied generally to light- or medium-weight fabrics of plain or twill weave having a slightly napped surface. Made in many varieties and qualities, some specific types being used for men's suiting and trousering, dresses, underwear, infants' garments, and so forth. 2. This term is also used for fabrics, either plain or twilled, of cotton, man-made staple, and various blends and combinations. Generally they are soft fabrics, with a nap that varies in denseness. Sometimes called flannelette.

Flat Cotton: Uncompressed cotton.

Flat Duck: Plain woven with two single ends weaving as one and with either single- or ply-yarn filling.

Flats: Narrow slats covered with card clothing that form the flexible, continuously revolving section of the card machine.

Flyer: Wicketlike frame placed over the bobbin on the roving frame and through which the roving is threaded in order to be laid on the bobbin in proper position.

F.O.B. Seller or Buyer: One who deals in spot cotton or fabrics according to local terms.

Full Fashion: Hosiery that has been fashioned to fit the shape of the leg.

Futures: Contracts, on a Cotton Exchange, to buy or sell so many bales of cotton to be delivered at a specified future date at a certain price.

G

Gabardine: A firmly woven, clear-finished, warp-faced cloth characterized by distinct, closely set, raised diagonal ribs or cords. Made from regular or steep twills and with a higher sley (warp) than pick (woof). Carded or combed cotton, man-made fibers, or worsted yarns may be used in single or ply. Usually piece dyed, especially in brown and olive-drab shades, to be made in dress and suiting or uniform weights. N.B.: Cotton gabardines are made with 63° steep twills on 11, 13 or 15 harnesses.

Gassing: Process of running yarn or cloth at high speed over gas flames to singe off excess fuzz.

Gin: A machine that removes cotton lint from cotton seed. First invented by Eli Whitney, the gins are now huge, electronically operated machines with very high fiber-production output.

Gin Fall: Trash from the gin box that remains in raw cotton.

Gingham: A yarn-dyed, plain-weave cotton fabric usually made with a colored check pattern. The patterns vary from simple two-color checks to quite elaborate plaids in many colors. Construction ranges from coarse carded-yarn styles to fine, lightweight combed-yarn styles. One of the most popular fabrics for sports apparel and play clothes.

Glass Cloth: 1. A plain-woven fabric of cotton, linen, rayon staple, or various combinations of the above. Should be very absorbent and comparatively free from shedding lint. Usually made in colorful stripes or checks, also in prints, and used for kitchen towels. 2. A fabric made of glass yarns. 3. A cloth covered with powdered glass used for smoothing or polishing.

Glass, Textile: Glass in a form suitable for spinning, weaving, and so forth. It is manufactured in two common forms: (1) continuous filaments and (2) staple fibers of comparatively short, but spinnable, length. Nonflammable.

Grade: The quality of cotton or fabric.

Gray Goods: Goods as it leaves loom or knitting machine prior to any finishing treatment. Term does not imply color, but rather an unbleached form. Also spelled grey, greig, greige.

Grind: To sharpen steel points or teeth on card clothing—that is, card grinding, a position in a textile mill.

H

Hank: A length of 840 yards.

Harness: Frame on loom from which heddles are suspended.

Heddle: Fine steel wires with an eye through which ends of warp yarn are threaded on loom.

Hedging: Use of futures contracts (buying or selling) to protect oneself against rise or fall of cotton market.

Humidifier: Machine, usually automatic, that supplies the proper amount of moisture to ensure required humidity.

Humidity (relative): Ratio of the quantity of vapor actually present in the atmosphere to the greatest amount possible at the given temperature.

I

Industrial Glove Fabric: Fabric—usually heavy cotton flannel or knit-cotton fabrics—used in manufacture of work gloves.

Intermediate: A machine used in the second step of obtaining roving. Such machines are now obsolete.

I

Jack-Frame: A machine used in the fourth step in obtaining roving. Only employed in the manufacture of fine yarns.

Jacquard: A machine (named for its inventor) on a loom that controls individual warp ends and thereby creates the pattern of the weave.

Jasper: A cotton code word of the industry meaning, "We do not offer firm but will probably accept if you offer us." Adopted as a slang term concerning propositions.

Jean: 1. A warp-face cotton cloth similar to drill but made from lighter yarns and having more threads per inch and a finer twill line. The weave is the 2/1 left-hand twill. 2. In Great Britain a filling-face cotton cloth made with the 1/2 twill, bleached or dyed, and used for linings.

Jeans: Work pants made of jean fabric, usually denim, and highly popular as young persons' sportswear.

Jute: A soft, long, multicellular fiber obtained from the bast, or inner bark, of two closely related plants, roundpod jute *(Corchorus capsularis)* and long-pod jute *(C. Olitorius).* Jute is grown extensively in India and practically all of it is water retted (a process used to remove gum and woody matter from the fibers). The fibers are from three to fifteen feet in length and creamy white to brown in color. Because of its cheapness, availability, and ease of manufacture, jute is used in tremendous quantities especially for cotton-bale covering, burlap bags of all kinds, and coarse yarns such as twine and rope. Jute is not a particularly strong fiber and because it lacks elasticity and durability, it is being replaced in rope and twine by nylon.

K

Kier: A tank holding from six to ten tons of fabric in which fabric is boiled during the finishing process.

Knitted Fabric: A fabric composed of a series of interlocking loops from one or more yarns. In general, such fabrics may be classified as filling (weft) knit or warp knit. In the former the yarns run generally crosswise and in the latter lengthwise.

Knitted Fleeces: A knitted fabric napped on one side.

Knitting: Creation of fabric through looping by needles.

Knitting Twist: Soft twist required for yarns to be used on knitting machines.

L

Lap: A continuous, compressed flat bat of cotton wound on a steel lap rod the width of the machine. The product of the Picker, Sliver lapper, and Ribbon lapper.

Latch-Needle: A tiny hooked needle with an actual latch at the hook, used on knitting machines.

Laundry Textiles: Fabrics used for covering rolls in laundry machines or for laundry bags.

Lawn: 1. Originally a fine, plain-woven linen of open texture. 2. A basic fine-yarn, plain-woven, gray cotton cloth made in various qualities and used in the conversion of fine, soft, sheer fabrics. Usually made from fine-combed singles yarn although some manufacturers use carded yarns. Often called by the name of the finish used: for example, organdy, batiste, nainsock, and so forth. 3. Name applied to a lightweight, plain-woven cotton or blended-fiber cloth that is bleached, dyed, or printed and given a crisp starched finish.

Leaf: 1. Particles of dried leaves found in raw cotton. 2. A term used in the same sense as *harness* or *shaft* when speaking of certain weaves. For example, a 2/1 twill may be called a three-leaf twill.

Lickerin: A revolving cylinder of the carding machine that pulls or "licks-in" the cotton stock to the carding sections.

Lint: Cotton fibers as fine as dust. A "linthead" is a mill worker on whom this lint dust settles. Breathing the lint may eventually cause lung disease.

Long: A situation where a person has bought more fiber than needed for booked cloth orders.

Long Staple: 1. Cotton $1\frac{1}{8}$ inches or longer. 2. Man-made fiber staple cut a certain length, usually 2 inches or longer.

Loom: Machine on which yarns are woven into fabric by a shuttle, or some type of carrier, that carries yarn back and forth, interlacing filling yarn between warp yarn.

M

Mercerizing: Running yarn or fabric through a caustic soda bath under tension. A process that gives cotton material a sheen. Named for its inventor, John Mercer.

Moleskin: A heavy filling-faced cotton cloth with a low-angle, right-twill effect. Made from coarse carded yarns with a high number of picks (cross threads per inch), about twice as many per inch as ends (lengthwise thread or warp), which gives a compact, dense surface. The common weave is the 8-harness satin with two ends weaving as one. May be given a short nap or napped and sheared to give a suede finish.

Motes: Foreign matter and trash removed from cotton lint in the Opening and Picking machines; often used as commercial fertilizer.

Mule Spinning: A system of spinning yarn (seldom used in the U.S.A.) employing the intermittent drawing and twisting of yarn. Used mostly in very fine numbers.

N

Nap: Fuzzy surface of fabric such as cotton flannel.

Narrow Fabrics: General term applied to materials woven or bonded on a narrow fabric loom such as tapes, webbings, ribbons, and so forth. Such fabrics usually are from $\frac{1}{2}''$ to 3" in width, but may run up to 12" or 18". A narrow-fabric loom weaves several pieces at a time, but each fabric has a true selvage on each edge. Called smallwares in England. Some narrow fabrics are obtained by slitting full-width fabrics, usually nonwoven but bonded fibers.

Neps: Tiny knots of fiber in raw-cotton fibers and yarns.

Noil: Waste fibers from the comber.

Number Duck: Plain woven from heavy carded ply yarns in warp and filling.

Nylon: The generic name chosen by the du Pont Company for a group of proteinlike chemical products classed as synthetic linear polymers. The term *nylon* includes a vast group of chemically related products whose physical properties differ considerably. Of special interest to the textile industry is nylon in filament form; this is made from a polymer in flake form that is melted and forced through a spinnerette. It is produced in deniers (sizes) ranging from 20 to 210, with an individual filament size of about 3 denier. Among the distinctive features of nylon are high tensile strength, elasticity and toughness, flexibility, high resistance to abrasion, and low water absorbency.

O

Opening: First process in cotton manufacture, that of beating and fluffing up the cotton as a cleaning process. From the opening machine the cotton goes to the Picker. Sometimes the machines are combined as in one-process picking.

Opening Room: Place where bales of fiber are stripped of bagging and ties and mixed by taking small layers of each bale, 20 to 100, and dropping these into the opening machine for cleaning and mixing.

OSHA: Government agency that regulates the safety of working conditions.

Osnaburg: A plain-woven, coarse-yarn, medium- or heavyweight cloth of low construction made wholly of short-staple, low-grade cotton, or of a mixture of this and fiber waste. Used in gray state for bags, as a base for linoleum, and so forth. Converted in various ways and used for draperies, slack suits, and coveralls. Also woven with colored stripes or checks. It is used for toweling and, in tubular form, for sacks and bags.

P

Pajama Check: A cross-barred dimity or muslin fabric made from carded print cloth yarns. Used for underwear or, when printed, for dresses.

Piano Machine: One that punches design holes in card boards; used in conjunction with the Jacquard. The newest method is by computer system.

Pick: One thread of filling yarn, or cross yarn, from selvage side to selvage side.

Picker: Machine that opens and cleans raw cotton and delivers it in the form of a lap.

Piker: A raw-cotton trader who makes a quick turnover on small capital.

Pile: Soft ends or loops of yarn that form the face of fabrics such as velvet and plush. In terry toweling these ends are on the underside as well as upper side of the object.

Pin Check: 1. A tiny check effect made by a combination of weave and color. Popular in clear-finish worsteds, in which the cloth appears studded with minute dots. 2. A cotton work-clothing fabric showing small white dots arranged in straight rows, vertically and horizontally, on a blue ground.

Piqué: A fabric, usually of cotton or man-made fiber yarns, characterized in its simple form by ribs or wales running crosswise from selvage to selvage or, if figured, by an embossed effect. It is a compound fabric made with two warps and two fillings. The face warp is lightly tensioned and weaves plain with the face filling. The back warp is heavily tensioned, and stitches with the plain face cloth according to a prearranged design. At the stitching points the face cloth is pulled down, forming welts or quilted effects. The second, or stuffer, filling is coarser than the other yarns and is used to make the wales or raised figures more pronounced.

Ply: Two or more yarns twisted together. Number of yarns is given by the expressions "two-ply," "three-ply," and so forth.

Points: Hooked wires with teeth on card clothing.

Pongee: Originally a plain fabric, hand woven by the natives of China and India from wild silk. Characterized by uneven yarns with many nubs and usually ecru or tan (natural) in color.

Poplin: A term applied to many qualities of fabrics in various yarns. The chief characteristic is a fine rib effect running across the cloth from selvage to selvage. The weave is plain. The rib is produced by having the warp yarn considerably finer than the filling and having two or three times as many ends per inch as picks (cross yarns).

Print Cloth Yarns: Carded cotton yarns, man-made or blends, usually ranging from 28 single ply to 42 single ply.

Put-Up: Type of holder on which yarn is shipped: for example, cone, cheese, tubes, or beams.

Q

Quill: Small bobbin that fits into the shuttle and carries filling yarn across the loom.

Quiller: Machine for winding yarn on quills.

R

Raw Stock Dyeing: The process of dyeing fibers in the unmanufactured state. There are several different methods such as immersing the loose fibers in the dye bath; packing the stock in a container and forcing the dye solution through it; or passing the stock through the dye bath.

Rayon: 1. The generic term for filaments made from various solutions of modified cellulose by drawing the solution through an orifice and solidifying it in the form of a filament, or filaments, by means of some coagulating or precipitating medium. 2. The Federal Trade Commission definition: "The generic term for manufactured textile fibers or yarn produced chemically from cellulose or with a cellulose base, and for threads, strands or fabric made therefrom, regardless of whether such fiber or yarn can be made under the viscose, acetate, cuprammonium, nitrocellulose or other process."

Repp: A fabric characterized by distinct ribs, usually running from selvage to selvage. The ribs may be made in various ways: (1) by having warp and filling arranged so as to alternate one fine thread and one coarse thread (plain weave); (2) by alternating slack and tensioned ends; (3) by using a low number of coarse filling threads per inch (plain weave); (4) by using a rib weave.

Ribbon Lap: A ribbonlike flat bat of cotton, cleaned and with fibers paralleled. The product of the ribbon lapper.

Ring Spinning: A system of spinning. The yarn is threaded through a traveler on a ring, which surrounds the bobbin, and thereby yarn is laid on the bobbin evenly. The drafting, or drawing out, of roving, twisting the yarn, and laying it on the bobbin are simultaneous and continuous processes. Invented by John Thorpe in 1828.

Ring Traveler: The tiny half circle of metal or plastic on the ring through which yarn is threaded.

Roving: A continuous strand of cotton or man-made paralleled fibers to which has been added the first twist in the manufacturing process.

S

Sanforizing: Preshrinking cotton or man-made fiber fabric at the mill with heat-wet processing. A generic term adapted from the originator's name.

Sateen: A cotton cloth made with the satin weave. The 5- and 8-harness weaves are used in either filling-face or warp-face effects. A filling-face sateen requires considerably more picks than ends per inch, while the opposite is true of a warp-face sateen. They are made from carded or combed yarns and the former are often made in heavy weights for work clothing as a base for coating and the like. The combed-yarn sateens, after mercerizing, have a smooth, lustrous surface and are used for wearing apparel, linings, and so forth. Also called glazed cotton.

Seamless Tubing: Seamless knitted fabric.

Seat-Cover Fabrics: A wide variety of fabrics used for covering seats, doors, and other upholstered surfaces in automobiles. Generally they are made of cotton and man-made fiber, paper, or leatherette and include such styles as stripes, checks, and plaids in plain, twill, and dobby designs.

Seersucker: A cloth generally of cotton, man-made fiber, or blends, characterized by distinctive woven-in crinkle stripes running warpways. Woven from two beams in stripes of plain ground and crinkle, which is also usually plain weave. The ground ends are held under ordinary weaving tension, while the crinkle ends are woven slack. Made in many different patterns including simple and fancy stripes, checks, and plaids. Popular for summer apparel or for sportswear. Seersucker stripe effects are also used in other cloths such as bedspreads and Bedford cords.

Selvage: Extra number of warp ends along the edge of woven fabric that gives it finish and strength.

Shed: V-shaped opening formed by warp yarns controlled by harnesses, through which shuttle (or yarn-carrying device) flies faster than the eye can see.

Sheeting: A plain-woven cotton cloth made in medium and heavy weights, usually from carded yarns, and extensively used for converting and for bed sheets. Made in a wide range of constructions and known as muslin sheeting, percale sheeting, soft-filled sheeting, and so forth.

Shuttle: Holds the bobbin or quill of filling yarn and carries it back and forth across the loom between shed lines.

Single Damask: Damask in which 5-harness satin weaves are used for both ground and figure. A lighter-weight fabric than double damask, less lustrous, and made of linen or cotton.

Slasher: Machine that starches or sizes yarn preparatory to weaving.

Sliver: A continuous untwisted strand (about one inch in diameter) of cotton fibers. The product of the card is carded sliver; of the comber is combed sliver; of the drawing operation is drawing sliver.

Sliver Lapper: Machine that lays many strands of sliver side by side to make a lap with width about ten inches.

Slubber: A machine used in the first process of obtaining roving.

Snake: Loose waste cotton from sample-room floor, packed for resale in sacks about nine feet long.

Snaps: A very low grade of cotton that was pulled from the stalk while still in the burr.

Solvent: A solution that dissolves other substances.

Spindle: A tempered, small steel rod, about fourteen inches in height, on which bobbin is placed on spinning frame. The spindle, revolving at great speed, gives yarn its twist.

Spinning Frame: Machine on which yarn is spun.

Spool: A package with a head at each end on which yarn is wound.

Spooler: Machine that transfers yarn from previous package to spool.

Spots (or Spot Cotton): Cotton bought or sold on the spot.

Squidger: 1. A cotton classer's helper or apprentice. 2. The first step in learning to class cotton fiber for staple length and grade.

Staple: The length of cotton or man-made fibers.

Stock: Cotton or man-made fibers in various processes of manufacture up to spinning.

Street Buyer: One who buys raw cotton from farm wagons on the street.

Stripe: 1. A line of a different color or structure from the ground; hence any linear variation of color, structure, and so forth. 2. A strip attached to something of a different color or material. 3. A pattern in a fabric with lines or narrow bands of a different color, structure, material, or weave.

T

Table Felt: Felted padding for billiard and dining tables.

Tailing Machine: One that strips bobbins of remnants of yarn that are then waste usable for filters, stuffing, and so forth.

Tarnish-Preventive Cloth: A flannel with finish for flat wear and for jewelry boxes to prevent metal tarnishing.

Tensile Strength: See Breaking Strength.

Tenter Frame: Machine that stretches fabric to prescribed width by drying it under tension. Part of finishing.

Terry Cloth: Fabric with a loop-pile face commonly used for towels, robes, or sportswear.

Thread: 1. A fine cord composed of fibers of cotton, wool, flax, or man-made fiber spun to a considerable length and spooled for sewing. The term applies also to a similar product from glass, asbestos, ductile metals, and so forth. 2. Specifically, such a cord composed of two or more yarns twisted together, finished, and used chiefly in sewing. 3. Each of the lengths of yarn that form the warp and filling of a woven fabric; hence, any one of these as an ultimate constituent of such a fabric. 4. A lineal measure of yarn, that is, the length of a coil of the reel, varying in amount according to the material and the locality.

Ticking: Fabric commonly used for covering box springs, mattresses, and pillows or upholstery. There are numerous types that may be classified as mill-finished ticking or converted ticking, commonly known as art ticking. When not specified, the term is understood to mean a mill-finished ticking made with the 2/1 or the 3/1 twill. This is a strong, closely woven, warp-faced cotton cloth characterized by a simple stripe pattern in white and dark blue.

Tire Fabric: Certain types of heavy duck made from multiple-ply yarns: for example, builder fabric, breaker fabric, chafer fabric. They are used in the manufacture of rubber-tread tires.

Tobacco Cloth: A loosely woven, thin, lightweight cotton fabric usually made in 36-inch width and quite similar to cheesecloth. Name comes from its use as a shade covering for tobacco plants.

Toweling: A general term applied to various fabrics used for making towels. They are usually of cotton or linen, quite absorbent and often rather coarse in texture. Commonly woven in continuous pieces in widths of twelve and twenty-four inches and cut to any desired size. Examples are crash, terry cloth, huck, honeycomb.

Twills: In general, all fabrics woven with a twill weave.

Twist: Obtained in roving or yarn by revolving same on own axis, thereby arranging fibers in a spiral manner.

Twister: Machine that twists two or more yarns together, making ply yarn and laying same on bobbins.

U

Upholstery Fabric: Any of a diverse range of fabrics used mainly for upholstering furniture or automobiles, pleasure boats, and so forth. Commonly yarn dyed but also printed or piece dyed. Examples are brocade, damask, chintz, frise, repp, tapestry.

Upland Cotton: See American-Upland.

V

Vat Dye: Fast-dye process used in dyeing cotton fabrics and yarns.

Vertical Opener: Machine that beats and shakes out trash and dirt in cotton, fluffs up cotton, and prepares it for the Picker.

Viscose Rayon: Filaments composed of regenerated cellulose that has been coagulated or solidified from a solution of cellulose xanthate. The basic raw material is a woodpulp product of high alphacellulose content. This is combined with sodium hydroxide solution and dissolved in carbon bisulphide solution to give cellulose xanthate. This is then mixed with diluted sodium hydroxide solution to give the spinning solution, termed *viscose,* which is forced through an orifice of suitable design into the spinning bath where it is coagulated into monofilament. Historically, this was the third method tried in the production of rayon, and the original patents were taken out by two Englishmen, Cross and Bevan. Now this method accounts for about two-thirds of the world's annual production.

W

Warp Beam: See Beam.

Warper: Machine that transfers warp yarn from small packages such as cones or cheeses to the warp beam prior to weaving.

Waste: Salable by-products of cotton manufacturing such as card strips and comber noils.

Weave: To create fabric by interlacing warp and filling yarns.

Wet Twisting: Running yarn through water immediately before yarn is twisted.

Whipcord: Term applied to fabric covering a wide range of qualities and commonly made of cotton blends or worsted. The characteristic features are a bold upright warp twill that is accentuated by suitable weave (often a 63° steep twill) structure (more ends per inch than picks) and a clear finish—to the extent that the twill of warp threads forms a cordlike appearance.

Winder: Machine that transfers yarn from one package to another by winding it on in a regular design, which allows it to unwind without tangling or knotting.

Winding: The operation of transferring yarn from one package to another.

Wiping Cloth, Industrial: A wiping material used in cleaning machinery and in manufacturing processes, made in an absorbent fabric, cut to a standard size or sizes such as 18″ x 18″, and overedged or hemmed.

Y

Yarn: A continuous twisted strand of fibers of any required tensile strength, employed in manufacture of a fabric.

Yarn Dyed: Fabrics, the yarn of which was dyed before weaving or knitting.

GLOSSARY OF LEAVERS MACHINE-MADE LACE*

The names given to Leavers lace are principally the names of the localities where the different styles originated as handmade laces and do not in any case indicate geographical sources of origin. Some of them are excellent imitations of the handmade articles of the same name.

Alençon: Independent-beam, single-warp bobbin-fining and double-warp bobbin-fining laces, made to imitate the products of the French bobbinet-Jacquard machine. In 1879 this name was applied to a narrow lace that was made on the Leavers lace machine.

Armenian: Narrow cotton lace of needlework type, made with independent beams and used principally for trimming handkerchiefs.

Binche: The name applied to cotton lace containing a distinctive fancy net or ground. Made by independent beams in narrow widths, as a variant of Valenciennes, or in wider widths as a thick-threaded, bobbin-fining lace.

Blonde: Natural-colored silk lace of light texture, made on an Ensor net background.

Bohemian: Cotton or silk lace made with warps in which the pattern consists of tape-like shapes.

Bourdon (Margot): Silk lace in which the pattern is outlined with very coarse threads.

Brabant (Loop): Cotton lace in which the ground work and the filled-in motifs, which are outlined with thick threads, are made by the warp; also called loop laces.

Carrick-Ma-Cross: Cotton bobbin-fining lace made in two varieties: solid outlined motifs on a net ground or on a guipure ground with cast-off purls.

Chantilly: Fine-quality silk lace with the motif outlined by thick threads of spun silk or cotton.

Cluny: Cotton lace of coarse texture, made by independent beams and largely used for articles of furniture and upholstery purposes.

---

*From *Leavers Lace*, a publication of the American Lace Manufacturers Association, and used with its permission.

Craquele: Cotton lace containing an irregular-shaped net having the outline of a coffin and sometimes termed *coffin net*.

Duchess: Cotton machine-made imitation of Brussels and Honiton lace. Bobbin-fining lace made with brides and tapelike effects with the motifs outlined with thick threads.

English Antique: Cotton lace made by independent beams or bobbin-fining systems. The net contains square effects known as *guipure d'art*.

Everlasting: Narrow cotton trimmings of the French banded style; so named because of their durable wearing qualities.

Filet: Cotton lace distinguished by a square mesh. Made by independent beams as a variant of Val laces, or on a bobbin-fining set-out.

Guipure: Cotton lace that is distinguished by brides covered with purls and by independent beams generally made of silk.

Hamburg: Cotton independent-beam laces made with a solid ground to imitate cloth.

Irish Point: Cotton lace sometimes called Irish crochet or baby Irish, made by independent beams or on bobbin-fining set-outs and with heavy purls.

Malines: Cotton lace made with a single warp and fine front gimps, with outlining threads for the motifs of the pattern. In the late nineteenth century, laces made of silk warp and bobbins with fine mesh net and cotton gimps with outlining threads were called Malines and Fedora laces.

Maltese: Cotton lace made on the independent system with bands and crosses similar to those that are characteristic of the handmade silk articles of the same name. Further distinguished by a beautiful arrangement known as "crown-front."

Mirecourt: Cotton lace made on a bobbin-fining set-out and distinguished by a fine woven net known as "half-fining."

Normandie: Cotton lace made on a bobbin-fining set-out, plain or outlined with thick threads, made as wide as eight inches with various characteristic meshes such as diamond, round hole, Point de Paris, or filet. The plain styles were at one time known as "Platt Valenciennes"; the same laces are also made with a warp as well as back and front gimps.

Paraguay: Cotton lace made with independent beams containing wheel designs similar to Teneriffe laces, with fine drawn-thread effects akin to a spider-web texture.

Point d'Esprit: Cotton lace made by independent beams on an Ensor net set-out with small spots on the net.

Point de Paris: Cotton lace made by independent beams or the bobbin-fining system. The distinguishing feature of the lace is an octagonal net ground.

Russian Point: Cotton lace made by independent beams. The pattern is composed of tapelike bands with a very heavy cord running down the center.

Spanish: A heavy silk lace with designs consisting of large motifs such as roses and leaves made on a warp ground, Ensor-net system, with back and front gimps or center gimps.

Torchon: Cotton lace made by independent beams according to the Cluny style of fine yarns and narrow widths.

Tuck Laces: Tuck nets are ornamented with parallel rows of tucks, arranged either close together and covering the surface, or in clusters with spaces in between, which may be of plain Ensor net or fancy nets made by independent beams.

Valenciennes: Cotton lace made by independent beams, Calais Vals, Vraie Valenciennes or fil passe, an imitation of handmade Belgian Valenciennes laces.

French Vals	diamond mesh
German Vals	round-hole mesh made half gauge, the motifs and details full gauge
Filet Mesh Vals	square mesh
Ensor Net Vals	hexagonal mesh

Val laces also contain motifs of the Cluny, Maltese, and Torchon styles.

Veilings: Silk lace of fancy meshes for use as face veils or on hats.

Venetian: Cotton lace made on a bobbin-fining net set-out and characterized by specially shaped motifs with fancy nets, the connecting stems being of a broad, braided style and joined by brides.

Yak: Cotton or wool lace made by independent beams, half gauge. So called because these laces were handmade of wool spun from the fleece of the yak. Used for articles of furniture and upholstery purposes.

BIBLIOGRAPHY

BOOKS

Acheson, Dean. *Morning and Noon*. Boston: Houghton Mifflin Company, 1965.

Andrist, Ralph et al. *200 Years: A Bicentennial Illustrated History of the United States*. Vol. 1. Washington: *U.S. News & World Report*, 1973.

Arnold, Pauline and Percival White. *Clothes and Cloth, America's Apparel Business*. New York: Holiday House, 1961.

Ashton, Barbara. *Of Men and Money and the Fall River National Bank*. Published by the bank in its centennial year, 1975.

Bagnall, William. *The Textile Industries of the United States, 1639-1810*. Vol. 1. Cambridge MA: Riverside Press, 1893; Ann Arbor MI: University Microfilms, 1963. Authorized reprint of original edition, produced by microfilm-xerography.

_____. "The Textile Industries of the United States, 1893-1895." Vols. 2, 3, and 4. Unpublished manuscripts microfilmed by Harvard University Press. Obtained through Old Sturbridge Village Museum Library.

Baird, Charles W., D. D. *History of the Huguenot Emigration to America*. Vols. 1 and 2. New York: Dodd, Mead and Company, 1885.

Barfield, Rodney and Keith Strawn. *The Bechtler and Their Coinage: North Carolina Mint Masters of Pioneer Gold*. Raleigh NC: North Carolina Museum of History, 1980.

Barnwell, Mildred Gwin. *Cotton Magic: The Elementary Principles of Cotton Manufacture*. Greenwood SC: Jacobs Press, 1944.

Bateman, Fred and Thomas Weiss. *A Deplorable Scarcity*. Chapel Hill: University of North Carolina Press, 1981.

Battle, Kemp Plummer. *Memories of an Old-Time Tar Heel*. Edited by William James Battle. Chapel Hill: University of North Carolina Press, 1945.

Beal, Fred E. *Proletarian Journey*. New York: Da Capo Press, 1971.

Bendick, Jeanne. *Electronics for Young People*. New York: McGraw-Hill, 1947.

Bendure, Zelma and Gladys Pfeiffer. *America's Fabrics*. New York: Macmillan Company, 1946.

Besson, J. A. *History of Eufala, Alabama*. Atlanta: Jas. P. Harrison & Co., Printers, 1875; Spartanburg SC: Reprint Company, Publishers, 1976.

Bettersworth, John K. *Mississippi: A History*. Austin: Steck Company, 1959.

Birnbaum, Leon. *Legacy in Lace*. New York: Fairchild Publishing Company, 1967.

Blanchard, Fessenden S. *The Textile Industries of China and Japan: Post-War Opportunities and Problems for America*. New York: Textile Research Institute, 1944.

Blicksilver, Jack. *Man-made Fibers: A Growth Industry for the Diversifying South*. Atlanta: Georgia State University, 1961.

Blount, Willie. *A Catechetical Exposition of the Constitution of Tennessee. Tennessee Beginnings*. Knoxville: printed by George Roulstone, 1803.

Blythe, Legette. *Meet Julius Abernathy: Trader and Philanthropist*. Charlotte: W. Loftin, 1970.

————. *Robert Lee Stowe: Pioneer in Textiles*. Belmont NC: privately published, 1965.

————. *William Henry Belk, Merchant of the South*. Chapel Hill: University of North Carolina Press, 1950.

Boddie, William Willis. *History of Williamsburg*. Columbia SC: State Company, 1923.

Botkin, B. A., ed. *A Treasury of Mississippi River Folklore*. New York: Bonanza Books, 1978.

Brandis, Buford, Ph.D. *Is the South Expendable?: A Study of Foreign Trade and Southern Progress*. Atlanta: Emory University, 1949.

Brandon, Ruth. *A Capitalist Romance: Singer and the Sewing Machine*. New York: J. B. Lippincott, 1977.

Brewer, Willis. *Alabama: Her History, Resources, War Record, and Public Men from 1540-1872*. Spartanburg SC: Reprint Company, Publishers, 1975. (1872 ed. in Tutweiler's Collection of Southern History and Literature, Birmingham Public Library, Birmingham AL).

Broomhead, W. H. and H. W. Nichols. *Standard Cotton Cloths and Their Construction*. Fall River MA: Dover Press, 1927.

Brown, Douglas Summers. *A City without Cobwebs: A History of Rock Hill, South Carolina*. Columbia: University of South Carolina Press, 1953; Spartanburg SC: Reprint Company, Publishers, 1973.

Brown, Harry Bates. *Cotton*. New York: McGraw-Hill Book Company, 1938.

Buresh, Francis M. *Nonwoven Fabrics*. New York: Reinhold Publishing Company, 1962.

Burgwyn, Mebane Holoman. *River Treasure*. New York: Oxford University Press, 1947.

Bush, George S. *The American Harvest*. Englewood Cliffs NJ: Prentice-Hall, 1982.

Byars, Alvin W. *Olympia: Pacific the Way It Was, 1895-1970*. Professional Printers, Ltd., 1981.

Cain, Andrew W. *History of Lumpkin County for the First Hundred Years*. Atlanta: Stein Printing Company, 1932.

Caldwell, Doreen. *And All Was Revealed*. New York: St. Martin's Press, 1981.

Cameron, E. H. *Samuel Slater: Father of American Manufactures*. American Saga Series. Portland ME: Bond Wheelwright Company, 1960.

Cameron, H. C. *Samuel Crompton.* London: Batchworth Press, 1951.

Campbell, Charles. *History of the Colony and the Ancient Dominions of Virginia.* Philadelphia: J. B. Lippincott & Co., 1860.

Candee, Helen Churchill. *The Tapestry Book.* First edition, Frederick Stokes and Company, 1912. Second edition, New York: Tudor Publishing Company, 1935.

Carter, Hodding. *Lower Mississippi.* The Rivers of America Series. New York, Toronto: Farrar and Rinehart, 1942.

Cash, James. *The Mind of the South.* New York: Alfred A. Knopf, 1941.

Cate, Margaret Davis. *Our Todays and Yesterdays: A Story of Brunswick and the Coastal Islands.* Brunswick GA: Glover Bros., 1930.

Chesnut, Mary Boykin. *A Diary from Dixie.* First edition, abridged, Appleton and Company, 1905. Second edition edited by Ben Ames Williams. Boston: Houghton Mifflin Company, 1949.

Childs, Marquis. *The Farmer Takes a Hand: The Electric Power Revolution in Rural America.* Garden City NY: Doubleday and Company, 1952.

Claiborne, J. F. H. *Mississippi: As a Province, Territory, and State, with Biographical Notices of Eminent Citizens.* Vol. 1. (Vol. 2 never published, destroyed by fire.) Jackson MS: Power & Barksdale, 1880.

Clements, J. B. *History of Irwin County.* Spartanburg SC: Reprint Company, Publishers, 1978.

Cole, Arthur Harrison. *The American Wool Manufacture.* Cambridge MA: Harvard University Press, 1926.

Cole, Donald B. *Immigrant City: Lawrence, Massachusetts, 1847-1921.* Chapel Hill: University of North Carolina Press, 1963.

Conway, Mimi. *Rise Gonna Rise: A Portrait of Southern Textile Workers.* New York: Doubleday, 1979.

Cooper, Walter G. *Official History of Fulton County.* Atlanta: W. W. Brown, 1934; Spartanburg SC: Reprint Company, Publishers, 1978.

Crawford, M. D. C. *The Heritage of Cotton: The Fibre of Two Worlds and Many Ages.* New York: G. P. Putnam's Sons, 1924.

Cromwell, Jarvis. *With a Great Deal of Luck.* Dalton MA: Studley Press, 1976.

Cross, Malcolm A. *Dan River Runs Deep.* Middletown NY: Whitlock Press, 1982.

Crow, Jeffrey J. *The Southern Experience in the American Revolution.* Edited by Larry E. Tise. Chapel Hill: University of North Carolina Press, 1978.

Dabney, Virginius. *Below the Potomac: A Book about the New South.* New York and London: D. Appleton-Century Company, 1942.

Davidson, Elizabeth H. *Child-Labor Legislation in the Southern Textile States.* Chapel Hill: University of North Carolina Press, 1939.

Davis, Burke. *The Southern Railway.* Chapel Hill: University of North Carolina Press, 1985.

Davis, Hiram S. *Economic Issues in Textiles: A Challenge to Research*. Philadelphia: Industrial Research Dept., Wharton School of Finance and Commerce, University of Pennsylvania, 1945.

_____. *The Industrial Study of Economic Progress*. Philadelphia: University of Pennsylvania Press, 1947.

Davis, Robert Scott, Jr., ed. *The Wilkes County Papers, 1773-1833*. Easley SC: Southern Historical Press, 1979.

_____ and the Rev. Silas Emmett Lucas, Jr., eds. *The Georgia Land Lottery Papers, 1805-1914*. Easley SC: Southern Historical Press, 1979.

Dembeck, Adeline. *Guidebook to Man-Made Textile Fibers and Textured Yarns of the World*. 2d ed. Rochester NY: Christopher Press, 1964.

Derrick, Samuel Melanchthon. *Centennial History of South Carolina Railroad*. Columbia SC: State Co., 1896; Spartanburg SC: Reprint Company, Publishers, 1975.

Dickson, Harris. *The Story of King Cotton*. New York: Funk & Wagnalls Company, 1937.

Dodd, William E. *The Old South: Struggles for Democracy*. New York: Macmillan Company, 1937.

Dorgan, Maurice B. *History of Lawrence, Massachusetts*. Second ed., Cambridge: Murray Print Co., 1924. (1st ed. of 1918 was entitled *Lawrence Today*.)

Dorsey, James E. *Footprints along the Hoopee: A History of Emanuel County, 1812-1900*. Originally published for the Emanuel Historic Preservation Society. Spartanburg SC: Reprint Company, Publishers, 1978.

Dowd, Jerome. *Sketches of Prominent Living North Carolinians*. Raleigh NC: Edwards & Broughton, Printers and Binders, 1888.

Duggan, I. W. and Paul W. Chapman. *'Round the World with Cotton*. Washington: GPO, 1941.

Dunwell, Steven. *The Run of the Mill*. Boston: David R. Godine, 1978.

Durden, Robert F. *The Dukes of Durham, 1865-1929*. Durham NC: Duke University Press, 1975.

Earle, John R., Dean D. Knudsen, and Donald W. Shriver, Jr. *Spindles & Spires*. Gastonia NC: John Knox Press, 1976.

Finkelman, Paul. *An Imperfect Union: Slavery, Federalism, and Comity*. Chapel Hill: University of North Carolina Press, 1981.

Fleming, Walter L. *Civil War and Reconstruction in Alabama*. New York: Macmillan, 1905; Spartanburg SC: Reprint Company, Publishers, 1978.

Fogel, Robert William and Stanley L. Engerman. *Time on the Cross: The Economics of American Negro Slavery*. Boston: Little, Brown and Company, 1974.

Galbraith, John Kenneth. *A Life in Our Times*. Boston: Houghton Mifflin Company, 1981.

Garlington, J. C. *Men of the Time*. Spartanburg SC: Garlington Publishing Company, 1902; Spartanburg: Reprint Company, Publishers, 1972.

Garrett, Franklin M. *Atlanta and Its Environs: A Chronicle of Its People and Events*. Vol. 3. New York: Lewis Historical Publishing Inc., 1954.

Garside, Alston Hill. *Cotton Goes to Market.* New York: Frederick A. Stokes, 1935.

George, James Z. *The Political History of Slavery in the United States.* New York: Neale Publishing Company, 1915.

Gibson, Count D. *Sea Islands of Georgia: Their Geologic History.* Athens: University of Georgia Press, 1948.

Gilman, Glenn. *Human Relations in the Industrial Southeast: A Study of the Textile Industry.* Chapel Hill: University of North Carolina Press, 1956.

Golden, Clinton S. and Harold J. Ruttenberg. *The Dynamics of Industrial Democracy.* New York and London: Harper and Brothers, Publishers, 1942.

Golden, Harry. *Our Southern Landsmen.* New York: G. P. Putnam's Sons, 1974.

Gouldrick, Paul F. *New England Textiles in the Nineteenth Century: Profits and Investment.* Cambridge MA: Harvard University Press, 1968.

Grass, Milton N. *History of Hosiery.* New York: Fairchild Publications, 1955.

Graves, John Temple. *The Fighting South.* New York: G. P. Putnam's Sons, 1943.

Greenman, Russell L. *The Worker, the Foreman and the Wagner Act.* New York and London: Harper and Brothers, Publishers, 1939.

Guess, William Francis. *South Carolina Annals of Pride and Protest.* New York: Harper & Brothers, Publishers, 1957.

Hall, Carrie. *A Review of the Follies and Foibles of Fashion: From Hoopskirts to Nudity, 1866-1936.* Caldwell ID: Caxton Printers, 1938.

Hall, James. *A Brief History of the Mississippi Territory.* Salisbury NC: F. Coupee, 1801; Spartanburg SC: Reprint Company, Publishers, 1976.

Harris, Joel Chandler. *Stories of Georgia.* New York, Cincinnati, Chicago: American Book Company, 1896; Spartanburg SC: Reprint Company, Publishers, 1972, 1974.

Hareven, Tamara K. and Randolph Langenbach. *Amoskeag: Life and Work in an American Factory-city.* New York: Pantheon, 1979.

Heron, Alexander R. *Sharing Information with Employees.* Stanford: Stanford University Press, 1964.

Herring, Harriet L. *Passing of the Mill Village.* Chapel Hill: University of North Carolina Press, 1949.

_____. *Southern Industry and Regional Development.* Chapel Hill: University of North Carolina Press, 1940.

High, Stanley. *Roosevelt—and Then?* New York and London: Harper and Brothers, Publishers, 1937.

Hogan, William Ransom and Edwin Adams Davis, eds. *William Johnson's Natchez: Source Studies in Southern History.* Vol. 1. Baton Rouge: Louisiana State University Press, 1951.

Howard, Robert West. *This Is the South.* Chicago, New York, San Francisco: Rand McNally & Company, 1959.

Hoye, John. *Staple Cotton Fabrics.* New York and London: McGraw-Hill Book Company, 1942.

Hudson, Arthur Palmer. *Humor of the Old Deep South*. New York: Macmillan Company, 1936.

Hullinger, Edwin Ware. *Plowing Through: The Story of the Negro in Agriculture*. New York: William Morrow and Company, 1940.

Hutchinson, J. B., R. A. Silow, and S. G. Stephens. *The Evolution of Gossypium*. Oxford, England: Oxford University Press, 1947.

Ireland, Marian P. *Textile Art in the Church*. Nashville and New York: Abingdon Press, 1966, 1967, and 1971.

Jacobs, William Plumer. *The Pioneer*. Clinton SC: Jacobs Press, 1935.

_____. *Problems of the Cotton Manufacturer in South Carolina*. Clinton SC: Jacobs Press, 1935.

Jones, Charles C., Jr. *Antiquities of the Southern Indians*. New York: D. Appleton and Company, 1873; Spartanburg SC: Reprint Company, Publishers, 1983.

_____. *Memorial History of Augusta, Georgia*. Syracuse NY: D. Massen & Co., Publishers, 1890; Spartanburg SC: Reprint Company, Publishers, 1980.

Jones, Katharine M. *The Plantation South*. Indianapolis, New York: Bobbs-Merrill Company, 1957.

Kane, Harnett. *Gone Are the Days*. New York: E. P. Dutton and Company, 1960.

Kephart, Horace. *Our Southern Highlanders*. New York: Macmillan Company, 1922.

Ketchum, Richard M., ed. *Picture History of the Civil War*. Vols. 1 and 2. Narrative by Bruce Catton. New York: The American Heritage Publishing Company, 1960.

Key, V. O., Jr. *Southern Politics: In State and Nation*. New York: Alfred A. Knopf, 1949.

Kimball, H. J. *International Cotton Exposition: A Report*. New York: D. Appleton & Company, 1882.

Kohn, August. *The Cotton Mills of South Carolina*. (Republished from the *News and Courier*, Charleston SC.) Columbia SC: South Carolina Agriculture, Commerce and Immigration Commission, 1907; Spartanburg SC: Reprint Company, Publishers, 1975.

Konkle, Burton Alva. *John Motley Morehead and the Development of North Carolina, 1796-1866*. Chapel Hill: University of North Carolina Press, 1922; Spartanburg SC: Reprint Company, Publishers, 1971.

Kornbluh, Joyce L. *Bread and Roses: The 1912 Lawrence Textile Strike*. Excerpt from *Rebel Voices: An IWW Anthology*. Ann Arbor: University of Michigan Press, 1964.

Lahne, Herbert J. *The Cotton Mill Worker: Labor in Twentieth-Century America*. New York and Toronto: Farrar and Rinehart, 1944.

Lamprey, L. *The Story of Weaving*. Stokes and Company, 1939.

Landreau, Anthony N. *America Underfoot: A History of Floor Coverings from Colonial Times to the Present*. Washington: Smithsonian Institution Press, 1976.

Landrum, Dr. J. B. O. *Colonial and Revolutionary History of Upper South Carolina*. Greenville SC: Shannon and Company, 1897; Spartanburg SC: Reprint Company, Publishers, 1977.

_____. *History of Spartanburg County*. Atlanta: Franklin Printing and Publishing Company, 1900; Spartanburg SC: Reprint Company, Publishers, 1977.

Lawrence, William. *Memories of a Happy Life*. Boston and New York: Houghton-Mifflin Co., 1928.

Lefler, Hugh Talmadge and Albert Ray Newsome. *North Carolina*. Chapel Hill: University of North Carolina Press, 1954.

Leiding, Harriette Kershaw. *Historic Houses of South Carolina*. Philadelphia: J. B. Lippincott Company, 1921; Spartanburg SC: Reprint Company, Publishers, 1975.

Linton, George E., Ph.D., and Joseph Pizzuto. *Applied Textiles: Raw Materials to Finished Fabrics*. Des Moines and New York: Duell, Sloan and Pearce (affiliate of Meredith Press), 1948. Fourth ed., rev. New York: Life & Time, 1963.

Little, Frances. *Early American Textiles*. New York: Century Company, 1931.

Lowry, Robert and William H. McCardle. *Mississippi: A History*. Jackson MS: R. H. Henry and Company, 1891.

Lucas, the Rev. Silas Emmett, Jr., ed. *The Third and Fourth or 1820 and 1821 Land Lotteries of Georgia*. Easley SC: Georgia Genealogical Reprints/Southern Historical Press, 1973.

_____, ed. *The Second or 1807 Land Lottery of Georgia*. Vidalia GA: Georgia Genealogical Reprints, 1968.

McIlwaine, Shields. *The Southern Poor White*. Norman OK: University of Oklahoma Press, 1939.

McLaurin, Melton Alonza. *Paternalism and Protest*. Westport CT: Greenwood Publishing Co., 1971.

McLendon, S. G. *History of the Public Domain of Georgia*. Atlanta: Foote & Davies Co., 1924; Spartanburg SC: Reprint Company, Publishers, 1974.

Malott, Deane W. and Boyce F. Martin. *Agricultural Industries*. New York: McGraw-Hill Book Company, 1939.

Marsh, J. T. *Mercerizing*. London: Chapman & Hall, 1941.

Matthews, J. Merritt, Ph.D. *Textile Fibers*. First edition, New York: Columbia University Press, 1904. Fourth edition, New York: John Wiley and Sons, 1924.

Meek, A. B. *Romantic Passages in Southwestern History*. New York: S. H. Goetzel & Co., 1857; Spartanburg SC: Reprint Company, Publishers, 1975.

Miller, Billy Robert. *McAdenville: Spun from the Wilderness*. Gastonia NC: E. P. Press, 1982.

Mitchell, Broadus, Ph.D. *The Rise of Cotton Mills in the South*. Edited by William D. Farnum. Baltimore: Johns Hopkins University Press, 1921; New York: Da Capo Press Reprint Series, 1968.

_____. *William Gregg*. Social Studies Series. Chapel Hill: University of North Carolina Press, 1928.

Mitchell, Frances Letcher. *Georgia Land and People*. Atlanta: Franklin Printing and Publishing Co., 1974.

Mitchell, George Sinclair. *Textile Unionism and the South*. Chapel Hill: University of North Carolina Press, 1931.

Montgomery, Florence M. *Printed Textiles: English and American Cottons and Linens, 1700-1850*. A Winterthur Book. New York: Viking Press, 1970.

Mowry, William A. *Nathaniel Mowry of Rhode Island*. Providence: Sidney S. Rider, 1878.

Murphy, William S. *Textile Industries: The Practical Guide to Fibers, Yarns and Fabrics*. London: Gresham Publishing Co., 1910.

Myers, Robert Manson, ed. *The Children of Pride*. Vols. 1, 2, and 3. New Haven: Yale University Press, 1972.

Newman, Edwin. *A Civil Tongue*. New York: Bobbs-Merrill Company, 1976.

Noland, Julia Tigner. *Confederate Greenbacks*. San Antonio: Naylor Company, 1940.

Oliver, Nola Nance. *The Gulf Coast of Mississippi*. New York: Hastings House, 1941.

Paxton, Col. A. G. *The Atlanta Campaign: The Retrograde of the Confederacy*. Greenville MS: N.p., 1940.

Payton, Boyd E. *Scapegoat: Prejudice, Politics, Prison*. Philadelphia: Whitmore Publishing Company, 1970.

Percy, William Alexander. *Lanterns on the Levee*. New York: Alfred A. Knopf, 1931.

Perry, Josephine. *The Cotton Industry*. New York: Longmans, Green and Company, 1943.

Pettit, Florence H. *America's Printed & Painted Fabrics, 1600-1900*. New York: Hastings House, 1970.

Plummer, Leigh S. *Getting Along with Labor: Practical Personnel Programs*. New York and London: Harper and Brothers, Publishers, 1939.

Polo, Marco. *Adventures of Marco Polo*. Edited by Richard J. Walsh. New York: Modern Library, 1926.

_____. *The Travels of Marco Polo*. George Marsden's revised translation. Edited by Manuel Komroff. Modern Library Series. New York: Random House, 1926.

Pope, Liston. *Labor's Relation to Church and Community*. Sponsored by the Institute for Religious and Social Studies, Yale University. New York: Harper and Brothers, Publishers, 1942.

_____. *Millhands and Preachers: A Study of Gastonia*. New Haven: Yale University Press, 1942.

Puett, Minnie Stowe. *History of Gaston County*. Charlotte NC: Observer Printing House, 1939.

Quigley, Thomas H. and W. S. Smith. *Cotton Mill Mathematics*. Atlanta: Turner E. Smith and Company, 1935.

Quimby, Ian M. G. and Polly Anne Earl, eds. *Technological Innovation and the Decorative Arts*. Charlottesville: University Press of Virginia, 1974.

Raven-Hart, Major R. *Down the Mississippi*. Boston: Houghton Mifflin Company, 1938.

Richardson, James M. *History of Greenville County, South Carolina*. Atlanta: A. H. Cawston, Publishers, 1930; Spartanburg SC: Reprint Company, Publishers, 1980.

Robertson, Ben. *Red Hills and Cotton*. New York: Alfred A. Knopf, 1942.

Rodier, Paul. *The Romance of French Weaving*. New York: Tudor Publishing Company, 1936.

Schwarz, Jordan A. *The Speculator Bernard M. Baruch in Washington, 1917-1965.* Chapel Hill: University of North Carolina Press, 1981.

Separk, Joseph H. *Gastonia and Gaston County, North Carolina: Past, Present, Future.* Kingsport TN: Kingsport Press, 1936.

Shuey, Audrey M. *The Testing of Negro Intelligence.* Lynchburg VA: J. P. Bell Company, 1958.

Simkins, Francis Butler. *The South, Old and New.* New York: Alfred A. Knopf, 1947.

Simon, William E. *A Time for Truth.* New York and Chicago: McGraw-Hill Book Company, Reader's Digest Press, 1978.

Simpson, William Hays, Ph.D. *Life in Mill Communities.* Clinton SC: Jacobs Press, 1941.

_____. *Some Aspects of America's Textile Industry with Special Reference to Cotton.* Columbia SC: R. L. Bryan Company, 1966.

_____. *Southern Textile Communities.* Charlotte NC: Dowd Press, 1948.

Smith, Allene De Shazo. *Greenwood Leflore and the Choctaw Indians of the Mississippi Valley.* Memphis: C. A. Davis Printing Company, 1951.

Smith, Daniel. *A Short Description of the Tennessee Government: The Constitution of the State of Tennessee.* Philadelphia: printed by Matthew Carey, bookseller, 1793; Spartanburg SC: Reprint Company, Publishers, 1976.

Smith, James F. *The Cherokee Land Lottery.* New York: Harper & Brothers, 1838; Vidalia GA: Georgia Genealogical Reprints, 1968.

Smith, Louise et al. *And Clover Began to Grow.* Clover SC: Westmoreland Printers, 1977.

Soule, George. *Sidney Hillman: Labor Statesman.* New York: Macmillan Publishing Company, 1939.

Spangler, Henry Wilson. *Elements of Steam Engineering.* 3rd ed., rev. and enl. New York: J. Wiley and Sons, 1910.

Spear, W. F. *History of North Adams, Massachusetts, 1749-1885.* North Adams MA: Hoosac Valley News Print House, 1885; Moscow ID: Clear Water, Publisher, 1974.

Springs, Katherine Wooten. *The Squires of Springfield.* Charlotte NC: William Loftin, Publisher, 1965.

Spruill, Julia Cherry. *Women's Life and Work in the Southern Colonies.* With a new introduction by Anne Firor Scott. First edition, Chapel Hill: University of North Carolina Press, 1938. Third edition, W. W. Norton & Company, 1972.

Squire, Geoffrey. *Dress and Society, 1560-1970.* New York: Viking Press, 1974.

Stevens, Horace Nathaniel. *Nathaniel Stevens, 1786-1865.* North Andover MA, 1946.

_____. *65 Years in the Stevens Woolen Industry.* North Andover MA: privately published, 1941.

Stevenson, Margetta, ed. *How the Fashion World Works: Fit Yourself for a Fashion Future.* New York and London: Harper and Brothers, Publishers, 1938.

Stockard, S. W. *The History of Alamance.* Raleigh NC: Capital Printing Company, 1900.

Stowell, Marion Barber. *Early American Almanacs: The Colonial Weekday Bible.* New York: Burt Franklin & Company, 1977.

Street, James, Jr. *James Street's South*. New York: Doubleday, 1955.

Taylor, Alrutheus Ambush, Ph.D. *The Negro in Tennessee, 1864-1880*. Washington: Associated Publishers, 1941; Spartanburg SC: Reprint Company, Publishers, 1974.

Thomas, Gertrude Z. *Richer Than Spices*. New York: Alfred A. Knopf, 1972.

Thomas, Z. V. *History of Jefferson County*. Macon GA: J. W. Burke Company, 1927; Spartanburg SC: Reprint Company, Publishers, 1978.

Tindall, George B. *The Emergence of the New South, 1913-1945*. Baton Rouge: Louisiana State University Press, 1967.

Tompkins, D. A. *Cotton Mill, Commercial Features: A Text-Book for the Use of Textile Schools and Investors*. Charlotte NC: Published by author, 1899.

_____. *History of Mecklenburg County and the City of Charlotte*. Vols. 1 and 2. Charlotte NC: Published by author, 1903.

Vance, Rupert, John E. Ivey, Marjorie N. Bond. *Exploring the South*. Chapel Hill: University of North Carolina Press, 1949.

Volbach, W. Fritz. *Early Decorative Textiles*. London, New York, Sydney, and Toronto: Hamlyn Publishing Group, 1969.

Wallechinsky, David and Irving Wallace. *The People's Almanac*. Garden City NY: Doubleday & Company, 1975.

Walton, Perry. *The Story of Textiles*. 2d ed. Boston: Walton Advertising and Printing Company, 1925.

Warburton, Gertrude and Jane Maxwell. *Fashion for a Living*. 1st ed. New York: McGraw-Hill Book Company, 1939.

Ware, Caroline F. *The Early Cotton Manufacture: A Story of Industrial Development*. Boston: Houghton Mifflin Company, 1931.

Weis, Frederick Lewis, Th.D. *Ancestral Roots of Sixty Colonists*. Lancaster MA, 1951.

Wertheimer, Barbara Mayer. *We Were There*. New York: Pantheon Books, 1977.

West, Uta, ed. *Women in a Changing World*. New York: McGraw-Hill Book Company, 1975.

Whisnant, David E. *All That is Native and Fine*. Chapel Hill and London: University of North Carolina Press, 1983.

White, Edwin E. *Highland Heritage: The Southern Mountains and the Nation*. New York: Friendship Press, 1937.

White, George S. *Memoir of Samuel Slater: History of the Rise and Progress of the Cotton Manufacture in England and America*. 2d ed. Philadelphia, 1836.

White, Nelson C. *Abbott H. Thayer, Painter and Naturalist*. Hartford: Connecticut Printers, 1951.

White, Theodore H. *In Search of History: A Personal Adventure*. New York: Harper & Row, 1978.

Whitridge, Arnold. *No Compromise: The Story of the Fanatics Who Paved the Way to the Civil War*. New York: Farrar, Straus and Cudahy, 1960.

Who Was Who in America. Chicago: Marquis Publication, 1943.

Williamson, Hugh, M.D., LL.D. *The History of North Carolina*. Vol. 2. Philadelphia: Thomas Dobson, 1812.

Wingate, Isabel B. and June F. Mohler. *Textile Fabrics and Their Selection*. Englewood Cliffs NJ: Prentice-Hall, 1984.

Woodhouse, Thomas. *The Finishing of Jute and Linen Fabrics*. London: Macmillan and Company, 1928.

Woodward, C. Vann. *The Burden of Southern History*. Baton Rouge: Louisiana State University Press, 1960, 1974.

_____. *Origins of the New South, 1877-1913*. Vol. 9 of *A History of the South*. Baton Rouge: Louisiana State University Press, 1974.

Woodward, W. E. *The Way Our People Lived*. New York: E. P. Dutton & Company, 1944.

Woolf, Douglas G., ed. *The Rayon Handbook*. (Including staple fiber.) New York: McGraw-Hill Publishing Company, 1939.

Yaseen, Leonard C. *Plant Location*. New York: Book Production Company, 1956.

Young, James R. *Textile Leaders of the South*. Columbia SC: The R. L. Bryan Company, 1963.

Young, T. M. *The American Cotton Industry*. London: Methuen and Company; New York: Charles Scribner's Sons, 1902.

Zimiles, Martha and Murray Zimiles. *Early American Mills*. New York: C. M. Potter, 1973.

PUBLICATIONS BY TEXTILE TRADE ASSOCIATIONS HISTORICAL, SCIENTIFIC, AND EDUCATIONAL GROUPS

American Economic Security. Washington: Chamber of Commerce of the United States, 1955, 1956.

The A.F.L. Textile Workers: A History of the United Textile Workers of America. United Textile Workers of America.

Andrews, Elmer F. "Tribulations of a Wage-Hour Administrator." *Public Opinion Quarterly* 4:1 (1940).

_____. "Wages and Hours." *Journal of Social Work* 75:1 (1939).

Andrews, Mildred Gwin. *The Anatomy of an Exhibition*. Washington: American Textile Machinery Association, 1969.

_____. *A Brief History of American Textile Machine Progress*. Washington: American Textile Machinery Association, 1955.

_____. *Profit Life of Textile Machinery*. Washington: American Textile Machinery Association, 1958.

_____. "Textile Almanac and Calendar of Events: Covering Important Events in the History of the Industry through the Ages and Including Present Times, 800 B.C. to 1952 A.D." Used as a textbook by the North Carolina State College School of Textiles, 1952-1954.

_____. *Visits to One Hundred Textile Mills*. New York: Cotton Mills Information Service, 1948.

"As Dr. Taylor Sees It." *Underwear and Hosiery Review*, 1935.

Association Activities and the Law. Washington: Chamber of Commerce of the United States.

Backman, Jules and M. R. Gainsbrugh. *Economics of the Cotton Textile Industry*. New York: The National Industrial Conference Board, 1946.

Barnwell, Mildred Gwin. *Faces We See*. Gastonia NC: The Southern Combed Yarn Spinners, 1939.

Bell, John. "Cotton Thread Industry in the United States." Paper commemorating the tenth anniversary of the Cotton Thread Institute. New York, 3 November 1943.

Bell, W. Ray. *25 Years: The Association of Cotton Textile Merchants of New York, 1918-1943*. New York: Association of Cotton Textile Merchants of New York and Parker-Allston Associates, 1943.

Bolton, John H., Jr. "The Machinery Builders' Responsibility in Textile Progress." Paper presented at the annual meeting of American Textile Machinery Association, Washington.

Brock, R. A., ed. *Documents Relating to Huguenot Emigration to Virginia and the Settlement at Manakin Town*. Edited and compiled for the Virginia Historical Society. Richmond, 1886; rev. eds., Baltimore: Genealogical Publishing Company, 1962, 1966.

Buck, George S., Jr. *Flammability of Consumer Textiles: Summary of Active Cotton Research*. Memphis: National Cotton Council of America, 1950.

Campbell, Malcolm. *Cotton Quality*. North Carolina State College School of Textiles, 1947.

The Case against Balance-of-Payments Controls. Machine & Allied Products Institute, Council for Technological Advancement. Washington, 1968.

Cope, Robert F. and Manly Wade Wellman. *The County of Gaston*. Gaston County Historical Society. Heritage Printers, 1961.

Cotton at the Crossroads. Charlotte: The American Cotton Manufacturers Association, 1937.

Cotton Counts Its Customers. Memphis: National Cotton Council of America, 1939, 1947, 1956, 1958.

Cotton: From Raw Material to Finished Product. Fourth edition, New York: The Cotton Textile Institute, 1947.

Cotton Inspirations. New York: The Cotton Textile Institute, 1947.

Cotton Thread Brands in the USA. New York: The Cotton Thread Institute.

Davis, Charles S., Ph.D. *The Cotton Kingdom in Alabama*. Montgomery: Alabama State Department of Archives and History, 1939.

Davis, Hiram S. et al. *Vertical Integration in the Textile Industries*. Washington: The Textile Foundation, 1938.

Dill, Col. D. B. "Properties of the Blood of Negroes and Whites in Relation to Climate and Season." *Journal of Biological Chemistry* 136:2 (November 1940).

Do You Know These Important Facts about Cotton? Washington: The Cotton Textile Institute.

"Early Industry Developed Slowly." *Hosiery Newsletter,* 8 November 1974.

Economic Outlook for the Capital Goods Industries. Washington: Machinery and Allied Products Institute, 1956-1965.

The Economic Outlook for U.S. Cotton. Washington: National Cotton Council of America, 1978.

Effect of the New Tax Depreciation Methods on the Earnings of Depreciable Assets. Washington: Machinery and Allied Products Institute, 1956.

Eisenhower, Dwight D. "Celebrating America's 350th Birthday." Foreword to *The Jamestown Festival.* Souvenir Program. Edited by Parke Rouse, Jr., 1957.

Encouragement of Domestic Industry. Transactions of the Rhode Island Society, 1861. Knowles, Aumody and Company, Printers, 1862.

Felkin, William, F.L.S., F.S.S. *A History of the Machine-Wrought Hosiery and Lace Manufacturers.* London, 1867. Preface by Gordon Hanes. Published for the American Society of Knitting Technologists. Research & Source Works Series, No. 148. Second edition, New York: Burt Franklin, 1967.

Fisher, Russell. *Satisfying the Salaried Employee.* Boston: National Association of Manufacturers, 1957.

Future of Georgia Is Woven in Textiles. Atlanta: The Cotton Manufacturers Association of Georgia, 1930.

Gilbane, Brendan F. *Pawtucket Village Mechanics: Iron, Ingenuity, and the Cotton Revolution.* Rhode Island Historical Association, 1975.

Goodhue, Charles E., Jr. *Ipswich: Proud Settlement in the Province of the Massachusetts Bay.* Newcomen Society in North America, 1953.

Hamby, S. *The American Cotton Handbook.* Vols. 1 and 2. First edition, Textile Book Publishers, 1949. Third edition, New York: Interscience Publishers, division of John Wiley and Sons, 1965.

Hammond, M. B. *The Cotton Industry.* Vol. 1, pt. 1. American Economic Association. New York: Macmillan Company, 1897.

Hanna, A. J. "A Diary of Tench Francis Tilghman: The Confederate Baggage and Treasure Train Ends Its Flight in Florida." *Florida Historical Quarterly* (January 1939).

Haskell, Ira J. *Hosiery thru the Years.* Lynn MA: Carole Mailing Service, 1956.

Hosiery Statistics. Charlotte: National Association of Hosiery Manufacturers, 1948.

Jackson, Floyd H., M.S. *Yarn and Cloth Calculations.* New York: Textile Book Publishers, 1947.

Keep the Cotton Mills in Georgia. Atlanta: The Cotton Manufacturers Association of Georgia, 1930.

Kpycinski, Joseph V. *Textile Industry.* Detroit: Book Tower, 1964.

Lawton, Mrs. James A. *Family Names of Huguenot Refugees to America*. Baltimore: Genealogical Publishing Company, 1963.

Leasing of Industrial Equipment. MAPI Symposium. Washington: Machinery and Allied Products Institute, 1965.

Lebhar, Bertram. "50 Years of Progress." *Hosiery and Underwear Review* (July 1950).

Lipscomb, Ed. *Grassroots Public Relations for Agriculture*. Little Rock AR: Pioneer, 1950.

McCord, Frank A. and Raymond Steinbach, Jr. *Cotton in the Converting Industry*. Memphis: National Cotton Council of America, 1948.

Manufacturing (U.S.) Investments Abroad and the Government Program for Balance of Payments Improvement. Washington: Machinery and Allied Products Institute, Council for Technological Advancement, 1965.

Merrill, G. R., A. R. Macormac, and H. R. Mauersberger. *American Cotton Handbook: A Practical Reference Book for the Entire Cotton Industry*. New York: American Cotton Handbook Company, 1941.

Muntz, Earl E. *Growth and Trends in Social Security: Studies in Individual and Collective Security, No. 6*. New York: National Industrial Conference Board, 1949.

Murchison, Claudius, Ph.D. "The Cotton Textile Industry and Foreign Economic Policy." Paper presented at a seminar held by The American Cotton Manufacturers Institute, Charlotte, North Carolina, 8 February 1954.

_____. *Spots and Futures*. New York: Cotton Textile Institute, 1940.

_____. *World Trade and the United States*. Charlotte NC: The American Cotton Manufacturers Institute, 1953.

A New Opportunity for All Textile Men through Research. Princeton: Textile Research Institute, 1944.

Ogburn, Charlton. *Railroads: The Great American Adventure*. Washington: National Geographic Society, 1977.

Old Hand-Knit Cotton Stockings Show Interesting Construction Details. Charlotte NC: National Association of Hosiery Manufacturers, 1945.

Penn, Theodore Z. "Calico Cylinder: The Introduction of Printing in America: Technological Innovation and the Decorative Arts." Seminar paper. Winterthur Conference Report. Baltimore, 1973.

Printing of Piecegoods and Related Processes. New York: The Cotton Textile Institute. (Merged with American Cotton Manufacturers Association in 1952. Now American Textile Manufacturers Institute, Washington.)

Proceedings of 41st Annual Convention, Washington, D.C., May 13-14, 1937. An Annual Report. Washington: American Cotton Manufacturers Association.

Products, Liability and Reliability. Washington: Machine and Allied Products Institute, Council for Technological Advancement, 1967.

Reaman, G. Elmore. *The Trail of the Huguenots: In Europe, the United States, Africa, and Canada*. Baltimore: Genealogical Publishing Company, 1966.

Report and Recommendations of the Hosiery Industry Postwar Planning Committee. Charlotte NC: National Association of Hosiery Manufacturers, 1945.

Rivard, Paul E. *Textile Experiments in Rhode Island, 1788-1789.* Author was director of Slater Mill Historic Site and Museum in Pawtucket RI.

Rosatto, Vittoria, ed. *Leavers Lace.* A study made by Professor Edward Golec and George G. Armstrong, Jr. Providence: American Lace Manufacturers Association, 1948.

Rowan, Richard L. *The Negro in the Textile Industry.* Industrial Research Unit, Department of Industry, Wharton School of Finance and Commerce, University of Pennsylvania. Philadelphia: University of Pennsylvania Press, 1970.

Rowland, Mrs. Dunbar. *Life, Letters and Papers of William Dunbar, 1749-1810.* Jackson: Press of Mississippi Historical Society, 1930.

Sappington, C. O. *Industrial Health—Asset or Liability.* Chicago: Industrial Commentaries, 1939.

Schenke, E. M. *The Manufacture of Hosiery and Its Problems.* New York: National Association of Hosiery Manufacturers, 1935.

Simpson, William Hays. *America's Textile Industry.* Columbia SC: Division of General Studies, University of South Carolina, 1966.

Small, Robert S. *U.S. Textile Opportunities in the '80's.* American Textile Machinery Association, 1979.

Smith, Harold DeWitt (chairman of the Committee of 13). *Textile Fibers.* An Edgar Marburg Lecture for the American Society for Testing Materials, vol. 44. Philadelphia, 1944.

Southern Combed Yarn Spinners Association Annual Reports. Gastonia NC, 1938-1946.

Southern Firms to Clothe Needy. Issued by American Association of Cotton Manufacturers. Published in *Christian Science Monitor,* 1932-1933.

Southern Mill Rules. Charlotte NC: The American Cotton Manufacturers Association, 1935.

The Story behind GATT. Publication No. 140. American Tariff League, 1955.

Sullivan, William K., ed. *The Facts about the New England Cotton and Man-Made Fiber Textile Industry Today.* National Association of Cotton Manufacturers, 1954.

Terborg, George. *Proprietary Manufacturing Know-How and the Requirements of National Defense: A Vital Issue in Government Contracts.* Washington: Machine and Allied Products Institute and Council for Technological Advancement, 1956.

Tested Knowledge of Business Cycles. 42d Annual Report. New York: National Bureau of Economic Research, 1962.

Testimony before House Subcommittee on International Trade, Investment, and Monetary Policy. American Textile Machinery Association, 1978.

Textile Design. New York: Federated Council on Art Education, and Connecticut College, New London CT: Institute of Women's Professional Relations, Research Headquarters, 1936.

Textile Design as an Occupation. New York: Federated Council on Art Education, 1936.

Textile Designs of Japan. Osaka, Japan: Japan Textile Color Design Center, 1959.

The Textile Economy: Restrained Recovery. Textile Workers Union of America, 1962.

Textile Markets: Their Structure in Relation to Price Research. New York: National Bureau of Economic Research, 1939.

Textile Research, Development, Education and Testing. New York: New York Board of Trade, 1949.

Textile Research Institute Annual Reports. Princeton, 1963.

Textile Research Journal. Monthly. Princeton: Textile Research Institute, 1958.

Textile Trends, 1952-1978. Washington: American Textile Manufacturers Institute, 1978.

Thompson, J. W. *The Clinical Status of a Group of Negro Sharecroppers.* American Medical Association, 1941.

Thruelsen, Richard. "Textile Trainee." *Saturday Evening Post,* 4 December 1948.

Trade Associations: Their Economic Significance and Legal Status. New York: National Industrial Conference Board, 1925.

Trademarks of Thread Brands, Manufactured by Thread Industry of the United States. Washington: The Thread Institute. (A series, 1922-1945.)

Traffic Committee Annual Report, 1949-1950. Charlotte NC: American Cotton Manufacturers Association.

The following series were published by the Council for Technological Advancement, Chicago.

Trends in Technology and Employment
Trends in Education and Utilization of Technical Manpower: Critical National Issue
Economic Outlook for the Capital Goods Industries, 1956-1965
Trends in Equipping the American Worker

Trumbull, Benjamin. *History of Connecticut, Civil and Ecclesiastical, from the Immigration of Its First Planters, from England, in the Year 1630 to the Year 1764.* 2 vols. in 1, rev. Reprint of 1818 ed. Research Library of Colonial Americana. New York: Arno Press, 1972.

Unionization of the Textile Industry: A Case Study of J. P. Stevens. The Heritage Foundation, 1977.

Walker, Caldwell, ed. *Record of Southern Progress.* 1963.

Wilhelm, Dwight. *Alabama Cotton Manufacturers Association 1949 Annual Report (including) Historical Sketches of Early Alabama.* Biloxi, Mississippi.

——————. *History of the Cotton Textile Industry of Alabama, 1809-1950.* Montgomery AL, 1949.

Wilken, Carl H. *Price Stability or Booms and Busts?* New York: Raw Materials National Council.

The following series of textbooks on cotton yarn manufacture was undertaken at the direction of The Textile Foundation, Washington, and written by members of the staff of Clemson Textile School, Clemson College, South Carolina.

Willis, H. H., Gaston Gage, and Vernette B. Moore. *Cotton Classing Manual.* 1938.

Willis, H. H., and Vernette B. Moore. *Combing.* 1937.

——————. *Cotton Carding.* 1936.

_____. *Cotton Opening, Cleaning and Picking.* 1937.

_____. *Drawing Frames.* 1937.

Willis, H. H., G. H. Dunlap, and Vernette B. Moore. *Cotton Spinning.* 1938.

Willis, H. H., R. K. Eaton, and Vernette B. Moore. *Roving Frames.* 1938.

COMPANY PUBLICATIONS
ABOUT THE TEXTILE INDUSTRY

Latham Alexander and Company. *Cotton Movement and Fluctuation, 1900-1905.*

The American Thread Company. *The Story of Cotton Thread.* Willimantic, Connecticut.

American Viscose Corporation. *Avisco Rayon: Short Story of Rayon.* Philadelphia, 1948.

_____. *Rayon Fabrics.* Philadelphia, 1944.

_____. *The Record of Rayon Cord in Tires.* Philadelphia, 1944.

Andrews, Mildred Gwin. *An Economic Analysis of Silk.* Irving Trust Company. New York: Dun & Bradstreet, 1946.

Arthur Anderson and Company. *Inventory Profitability Study.* Gaffney Manufacturing Company, Gaffney, South Carolina, 20 March 1959.

Battle, Kemp Daves. *A History of the Rocky Mount Mills.* Rocky Mount NC: Rocky Mount Mills, 1944.

Burlington Industries. *Swifter Than a Weaver's Shuttle: The Story of Burlington Industries.* Greensboro NC.

Canton Cotton Mills. *The Story of a Man, a Town, and a Mill: 50th Anniversary of Canton Cotton Mills.* Canton GA, 1949.

Chase, H. M. *The Treatment of Cotton Roving and Yarns with Bonding Agents.* Danville VA: Riverside & Dan River Cotton Mills.

Chase, William H. *Five Generations of Loom Builders.* Draper Corporation, Hopedale MA. Cambridge MA: University Press, 1950.

Clifton Mills. *80th Anniversary.* Spartanburg SC, 1960.

Clinton Mills. *Clinton Mills, Clothmaker.* Clinton SC, 1976.

Collins Brothers Machine Company. *History of the Collins Family,* chs. 3 and 4. Pawtucket RI, 1976.

Cone Mills Corporation. *81st Annual Report.* Greensboro NC: Cone Printing Service, 1975.

_____. *Handbook: You . . . and Your Company.* Greensboro NC.

_____. *World Leadership in Denims.* Dedicated to the founders of Cone Mills. Greensboro NC, 1925.

Cramer, Stuart W. *Useful Information for Cotton Manufacturers.* First edition, 1898. Second edition in 3 vols. Vol. 1: *Textile Machinery.* 1904. Vol. 2: *Sundry and Miscellaneous Equipment and Power Plants.* 1904. Vol. 3: *Dyeing and Special Finishing Machinery.* 1906. Charlotte NC: Queen City Publishing and Paper Company.

Crawford, M. D. C. *Highlights in the Progress of Cotton Spinning.* Introduction by Hyman Battle. Rocky Mount NC: Rocky Mount Mills, 1944.

Crompton, George. *The Crompton Loom.* Worcester MA: Davis Press, 1949.

Curtis and Marble Corporation. *History of Curtis and Marble.* Worcester MA, 1956.

Dan River Mills. *The Dan River Pattern.* Danville VA.

Davis & Furber Machine Company. *The Davis & Furber Machine Company and the Men Who Made It, 1832-1908.* North Andover MA.

E. I. du Pont de Nemours and Company. *About du Pont Nylon.* Wilmington DE, 1946.

——————. *Nylon: Development, Physical Properties, and Present Status.* Dr. James K. Hunt, director.

——————. *Nylon: The First Twenty-Five Years,* 1963.

——————. *Nylon Textile Fibers in Industry,* 1947.

The Exposition Cotton Mills Company. *Seventieth Anniversary, 1882-1952.* Atlanta GA, 1952.

Fieldcrest Mills. *Educational Workshop, Industry in Action—Guided Tours.* 1949.

Gianino, Salvatore. *Signs of the Times.* New York: Textile Banking Company, 1976.

Gibb, George Sweet. *The Saco-Lowell Shops.* Cambridge MA: Harvard University Press, 1950.

Harris, Milton, ed. *Handbook of Textile Fibers.* Washington: Harris Research Laboratories, 1954.

Haven, George B. *Handbook of Industrial Fabrics.* WestPoint Pepperell. New York: Wellington Sears Company, 1941.

Indigo in America. Parsippany NJ: BASF Wyandotte Corp., 1976.

James Hunter Machine Company. *Heritage of Dependability, 1847-1947.* North Adams MA, 1947.

Hutton, Alfred, Jr. *The Evolution of Hosiery Machinery.* New York: Bentley Knitting Machinery Organization, 1962.

Kennedy, Stephen J. and Hiram S. Davis. *Textile Markets.* Boston: Pacific Mills Company, 1940.

Knowles Loom Works. *Knowles Open Shed Fancy Looms.* Worcester MA, 1895.

Knowlton, Evelyn H. *Pepperell's Progress: History of a Cotton Textile Company, 1844-1945.* Cambridge MA: Harvard University Press, 1948.

Lamb Knitting Machine Company. *Lamb Knitting Machine Company.* 2 vols. Chicopee MA, 1884 and 1919.

Lincoln, Samuel B. *Lockwood Greene: The History of an Engineering Business, 1832-1958.* Brattleboro VT: Stephen Greene Press, 1960.

Marshall Field & Company. *Annuity Plan for Employees of Marshall Field & Company.* Chicago, 1947.

——————. *Pension Plan for Employees of Marshall Field & Company.* Chicago, 1946, 1951.

Milliken & Company. *The Milliken Story.* Tape Recording. New York, 1978.

Moore, James Lewis and Thomas Herron Wingate. *Cabarrus Reborn: A Historical Sketch of the Founding and Development of Cannon Mills Company and Kannapolis*. Kannapolis NC: Kannapolis Publishing Company, 1940.

National Drying Machinery Company. *Textile Finishing Equipment: Automatic Loop Dryers for Piece Goods*. Philadelphia.

Navin, Thomas R. *The Whitin Machine Works Since 1831*. Cambridge MA: Harvard University Press, 1950.

New Orleans Cotton Exchange. *History of New Orleans Cotton Exchange*. New Orleans LA.

Our Railroad. Norfolk & Western Railway, 1950.

Pacific Mills. *Memoirs of a Corporation*. 12 installments. Boston MA, 1950.

Palmer, Albert. *Know Your Weaving Costs!* Charlotte NC: Crompton & Knowles Loom Works, 1950.

_____. *Measuring Weave-Room Efficiency*. Charlotte NC: Crompton & Knowles Loom Works, 1950.

_____. *A Practical Plan for Regulating Work Assignment*. Charlotte NC: Crompton & Knowles Loom Works, 1950.

Parks-Cramer Company. *A Brief History of Parks-Cramer Company*. Charlotte NC and Fitchburg MA, 1937, 1943.

Pendleton Woolen Mills. *The Wool Story . . . from Fleece to Fashion*. Portland OR, 1971.

Pepperell Manufacturing Company. *The Romance of Pepperell*. New York: William Ridge and Sons, 1921.

Redstone, Al. "Problems and Progress: Proctor and Schwartz Since 1802." Philadelphia: Proctor and Schwartz, 1970.

Robinson, G. O. *The Character of Quality*. Greenwood Mills. Columbia SC: R. L. Bryan and Company, 1964.

Russell, Benjamin. *Whale Ships and Whaling Scenes*. Boston MA: State Trust Company, 1955.

Saco-Lowell Shops. *Cotton Mill Machinery*. Boston MA, 1920. (Now Platt Saco-Lowell Corporation, Greenville SC.)

_____. *Saco-Lowell Bulletin. 150th Anniversary Issue, 1813-1963*. Special edition of monthly series. Easley SC.

_____. *Saco-Lowell Bulletins*. October 1963 to October 1973. Easley SC.

Scott, R. C. *Incentives in Manufacturing*. The Eddy-Rucker-Nickels Company, 1966.

Singer Manufacturing Company. *The Invention of the Sewing Machine*. New York.

_____. *The Singer Company History*. New York, 1965.

Smith, Robert Sidney. *Mill on the Dan: A History of Dan River Mills, 1882-1950*. Durham: Duke University Press, 1960.

The Southern Serves and Sells the South. Southern Railway System, 1949.

The Spool Cotton Company. *The Story of Cotton Thread*. 2d ed. New York, 1939.

Springs, Elliott White. *Clothes Make the Man*. Springs Mills. New York: J. J. Little & Ives Company, 1949.

Sutton, Louis V. *Carolina Power and Light Company, 1908-1958*. Raleigh NC: Newcomen Society in North America, 1958.

Sykes, E. T., Jr. *Sykes' Lightning Cotton-Seed Calculator*. 2d ed. Charleston SC: Walker, Evans and Cogswell Company, 1901.

Tallassee Mills. *Briefs*. Tallassee AL, 1926.

Taylor, Wesley. *The Story of Hosiery*. May Hosiery Mills. High Point NC: Houck and Company, 1931.

Ted A. Podbereski & Associates, Textile Management Engineers. *The Singer Company: Knitting Technology*.

Teplitz, Irving. *Principles of Textile Converting*. New York: Textile Book Publishers, 1947.

Thompson, Albert W., ed. *Air Conditioning Textile Mills*. 2d rev. ed. Charlotte NC and Fitchburg MA: Parks-Cramer Company, 1925.

Tinsley, John F. *Looms for the World*. Crompton & Knowles Corporation. Newcomen Society in North America, 1949.

Tymeson, Mildred McClary. *The Wyman-Gordon Way, 1883-1958*. Worcester MA: Commonwealth Press, 1959.

The United Piece Dye Works. *Guidebook to Man-Made Textile Fibers and Textured Yarns of the World*. New York, 1964.

Walker, S. J. *History of Joseph Sykes Brothers and Ashworth Brothers Incorporated*. Greenville SC and New Bedford MA, 1939.

Werner Textile Consultants. *A Look at the 1960's*. New York, 1960.

West, Thomas H. *The Loom Builders: The Drapers as Pioneer Contributors to the American Way of Life*. Draper Corporation. Hopedale MA and Spartanburg SC: Newcomen Society in North America.

Whitin Machine Works. *A Look at the United States Textile Industry through 1970*. Whitinsville MA, 1963.

——————. *In This Quiet Valley*. Whitinsville MA, 1945.

——————. *Whitin Cotton Card-Room Machinery*. Whitinsville MA, 1928.

——————. *Whitin Cotton Picking Machinery*. Whitinsville MA, 1928.

——————. *Whitin Spinning Frames for Cotton*. Whitinsville MA, 1928.

Whitin-Roberts Company. *Whitin Review*. Charlotte NC.

Wonalancet Company. *Wonalancet Cotton Tables*. Nasua NH, 1923.

Wright, Mrs. Breene L., ed. *Lace: Aristocrat of Textile Fabrics*. United States Testing Company, Consumers Service Division. Hoboken NJ, 1949.

Yorke, Dan. *Men and Times of Pepperell: An Account of the One Hundred Years of the Pepperell Manufacturing Company, Incorporated, 1844-1944*. Boston, 1945.

ARTICLES IN TRADE AND OTHER PERIODICALS

"America's Textiles: 200 Years of Textile Manufacturing." *America's Textile Reporter/Bulletin* 5:3 (March 1976): 29.

"Annual Textile Statistics Section." Ibid. (1968).

Andrews, Elmer F. "What Amendments to the Wage and Hour Law?" *Dun's Review* 48:2144 (April 1940).

Andrews, Mildred Gwin. "Can a Textile Man Make Money?: Yes, If Merchandising Policies Are Renovated." *Textile World Annual Issue,* "Way to Profit" Section (August 1939): 96.

_____. "Cotton-Breeding Research Pays Off." *Textile World* (May 1942): 73-76.

_____. "Cotton Picker Portents." *Business Week* (5 September 1936): 15.

_____. "Exploring the Textile Community." (Monthly series.) *Textile World.* New York: McGraw-Hill, 1943-1958.

_____. "Full-Fashioned Lisle . . . " *Textile World* (February 1938).

_____. "International Harvester Cotton Picker." *Textile World* (January 1943).

_____. "King Cotton Weekly." Syndicated column with 125 newspaper subscribers (1930-1933), Gastonia NC.

_____. "Machinery Association Touches Every Phase of Textile Manufacture." *ESC Quarterly*, textile edition, 25:1-4 (1969): 31-32. Issued by Employment Security Commission of North Carolina.

_____. "New Textile Machinery Stages Debut." *Cotton Trade Journal—36th International Edition* (1969): 102-105.

_____. "Picker Progress: Checking Up on 1937 Status of One of the Big Stories of 1936." *Textile World* (June 1937): 81.

_____. "Rust Cotton Picker—Means Gradual Motorization, But Not Violent Economic Upheaval." *Textile World* (1936): 66-68.

_____. "Sea Island Cotton Revival." *Textile World* (January 1937): 76-77.

_____. "The Situation as Seen Across an Executive's Desk." (Monthly series.) *Cotton* (now *Textile Industries*). Atlanta: W. R. C. Smith Publication, 1938-1945.

_____. *Textile World.* (Periodic miscellaneous articles.) New York: McGraw-Hill, 1934-1958.

_____. "Watson's New Centrifugal Cotton Gin." *Business Week* (December 1937): 40; *Commercial Appeal* (Memphis TN), December 1937; and *Textile World* (December 1937).

_____. "Arguing Merger Guides." *Business Week* (August 1968).

"Byssinosis." *Textile Industries* (August 1978).

Chamberlain, Anne. "Panty Hose: See How They Run." *McCall's Magazine* (March 1971).

"The Changing Textile Industry's Challenge to Machinery Manufacturers." *International Textile Publications.* (Report of I.T.P. Seminar, American Textile Machinery Exhibition-International, 21 October 1969, Greenville SC.)

Crawford, M. D. C. "Cotton and Spices: East Meets West." *The Carolinas* 1 (1932).

Dearing, Gerald L. "The Oscar Johnston Cotton Foundation: Opening New Vistas for Cotton." *Commercial Appeal* (Memphis TN), 1945.

"Decisions of Southern Educators on Study of Cotton." *Cotton Trade Journal* (1944). The Cotton Educational Conference, Memphis TN.

"Dixie Spins the Wheel of Industry." *National Geographic Magazine* (March 1949).

Doar, Harriet. "The Servants of King Cotton." *Charlotte Observer* (NC), August 1978.

"Fact File." *Textile World* (annual edition).

"George Dockray: Textile Machinery Industry Gadfly." *Textile Industries* (August 1978).

High, Stanley. "A Kind Word for the South." *Saturday Evening Post*, 1938.

Hildebrand, J. R. "Cotton: Foremost Fiber of the World." *National Geographic Magazine* 79:2 (February 1941).

Jeremy, David J. "British Textile Technology Transmission to the United States: The Philadelphia Region Experience, 1770-1820." *Business History Review* 47:1 (Spring 1973).

_____. "Innovation in American Textile Technology during the Early Nineteenth Century." *Technology and Culture* (January 1973).

Keebler, James C., ed. "What Automation Means to America." *Automation* 11:4 (April 1964).

King, Augusta Wylie. "International Cotton Exposition." *Atlanta Historical Bulletin* 18 (1939).

Lawrence, David. "Limiting Wage Increases and Sharing Profits." *U.S. News & World Report* (April 1972).

Lesesne, Henry. "Lou Brissie." *The State Magazine* (March 1949).

Love, James Lee. "Some Bits of Gaston County Textile History." *America's Textile Reporter/Bulletin* (March 1948).

"Maremount Trips over Auto Parts." *Business Week* (20 July 1968).

"Market and Media Data." *Modern Knitting* (July 1976).

"Men Go on a Fashion Kick." *Business Week* (20 July 1968).

Mettler, Alexandra. "The Textile Woman: An Expanding Role." *Textile Industries* (October 1977).

"Modern Bleaching, Dyeing, and Finishing Techniques." *Textile World* (1924).

Modern Textiles. Fiftieth anniversary issue (August 1975).

"New Products and New Sales Ideas." *Journal of Commerce* (1963).

"North Carolina Produces Forty Percent of Nation's Hosiery." *ESC Quarterly* 11:1-2 (Winter-Spring 1953). Issued by Employment Security Commission of North Carolina.

"The Pace of Change: Textiles, 1868-1968." *Textile World*. Centennial issue.

Philip, Robert. "United States Textile Mission to Japan." *Cotton* (1937).

"Running Hard But Standing Still." *Business Week* (10 August 1968).

"Southern Story Becomes Textile Story Rather Than Cotton Story." *Southern Textile News* (2 October 1954).

"Southern Textile Progress: New Plants Led by Knits." *America's Textile Reporter/Bulletin* 97:12 (December 1971).

"The South's Development." (Part two.) *Manufacturers Record* (11 December 1924).

"A Special Study of America's Textile Industry." *America's Textile Reporter/Bulletin* (1977).

"Staple Cotton Review." Staple Cotton Growers Association, Alfred Stone, ed. (Weekly for members.)(1920–).

"Textile Machinery." *Textile Industries* (August 1978).

"Twenty-Five Years of Southern Textile Progress." (Reprinted from the twenty-fifth anniversary issue of *Textile Industries*, January 1924).

"United States Textile Job." *Textile Industries* (August 1978).

Urlaub, George A. "Women's Stockings (over Last 25 Years)." *Knit Goods Weekly* (5 April 1948).

Ward, Derek. "Non-Wovens International: A Report on Index '78." *Modern Textiles* (June 1978).

"Will Clayton's Cotton." *Fortune Magazine* (1945).

"The Woolen and Worsted Mill Handbook." *Textile World* (1940).

BULLETINS, ARTICLES, AND OTHER INFORMATION FROM ORGANIZATIONS, MUSEUMS, AND PRIVATE COLLECTIONS

Alabama Textile Manufacturers Association. Bulletins and general data.

American Federation of Hosiery Workers. *Making History in Hosiery.* 1938.

American Textile Machinery Association, Washington. Bulletins and general data.

American Textile Manufacturer's Institute, Washington. Bulletins and general data.

American Wool Manufacturers. Bulletins and photos.

American Yarn Spinners Association, Gastonia NC. Annual reports.

Andrews, Elmer F. "Scrapbooks 1930-1940." Wage and Hour legislation; newspaper and textile publication clippings; eight scrapbooks.

Andrews, Mildred Gwin. "A Study on Housing Developments in Textile Mill Areas." For the Committee on Public Relations of the Cotton-Textile Institute, New York, 1948.

_____. "Educational Developments Made Possible through the Efforts of the Textile Industry." For the Committee on Public Relations of the Cotton-Textile Institute, New York, 1947.

Brooks, Lester (chairman, Jefferson Standard Life Insurance Company of Charlotte). "Scrapbook." Owned by his daughter, Mrs. Martha Jean Brooks Miller, Charlotte NC.

Chapelle, Howard I. *The National Watercraft Collection*. Washington: Smithsonian Institution, 1960.

Cherington, Paul T. *The Commercial Problems of the Woolen and Worsted Industries*. Washington: Textile Foundation, 1932.

Cross, Malcolm. "Textile Pioneers of Greenville: Civil War to World War I." Talk given before the South Carolina Textile Manufacturers Association, 1976.

Federated Council on Art Education and the Institute of Women's Professional Relations. *Textile Design as an Occupation*. 1936.

Georgia Textile Manufacturers Association. Bulletins and historic material. Atlanta GA.

Gossett family of North and South Carolina. "Scrapbook 1900-1946." Letters, family photos, and papers of James P. and Ben Gossett.

Holt, Edwin Michael. "Occasional Diary 1844-1854." Family papers of his great-granddaughter, Mrs. Julian Robertson, Salisbury NC.

Lepawsky, Albert. *State Planning and Economic Development in the South*. Washington: Committee of the South, National Planning Association, 1949.

Loper, Ralph E., Consultants, Engineers. Special studies and reports. Greenville SC.

Machinery & Allied Products Institute. Bulletins, seminars. Washington.

Merrimack Valley Textile Museum. Bulletins, reproduced articles. Lowell MA.

Montgomery, Walter, Sr. Photographs and reports of overseas missions, World War II; letters and papers of his grandfather, Captain John Montgomery. Spartanburg SC.

National Association of Wool Manufacturers. Bulletins and general data. Boston.

North Carolina Textile Manufacturers Association. Bulletins and general data. Raleigh NC.

Northern Textile Association. Bulletins and general data. Boston.

Old Sturbridge Village Textile Museum. Papers and other data prepared by Ted Penn, director. Sturbridge MA.

Pullan, Mrs. *The Lady's Manual of Fancy-Work: A Complete Instructor in Every Variety of Ornamental Needle Work*. New York: Dick & Fitzgerald, Publishers, 1858.

Ragan, R. A. *Gaston County Textile Leaders*. 2 vols. (Period after 1904.) Reproduced newspaper clippings. Raleigh NC: North Carolina State University, 1975.

_____. *The Pioneer Cotton Mills of Gaston County: "The First Thirty," 1848-1904*. Reproduced newspaper clippings. Raleigh NC: North Carolina State University.

Silk, Ed, ed. *Nonwovens and Disposable Soft Goods*. Denville NJ, 1979.

South Carolina Textile Manufacturers Association. Bulletins and general data. Columbia SC.

The Splendor of Rare Tapestries Created from the Priceless Treasures of the Louvre. Photographic reproductions of famous sixteenth-century Flemish tapestries.

Stickley, John. Scrapbooks of yarn sales, 1920-1960.

Textile Economics Bureau. *Textile Organon*. (Monthly.) Stanley B. Hunt, ed. New York, 1940-1963.

The Thread Institute. (Merged with American Textile Manufacturers Institute.) *Documentary Materials*. Washington.

Werner, Jack, textile consultant. Papers and statistical material. New York.

Wright, Joseph. "Scrapbooks 1890-1920." 9 vols. Newspaper clippings about U.S. finishing companies. Owned by his grandson, Joseph Wright, Charlotte NC.

TRADE PUBLICATIONS

American Cotton Grower. Seton Ross, ed. Memphis. (Succeeded *Cotton Trade Journal*.)

American Fabrics and Fashions. Cecil Lubell, ed. New York.

America's Textiles. Randolph Taylor. Greenville SC.

Canadian Textile Journal. Bill Davidson. Montreal, Canada.

The Carolina Financial Times. William B. Givson, marketing director. Raleigh NC.

Charlotte Magazine. James L. Townsend, ed. Charlotte NC.

Cotton Trade Journal (international editions). Francis Hickman, ed. Memphis, 1935-1955.

Daily News Record. Matthew Kasten, ed. New York.

Dun's Review. Dun & Bradstreet. New York, 1940.

Fairchild Publications. John B. Fairchild, president. New York.

Fibre Market News. Anthony Abitante, ed. New York.

Forbes. Dero A. Saunders, exec. ed. New York.

Hosiery and Underwear Magazine. Jerald M. Bloom, ed. New York.

Knitting Times. Charles Reichman, ed. New York.

Metal Working News. Al Mari, ed. New York.

Modern Knitting. "Covering the Complete Knitting Spectrum from Fiber . . . to Fabric . . . to Finished Apparel." (Annual.) New York, 1977, 1978, 1979.

Modern Knitting Management. Harold E. Mitchell, regional manager. Atlanta.

Modern Materials Handling. Gordon C. Thomas, assoc. ed. Boston.

Modern Textiles. (Monthly.) A. H. McCullough, publisher. New York.

Phi Psi Quarterly. Cleveland Adams, ed. Published by Phi Psi Fraternity, textile school deans. (Spring 1978).

Southern Textile News. (Weekly.) Ernest E. Elkins, publisher. A Mullen Publication, Charlotte NC.

Textile Chemist and Colorist. Jack Kissiah, editorial director. Research Triangle NC.

Textile Engineer. Judith W. Kip, ed. Philadelphia.

Textile Equipment. James L. Prendergast, publisher. Charlotte NC.

Textile Industries. Robert J. Edsall, ed. A W. R. C. Smith Publication. Atlanta.

Textile Machinery Index. James Holdsworth & Sons. John Worrall Limited. New Bank, Halifax, Yorkshire, 1958.

Textile Research Journal. Richard K. Toner. Published by Textile Research Institute. Princeton NJ.

Textile Technology Digest. Dennis C. Loy, ed. Charlottesville VA.

Textile World. Lawrence A. Christiansen, Jr., editor-in-chief. A McGraw-Hill Publication. Atlanta.

GOVERNMENT, FEDERAL, AND STATE
REPORTS AND HEARINGS

Alabama Department of Industrial Relations. *History of the Child-Labor-Law Movement in Alabama.* Child Labor Agency reports, 1887-1947.

The American Civil War—A Centennial Exhibition. Library of Congress, 1961.

Andrews, Mildred G. *Netherlands Textile Industry Modernization, Expansion, Open Market to Machine Builders. International Commerce.* A special report prepared at the request of the United States Department of Commerce. June 1963.

Anglo-American Cotton Textile Conference. (Report of) April 2-13, 1948. Manchester and London.

Civil War Centennial Commission. *The U.S. on the Eve of the Civil War as Described in the 1860 Census.* Washington: GPO, 1963.

Davis, Charles S. *The Cotton Kingdom in Alabama.* Montgomery: Alabama State Department of Archives and History, 1939.

Dill, Lt. Col. D. B. 1. *Report on Observations in Southwest Pacific and Pacific Ocean Areas.* 2. *The Combat Uniform.* Office of the Quartermaster General, Research & Development Branch Military Planning. October-December 1944.

Federal Environment Resources Administration. *Reminiscences of Pioneer Residents of Leflore County, Mississippi.* Historic Research Project. Washington: GPO, 1933.

Federal Trade Commission. *Report of National Conference on Weights and Measures.* Washington: GPO, 1947.

_____. *Rules and Regulations under the Textile Fibers Products Identification Act.* Washington: GPO, 1960; amended, 1974.

_____. *Trade Practice Rules, 1937-1941.* Washington: GPO.

Forbes, W. H., R. E. Johnson, and F. Consolazio. *Leukopenia in Negro Workmen.* Report prepared for U.S. Health and Welfare Department. Washington: GPO.

Geyer, Lee E. Remarks on "the phoney farmer lobby." *Congressional Record.* 75th Cong., 2d sess., 1939.

Holland, James W. *Andrew Jackson and the Creek War: Victory at the Horseshoe.* Eastern National Park and Monument Association and Horseshoe Bend National Military Park, 1968.

Howell, L. D. *Changes in American Textile Industry—Competition—Structure—Facilities—Costs.* Technical Bulletin No. 1210. Marketing Research Division, Agricultural Marketing Service. Washington, 1959.

Lepawsky, Albert. *State Planning and Economic Development in the South.* Report prepared for the National Planning Association, Committee of the South. Washington, 1949.

McKeough, Raymond S. Remarks on "Wage and Hour Law amendments." *Congressional Record.* 75th Cong., 2d sess., 1939.

McLaughlin, Glenn F. and Stefan Robock. *Why Industry Moves South.* Report prepared for the National Planning Association, Commission of the South. Washington, 1949.

Ministry of Production. *Report of the Cotton Textile Mission to the United States of America.* London, 1944.

Molyneaux, Peter. *The Cotton South and American Trade Policy.* Report prepared for the National Peace Conference. New York, 1936.

National Emergency Council. *Report on Economic Conditions of the South.* Washington: GPO, 1938.

Nevins, W. *The Federal Wage and Hour Law: The Fair Labor Standards Act of 1938.* Report prepared for the U.S. Department of Labor. Washington: GPO, 1941.

Office of the Quartermaster General and War Production Board. *First Report of Textile Team Sent to Germany by Quartermaster General.* Washington: GPO, 1945.

Organization for European Economic Co-operation. Textiles Committee. *Interim Report on the European Recovery Programme.* December 1948.

South Carolina Department of Labor. *42nd Annual Report.* 1 July 1976 to 30 June 1977.

U.S. Congress. House. Committee on Agriculture. *Research and Related Services in the United States Department of Agriculture.* 81st Cong., 2d sess., 1959. Vol. 3.

_____. Committee on Ways and Means. Subcommittee on Foreign Trade Policy. *Compendium of Papers on United States Foreign Trade Policy.*

_____. International Trade Committee. Subcommittee on Investment and Monetary Policy. *Testimony of American Textile Machinery Association.* 96th Cong., 2d sess., 1978.

_____. Subcommittee on Education and Labor. *Hearings on the Impact of Imports and Exports on American Employment.* 87th Cong., 1961.

U.S. Congress. Senate. Subcommittee on Interstate and Foreign Commerce. *Hearings on the Problems of the Domestic Textile Industry.* 85th Cong., 2d sess., 1958; 87th Cong., 1st sess., 1961; 87th Cong., 2d sess., 1962; 88th Cong., 1st sess., 1963.

U.S. Department of Agriculture. *Cotton Classers.* (Handbook.) Washington: GPO.

_____. *Cotton: Compilation of Statutes Relative to Soil Conservation, Marketing Quotas and Allotments, Soil Bank, Community Credit Corporation, Price Support, Export and Surplus Removal, Crop Insurance, Sugar Payments and Quotas, Marketing Agreements and Orders, School Lunch, and Related Statutes.* (Handbook.) Washington: GPO, 1961.

_____. *Cotton: (including Cottonseed) and Other Fiber Plants.* Ch. 10, pt. 2. (Known as the Pace Report.) Washington: GPO, 1950.

_____. *Cotton: Statistics & Related Data.* Statistical Bulletin No. 99, 1951.

_____. *Women's Preferences among Selected Textile Products.* Washington: GPO, 1947.

U.S. Department of Commerce. *Industries Profiles—1958-1965.* Washington: GPO.

_____. *Principal Sources of Statistical Data on Textiles & Apparel.* Washington: GPO, 1964.

U.S. Department of Labor. *The American Workers' Fact Book.* Washington: GPO, 1960.

_____. *Health & Welfare Funds in the Needle Trades.* Seminar held in October 1946.

_____. *Impact of Automation.* Bulletin no. 1287, 1960.

_____. *Industry Wage Studies.* Washington: GPO, 1947.

_____. *Labor in the South: Labor Supply; Development of Trade-Unionism.* Bureau of Labor Statistics. *Monthly Labor Review* 63:4 (October 1946).

_____. *Mill Earnings: In Cotton Goods.* Bulletin no. 798.

_____. *State and Regional Variations in Prospective Labor Supply.* Bureau of Labor Statistics. Bulletin no. 893.

_____. *Union Agreements in the Cotton Textile Industry.* Bureau of Labor Statistics. Bulletin no. 885, 1946.

_____. *Wages in Cotton-Goods Manufacturing.* Bureau of Labor Statistics. Washington: GPO, 1938.

_____. *Work and Wage Experience of Cotton Textile Workers.* Bureau of Labor Statistics. *Monthly Labor Review* 63:4 (October 1946); 63:1 (July 1946).

_____. *The Workers' Story—1913-1953.* Labor Yearbook no. 2.

U.S. Interdepartmental Trade Agreement Organization. *The General Agreement on Tariffs and Trade (GATT).* Washington: GPO, 1954, 1955.

U.S. State and War Departments. *Textile Mission to Japan.* Washington: GPO, 1946.

U.S. Tariff Commission. *The Rayon Industry.* Washington: GPO, 1944.

War Production Board. National Security Resources Board, World War II. *Directory of Industry Advisory Commission.* Washington: GPO.

_____. *Wages in a National Emergency.* Wage Stabilization Board. Washington: GPO, 1951.

Work Projects Administration. *North Carolina—A Guide to the Old North State.* The Federal Writers' Project of the Federal Works Agency. Washington: GPO, 1940.

_____. *Palmetto Pioneers: Six Stories of Early South Carolinians.* The Federal Writers' Project of the Federal Works Agency. Rpt., Washington: GPO, 1972.

Wulsin, Frederick R. *Responses of Man to a Hot Environment.* Report prepared for the Office of the Quartermaster General. Published by Climatic Research Unit, Research and Development Branch, Military Planning Division, 1940.

Zeizel, Rose. *Technological Changes in Manpower Trends.* Report prepared for the U.S. Department of Labor. Bulletin no. 1817, 1974.

_____. *Technological Trends in Major American Industries.* Report prepared for the U.S. Department of Labor. Bulletin no. 1474, 1968.

DICTIONARIES, DIRECTORIES, ENCYCLOPEDIAS, GENERAL AND TEXTILE

American Textile Machinery Association—Its Members and Their Products. Annual edition.

American Textile Manufacturers Institute. *Annual Directory.* Washington.

Andrews, Mildred G. "Cotton." *Encyclopedia Brittanica,* 1938.

Carmichael, W. L., George E. Linton, Isaac Price. *Callaway Textile Dictionary.* La Grange GA: Callaway Mills, 1947.

The Chicago Manual of Style. 12th ed., rev. Chicago and London: University of Chicago Press, 1969.

Clark's Directory of Southern Textile Mills. Annual issue. Greenville SC.

Daugherty, Margaret M., Julia H. Fitzgerald, Donald O. Bolander. *Instant Spelling Dictionary.* Mundelein IL: Career Institute, 1964.

Davison's Textile Blue Book. Annual issue. Ridgewood NJ: Davison Publishing Company.

Donald, W. J. *Trade Associations.* New York and London: McGraw-Hill Book Co., 1933.

Linton, George E. *The Modern Textile Dictionary.* New York: Duell, Sloan and Pearce, 1963.

Man-Made Textile Encyclopedia. J. J. Press, ed. New York: Textile Book Publishers, 1959.

Marquis, Albert Nelson. *Who's Who in America.* Annual issue. Chicago: A. N. Marquis Company.

Mauersberger, Herbert R. *Matthews' Textile Fibers.* 5th ed. New York: John Wiley & Sons, 1947.

Miller, Bessie May. *Private Secretary's Encyclopedia Dictionary.* Englewood Cliffs NJ: Prentice-Hall.

Random House Dictionary of the English Language. Unabridged edition. New York: Random House, 1966.

Rodale, J. I. *The Glossaries.* Emmaus PA: Rodale Books, 1967.

_____ and Edward J. Fluck. *The Synonym Finder.* Emmaus PA: Rodale Books, 1961.

_____ and staff. *The Word Finder.* Emmaus PA: Rodale Books.

Textile Machinery Index. Second edition. Oldham, England: John Worrall Ltd., 1958.

Textured Yarn Directory. New York: Rayon Publishing Company, 1979.

Webster's New Collegiate Dictionary. Springfield MA: G. & C. Merriam Company, Publishers, 1974.

Webster's New International Dictionary. Second edition, unabr. Springfield MA: G. & C. Merriam Company, Publishers, 1934.

Webster's Synonyms, Antonyms, and Homonyms. New York: Ottenheimer Publishers, 1953, 1962.

Wingate, Dr. Isabel B. *Fairchild's Dictionary of Textiles.* New York: Fairchild Publishers, 1967.

Working Press of the Nation. Annual edition. Chicago: National Research Bureau.

INDEX

Abbott Machinery Company (New Hampshire), 224

Aberfoyle Manufacturing Company, 259, 265

Absentee ownership, 81, 86-87

Acme Spinning Company, 262-63, 287

Adams, J. A., 127

Adams-Millis Corporation, 127, 247

Addison Mills (of Hampton Group), 185

Aderholt, Police Chief, 89

Adrian Mill, 267

Advisory Commission to the Council of National Defense, 135-36. *See* Council of National Defense; Textile Advisory Committee

A. G. Myers and Associates, 265

Agricultural Adjustment Act (AAA), 98-102. *See* Agricultural Adjustment Administration

Agricultural Adjustment Administration (AAA), 161. *See also* Agricultural Adjustment Act

Aiken brothers, 124

Aiken, Walter, 124

Ainley-Jacquard loom, 3

Albemarle, North Carolina, 268

Albert G. Myers Foundation, 266n

Air-conditioning, 27, 214

Alabama, 65; Cones invested in mills in, 67; Opelika Mills of, 84, 107; Textile Association of, 153

Alabama-Georgia Company, 65-66

Alabama-Georgia Mill, 66

Alamance County, 44, 81, 126

Alamance Mill, 67-68

Alamance Plaids, 44, 68. *See* "Plaid Trust"

Alchem Corporation, 241, 285, 290. *See* Delta Woodside

Aleo Mills, 272. *See* Entwistle Manufacturing Company; M. Lowenstein & Sons Incorporated

Alexander, David, 17

Alice Manufacturing Company, 279

Alsace Mills, 267. *See* Mount Holly Mills

Alsatian Machine Works, 213

Alta Vista, Virginia, 235

Amalgamated Clothing and Textile Workers Union, (ACTWU), 276

Amazon Cotton Mills, 267

American-Casablancas, 212

American Cotton Manufacturers Association, 20, 92-93, 98, 105, 151, 155-57, 178. *See also* American Textile Manufacturers Institute; Cotton-Textile Institute; National Council of American Cotton Manufacturers; Southern Cotton Spinners Association

American & Efird Mills, 268-69

American Enka, 129

American Federation of Labor (AFL), 80-81, 88, 96, 105, 121, 236

American Manufacturing Company (New York), 186

American Print Works, 84, 107

American Processing Company, 267

American Red Cross, as Central Cotton Distribution Office (1932), 92

American Textile Machine Builders, 165. *See* Textile Exhibitors Association

American Textile Machinery Association (ATMA), 114, 146, 164-67, 169-71, 174, 216, 219, 230-31, 243, 281, 284

American Textile Machinery Exhibition-International, 167, 171-72

American Textile Manufacturers Institute

Gerrish Milliken Mill, 183
Giffen, Terry, 129
Gillespie, Ralph, 184
Gilliland, Dr. Ed, 183
Gilmore-type looms, 47
Gilmore, William, 45
Gin, 45, 111, 207, 209-10
Glass, North Carolina, 28,
  201. *See* Kannapolis
Glen Raven Silk Mills, 117
*Gliederung der Winschafts-
  grappe Textilindustrie,* 147
Globe Mills, 189
G. M. Parks Company
  (Massachusetts), 214
Goldberg brothers, 265
Goldberg, Max, 159
Goodall-Sanford Mills, 121
Goodwin & Clark & Com-
  pany, 44
Gordon Cotton Mills (Mis-
  sissippi), 7
Gossett, Benjamin Brown ,
  21-23, 92-93, 98, 153, 253
Gossett, James Pleasant,
  19-21, 62, 156, 157 n. 4
Gossett Mills, 20, 92-93,
  143, 253
Gossett, Ralph, 21
Gould, Mrs. Jay, 86
Government allocations
  (post World War II), 177
Government contracts, 142
Government controls,
  elimination of (1946), 178
Government standards
  (cotton), 111
Grady, Henry, 9, 116
Granby Cotton Mills, 31
Graniteville Company, 61,
  193, 287
Grants, 125
Gray, Charles, 159
Gray, George A., 17-19, 86,
  113, 264
Gray, Ira, 46
Gray, J. Lander, 19 n. 13
Gray Manufacturing Com-
  pany, 19
Gray Mills, 267

Gray-Separk chain, 264
Grease-wool, 136
Great Falls Mills (New
  Hampshire), 189
Greek Revival Mill (Rhode
  Island), 189
Green, Samuel, 47
Green, William, 95-96
Greenberg, Frank, 285
Greene, Edwin Farnham,
  28, 31, 157 n. 4
Greene, Stephen, 12-14, 28
Greenhalgh & Shaw (En-
  gland), 143-44
Greensboro Daily News
  (North Carolina), 121
Greensboro, North Caro-
  lina, 67-68, 80, 228, 242,
  244, 247
Greenville, South Caro-
  lina, 21, 80, 238, 241, 281;
  influx of foreign ma-
  chine companies to, 219;
  Milliken's man-made fi-
  ber venture in, 182; as
  textile center in 1902, 65,
  in 1984, 275-77
Greenwood Cotton Mill,
  16, 73-75
Greenwood Mills, 289
Greenwood, Mississippi, 4
Gregg, John, 234
Gregg, William, 9, 26, 193,
  271
Gregory, Lt. General Ed-
  mund B. (quartermaster
  general, World War II),
  136-37, 147
Greige goods, compilation
  of statistics on (1920s),
  155
Grier's Candlewick Fac-
  tory, 17
Grimm, W. T. and Com-
  pany. *See* W. T. Grimm
  and Company
Griswold, Henry, 3
Groves, J. Alonzo ("Gov-
  ernor"), 127-28

Groves Thread Company,
  268
Gulf & Western, 276
Gullick, G. M., 69
Gurney/Girard (Gold-
  berg), 268. *See* Goldberg
  brothers
Gurney group, 267
Gwaltney, Eugene, 209

Hacker, Gordon, 213
Halcomb, David, 12
Hale, Ezekial, 186
Hall, David, 71, 259, 262
Hall, F. P., 71
Hall, J. B., 70
Hall, J. Q., 70
Hall, M. N., 69-70
Halsey, Admiral William
  Frederick ("Bull"), 22
Halstead, Paul, 158
Hamby, Dame, 219-20, 283
Hamilton, Alexander, 39
Hamilton, Joe, 247
Hamilton Mills (Massa-
  chusetts), 189
Hammett, Henry P., 58
Hammond, Edward, 186
Hampden County Cotton
  Manufacturers Associa-
  tion, 151. *See also* Na-
  tional Association of
  Cotton Manufacturers;
  New England Cotton
  Manufacturers Associa-
  tion; Northern Textile
  Manufacturers Associa-
  tion
Hampton Mills (South
  Carolina), 185
Hamrick Mills, 272
Hancock, John, 94
Hanes Corporation (North
  Carolina), 247. *See* Hanes
  Hosiery Mills; Hanes
  Knitting Company; Sara
  Lee Corporation
Hanes Dye & Finishing
  Company, 247

industry of, 108; exodus of textile industry of, 188-90

New England Cotton Manufacturers Association, 151. *See also* Hampden County Cotton Manufacturers Association; National Association of Cotton Manufacturers; Northern Textile Manufacturers Association

Newmarket Manufacturing Company, 143

New Orleans, 11, 184, 233

New Republic, 89

Newton, Russell, 235-37

New York, 11, 238

New York Times, 156

Night work, women and minors (1930), 92-93

NIRA. *See* National Industrial Recovery Act

Noise control, 226

North Adams Mills, 189

North American Rockwell, 216-17, 228

North Carolina, 67, 79, 107; importance of hosiery/knitwear industry in, 126-29, 131; textile association of established, 153. *See also* Gaston County

North Carolina Cotton-Manufacturers Association, 155. *See* North Carolina Textile Manufacturers Association.

North Carolina Employment Securities Commission, 252

North Carolina Finishing Company, 249

North Carolina State University, 267

North Carolina Supreme Court, 227

North Carolina Textile Ed-ucation Foundation, 263

North Carolina Textile Manufacturers Association, 244. *See* North Carolina Cotton Manufacturers Association

North Carolina Transportation History Museum (Spencer yards), 249, 256

Northern mill interests move south, 185, 200

Northern Textile Manufacturers Association, 151, 160. *See also* Hampden County Cotton Manufacturers Association; National Association of Cotton Manufacturers; New England Cotton Manufacturers Association

Northrop, James, 54-56

Northrop loom, 56, 58, 85, 118, 215, 229

NRA. *See* National Recovery Administration

NTWU (National Textile Workers Union), 88

Nums Mill, 267

Oakboro Mill, 127-28

Oakdale Mills, 75

Oates, D. W., 17

Oates, J. E., 17

Oates, J. M., 17

Oates, R. M., 17

Obsolescence: during the depression of mid-1950s, 217; dissolution of New England cotton-textile industry caused by, 186; leads to use of foreign equipment, 219

Occidental Petroleum, 250

Occupational Safety and Health Administration (OSHA), 214, 242, 250; standards for noise and dust control set by, 226-29

Ocean Mills, 12. *See* Whitefield Mills

Odell chain, 252

Office of Price Administration (OPA), 137-38, 142, 175-76, 179

Oglethorpe Park, 2, 4

Olympia Mills, 31

OPA. *See* Office of Price Administration

Opelika Mills (Alabama), 84, 107

Opening-cleaning systems, 209-11

Opening room, 37. *See* Processing cotton

Open-shed principle, 51

Orr, Hugh, 45

Orr-Lyons Mills, 272

OSHA. *See* Occupational Safety and Health Administration

Outlook Manufacturing Company, 262

Overexpansion of mill capacity, 85

Ozark Mill, 19

Pacific Holding Company, 250, 287

Pacific Mills, 30, 107, 120-21, 176, 185, 272

Pacolet Manufacturing Company, 12-14, 60, 182

Palm Beach fabrics and clothing, 121

Palmetto Mill, 269

Pamplin, R. B., 284, 289

Panty hose, 129

Parachutes, 141-42

Paris Exposition (1867), 50

Parity, 98, 180. *See also* Agricultural Adjustment Act; Processing tax

Parkdale Mills, 248, 267, 284, 287

Parker Cotton Mills (Hampton Group), 31, 121, 184-85

Parks Company, G. M. *See* G. M. Parks Company

32 n. 4, 225
Whitinsville Spinning Ring Company, 224
Whitney, Eli, 45, 111
Whitney (South Carolina) Mills, 14
Whittier Cotton Mill, 31
Wickes Companies, 291
Wiggins, Ella May, 90
Wildman-Jacquard Knitting Company, 126; as acquired by North American Rockwell, 217
Wilkins, Sir Hubert, 141
Wilkinson, David, 47
William C. Langley and Company, 59
Williamsburg, Virginia, 201
Williamston Mills, 21-22
Williamston Oil and Fertilizer Company, 21
Wilson, President Woodrow, 83, 154
Winant Board, 101
Winant, Governor John (New Hampshire), 101
Winder, 38. See Processing cotton
Windfall tax, 102, 107
Winget, A. K., 268
Winston-Salem, North Carolina, 247
Winston-Salem Southbound Railroad, 75
Wire screen, 130
Wiscassett Mills, 127-28, 198, 287n
Wittekind, 79, 194
WIX, 159

Wofford College, 20
Wolhman, Dr. Leo, 94
Women's Army Corps (WAC), 142
Woodcock and Smith, 52
Woodlawn Mill ("Pinhook"), 17-18
Woodside Division/Dan River, 240-41
Woodside Mills (South Carolina), 237-38, 290
Woodward & Baldwin, 58-59
Woodward, W. S., 124-25
Wool, 111-12, 131
Woolf, Douglas, 170, 173
Woolworth, 125
Woonsocket Machine Company, 27
Worcester, Massachusetts, 219
Workmen's Compensation Law, 229
Works Progress Administration (WPA), 107, 230
World War I, 114, 116, 137; effect of on textile industry, 151-53; need for combed sales-yarn during, 264; strike at Loray Mills soon after, 86-88
World War II, 249, 250, 272; acquisitions of mills during (1940–1946), 187-88; Bancroft Mission during, 145; Certificates of Necessity during, 180; Cotton and Synthetic Textile Division of the War Production Board

of, 117; government allocations following, 177; government impounded raw silk stockings during, 178; Jekyll Island as antisubmarine base during, 182n; production achievement for, 175; reconversion to peacetime production following, 176; research on textile machines for civilian goods halted by, 215; sales of mill-village houses to employees slowed during, 199; silk supply cutoff during, 129; textile-machinery builders participation in, 166; U.S. as textile supplier for, 110; use of nylon in, 122. See also chs. 9 and 11
Worth Street (New York City), 11, 91-92, 116
WPA. See Works Progress Administration
W. R. C. Smith Publishing Company, 169
Wright, Joseph, II, 247
Wrinkle-Shed cotton fabric, 236
W. T. Grimm and Company, 285
Wyman, Horace, 50-52
Wynn, Billy, 162

"Yellow dog" contract, 80-81
York Mills (Maine), 189
Young Communists League, 88